Global Ideas:
How Ideas, Objects and Practices
Travel in the Global Economy

SERIES EDITORS:
Stewart R. Clegg &
Ralph Stablein

Edited by
Barbara Czarniawska and Guje Sevón

Global ideas

How Ideas, Objects and Practices Travel
in the Global Economy

ADVANCES IN ORGANIZATION STUDIES

Liber & Copenhagen Business School Press

Global Ideas: How Ideas, Objects and Practices Travel in the Global Economy
ISBN 91-47-07719-0 (Sweden and Norway)
ISBN 87-630-0166-7 (Rest of the world)
© 2005 the authors and Liber AB

Publisher's editor: Ola Håkansson
Series editor: Stewart Clegg and Ralph Stablein
Typeset: LundaText AB

1:1

Printed in Sweden by
Daleke Grafiska AB, Malmö 2005

Distribution:
Sweden
Liber AB, Baltzarsgatan 4
205 10 Malmö, Sweden
tel +46 40-25 86 00, fax +46 40-97 05 50
http://www.liber.se
Kundtjänst tel +46 8-690 93 30, fax +46 8-690 93 01

Denmark
DBK Logistics, Mimersvej 4
DK-4600 Koege, Denmark
phone: +45 3269 7788, fax: +45 3269 7789
www.cbspress.dk

North America
Copenhagen Business School Press
Books International Inc.
P.O. Box 605
Herndon, VA 20172-0605, USA
phone: +1 703 661 1500, toll-free: +1 800 758 3756
fax: +1 703 661 1501

Rest of the World
Marston Book Services, P.O. Box 269
Abingdon, Oxfordshire, OX14 4YN, UK
phone: +44 (0) 1235 465500, fax: +44 (0) 1235 465555
E mail Direct Customers: direct.order@marston.co.uk
E-mail Booksellers: trade.order@marston.co.uk

Table of Contents

PART II
HOW DO IDEAS TRAVEL
AND HOW DO THEY LAND?

Chapter 1

Translation Is a Vehicle, Imitation its Motor, and Fashion Sits at the Wheel

Barbara Czarniawska, Göteborg University and
Guje Sevón, Stockholm School of Economics, Sweden

In William Gibson's *All Tomorrow's Parties* (1999), the global chain Lucky Dragon installs in its store the Lucky Dragon Nanofax, which will be able to reproduce the matter at any branch of their chain throughout the world. While the manager is planning to reproduce a gold statue of the Lucky Dragon, the idoru Rei Toei sneaks in and reproduces herself to every Lucky Dragon in the world.

While teletransportation is still a remote possibility,[1] it is said that globalization is a process that contributes to the compression of the world (Robertson, 1992). This is possible due to progress in communication, both in the sense of information exchange and transportation: more things, people, ideas travel more and quicker. But what makes them move? And what happens to them when they travel?

In management studies, the traditional explanation of the circulation of ideas, objects, practices, customs, and even institutions employed the notion of *diffusion*. This physicalist metaphor, dating from an old school of thought in anthropology (on the history of the concept, see Rogers, 1962), was embedded in many a physical and chemical connotations of doubtful utility in a social context, and has recently been replaced by the notion of *translation*.

Translation, as used currently in social sciences, is a loan from Michel Serres, who introduced it in his series of Hermes books (Serres, 1982;

---

[1] Nanofaxes exist, though, and were in use for at least a few years before being described in the novel. The technology is called stereolithography, and it is used to create a three-dimensional plastic model from a three-dimensional computer-aided design (CAD) drawing. The machines cost about $250,000 and the polymer is about $800 per gallon. The authors of this information (http://www.technovelgy.com/ct/content.asp?Bnum=112) remind the readers that computers no more powerful than a $5 calculator once cost millions of dollars.

Brown, 2002). For Serres, translation is a generalized operation, not merely linguistic, and it takes many different forms. It may involve displacing something, or the act of substitution; it always involves transformation. Consequently, that which is involved in translation – be it knowledge, people or things – has an uncertain identity. Each act of translation changes the translator and what is translated.

This notion has been adopted by French sociologists of science and technology, Michel Callon and Bruno Latour. Callon has put it primarily to use in actor-network theory and emphasized its homologizing effect:

> ... [translation] postulates the existence of a single field of significations, concerns and interests, the expression of a shared desire to arrive at the same result. ...Translation involves creating convergences and homologies by relating things that were previously different (1980: 211).

Latour, on the other hand, is not so certain about the results of translation, although the desire to become similar might be at its origins. According to him,

> ...the spread in time and space of anything – claims, orders, artifacts, goods – is in the hands of people; each of these people may act in many different ways, letting the token drop, or modifying it, or deflecting it, or betraying it, or adding to it, or appropriating it (1986: 267).

We have adopted this latter way of understanding translation in an attempt to understand a continuous circulation of management ideas and practices and put it to use in the volume entitled *Translating Organizational Change* (Czarniawska and Sevón, 1996). In that volume, together with our contributors, we watched management ideas translated into objects (models, books, transparencies), sent to other places than those where they emerged, translated into new kind of objects, and then sometimes in actions, which, if repeated, might have stabilize into institutions, which in turn could be described and summarized through abstract ideas, and so on and so forth (Czarniawska and Joerges, 1996).

Together with many others, we have attempted to follow those fascinating trajectories, and on the way we have been composing a more detailed picture of such travels. We have noticed that the concept of translation is a good way to describe the emergence and construction of various types of connections around the globe exactly because it is polysemous: albeit usually associated with language, it also means transformation and transference. It attracts attention to the fact that a thing moved from one place to another cannot emerge unchanged: to set something in a new place is to construct it anew. Thus, translation is a concept that immediately evokes symbolic associations, while at the same time being stubbornly material: only a thing can be moved from one place to another and from one time to another. Ideas must materialize, at least in somebody's head; symbols must be inscribed. A practice not stabilized by a technology, be it a linguistic technology, cannot last; it is bound to be ephemeral. A practice or an institution cannot travel; they must be simplified and abstracted into an idea, or at least approximated in a narrative permitting a vicarious experience, and therefore converted into words or images. Neither can words nor images travel until they have materialized, until they are embodied, inscribed or objectified, as only bodies or things can move in time and space (Czarniawska, 2002: 7).

What puts the vehicle of translation in motion? As Callon (1980) already pointed out, it has to do with a shared desire. Behind translation there is imitation, this fundamental learning mechanism, brought to attention by Gabriel Tarde, but soon abandoned for "norms", and only recently saved from oblivion by Latour (2002). Tarde (1890/1962) differentiated between imitation of beliefs and imitation of desires. The latter notion has been developed further by René Girard (1977) in psychoanalytic theory, and in organization theory by Guje Sevón (1996). Both kinds of notions explain imitation of practices, through copy or through contact (Taussig, 1993).

With myriads of models surrounding us from the early childhood, says Clark, commenting on Tarde's work (Clark, 1969: 18), how does one know what to imitate? What is translated and what is not? Tarde (1890/1962) said that what is imitated is allegedly superior – on the grounds of its qualities (Tarde calls these "logical reasons"; we would call them "pragmatic") or on the grounds of their provenance in time and place (Tarde's extra-logical reasons; we would call them power-symbolic). It is impossible to tell the difference between the two at any given time, as the power-symbolic superiority tends to masquerade as a superiority of quality. The third type of superiority characterizes ideas that have many allies in other ideas – that is, ideas that are well anchored in an institutional thought structure.

Still, the question remains unanswered: how do people know what is superior and how do they learn about things to imitate? It is here that the notion of fashion – as used by Tarde, and after him by Simmel (1904/1971) and Blumer (1969) – enters in. Fashion is a collective choice among tastes, things and ideas; it is oriented toward finding but also toward creating what is typical of a given time. Fashion creates "a time collective", as Sellerberg (1994) called it, making an allusion to Tarde's differentiation between a "timeless society" and "times we live in".

In management, fashion is one of the ways of introducing order and uniformity into what might seem like an overwhelming variety of possibilities. In this sense, fashion helps to come to grips with the present. At the same time, it "serves to detach the grip of the past in the moving world. By placing a premium on being in the mode and derogating what developments have left behind, it frees actions for new movement" (Blumer, 1969: 289). It also introduces some appearance of order and predictability into preparations for what is necessarily disorderly and uncertain: the future. Fashion, in its gradual emergence, eases up the surprises of the next fashion, and tunes in the collective by making it known to itself, as reflected in the present fashion and in the rejection of past fashions (Czarniawska and Joerges, 1995).

The image we are evoking is as follows: guided by fashion, people imitate desires or beliefs that appear as attractive at a given time and place. This leads them to translating ideas, objects, and practices, for their own use. This translation changes what is translated and those who translate. However, the more imitated something is, the less attractive it becomes with time (Tarde, 1890/1962: 210); therefore there is always room for new fashions and for subsequent translation. This circular, or perhaps spiral, process produces an enormous variety of different results, some of which we shall examine in this book in relation to management.

The book consists of two parts. In the first part we scrutinize that which travels, and how it changes forms and/or content during the process. The second part focus on how something can travel, it describes the "engine" and "steering wheel" of the vehicle that transports the traveller.

In the first part of the book, we inspect what is traveling. It is easy to say that ideas must be materialized in order to travel, but the fact that they are turned into objects such as documents or pictures is not very surprising. The point of debate, in theory as in practice, is: what is spreading? Only forms, as the pessimists say, or the content (in the case of organizing, the organizing practices), as the optimists would have it? Our cases show that the answer is far from simple. One thing that travels easily and with great speed are names: Orvar Löfgren shows how the idea – and the label – of experience economy arrived to Scandinavia. But Rolf Solli, Peter Demediuk and Robert Sims wonder: what if people do different things and call it the same name, such as in the case of Victoria, Australia, the state that imitated the Best Value reform from England but did it "their own way"? What, on the other hand, about Sweden, whose state administration faithfully followed the UK example but never used the name?

Gudbjörg Erlingsdóttir and Kajsa Lindberg provide one answer: names do travel and so do forms, but also practices, when incorporated in human bodies or prescribed in detail. They postulate three different mechanisms, and show, with examples from the Swedish health sector, that these mechanisms do not necessarily exclude one another. A replication of practices might be enough when there is a call for the use of a certain name, or when a certain form must be recognizable to the reformers.

Hokyu Hwang and David Suarez, who studied non-profit organizations in the San Francisco Bay Area, develop some of the themes identified by Erlingsdottir and Lindberg. What is translated in case of e.g. strategic plans and websites? Are they practices or artifacts for show? The answer depends to a large extent on who is doing the translation, the "travel agents", as it were. Such standard traveling artifacts can acquire different roles and contents depending on whether it is consultants who translate them for the benefit of a given organizations, or the organizational members, and in the last case, what kind of "translation habits" they have.

One would imagine that it is all much simpler when "genuine" objects, and not quasi-objects such as management tools, travel around. Is it, though? Petra Adolfsson's unique photo-reportage shows how the water and air of Stockholm is translated into measures and values, and then into reports, and then into a variety of most fantastic forms, including ornamental pictures on the wall and the obelisk in the middle of the city. All these trajectories, she shows, are then geared into the collective effort – an action net – of organizing and managing a big city.

The complications grow when objects are animated; fish is one example. While it has been recently suggested that our time has seen a construction of a cyberfish (Holm and Nielsen, 2004), the cod described by Korneliussen and Panozzo has many amazing properties. In its journey from Norway to Italy, it transforms, and in doing that it connects, builds and maintains several communities – economically and culturally.

In the second part of the book, the focus then changes from the question "what" is traveling to the question "how": how does it travel? And what is the "motor" of the "vehicle"? As signaled above, we see imitation as such motor, and fashion as the steering wheel, directing the movement and the ensuing transformation.

Czarniawska's chapter suggests applying a cultural analysis to the phenomenon of fashion in organizing in place of the more common market analysis. Such shift of focus will shed more light on the processes involved, rather than on their results. A better understanding of fashion as a cultural phenomenon might aid a better understanding of the current "spirit of the times". Michal Frenkel answers her plea by focusing on the pivotal role of time distancing between one fashion and another, showing how Israeli companies, in order to be able to follow the US fashion of "family friendly organizations", needed to distance themselves from identical practices already well-established in their organizations for a long time.

Another case is presented by Kris Olds who takes up the issue of the "Americanization"of higher education in his analysis of Singapore university where "academic freedom" acquires a local twist that might actually strengthen rather than question the hegemony of the state. The explosion of management education in Europe is the topic of the chapter by Tina Hedmo, Kerstin Sahlin-Andersson and Linda Wedlin. The ways of imitation are multiple: there is straightforward "broadcasting", mostly from US centers; there are chains of translations, where each imitator knows only the previous translator; and there is imitation mediated by a new kind of organized bodies that take care of accrediting and ranking within the field of management education. In this process the imitation reaches wider and wider circles, forming its own "imitation fields".

Mediating organizations, fixed or temporary, that exist with the sole scope of facilitating the circulation of ideas, have become a common staple of our times. Thus the city of Stockholm has repeatedly initiated competitions in e-modernization of public administration. Hans Krause Hansen and Dorte Salskov-Iversen show how two state authorities, in Mexico and in Denmark, enter such created space, and perform local translations, at the same time joining a newly created network that differs from traditional transnational networks.

One thing is certain: the state authorities shared a belief that they participated "in the same thing". But did they really? Walter W. Powell, Denise L. Gammal, and Caroline Simard show how various non-profit organizations differently translate what they see as "managerial practices" into their actual activities. Some take the practice, some take the name; with many other possibilities in between. While a "managerialization" of practices is seen as necessary or even desirable, the actual translation can vary strongly, and the results actually do change the translator.

All is well, says Richard Rottenburg, provocatively, in the last chapter of the book, for those who theorize about translation. You may well point out that translation is never identical to the original, and that globalization produces as much variety as standardization. You can sit comfortably in your relativist armchairs, knowingly shaking your heads over the naive idea that there exists a universally understood message, which then will be uniformly translated into practice. He claims that without such a belief, whether it is naïve or not, people would not be motivated to translate at all. Once translations are in place, one can withdraw to the same-language territory where the universalistic assumptions can be abandoned, and join the theoreticians in their ruminations.

Rottenburg makes a strong argument, but his framing of the rest of us as armchair-theoreticians might be exaggerated. Between us, and at different points in time, we represent fifteen different nationalities, ten academic disciplines, and we speak of management practices on five continents. Researchers travel, and research becomes translated, too.

PART I

*What Is Traveling?
Names, Practices, Objects,
and People*

Chapter 2

Cultural Alchemy: Translating the Experience Economy into Scandinavian

Orvar Löfgren, Lund University, Sweden

Two Scenes from the Experience Economy

1.

The walls of the conference room are plastered with pink, orange and yellow Post-it-Notes. As the meeting starts I listen to the rustle as they lose their grip and flutter down to the floor, like autumn leaves. I collect some, and notice that they have scribbles on them, such as *Space Voyage, A Feast for All Senses, Cartoon Land, Bicycles, Love at First Sight, Senior Citizens, Vikings, Fire* and *Transgressions*. These wall decorations are the result of the brainstorming of a group of "ordinary citizens", producing ideas for a future theme park project. Here, in the afternoon, ten middle-aged men in grey suits are gathered around the table. We are supposed to harvest the ideas from this morning's session and process them before the consultants fly in from the US next week, to decide if the project is worth continuing. Most people in the group are city administrators, planners, project managers etc., but the person leading us wears striped socks, big boots and a red sweatshirt. He is the outside facilitator brought in to keep our energy levels up.

Words like *edutainment, the IT-factor* and *the experience generation* whizz around the table. Most of us are rather slow in responding to the enthusiasm of the facilitator, and I cannot help thinking about the absurdity of the situation: a number of city administrators and a few outsiders being asked to let their hair down and brainstorm about the content of a theme park – a huge investment adventure that is part of the city's redevelopment.

"The Manchester of Sweden" ran an old advertising campaign for the indus-trial city of Norrköping in the mid 20th century. The image of a forest of factory chimneys belching optimistic smoke illustrated the slogan. Today the smoke is gone, but most of the chimneys still occupy the traditional indus-trial complex that sprang up around the town centre's waterfalls. While all the old industries – workshops, textile and paper mills – that made Norrköping famous and wealthy have now disappeared, the old factory buildings have been injected with new life. The industrial core of the town is often presented as the perfect example of how old industries give way to the creative industries of the New Economy. On walking the riverside streets, one encounters names and logos like, *The Knowledge School, Aikido Academy, Kulturama, The Textile Craftshop, The World Bar, Feel Good, The IT-Compass* and *The Museum of Work* (housed in "The Most Beautiful Industrial Building in Sweden"), as well as new university departments that have moved into town. *ProNova Knowledge Ecology & Science Park* is another typical institution and represented in the promotional brochure, *Experience Norrköping*, as "an enterprise of the future, designed for inno-vative people" as well as a "greenhouse" for new projects and companies. Artists are redecorating the settings and creating new installations, as for example *The Cathedral of Electricity*. The old steam boiler building "now houses one of the country's best symphony orchestras".

There is, however, a slightly desperate note about all this. Norrköping is facing difficulties in its transformation from a traditional working-class city of the Old Economy and attempts to attract new kinds of business and actors. The world is littered with attempts to reinvent cities such as this, where the marketing poetics sound pretty much the same and a similar fear of failure hangs in the air. I have a sense that some of the places with trendy and optimistic names will have vanished on my next visit to the city.

Such scenes can be witnessed worldwide, as local councils try to develop their community or region in order to become part of a New Economy. While waiting for the American consultants, local politicians and adminis-trators try to navigate in unknown waters. How do we brand our city? Can we develop an adventure park, or at least a new tourist trail? How do we make our corner of the world attractive not only to tourists but investors and career-movers?

This chapter discusses how the idea, or blueprint, of the 1990s invention "The Experience Economy" journeyed into local settings and became an important element in the New Economy boom years of experimentation and expansion. It looks at some of the transformations that occurred in this process, using examples from Scandinavia.

* * *

I come from a discipline that has always been obsessed with studying the movements of cultural phenomena in time and space, across borders and between contexts. Different eras adopted different metaphors and theoretical approaches for such movements. At first they were often discussed in terms of the movements of "cultures" that wandered, met, clashed, conquered or merged. Later on there was more focus on the journey of cultural traits or elements, and discussions about the difference between ideas, objects and people moving. In the culture theories of recent years, the prefix *trans-* has become increasingly popular: cultural phenomena are not only being translated, but transplanted, transported, transformed and transgressed. In this volume, the focus is on the metaphor of translation. Although it is used in Latourian ways that are meant to transcend its linguistic origin, it may, however, still carry a faint echo of that background, which we need to scrutinize. Metaphors are good at hiding their original meanings, like stowaways on journeys to new territories.

We also need to explore the micro-physics of movements between contexts (see the discussion in Czarniawska & Joerges, 1995: 32 ff). Why is it that some phenomena seem to travel light, are easily uprooted and re-embedded, while others carry such a heavy cultural load that they rarely make it across borders? We have to discuss the differences between the materiality and technology of such journeys. There is, for example, the interesting discussion of how ideas and objects travel. All too often objects are reduced to the role of carriers of cultural meaning. Instead we need to reflect on the materiality of traveling objects. Do ideas that come attached to an object or a set of practices have a different impact than those traveling on their own? Another question concerns the problems of timing and "ripeness" of cultural imports, and in this context the concept of cultural resonance (Wikan, 1992) may be useful.

As the editors of this volume point out, an imported idea will always change in translation. In looking at the concept of the Experience Economy, we need to ask what kinds of changes its introduction into Swedish local settings brought about. What does it mean to view a city, a local museum or corporation through the lenses of this concept? What stands out and what recedes into the background? What opportunities are created and what possibilities are blocked?

The Magic Word

During the New Economy years at the end of the 1990s, culture and economy were combined in new ways (see for example du Gay & Pryke, 2002; and Thrift, 2005). Verbs like *branding, styling, designing, theming, performing and imagineering* appeared everywhere. (This plethora of *-ing* forms was also used liberally in Academia during these years, celebrating cultures and economies in flux, at work and in a constant state of becoming.)

The New Economy concept became an umbrella term, or a figure of speech, that encompassed a number of different trends and united very diverse enterprises and economic arenas. Some of the fields singled out as hotbeds of the New Economy, such as IT and biotechnology, e-commerce and "the Experience Economy," labored under rather different conditions, although they shared the benefits of new digital technology with speedier and more efficient possibilities of storing, using, developing and circulating information. They also benefited from the possibilities that "post-Fordist production" offered, in terms of a much more flexible organization of work and capital, both slimming and flattening corporate structures. There was a focus on speed, innovation, creativity and intensity. Discussions of an "emotional" or "passionate economy", highlighted processes of aestheticization and performative qualities (see Löfgren 2003).

Another central characteristic of this New Economy was the will to remodel what was regarded as an antiquated or unimaginative division of labor in the Old Economy. The emphasis was on creating crossovers and mixes, not only with new combinations of media and technologies, but also in the restructuring of trade sectors. The concept of the Experience Economy was one example of this, where a new label was invoked to transform old divisions between production and consumption and aimed at bringing tourism, the retail trade, architecture, event management, the entertainment and heritage industries as well as the media world together under a common umbrella – that of producing and selling experiences rather than just goods or services (see O'Dell, 2005).

But how did the concept of the Experience Economy become such a striking part of the New Economy? This label included economic activities that, in many ways, belonged to "The Old Economy". In the fields of tourism and entertainment, discussions about the production and consumption of experiences have a long history. In the world of tourism, the last two centuries have been marked by a continuing debate about the nature of good experiences and what constitutes a rich or elevating event, as well as the framing and ritualization of the eventful. Tourist and tour organizers tirelessly described, measured, compared, ranked, or criticized the forms and contents, flavors and feel of experiences (see Löfgren, 1999: 13 ff).

The word "experience" got a boost in the late 1980s. The German sociologist Gerhard Schulze (1995) created the concept of *Die Erlebnisgesellschaft* (The Experience Society); a society obsessed with the need to have rich and numerous experiences. His argument was that since the 1980s there had been a rapidly rising demand for the eventful. Schulze's analysis was, however, too sweeping and also rather ahistorical – the quest for authentic experiences has a long history – although his book nicely outlined a striking pattern of intensification. (Interestingly enough, his study never made it onto the global stage as it wasn't translated into English, reminding us that social and cultural research is often confined by the barriers of language and thus confirming and creating German, French and Anglo-American spheres of knowledge.)

Within the tourist industry, "experience" had become a popular prefix that signaled an intensified or more authentic scene or situation. In a world flooded by virtual messages and mass mediated impressions, "the real experience" ought to stand for something different – a truly personal occasion, something that engaged people or an antidote to the shallowness of mass produced sights and entertainment.

In this sense, the world was more than ready for the launch of the next concept. In 1999, two US economists published *The Experience Economy* (Pine & Gilmore, 1999). Pine was soon touring Europe and marketing their new ideas. "You are sitting on a gold mine!" was the theme of his business seminar in Stockholm, held in the autumn of 2000. Here actors in tourism, the heritage world etc., were offered a chance "to go from products and services to offering attractive experiences".

The US concept was about to be translated into Swedish reality, and it is striking that this process was both faster and stronger in Sweden than in most other European countries. Searching the Net for translations of the concepts of experience, economy or experience industry in Norway and Denmark in the spring of 2003 gave only a handful of hits, whereas there were hundreds of links to Swedish sites. In a Danish government report from the autumn of 2003, *Danmark i kultur- og oplevelsesøkonomien – 5 nye skridt på vejen. Vækst med vilje*, Sweden is described as the European frontrunner in attempts to develop "an experience industry", together with the UK, where the term used is "creative industries'" Why such a strong Swedish position? This enthusiastic embrace of the new concept had to do with local Swedish politics and economic strategies, as well as the problem of translation.

I'll start with money. In the 1990s, a number of public foundations for research and economic innovation were created by the Swedish government. One of them was the KK Foundation (short for The Foundation for Knowledge and Competence Development), established in 1994 and aimed at creating new dialogues between business, the art world and academic research. In 1999, the Foundation carried out a pilot study of the new territories of the Experience Economy, and decided to invest five million euros to enhance what was called a "Swedish experience industry". A string of events, workshops, kick-offs and very different actors gathered under this umbrella and the KK Foundation's list of participant fields looked something like this:

fashion and design, architecture, computer games, film and other media, writing and publishing, art, music, PR, advertising, theatre, event, tourism (including food, museums, nature and theme parks), retail, education and "edutainment".

Within this broad definition it was stated that more than 370,000 Swedes worked in this industrial field in 1998 – around ten percent of the total workforce – while traditional manufacturing industries only provided 260,000 jobs. The Experience Industry was to be a Swedish profile and a future export, and was already manned by a very mixed crew of web designers, hotel maids, artists, waiters, copywriters, sound technicians and museum guides. They were labeled "the creative force of Sweden" and the slogan announced that "Sweden can become the world leader in the experience field!"

Why such enthusiasm? First of all, one shouldn't underestimate the optimistic sound of the Swedish word for experience. Just as in German, two words represent the English term: *erfarenhet* (Erfahrung) and *upplevelse* (Erlebnis). *Upplevelse* can be literally translated as "enlivening" or "uplifting" and sounds much more fun than the generic "experience". It is a word that embodies upward and forward movement. Although *upplevelse* denotes any experience – both good and bad – the market gave it a new, optimistic slant, so that it started to signify good, or fun, experiences. (A Norwegian academic involved in developing the Experience Economy complained of the lack of the concept of "upplevelse-industri" in the Norwegian setting. Here, the traditional term of "leisure economy", was still used, which did not have the same rallying power; see Mathiesen Hjemdahl, 2004). One of the reasons that Schulze's discussion of Erlebnisgesellschaft was so slow in crossing both the Channel and the North Atlantic could have been due to the differences between the Germanic and Anglo-Saxon languages.

But there were also other reasons for the Swedish popularity of the new concepts translated out of the Experience Economy: *upplevelse-marknad, upplevelse-industri, upplevelse-ekonomi*. In the invocations of a New Economy during the 1990s, The Experience Economy had been seen as an important complement to the smaller and more exclusive fields of IT and biotech. In the experience sector, parts of the Old Economy could be integrated with the new. With the magic of re-labeling, the old actors belonging to a service sector of low wages and unskilled jobs were given a new life in "the industry without smoke-stacks", as the KK Foundation put it. At the same time there was a marked ambivalence about using the suffix "-industry". One good thing about the word was its forceful chime. We are not talking about a motley collection of trades and actors, but a new *industry*. On the other hand, "industry" had an old and derogatory sound to it that could be traced back to the critique of mass culture in the 1920s and 1930s. At

20

that time another German sociologist, Sigefried Kracauer, used the term "entertainment industry" in his studies of urban work and leisure in Weimar Germany. He depicted office clerks and typists as easy targets for shallow, mass-produced experiences, "cheap thrills" and "pseudo-glamour". His concept was further developed by the Frankfurt School of Critical Theory (see Kracauer, 1930/1998: 88 ff). Because of this association with mass-production and unbridled commercialism, some of the actors in the new Experience Economy of the 1990s shied away from talking about it as an "industry", preferring to use words like "experience sector" or "market". On the whole, however, the various suffixes were used interchangeably in the debate.

Whatever the word chosen, it became clear that the popularity of the Experience Economy as a buzzword increased in Sweden as the dotcom-era started to falter around the year 2000. It thus became even more important to find a long-term winner. The new concept had another trump card: it could be used for the regional development that was so important given the Swedish political situation of the time. (The governing Social Democrats had to rely heavily on the Green and the Socialist parties to stay in power, and both these parties had the issue of a more equal regional development on their agendas.)

As information technology developed during the 1990s, there was a lot of talk about its placelessness: its potential for being located anywhere and giving the peripheries of nation states a new chance. The hot spots of the New Economy, however, were often cities; something that not only had to do with the need for a cosmopolitan audience in the Catwalk Economy and the focus on the art of WorkPlay – a fun-loving and youthful business culture needing FunCities – but also the fact that the New Economy produced a high degree of specialization, and demanded settings large enough to provide a base for all these special services. The paradox is that mobile technology led to a further urban economic concentration.

The experience industry was seen as a way of redressing the balance and giving local communities a share of the new world. In 2002, five small Swedish towns were funded by the KK Foundation as centres of innovation in fields like the music industry, computer games, gastronomy and design. It is easy to be ironic about this attempt to create "local centers of excellence". Concepts from the global economy, like "cluster" or the icon of Silicon Valley, encouraged many small communities to dream about creating their own little Valley or "local cluster". While many such attempts failed, there were also local attempts that succeeded. In the small community of Hultsfred, in central Sweden, local kids slowly established a rock festival tradition that eventually became the biggest music event in Sweden, and formed the basis for investment in a college training program for the music industry under the brand of "Rock City".

The magic of the Experience Economy made many small communities eager to cash in on the future. In Sweden, a number of handbooks were published that described success stories and provided recipes for action. Suddenly people looked for "the experience potentials" of their local settings. Couldn't we arrange a folklore festival, a harvest week, build a small heritage centre or a spa? Tourists usually left the Swedish west coast in August until someone came up with the idea of arranging lobster catching safaris and seafood gastronomy events during the dark and wet October weeks – which suddenly prolonged and expanded the tourist season.

This new interest was also mirrored in the activities of new and small university colleges eager to develop new profiles. Especially in the humanities, programs emerged in "experience production" or "experience technology".

Cultural Alchemy

The travels and transformations of concepts like the Experience Economy and the creative industries can also be seen as the accumulation of a tool kit, or a kind of chemistry of innovation that I prefer to label *cultural alchemy* (see the discussion in Löfgren & Willim, 2005). As Per-Olof Berg (2003) has pointed out, there was a marked focus on magic, on ways to invoke new products, markets and skills. The KK Foundation's strategy was to use the old trick of putting a number of separate and traditional items into the new hat of the Experience Economy, waving a magic wand, and then watching as, hey presto, something new emerged. Another strategy was to draw a magic circle around the list of activities mentioned earlier, and cast a spell to bind them in a new and shared identity.

The euphoric years of the New Economy carried with them an obsession for experiments, crossovers and new combinations. Venture capital flowed freely in a search for alchemists who were ready to experiment with new mixes. The alchemists were brokers, project leaders and romantic entrepreneurs. On surveying the experiments within the experience industries, we can find a number of different mixing strategies. It might be a question of trying to blend two substances, as when traditional heritage institutions enlist the help of young IT-firms in order to provide high-tech experiences. Sometimes this mix can be trivialized, such as when laptop computers are combined with medieval role-play. Some mixes might slowly separate, while others become irreversible amalgamations. There is also the process of osmosis, the slow trickle of one substance into another. We can observe this in the powerful logic of commodity branding that slowly colonizes new fields – from cities to universities. There are catalytic processes, in which a third element, such as a creativity consultant, is needed to speed up the reaction. Another process is expressed in the popular metaphor of synergy, which is the activity through which two combined agents produce greater results than could be obtained by those same agents separately. In such cases synergy often results in something unexpected. There is also the alchemy of creating coherence and integration. How do you blend the various ingredients of a city brand or an event into "the total experience"? An example of such a strategy is the narrative of the project, "Experience Norrköping", where the alchemy of coloring is used to knit the message together:

> The color of Norrköping is a warm yellow. Yellow is: *energy* and *heat* (the sun), *appetizing* (we like to eat yellow, yellow smells of lemon and vanilla), *creative* (yellow speeds up the creative parts of the brain), *visible* and *communicative* (yellow is the color that the eye registers the quickest?). We also have a historical link to yellow – the traditional "Norrköping yellow" (From *Upplev Norrköping – en idébroschyr*, Norrköping Municipality 2004).

Almost as an afterthought, this message is followed by a quote from a color psychologist, as if to ensure that the text isn't just seen as another branding trick: "As a clear and piercing ray of light yellow mercilessly cuts through all the wishy-washy philosophy."

Alchemy is, therefore, about transformation, but we also need to analyze what gets lost in the process of translating a concept or a perspective into a local context. When the marketing organization *Wonderful Copenhagen* tried to improve Copenhagen's standing as an attractive destination, they decided to create what they called "the experience capital" of the city, defined as the production capacity of experiences:

> We want to make it a Copenhagen core competence to realize itself through experiences, and this should be done by first making inventories of the city's potential experience capital because the future is an Experience Economy, in which people will fulfil themselves and invent new needs (From the report *Copenhagen Eventures* 2000).

The Experience Economy is here defined as the production of economic value in terms of experiences, events, feelings and dreams. The metaphor of capital brings other concepts to the fore, like accumulation, investments, yields, growth, book-keeping and auditing. With such a perspective, certain settings and situation are defined as having "event power" or "experience potential", and we need to ask which situations, actors and milieus are chosen and which are dropped in this process. Who fits in and who doesn't?

Helsinki is another example. In the early 1990s the city planners lamented the lack of a vibrant urban culture in the city: "Compared to major European cities, Helsinki has been found to be boring, inactive, but also green, clean and safe". According to a planning document from 1992, the remedy was a new policy: "the city will harbour a more active policy towards commercial activities inherent in urban culture, street life and events ..." More of the elusive capital called "city culture" was needed. In 1996 an urban researcher stated: "An image of an active city where there's always something going on is at least partially created by culture". In short, Helsinki should become more European and cosmopolitan (the quotes come from a study by Lehtovuori, 2001). In 1999, an ad running in *The New Yorker* urged tourists to visit Helsinki in 2000 because by then there would be "more than 20,000 events".

The Helsinki case illustrates what may happen when "an event grid" is placed over the city map. Which public places have event-power? What kinds of situations, mixes, stories and actors are needed to make the city eventful? No doubt Helsinki emerged from the process as a more entertaining city milieu, but at the same time the very attempt to classify, organize and distribute "the eventful" throughout the city risked killing the whole process.

The ethnologist Lisa Högdahl (2003) has studied what happens when a neighborhood is redefined as a tourist experiencescape. In a study of a part of Cape Town, she has followed the activities of different actors who are either written in or written out of the new script of appetizing colorfulness: street kids, security guards, local inhabitants and incoming entrepreneurs. Her close ethnographic readings illustrate the micro-processes of reorganizing street life to fit a new model, as well as identifying the winners and losers in this process. In a similar manner we might follow the impact of another recipe-maker, Richard Florida (2002), who traveled around the world presenting his concept for making cities creative and colorful. Again, the question of the right mix of people, arenas and activities was crucial, and Florida's research results were often trivialized into a few one-liners.

In analyzing the alchemy of the Experience Economy, we need to scrutinize what happens when experience is redefined as capital, creativity as a commodity and an art form as event-management. How is the potential magic of the mix perceived and harnessed? In modern economic alchemy, "re-"processes are often prominent. There is a lot of re-cycling, re-imagining and re-inventing. Traditional skills and props are put to work in new settings.

Cloning?

On looking back at some of these experiments, it is obvious that local translations often attempt a kind of cultural cloning. Ready-made blueprints are copied as local actors try to imitate success stories. There are several reasons for this routinization. In the Experience Economy you have to turn cultural software, such as adventures, experiences and events, into commodity forms – units that can be stored, marketed and consumed. In such a transformation there is a striking paradox: the strong experience, the great adventure or the eventful day usually builds on surprises and improvisations. The experience industries routinize such happenings and thus risk trivializing them. The cultural packaging of experiences also calls for creating a manageable arena in time and space. How do you organize a memorable weekend, a fun family outing or a great kick-off? In such a process, activities and experiences that cannot be squeezed into workable forms tend to be discarded. Local actors eager to join the New Economy often copy global or national successes, although many are quite aware that such a cloning may have a short life span. The high degree of cultural wear and tear creates an insatiable desire for new key concepts and new recipes for change. Sometimes new buzzwords act as appetizers or energizers in that they are used to set ideas and activities in motion, and are then discarded as one starts to look for new energizers. *Copenhagen Eventures* started out as a media event, and was presented as involving an international auditing firm and long-term perspectives. A year later the project had faded out, having done its job as a temporary energizer and media eye-catcher.

But we should not overexploit the cloning metaphor, as again, translation means transformation. It is also easy to get trapped in a trickle-down narrative – from Harvard Business School to the local lobster safari. A word like Experience Economy, or rather its much more attractive Swedish translation, opened up associations and possibilities as it started traveling. Copying the concept of lobster safari, two partners started to arrange successful "oyster safaris" for corporations, albeit in a very improvised manner. When one of them discusses her experiences it sounds as if she has followed the recipes in Pine and Gilmore's book down to the minutest detail. (Put on a fun performance and keep the setting messy and improvised to give the event an authentic flavor...) She has, of course, never heard of the book, but develops her own local contribution to the Experience Economy after being stimulated by the buzz around "upplevelse-industrin". A concept may either open up a new local field, or have a triggering effect. The oyster safari would just as probably have got off the ground with the help of another concept, due to the general trend or *Zeitgeist*.

So, what kinds of transformative processes might we observe in a local translation? One of them is *miniaturization*. What happens when actors who work on a very much smaller scene borrow concepts such as synergy, cluster or "valleyfication" from The Grand Economy? One example is when a local politician talks about "creating the synergy of an entertainment cluster", as a way of describing how the new ice hockey arena, the local mall and the bowling alley should work together. Outside observers often make fun of such local adaptations, and see them as ways of trivializing a powerful concept. There can be no cluster or Silicon Valley out in the woods. It is more fruitful, however, to discuss how concepts change meaning as they are scaled down.

Similarly, certain kinds of alchemy came to dominate in local translations, often focusing on the need for *intensification*. The Experience Economy set out to create marketing situations that could not only be heard or seen, but *felt* in the massive outpouring of media messages and market offers. The aim was to make a strong and lasting impact. One strategy was to emotionalize, often in the form of adding new ingredients or engaging other senses. What about supplying new IT-technology or adding music or gastronomy to the event? A popular version is the addition of more sensuality: let us add new colors, tastes, sounds, smells or tactile experiences. A favorite concept in the energetic activities of the KK Foundation was "fusion". Their workshops were often called "fusion days", when people from different corners and traditions of the Experience Economy could mingle and discover new forms of synergy.

As I have already pointed, out the most effective tool of invocation had to do with the magic of the circle; the circle that was drawn around activities thus defining their common economic field. This spellbinding could take many cultural forms: a list of included and excluded activities, as in the KK formula, or a graphic design, as in the Danish government report. In the KK plan, not only economic but also moral or ethical considerations determined the drawing of the circle. Computer games were seen as part of the new Experience Economy – but not gambling. Romance was an important element – but definitely not pornography. At the same time, the extremely successful mega-industries of gambling and pornography cast their long shadows. Here were industries expert in packaging and marketing experiences. These strong actors created a market for new technologies – from surfing the net to transmitting images via cell phones. Just think about the insatiable demand for hotel sex videos, new on-line escort services and phone-line sex directed through small states in search of new incomes.

A striking element in the alchemy surrounding the Experience Economy was the strong hands-on approach supplied by consultants and writers of handbooks. This economy was rather about fleeting or ephemeral phenomena, although hardware words from the construction trade were used in the marketing: *building* a brand, *producing* an event, *crafting* a feeling, *constructing* an experience or *managing* a mood. Such craftsmanship was often very detailed. A good example is the handbook, *Brand Lands, Hot Spots & Cool Spaces*, where the reader is taught how to produce "a wow effect", "an open sesame feature" or "a golden touch" (Mikunda, 2002: 119 ff).

There was also a tension between global standardization and local difference. The tool kit provided materials for creating "the generic event" or "the generic experience". It contained tools for choreographing "multi-sensuality" or other attractive elements. It contained processing devices through which you could transform local life into "a theme" or "a heritage", and ways of framing the local experience into patterns that were recognizable and marketable. If you carried this too far, however, there was the risk of losing the "special local flavor" that was supposed to give you a unique competitive edge.

Theatrical Work

In retrospect, much of the buzz surrounding the Experience Economy was manufactured by magic metaphors. One had to produce concepts that were energizing as well as powerful. Many of these concepts have a short life span, but it is important not to reduce this to "mere words" or "just a fad". The emergence of the Experience Economy was not only about dreams and visions, but also about economic practices and reallocations of resources and power. Comparing the history of the concept in Sweden and Denmark, it is striking that local translation was helped by a strong state interest, but colored by different political agendas. The new Conservative government in Denmark not only defined the Experience Economy as a possibility to marry the cultural world and business, but also as a way of disciplining the left-wing world of culture. In a red-green Sweden, the politics of regional development became an important element.

Both political settings shared the view of culture as both software and a means of production. It was not only a question of creating new commodities, services and "added value", but also of harnessing the elusive cultural energies of creativity, passion and artistry. A national comparison also illustrates the question of the life cycle of a concept. Early introduction in Sweden also meant that the enthusiasm for this new concept peaked before it did in, for example Norway, where its impact was a couple of years later.

Looking back at the translation processes and ways in which the formulas of The Experience Economy were turned into local practices, we need to reflect on the inherent logic of this buzzword. First of all there was a clear focus on the production of experiences, and this production had a marked theatrical flair, or as the Pine and Gilmore slogan put it: "Work is theatre & every business is a stage." The crafting and marketing of experiences was perceived through the web of theater metaphors. How did this framing highlight some aspects and obscure others? The perspectives of scenography, dramaturgy and choreography became dominant and consultants were able to take on the roles of scriptwriters, directors or stage hands. Producing an experience called for putting on an act, setting a scene and finding a good back-drop or the right props. Through this lens, Copenhagen and Helsinki were viewed as urban theaters, where the public was supposed to move from scene to scene, and where experiences occurred in clearly delineated time and space frames. Everything else became an uneventful interspace. Events and experiences could also be woven together through a dramaturgy of storytelling. Certain verbs signaled the choreography needed to consume such scenes, as for example in a promotional leaflet for the city of Malmö:

> Swarm in the shopping districts of Malmö until your feet ache, dive in among the market stalls of Möllevångstorget, smell spices from the whole world, stroll the short distance to the art gallery, sink into the restaurant, check out the evening programme of the theatre across the street... (from the leaflet *Skåne – ett land i Europa. Skånes turistråd*).

"Swarm, rest, dive, smell, stroll, sink in, check out ...", this is the Experience Economy's *mis-en-scène* of pulse and multi-sensuality, changes of tempo and scenes.

Above all, theater metaphors emphasized the role of a rational planning process. Even if consumers were not seen as just an audience, but rather as active actors, their movements could be choreographed, their moods managed and their senses triggered. In an ambition to control and delineate, a rather special view of what it means "to have an experience" developed, based upon the dichotomy of production and consumption – something that often had a trivializing or dulling effect. This paradox of planning the unplanned haunted the producers. After all, their interest in the focus on experiences was connected with a will to provide something that would engage and absorb consumers; something much more "authentic" than just exposure to images or texts. "Action speaks louder than words" or "we can build a universe, where people *use* the product and experience it. It is *genuine*", as two event-marketing men succinctly put it (Hansen, 2004: 47).

The translation process also includes ways in which other popular perspectives and buzz-words are incorporated in, or subordinated to, the frame of The Experience Economy. I have given examples of the ways in which concepts like heritage, aura, creativity or brand are reorganized when they are seen as parts of such an economy.

Looking back at these years of intense experiments and crossovers, we may note a high burn-out rate in the ventures developed – as in many other fields of the New Economy. We should remember, however, that as in traditional alchemy, the drive to experiment and the risk of miscarriage is part and parcel of the game. In medieval alchemy there were a number of creative failures, some of which resulted in surprising innovations. As Carl Jung once pointed out, the most important change was not that occurring in the laboratory, but in the mind of the alchemist (see Hark, 1997: 12). Energetic mixing results in mental changes, and even if the local city never gets a theme park, an IT-innovation centre or a gastronomy cluster, just letting your hair down and experimenting with some new and crazy ideas might be well worth the investment in the long run. Although most of the projects started by the KK Foundation were not really viable – they had problems in changing from innovation attempts into regular market possibilities – the alchemy involved had some interesting side effects.

The concept of The Experience Economy has thus been translated in many ways. It has been nationalized and localized, and has taken the shape of a rallying cry, a magic invocation, a spellbinder, a kick-off or a recipe. In all its various shapes and forms it has been an energizer, a filter or an arrow towards the future. It has also been a convenient bandwagon to jump on – even though it has often been difficult to identify the driver or the passengers, and who decided where the wagon was heading.

Chapter 3

The Namesake: On Best Value and Other Reformmarks

Rolf Solli, Göteborg University, Sweden;
Peter Demediuk and Robert Sims, Victoria University, Australia

The Name

After taking part in his very first battle, Tatanka-Iyotanka, better known as Sitting Bull (1831–1890), received his name by (and after) his father. The name refers to "an animal possessed of great endurance, his build much admired by the people, and when brought to bay planted immovably on his haunches to fight on to the death" (Utley, 1993: 15). The naming was a combination of labelling the merchandise and describing a mission to fulfil. The point was to state a human identity by generalizing animal qualities.

Shakespeare questioned the significance of the name as he had Juliet pronounce "What's in a name? That which we call a rose by any other name would smell as sweet" (*Romeo and Juliet*, Act II, scene II). The name of the first author of this chapter is a mix of Old Norse, German, and Norwegian and means, freely translated, the honourable wolf on the sunny slope. Neither the author's name-givers nor he who received the name have given it any thought until now. They saw it more as a practical designation, handy when it came to calling him in for supper. Who is right when it comes to naming and the role it may play? Shakespeare, the author's parents, or Tatanka-Iyotanka's father?

Public sector reforms also have names, and, by the way, so have hurricanes of some magnitude.[1] Reforms can be called city district reform, municipal committee reform, management by objective, balanced score card, and so on and so forth. Even when reforms have the same names, researchers have proved again and again that they take different shapes in practice, regardless of which organizations are compared. Translation – of abstract ideas to concrete practices, of words to actions, from one place to another – inevitably leads to difference in relation to the original (for examples, see Czarniawska & Joerges, 1996; Latour, 1998; Engwall & Pahlberg, 2001).

---

[1] Ivan was the one on a visit while this chapter was written.

The aspect of the complex translation process that we would like to pay attention to in this chapter is the significance and function of a *name*, which constitutes the main part of reforming. We will thus consider reforms from the nominalistic perspective advocated by, for example, Hacking (1999). Nominalism assumes that a name has constituting qualities, that is, through its connections to other words and public discourses it affects the way we perceive what it designates. Such a belief is seen by many as a pre-modern phenomenon – in modernity a name is assumed to reflect, not construct, the "essence" of a thing.

In this chapter, we would like to show that nominalism is not a thing of the past as one may be led to believe. Visible traces of nominalism can be found in one of modernity's most comprehensive inventions – the public sector.

The Beginning – NPM and Best Value

During the past decade modernization within public administration has been performed under the label of New Public Management (NPM). The activity behind the concept NPM is not as easily found as a reference to it. In one of the articles on NPM that have attracted the most attention, Hood (1995) claimed that Sweden was one of the more NPM-oriented countries in the world. This is hardly the case, if we are to believe Ståhlberg (1999) who names Finland as way ahead of Sweden in this aspect. Sweden seems more a case of talk rather than action (Christensen and Lægreid, 2001). Is Hood right and Ståhlberg, Christensen and Lægreid wrong? Or is it the other way around? To answer this question we first have to know if they all intend one and the same thing. What is "NPM"?

One explanation why it is difficult to establish what NPM means in practice seems to be the impossibility of finding an original idea that could give the concept NPM a clear meaning. Of course, it is not unusual that it is difficult to say what is original, and what is a copy (Eco, 1990). However, in this case it is *entirely* unclear what NPM means. There are many indications that it has to do with a collection of activities that researchers have brought together under the label, the name, NPM (see e.g. Hood, 1995; Olsen & Peters, 1996; Power, 1997; Christensen & Lægreid, 2001). Perhaps NPM as an invention of researchers is not the best term with which to understand the point of recurring reforms.

An alternative way to go about this would be to start with a concrete reform that is perceived as part and parcel of NPM. We have chosen the reform Best Value, which reportedly has been implemented in England as well as Australia. Sweden makes up a third case just because there is no reform called Best Value there (for a methodological explanation of this selection see Glaser & Strauss, 1967). Two of the cases seem, at a first inspection, to be similar and the third, that of Sweden, serves as an illuminating contrast.

The approach used in this study was exploratory. The starting-point has been that there was a reform that has been allocated more resources than any other reform that we have seen in a very long time. At the reform hub in London, the "Audit Commission", slightly more than 1,000 people were hired to work with questions concerning Best Value in 2002, at a cost of 97.3 million pounds. The reform in question has a name, and what is usually associated with this name is what will be discussed here. This exploratory approach means letting the field material speak most and first, and the literature second. The descriptions below may seem long and detailed here and there. The limit for how detailed and long the descriptions are allowed to be is defined by how much we believe a reader can endure. Our motive for using detailed description leans on a conclusion drawn by Latour (1998: 176) that explanations appearing first as descriptions become saturated.

What have been caught in the fieldwork's fishing net are, foremost, stories of different kinds told by initiated actors. In this chapter, Best Value in England is regarded as the original and thus becomes the frame of reference for the descriptions of the other two cases. As we said above, referring to Eco (1990), it is questionable whether it is possible to tell which is original and which is the copy. In this context, we have quite simply let the interviews and texts that we have studied speak. Nothing that we have encountered, and nobody with whom we have spoken, or anybody that we have read has questioned that it was in England that the concept was coined first, at least when it comes to reforms in the public sector.

England: Central Control

Data concerning Best Value in England have been collected by way of asking people who were clearly initiated whom they thought was even more initiated. The study began in the Fall of 1998 with interviews; mostly with employees at the Audit Commission, but also at accounting companies of various kinds and in one municipality. In the Spring of 2001 a more comprehensive series of interviews was conducted in London and some surrounding areas, where people presumably knew a lot about Best Value. The interviewees were found in municipalities, the Department of the Environment, Transport, and the Regions (DETR), the Audit Commission, the Improvement and Development Agency (IDeA), and the Municipal Association. Before, during, and after the interviews, the reform was followed over the Internet. It turned out that it is not at all certain that one needed to go to England to study Best Value – it was possibly necessary only to be able to orient oneself among all the homepages that in some way or other deal with the term.

Best Value can be seen as part of the Blair government's reform work with English municipalities (Boyne, 1999; Boyne et al., 2001). It was not only an issue of implementing new technology, but part of a plan presented in "The White Paper" in 1998 that defined the role of the municipalities in the following way:

> Modern councils should be in touch with the people, provide high quality services and give vision and leadership for local communities. Modern local government plays a vital role in improving the quality of people's lives.

An expression that recurs in presentations and documents is "responsive to the needs of citizens" or words to that effect, and modernization and Best Value is named as the best method to achieve this. Part of the plan was to break up the policy that was implemented by the Thatcher government, which has been done, for example, by winding up the regulation on Compulsory Competitive Tendering (CCT). In consequence, the law no longer prescribes that parts of the municipal operation *shall* be exposed to competition from outside of the municipality, merely that they *can*. The Thatcher government advocated strong state government control of the municipalities. The Blair government does not show any intention of wanting to decrease this control. The state still controls the municipalities quite tangibly, or, as one of our informants expressed it, "the municipalities are what the state has left of the old British Empire", but it does so with other instruments.

Best Value was presented by our informants in very rational terms. In their presentations, "strategies" came before "principles" that, in turn, were followed by a number of "supporting techniques". Wherever we turned, we got very graphic and rhetorically well executed presentations of what Best Value is. The cornerstones of the Best-Value reform rhetoric are the four C's ("4C"), which stand for *c*ompare, *c*ompete, *c*hallenge, and *c*onsult.

Compare represents the requirement to consciously compare. Municipalities are to be compared to one another in order to encourage learning from those who prove to be the best. Benchmarking is an example of the activities named in this context. Another activity that most likely can be included among these is the very comprehensive system of obligatory ratios, so called Best Value Performance indicators (BVPI).

Several indicators were generated. What they have in common is that they are mandatory for the municipalities. For example, these indicators are described in a 122-page long text published by the DETR. They are for the most part worked out by the Audit Commission.

The second C stands for *compete*. This in itself is nothing new and is not only about creating competitive units through procurement procedures, but literally about competing. There is an annual competition where the participating municipalities can win *Beacon Status*, that is, become a model municipality for a year. For example, the municipality of Harrow won Beacon Status in December 1999 – "for modern services delivery by its Benefits Administration service". To achieve Beacon Status entails, apart from having to tell others how things are done, winning a small sum of money, and liberalization of municipal regulations. The ranking lists, which are based on different kinds of BVPI, are widely distributed. The lists are continuously updated throughout the year on the home page of the Audit Commission.

Challenge stands for continuously challenging and questioning both what one does and how one does it. The reasoning behind this is confusingly similar to what once upon a time was called zero-based budgeting (see e.g. Pyhrr, 1973). Everything is to be scrutinized and alternative methods tried.

Finally, there is the C as in *consult*. This quite simply stands for asking customers/clients/subscribers about anything. Their opinions are to be used to influence the design of the operations.

The text presenting these four C's goes on to explain that they can be realized in practice, if connected to twelve principles. They are called principles, but in most cases they are unambiguous rules that *shall* be applied. One such principle is that the so called Performance plans are to be drawn up, and say something concrete, quantifiable, about which standards the municipality intends to live by and which goals it aims to fulfil. These goals are also to be compared with established national goals. In cases of a divergence, the national goals have precedence. It should be noted that these twelve principles were published already in June 1997, that is, before the "The White Paper" that presented the four strategies (Boyne, 1999). That is to say that tactics can sometimes come before strategy.

The accountants play a very special role in this context (see Power, 1997). They work out of the Audit Commission that runs the auditing of English municipalities. The Audit Commission is a complex trust, including representatives from different parts of society, with far-reaching authority. The Audit Commission decides, for example, which auditing firm will audit which municipality and how much it is allowed to cost. The Audit Commission is mainly financed by fees that have to be paid by the municipalities. The auditors examine whether the municipalities are working according to the Best Value Performance Plan. Parallel to the work performed by the auditing firms, the Audit Commission has at its disposal a great number of inspectors whose work it is to investigate how operations are developed. The inspectors' report is public and submitted to the board of the Audit Commission. It has to contain evaluations of whether the municipality has achieved Best Value or not. If there are glaring deviations, the Audit Commission should call it to the attention of the Secretary of

State. S/he has the formal authority to make direct interventions in each separate municipality, for instance to turn over an operation from the municipality to another principal. None of our interviewees could remember that this drastic instrument ever had been used, but it exists.

The inspections of the Audit Commission are very central to Best Value in the UK (see Davis et al., 2001). The first inspection was published the day before September 11, 2000. After two years in business, 1,655 different inspections had been published. The inspectors produce more and more reports. In 2000, fully 10 reports were published each month, in 2001 the number was 69, and in 2002 an average of 83 reports were generated each month. The reports are based on a template and almost always summarized in a diagram with the axes: "Prospect to improve" and "A good service" (see Table 1). The terms of evaluation have varied over time and in Table 1 we use the terms that were introduced in February 2002. These diagrams make the conclusions of the report very clear and correspond well to the principle that reports should be public. All reports are systematically and continuously published on the homepage of the Audit Commission.

Table 3.1. Summary of Best Value inspections performed between 2000-09-10 – 2002-09-10.
Distribution in per cent, N = 1,655 (30 reports lack concluding assessments).

Prospect to improve	A good service?			
	Poor	Fair	Good	Excellent
Excellent	1	5	5	1
Promising	2	23	22	1
Uncertain	2	22	11	0
Poor	1	3	1	0

But what gives rise to a certain value? How do you label something "fair" or "uncertain to improve"? These evaluations are most common; 22 per cent of all inspections the last two years have received this mark. We picked out one of them for closer study.

London Borough of Harrow

Harrow is a municipality with 220,000 inhabitants located North West of London. It takes approximately an hour by train to get there from central London. The report (Audit Commission, 2001) concerned refuse collection and was authored by two people who, according to their account, took six weeks each to carry out their inspection. One of them is employed as an inspector at the Audit Commission; the other is temporarily hired as an expert in the area. The inspection report is concluded as follows:

> The refuse service is a "fair" service because whilst it is relatively low cost with good standards of customer care, there are too many missed domestic wheeled bin collections. These tend to be of a large scale when they do occur with whole streets being missed. The trade refuse collection service works well and generates a surplus. The whole service is operating at full capacity at present and there is very little capacity to deal with even minor operational difficulties. Progress has been made in recent months regarding aspects such as high sickness and absence levels. However there is continued reliance on agency drivers to operate the domestic service with driver vacancies on 5 of the 12 domestic routes. We also consider that performance against the standards the council aspires to for this service is "unlikely" to improve significantly in the short term. A decision is required by the council to either to adjust the service levels advised to residents or fund the service to a higher level. We are aware the council is currently considering the options but is unlikely to be resolved until April 2001 at the earliest. The intention is to market test the service again to be effective in 2002. Whilst we accept the need to handle this matter carefully we do feel the council's proposed timetable is too long (Audit Commission, 2001: 4–5).

It should be added that the number of missed refuse bins deviated grossly from the norm. The rule is that the service should belong in the upper quartile of the country, which means that in this line of business one is allowed to miss 20 bins per 100,000. In Harrow, between 2,467 (fiscal year 95/96) and 752 (99/00) bins were reported as having been missed in the last four years. There were good explanations, one of them being that a private contractor opted out in 1995, forcing the municipality to quickly organize the service itself, resulting in a less successful financial year 1996/97. The year after, several refuse collection lorries were attacked; somebody had set them on fire. One year later, a refuse dump caught fire, which meant that the refuse collectors had to drive further to unload their trucks. These were good explanations, according to the inspector that we interviewed, but added that neither cars nor dumps should catch fire! Still they were given the assessment "fair" and this was because the cost per collection, despite everything, was among the lowest in the London area. The complementary "uncertain to improve" was given just because of those low costs since it is no great art to use maximum capacity if it is consistently too low. The inspector told us that a certain measure of challenge was embedded in the evaluation, particularly in the "uncertain to improve". When we asked the head of the service what he thought of the evaluation he answered that it was the best thing to happen in a long time – the executive board immediately had increased the allocation of funds by eight per cent.

As we have seen, inspectors can be challenging, but they also have reason for concern. Given that the costs born by the Audit Commission for the Best Value inspections are named at approximately 50 million pounds a year (Davis et al., 2001), and that the 400 inspectors make up a large part of this expense, what is done must be done impeccably, as far as facts go. To make an obvious mistake would be a disaster for legitimacy. Another concern comes from the fact that sooner or later the inspections have to prove that they are worth what they cost. To fail that task could become a very uncomfortable experience for the Audit Commission.

The reform is not entirely based on authoritative language in the shape of regulations and threats of sanctions. In the same breath as the reform is presented as launched with constitutional support, the good examples are introduced. The best example is Newham. Not too long ago Newham was second to worst among the 33 municipalities in the London district. With methods that are part of Best Value, Newham managed, against all odds, to pull itself up to third place. Apart from the flag ship Newham, there are said to exist at least 110 individually good examples that have worked with Best Value.

Not surprisingly, large efforts and investments such as inspections, comparative figures, plans, management by objectives, benchmarking, and many other control techniques that we are familiar with, feed a need for support felt by the municipalities. The formation of the Improvement and Development Agency (IDeA) is an example of this. IDeA introduces itself as created by and for the municipalities to help them "navigate successfully through the challenges of a fast changing environment, delivering leadership, cultural change, and performance improvements" (www.idea.gov.uk 2002-07-31). IDeA is far from the only supporting actor. Audit firms and consulting organizations have quite clearly also found a market because of Best Value. In August 2002, eleven new organizations had appeared that saw as their task to help the municipalities in their work with Best Value (Rogers, 2002).[2]

To conclude, Best Value in England is, according to our interviewees, characterized by keywords such as indicator control, rational planning ideals, inspections, large reform investments, www-publishing, and last but not least, governmental control of the municipalities.

Victoria: A Legitimation Project

Australia is a federation. Particularly when it comes to municipalities, there are great variations from state to state. Victoria, which this paper deals with, is no doubt one of the more reform-friendly states in the world in terms of municipal organization (Solli et al., 2000).

---

[2] Read more about this kind of organizations in Hedmo et al. in this volume.

Data presented in this section comes largely from a series of interviews that we conducted in the Fall of 2001 and the Spring of 2003. In total 31 people were interviewed, most of whom came from the 13 municipalities in and around Melbourne, but also other people were included who worked with municipal questions on a state level. In all cases, Best Value constituted a significant part of the interviewees' daily work.

Stories differ on how Best Value Victorian (BVV) style came about. One story is that the chairman of the council of the City of Melbourne visited England in 1998. Once back in Australia he ordered that Best Value be introduced in Melbourne City. It would have to be a local version/brand. With a single municipality as initiator, a few of the ingredients in the English version can be counted out. The inspection system did not seem natural to adopt. The same thing, of course, applied to the obligatory comparative ratios in England. On the other hand, the idea of consulting the users and voluntarily creating comparisons in terms of, for example, benchmarking, worked perfectly as directly translateable.

Another story of the birth of BVV is a bit more circumstantial, but as credible as the first one. This story began when the former state government took up its duties in the first part of the 1990s. The Kennett government, named after its Premier, very quickly enforced several laws aimed at modernizing the municipalities of Victoria. One move was to merge municipalities with 210 municipalities being made into 78. They were forced to lower their taxes by 20 per cent with the motivation that the mergers entailed savings of this magnitude. Labor legislation was reworked which, among other things, meant that a large number of municipal officers in managing positions were to be employed on time limited contracts. In principle, these contracts were to be announced after they had run out. Finally, compulsory competitive tendering (CCT) was introduced, according to the English model, but with the difference that a fixed percentage (50%) of the operating budget was to be exposed to competition. As many major items within a council budget (especially depreciation and consumables) are not possible to be tendered, a 50% requirement effectively meant that *all* activities had to be put up for public tender, which was never the case in England (Bryntse, 2000). Keywords in this reform were "customers", "competition" and "efficiency".

Preparing for the state election in 1999, the opposition Labor party strongly criticized the reforms enforced by the Kennett government, not least the CCT. In some cases CCT had apparently lead to lower costs at a reasonable quality, but there were plenty of examples to the contrary (Sims, 2000). Interest organizations such as the Local Government Professionals (LGPro), an organization which consists of higher municipal officers, lobbied resolutely to make the Labor party oppose the CCT, and so they did in the 1999 election. To the surprise of many, Labor won the election and a government headed by Premier Bracks took office.

One of the very first steps taken by the Bracks government was to remove the part of the law that dealt with CCT and without ceremony replace it with a new section: the Local Government Act 2:6, which concerns the introduction of Best Value. The law became effective on January 1, 2000. Note that the law was enacted, in effect, three months before the law concerning Best Value in England. The new law builds on six principles that in short can be summarized as follows:

1. All services must meet quality and cost standards.
2. All services must be responsive to the needs of the community.
3. A service must be accessible to those for whom it is intended.
4. A council must achieve continuous improvement of its provision of services.
5. A council must regularly consult with the community about services.
6. A council must report regularly, at least yearly, on its achievements to its community in relation to the Best Value Principles.

According to several of the people that we interviewed, the difference between the English Best Value and BVV is a difference very consciously intended by the Australians. We participated in a meeting where those who were responsible for the implementation of BVV in eight municipalities were coming together to exchange experiences. One of the participants had made an educational visit to England and poked fun at the English inspection system and the system of indicators, and the rest of the participants clearly agreed with this negative attitude. The system of indicators was described as comparing "apples and oranges and it ends up in a fruit-compote". The inspection system was criticized partly because it was too expensive, and partly because it was considered rather easy to manipulate the inspectors. No concrete evidence was cited, but the attitude was crystal clear. In short, to create Best Value was something the Victoria municipalities thought they could do on their own. On the whole, this perspective was also espoused on the state level.

Our informants from the state level also added another dimension to the motivation for the legislation. As the 1990s reforms were enforced, the municipalities had been made anonymous. The Victoria municipal governments had in the 1990s experienced a low degree of legitimacy among their citizens (Solli et al., 2000). The municipal mergers contributed to this anonymity, as did the old national government's very firm control of the municipalities. The new law merely assumed that activities would be reviewed in the form of an analysis, perceived as a way of making operations more expedient but also making the municipality more visible to the citizens. By asking citizens a whole number of things, they were expected to become interested in what the municipality is and does.

Even when the story is as told in this latter version, BVV stands out as an activity that largely depends on the individual municipality, without any major involvement from the state. How the municipalities deal with the questions varies enormously. According to our informants (in the Municipal Association) the activity is the highest in and around Melbourne, whereas municipalities farther out in the state are moderately interested and are moderately active. All of the eleven municipalities that we visited showed activity in terms of presentations of how they went about introducing BVV.

The most common conception was that BVV was not really anything extraordinary, just "good management". The trick was to get the review process into the ordinary control process. We have seen a lot of PowerPoint-transparencies describing this. Sometimes these were flow charts with an abundance of squares, sometimes they were simple pictures. In one municipality we were shown a (rather amateurish but still interesting) video that had been used to introduce BVV to all the municipal employees. The film concluded by summarizing what BVV is about for them. The sequence was simple: "Review – Improve – Deliver". By reviewing services, partly by consulting its users and citizens, partly by comparison with others, operations are to be improved.

There was a lack of examples of improvement. The typical attitude was that the reform had not yet reached maturity. Very often, it had started with services that never were exposed to external competition under CCT, a situation that varied from municipality to municipality. It is important to note that all operations were to be reviewed, and according to the law this should be done in a five-year period. In one municipality the department of planning was the first to be reviewed, but what this led to was not quite clear, other than that the planners realized that they did not exist merely for themselves. Another municipality started with the library service. One particular problem was that the service consisted, at first glance, of an unreasonable number of branches. The review was in this case carried out with the help of so called focus groups that showed that these libraries were not only intended for traditional library services. For users it was also important to have access to a place with clean bathrooms. At the same time, the library was considered to be a safe haven away from troublemakers. What could be learned from this was thus that branches that were perhaps not fully functional from a library service point of view could yet be important to their users.

To conclude, BVV entailed a local focusing on reviews expected to lead to improved services for the citizens. Keywords of BVV were words such as: review, improvement, decentralization, and, not the least, identity shaping. The reform has the same name as it has in England and the English version has in some way inspired Victoria. But, both in the concept description and practical action, there are more differences than similarities between the two cases.

Sweden: Sneaking in Control

Swedish municipalities differ radically on several accounts from the English and Victorian municipalities. The turnover in Swedish municipalities is, for instance, twice as large, counted per capita, compared to an English municipality and approximately five times as big as an Australian one. Another important distinction between them is that in Sweden there are full-time politicians. As a rule, there are at least two full-time politicians in each municipality. Full-time politicians are rare in English municipalities and they barely exist any longer in the Victoria municipalities.

In Swedish municipalities, the banner of autonomous local government is held high. Knowing the specificity of their own municipality and aware of their local tax power, the municipalities are expected to handle their own affairs. This situation is protected by the Constitution of Sweden. The state is supposed not to interfere with municipal business unless absolutely necessary. Even if the state in recent years has resumed more and more of the legal control that dominated the relations between the state and the municipalities up to the beginning of the 1980s, Swedish municipalities are still autonomous compared to their English and Victoria counterparts.

Although Swedish municipalities see themselves as positive about change (Brorström & Siverbo, 2001), this is a relative statement: as Sahlin-Andersson (2001) claims, it is symptomatic of municipal change that it consists more of talk about change than change itself. In one area, Sweden has performed comprehensive changes, perhaps more than any other country and that is the area of accounting and financial control (Olson et al., 1998, Brorström & Solli, 2000). Best Value is not an exception to this rule. We have yet (Fall of 2004) to see a municipality that has introduced Best Value, although, as we shall see, it exists in what we call municipal discourse. In one of the interviews at the Audit Commission in London our informant told us that they often had visitors from other countries and that in eight cases out of ten these were from Sweden, information offered in a humorous tone, but still, the implication was clear. Hence, in the discourse we can expect to find what is on the agenda right now and it proves to have elements of Best Value.

In the beginning of the 1990s, when the financial crisis was at its worst in Sweden, the so called Lindbeck commission was appointed. The Lindbeck commission was made up of well-known economists, political scientists and others with the mission to come up with recipes on how Sweden should get out of the crisis. They delivered their recipe very quickly (SOU 1993: 16) and had thereby fulfilled their task. Apparently it was an appealing way of working, because the commission has continued delivering recipes on how Sweden could improve, although under a different name, *Ekonomirådet* (Economic Council). They wrote in their report for the year 2000:

> Moreover, establish a national service for auditing municipalities with the task of surveying municipal self-audits and accounting for the efficiency review of municipal operations (Lindbeck et al., 2000: 162).

This has some resemblance to the UK Audit Commission mentioned above, does it not? Similar thought can be found in the Swedish Government Official Report (SOU) 2001: 76 entitled "Good financial management in municipalities and county councils" in which it is suggested that the government establishes:

> ...a State council for municipal economy. This council would have among its purposes to follow and analyse developments in the area of municipal economy. Furthermore it should serve as a conversation partner and advisor to municipalities and county councils in need of expert help to analyse their financial situation, especially cases where the state may come to play a role (SOU 2001: 76, p. 20).

It is also suggested that

> Accountants should judge whether the political majority has lived up to the goals of the financial administration. Negligence to balance the economy during a four-year period may lead to consequences (SOU 2001: 76, p. 18).

As regards indicators, this is nothing new really. In Swedish municipalities these have been part and parcel of the administration since the 1930s (Bergevärn & Olson, 1987). But in recent years they have been brushed off, by for example the Swedish Association of Local Authorities. In a SOU (2001: 75) a single investigator [an unusual practice] writes:

> I propose in all 157 different performance indicators for child care services, schools, nursing and care for the elderly, care for the physically impaired, and individual and family care, distributed as 65 volume indicators, 49 economic indicators and 43 quality indicators (SOU 2001: 75, p. 44).

This proposition has also been realized, see http://www.kommundatabas.se. But not only indicators are to be developed, the same investigation also suggests

> ...that, as a support to the municipalities, purchase a number of suppliers of surveys according to the model that Statistics Sweden (SCB) has worked out

for the investigation that the municipalities then may suborder (SOU 2001: 75, p. 44).

The investigation goes on:

> The organization that will be responsible for the municipal database also is responsible for setting up and publishing cross-sectional analyses, and initiating and running a knowledge in which concrete benchmarking projects are reported and made available (SOU 2001: 75, p. 61).

Sometimes there is little talk and lots of action. After a number of much noted cases of neglect and deficiencies in the care of the elderly, the Social Democrats and Prime Minister Göran Persson entered the election campaign 2002 with promises of appointing 100 ombudsmen for the protection of the elderly in the case of a victory. There was an election victory and 50 million crowns were allocated but it was not enough to appoint 100 ombudsmen, only 68. The purpose of the ombudsmen for the protection of the elderly is to ensure that deficiencies and anomalies within the care of the elderly are revealed and attended to. This is to be achieved mainly through announced and unannounced inspections of various activities.

In this context the Committee on Public Sector Responsibilities should be mentioned. This investigation concluded in its partial report (SOU 2003: 123) that the governmental control of the municipal sector is very fragmented. The government uses many different control techniques at the same time and often with a loss of efficiency as a result. The report on divided control is interesting because it gives room for the establishing of new control techniques, for instance, ombudsmen for the elderly and support for performance indicators; although in other contexts the topic is managing by objectives and results.

In the discourse we thus find proposals from various sources of something similar to the Audit Commission, indicators, and the consulting of citizens. These ingredients could go together quite well under the umbrella term Added Value or Surplus Value, if they did not sounded so much like an old Swedish tax or a Marxist concept. But the most important argument against Best Value as a recipe is likely that it entails such strong governmental control that each and every municipal officer – man or woman – would be against it.

The Sake of the Name

If we look for Best Value components in all of the three countries (reported in table 2), an interesting pattern appears. Regarding the six reported components, England naturally has checks on all of them, Sweden almost on four, and Victoria barely on two. If you combine Victoria and Sweden, they more or less make up the case of England. No matter how you turn the comparison in your mind, England is a case of its own when it comes to investments, but, apart from that, the properties of the reform, that is the similarities between the work performed, show clear kinship. The large investment makes England, we would say, the "market leader". Both Victoria and Sweden are followers of what is taking place in England.

Table 3.2. The reforms in conclusion.

	England	Victoria	Sweden*
Name	Best Value	Best Value	None
Performance indicators	Yes	No	Yes
Inspections	Yes	No	Yes and no
Investment	Large	Small	Small
Internet-based	Yes	No	Yes
Governmental control	Yes	Yes and no	Yes

*For Sweden we have considered the discourse in progress during the Spring 2004.

Then, how can it be that a country such as Sweden which has not introduced a reform still fulfils its criteria? And, how is it that Victoria, that claims to have introduced it, does not?

One thing is certain: reforms spread. Equally certain is that similar management recipes often turn out different dishes, not the least because institutional expectations lead to different translations. Røvik (2000) writes that in our time organizational recipes and standards travel both far and quickly. In this case we have an organizing recipe that arrived in Australia even before they had time to get the original ready in England.

What then, is the value of names in municipal practices? In business administration it is traditionally marketing that pays attention to the role of the name in discussions of trademarks. The great significance of trademarks is described by Aaker (1991, 1996), for example, who sees it as the company's single most important asset. In *Business Week* (July 2003) it was stated that, for example, the Coca Cola trademark is worth 70.5 billion dollars. In some cases the trademark is even taken up as an asset in the balance sheet and its worth set at several times the value of all other assets taken together (see Melin, 1999). The significance of the trademark is obvious. Del Río et al. (2001) observe that it is easier for consumers to name properties of a certain brand than of an individual product. The trademark simplifies for us who need to remember more than we do. But it does more than that. The trademark grants recognition and thus identity, as it demonstrates that its users belong to the group that buys these products. In our case, this means that you belong to a group that has introduced the Best Value reform.

Can Best Value be called a trademark? A singularity of trademarks is that most of the time they are protected by some kind of legislation that impedes others from using the trademark for their own benefit. When it comes to public sector reforms and most modern management techniques, the case is rather the opposite. We suggest designating public reforms by the concept *reformmark*. Nevertheless, what we call a *reformmark* has a lot of similarities to a trademark. It concerns an identity that one wishes to build up, which is supposed to signal progress and excellence although not necessarily must have very much to do with the product itself. While the view that the trademark in itself is an asset does not seem disputed, its use has been debated. Klein (2000) describes how large companies whose business is entirely based on taking the trademark to ever new heights use dubious methods, to say the least, to introducing new products, since they produce increasingly less themselves. Klein (and others) predict that a counter-reaction will occur in terms of people becoming more and more fed up with trademark exposure in the shape of, for example, commercials. Identity is thus signified by not using a trademark. "No Logo" is also part of an identity and a trademark in itself.

England has made the *reformmark* Best Value well known. By displaying great power, at least in terms of funding, the state has proved that municipalities can be modernized in other ways than through competition and privatization. In Victoria the *reformmark* is appropriate in the sense that they too want show that one can modernize without the instrument of CCT. At the same, they prove their autonomy by rejecting the "elements" of the *reformmark*. If you have been a colony, it is important enough to show that you no longer are one. The governmental control-part of the *reformmark* does not pose a problem; historically it has been even greater than in England. In Sweden, the governmental control aspect of Best Value becomes a problem that, at least for now, is insurmountable. It is contrary to the institutional arrangement called local self-government. That does not stop them from imitating the product, learning everything else that has to do with Best Value. To see the *reformmark* as separate from activity is, in our opinion, a way to understand similarity and difference as practices are compared. Hacking's (1999) view of nominalism thus fits well in here; the concepts are divorced from the activity they refer to, but despite this, they have a function.

Thus we want to pay attention to the name of the reform and propose that it is the name that plays a role for the understanding of reforming. Our reasoning amounts to the notion that names in themselves give identity, while apparently different local circumstances legitimate a disengagement from the activities of the "original". The case of Victoria can be understood in this way. Seen the other way around, it is entirely possible to emulate a large part of the original's actions, while not having to assume its identity, which could entail, for instance, strong governmental control but avoiding its name. It seems to be a well-founded speculation that this is the reason the name Best Value is not used in Sweden, although it imitates the practice. Here we will admit that now that our description of Sweden as a case of sneaking control is motivated. Step by step governmental control is being snuck into Swedish municipalities.

Another kind of conclusion about the descriptions and their trademark application has to do with how we understand the spreading of reforms. To understand how reforms are spread we first have to study their individual components, the more detailed the better. In the details we can see the plans of action. Without details, we run a great risk of missing that which is done without a trademark.

So, who is right? Shakespeare, the first authors' parents, or Tatanka-Iyotanka's father? In our opinion, Tatanka-Iyotanka's father best understood the significance of the name. Sitting Bull never became a sitting bull, but probably benefited from being perceived as one. To be fair, Shakespeare also knew what was going on, why else would he make such a big deal out of the fact that Romeo was a Montague? As far as the author's parents are concerned, they were right in so far that he sometimes came running when called in for supper.

Chapter 4

Isomorphism, Isopraxism, and Isonymism: Complementary or Competing Processes?

Gudbjörg Erlingsdóttir, Lund University and
Kajsa Lindberg, Göteborg University, Sweden

In today's global economy, ideas and models about how one should act and present oneself are generously offered to all organizations. Organizational models, management principles, and quality standards travel among countries, fields, and organizations (Czarniawska and Sevón, 1996). Public administration organizations are faced with demands to achieve higher productivity and greater customization with reduced resources, and often look for solutions in ideas that are circulating in their particular organization field (Jacobsson, 1995; Sahlin-Andersson, 1996). In this chapter, we focus on the Swedish health care sector as a case in point.

The notion of organization field comes from the new institutional perspective in organizational research. According to this body of theory, organizational change occurs because of a desire for legitimacy and survival (DiMaggio, 1983). Organizations are dependent on acceptance and legitimacy in the field in which they operate – otherwise they would have difficulty in attracting qualified personnel and other resources. In order to gain legitimacy, organizations may seek congruence with the institutions upon which they are dependent and those with which they want to be associated. Thus, change in organizational processes and structures are explained by the prevailing institutional forces (Meyer and Rowan, 1977).

It has also been claimed that this process creates a growing homogeneity of form, as organizations, both within and between different fields, are influenced by the same set of institutions. Thus, according to Meyer and Rowan (1977), many organizations base their formal structure on the "institutional myths" of their environment rather than on their needs. The fact that organizations are becoming increasingly homogeneous, a phenomenon called institutional *isomorphism*, can be attributed to lack of both innovation and effective management (DiMaggio and Powell, 1991). It has also been observed that organizations cope with external demands for control by decoupling: they adapt structures that fulfill a legitimizing role towards their organization field, while simultaneously protecting their core activities through buffers of various kinds (Meyer and Rowan, 1977).

New institutional theory has been criticized, however, for describing institutionalization as a static qualitative state rather than a process, on charges that a compression of the time dimension leads to an oversimplified description of the institutional process (Tolbert and Zucker, 1996). The so-called Scandinavian School within new institutional theory has expanded the theoretical perspective, first by focusing on the institutionalization process rather than its results, and second, by viewing both stability and change as an institutional norm (Czarniawska and Sevón, 1996). Additionally, the mechanical concept of diffusion has been replaced by such concepts as translation (Czarniawska and Joerges, 1996), imitation (Sevón, 1996) and editing (Sahlin-Andersson, 1996) in order to provide an extended understanding of the process of institutionalization. Czarniawska and Joerges (1996: 46) use these concepts in their model of "travels of ideas", which describes how ideas become disembedded, sent away, and then reembedded in a series of translations as they "travel" in time and space. In order for an idea to travel across an organization field, it must be separated from its institutional surroundings (disembedded) and translated into an object such as a text, a picture, or a prototype (packaged). Such an object then travels through the relevant field of organizations to another time and place, where it is translated to fit the new context (unpacked). Finally, the object is translated locally into a new practice (reembedded), and, with time, the black box of institution may close itself around the idea. Such an idea will then be taken for granted in its new surroundings and will, in its turn, be disembedded in order to travel through time and space again.

In this chapter, we suggest additional effects caused by the travel of ideas – possible complements or even competitors to isomorphism. An idea driven by isomorphic tendencies is usually buffered from the daily routines of an organization and often translated into a ritual rather than a new practice. But we have also seen cases in which an idea has actually been transformed into action, generating new routines. Erlingsdóttir (1999) called this process of creating homogeneous practices *isopraxism*. Processes of imitation can also lead to the adoption of the same names but for different forms and practices – an *isonymism* (from Greek, meaning "the same name"). In this chapter we attempt to trace various homogenizing and heterogenizing processes which reproduce organizational ideas, models, and practices.

Before we engage in this endeavor, however, we need to specify what we mean by "practice".

Although it has been said that there is a "turn to practice" in contemporary social theory (Schatzki *et al.*, 2001), there are a great number of definitions of practice in circulation. Among them is one that we find especially convincing because, as Paul Rabinow (1997) pointed out, it reverts to a language of virtues. This is the definition of practice presented by Alasdair MacIntyre (1981), who emphasizes the quest for betterment inherent in the way people, and only people, conceive of their practices:

> any coherent and complex form of socially established human activity through which human goods internal to that form of activity are realized in the course of trying to achieve those standards of excellence, which are appropriate to, and partially definitive of that form of activity (p. 175).

MacIntyre plays here on the meaning of the word "goods". A practice may produce concrete effects in terms of material products, even commodities, but these products also have a moral or aesthetic value: they must be "good". It is the practitioners who define – and redefine through practice – the meaning of "good". One can imagine that the concept of "good" as conceived by classic musicians differs from that shared by rappers.

MacIntyre's definition of practice is somewhat at variance with the sociological concept of translation which insists on a symmetric treatment of all actants involved in an activity. Yet we agree with MacIntyre. Although, in his definition, practice can be performed in part by cooperation among humans, things, and machines, the notions of "good" and "excellence" apply only to the human participants. On the other hand, certain aspects of performance – the ability to compute complex calculations instantly, for instance – belong only to machines. The symmetry is maintained, but symmetrical parts need not be identical.

The Studies

In our study, we use field material from three cases of translation of ideas in the Swedish health care sector: the introduction of "quality assurance" to the sector as a whole, the introduction of accreditation to clinical chemical laboratories, and the "chain-of-care" project in one region of Sweden.

The study on which the first case was based (Erlingsdóttir, 1999) was carried out in the period 1994 to 1999, and its aim was to trace the circulation of the idea of quality assurance within the health care sector since the mid-1980s. First, various authorities were engaged in formulating and testing the idea. A national board was formed, and it sought a national solution: a national quality assurance model. A model called Organizational Audit was borrowed from England and tested at the Lund University Hospital, and this part of the process was the focus of the field study.

In order to study the eventual translation of the model down to shop floor practice, it was necessary to observe the work in a ward for a continuous period. Therefore, direct observation was used as the main fieldwork method. Direct observations were conducted at three clinics at Lund University Hospital; the Medical Clinic, the Surgical Clinic, and the Clinical Chemical Laboratory, settings that represent different working methods and different routines within health care.

Observations at the Laboratory revealed that it was using a different quality assurance model than the rest of the hospital. In particular, the laboratory was engaged in accreditation monitored by the Swedish Board for Technical Accreditation (SWEDAC). Tracing this model back to its origins revealed differences in the origins of the two models. The two ideas are hereafter called "quality assurance" and "accreditation" – although both can be seen as types of quality assurance.

New questions arose during the direct observation, leading to a continuous reformulation and restructuring of the research, which not uncommon for this type of study (Schatzman and Strauss, 1973). Thus, in parallel with the direct observations, interviews were conducted and written material gathered at different central agencies and at the management level at the hospital, in order to identify the origins of these quality assurance ideas in health care, and the paths by which they have spread through the organization field.

The study of the chain of care[1] originated in an observation that the public administration sector in Sweden, including its health care sector, is presently under the influence of several different organizational trends. There is, on the one hand, a tendency to introduce clearly demarcated units which have their own budget and management and which work towards specified objects. This trend can be interpreted, as Brunsson and Sahlin-Andersson (2000) suggest, as a creation of formal organizations. On the other hand, there is a strong emphasis on the importance of cooperation among various units, organizations, and professional groups, based on the assumption that by cooperating they will better fulfill their mission to give patients, clients, and customers as good service as possible. This means that there is a need for connections that cross organizational and professional boundaries, and projects exploring such possibilities are encouraged and financed by Sweden's public sector authorities.

The study reported here aimed at a description and analysis of the so-called Högsbo project, which had the objective of creating coordination among the care units. Employees from three organizations participated in the project. Different laws regulated their tasks and their operations were financed from different principals. The everyday work activities of care personnel were separated in time and space. Nevertheless, they were – at least in part – dependent on each other to be able to produce "good" care. Thus

---

[1] "Chain of care" is a literal translation from the Swedish *vårdkedja*.

they were required to create connections, while retaining their separation in time and space.

The project was initiated and financed by the National Institute of Working Life (NIWL). The stated aim of the project was to develop a "chain of care" for elderly people. The project was located in a district of Gothenburg, where one-third of the citizens were over 65 years of age. Thirty-five persons participated in the project: people from the local hospital, from primary care units, and from municipality-run care centers. Kajsa Lindberg observed their project meetings during one year, interviewed twelve of them, and studied protocols and other documents from the project and from NIWL (for a more complete discussion of the entire study see Lindberg, 2002).

To assume that organizing is a social process has implications for the ways in which organizing is studied. Thus actions were a primary focus in this study. Observing actions and how they were connected to each other made it possible to highlight the dynamics of organizing across organizational borders. This meant not only that borders were trespassed, but also that they were constructed and reproduced. The picture of organizing that emerged from the study is one of an ongoing process whereby structures, people, and actions are constantly connected and re-connected to each other.

Quality Assurance in Health Care

Quality assurance programs have been of great interest within Sweden's health care sector since 1986 when the Swedish Planning and Rationalization Institute of Health and Social Services (Spri) started investigating different ways of enhancing the quality of health care. This interest arose because, in the 1980s, new demands and considerably increased costs led to what has been referred to as the "cost crisis" in Swedish health care (Spri 287, 1990). In 1986, the National Audit Office (RRV) published a report on productivity within the health care sector in Sweden between 1960 and 1980, which claimed that productivity had decreased over this twenty-year period. Organizations within the health care sector reacted defensively by claiming that the report was misleading, as it did not show and give credit for the increases in quality during that same period.

Spri's main task was to provide advice and support for decision makers within the health care sector, and, in doing so, Spri kept close contact with organizations in the field as well as the general state of affairs within the health care sector. The problem was later formulated in one of Spri's reports as follows: "The system is lacking devices for measuring and evaluating the quality of health care" (Spri 287, 1990).

Consequently, Spri assigned a group to work on quality issues. It took its inspiration from quality assurance in industry and various quality assurance programs applied to health care in other countries. Spri became especially interested in one of the models whereby the participating units are externally audited once a year by staff from other hospitals. Spri got its inspiration from King's Fund in UK, which was inspired by a Canadian model, which was adopted from an Australian model, which in turn had a US model as a prototype. Because Spri could not test the model, it turned to the health care organization – the Lund University Hospital.

The Lund model

A "local quality board" was formed in Lund University Hospital to translate and adjust the English version of the quality guide to Swedish circumstances. A project leader was assigned to supervise and coordinate the translation and implementation processes. This work started in December 1992 and was conducted in cooperation with the National Board of Quality in Health Care and Spri, which supervised the translation of the document. In the written contract between the parties, the Organizational Audit model was positioned as "being in line with the quality assurances used in the industry". The Quality Assurance Board, including a representative from all the hospital clinics, worked centrally on the implementation of the Lund model. The clinic representatives each had the responsibility of informing their respective clinics about the program. The Quality Assurance Board in Lund circulated an internal "quality newsletter" and established a "See our quality work" exhibition at the large entrance area of the hospital.

According to the project leader, the Organization Audit model (which was called the Lund model at the hospital) spread down to the wards. Lund University Hospital was audited by external auditors early 1995. The auditors' main critique was the lack of pronounced goals for the quality assurance process and the lack of involvement of the hospital board and the senior physicians in the process. The model was, therefore, a disappointment to the authorities, and was never used as a national model in Sweden. The observations taken at the hospital at that time did not reveal any traces of the model in the concrete, day-to-day activities of the wards. Several work routines and quality control activities were conducted in the wards, but none of them could be linked directly to the Organizational Audit model.

When asked about the quality assurance procedure, the nurse at one of the wards replied that she had completed the forms herself, saying that she wanted to spare the other nurses the job. The only time the quality assurance model was mentioned by the personnel was during the same week the audit was carried out at the hospital. The personnel believed that the auditors would turn up, which they did not. As it turned out, the auditors had talked to somebody at the administrative level at the clinic and saw no reason to visit the department on that occasion.

It was said within the Lund University Hospital community that one reason for implementing a quality assurance model of this kind in Lund was to bring benefits to the hospital in relation to the customers – the municipalities and county councils that were the potential buyers of the hospital's services. Another reason was to show others in the field that Lund University Hospital had engaged itself in quality assurance work. In the administration offices, the quality assurance project was seen as part of the change toward a market economy within the Swedish health care sector. Thus interpretations at the local level differed significantly from those of the higher authorities who connected quality assurance to efficiency, cost cutting, measurability, and a possible comparison among various wards and hospitals.

In the beginning – that is in the early 1990s – the doctors did not seem to pay much attention to quality assurance (with the exception of some doctors who acted locally as spokespersons for quality assurance at their own hospital or clinic). When mentioned at all, quality assurance was described as an administrative "gadget", not connected to the quality of their work. The interviews with chief doctors showed that they were not particularly interested or startled by the fact that quality assurance was spreading in health care organizations. Quality assurance would fall under the administrative category of their job – time-consuming and necessary, but not as important as the medical part of their role. They connected the idea with the introduction of a market economy in health care, and thus referred to it as one of many ideas that happened to be in vogue at the time: "It's a sort of a trend for the moment, you see. A couple of years ago everything was ethics. Now there's no talk of ethics; it's all about quality assurance." Another comment was that "We have always worked with quality; that's what we do. We just don't call it quality assurance".

From an idea to a law

The general lack of engagement in quality assurance from the doctors at the Lund University Hospital was representative for Swedish health care sector. The National Board of Health and Welfare demanded that the Swedish Medical Association create The Medical Quality Board in order to deal with these matters. Furthermore, it decided to formulate a practical recommendation for the Swedish health care sector, according to which any person or organization responsible for medical care had to have a quality assurance plan. But not even this recommendation created much interest, and an investigation conducted in 1996 showed that many senior physicians had not even heard of the plan. This was considered a shortcoming in the internal efficiency of the National Board of Health and Welfare, according to an investigation by the National Audit Office.

Harsher measures were needed. In the summer of 1996, the government commissioned a change in the Swedish Health and Medical Services Act. The time was short, there was no public debate on the new law, and the changed Act was published in January 1997. It made it compulsory for any individual or organization responsible for medical care to have a quality assurance plan. However, there was, and still is, no agreement between authorities and health organizations as to which model or method should be used.

This state of affairs accompanied the introduction of the idea of quality assurance into the Swedish health care sector in the mid-1980s. Various authorities promoted different methods and models at different times. Spri propagated the Organizational Audit model, while the Swedish Federation of County Councils developed a Swedish model similar to the Swedish Institute for Quality (SIQ) model called QUL. The QUL model was launched as "a quality management tool", but included a form of a competition that rewarded the best organization as the "winner". QUL was launched in 1996, became the model recommended by the Stockholm County Council, and probably became the most widely adopted quality program in the Swedish health care sector. It has also had the greatest effect on the practices of health care organizations because doctors have been forced to fill in the documents required.

However, an evaluation of the health care organizations using QUL in Stockholm, conducted in 1999, showed that the benefits of using the method were insignificant in comparison with the amount of time and money required. Still, the law remains, and there is a continued search within the health care sector for a quality assurance method or model that can fulfill its demands. This search has resulted in a vast array of translations and interpretations of the concept of quality assurance amongst organizations within the health care sector. Often, the models or methods are introduced and tried sequentially, as each one has been found to be a failure and abandoned. Thus several hospital clinics have tried more than two and even as many as five quality assurances methods in succession. Thus, over the past ten years or so, quality assurance has become a common practice within the health care sector in Sweden, although the methods and models vary.[2]

---

[2] For the latest turn of events, see Erlingsdóttir and Jonnergård (2006). Most models for quality assurance focused on the organization or structure of the activities rather than on the quality of medical practices because of the difficulty in measuring and controlling the quality. Recently, however, the National Board of Health and Welfare have clearly formulated their interest in making the quality of medicine open to public scrutiny and control. There seem to be three main areas of quality of medical practice in which the medical profession is now taking interest: 1) gathering and documenting data for the national quality registers, 2) the development of quality indicators, and 3) drawing up guidelines for medical quality audits.

Isomorphism or isonymism?

The Lund University Hospital case illustrates an introduction of a novelty – quality assurance – that spread and established itself in spite of a series of its failures. The winds of change were stronger than professional resistance and organizational reluctance were. Several questions arise from this case: is "quality assurance" an organizational form or organizational practice? One answer is that it is an administrative (managerial) practice intended to affect (homogenize) another organizational practice: medical care. This effect has not yet materialized. Neither is the practice of quality assurance itself homogenous; it exists in many variations. What is more, not even the form is the same. This case resembles the study described by Solli, Demidiuk and Sims in this volume; the same name does not necessarily indicate the same practice – not even the same form. Thus we suggest that organization imitation may lead not only to homogenization of forms (isomorphism), but, in some cases, may lead simply to the spreading of a name, like "quality assurance". Although it illustrates materialization of an idea, the object is minimal: a word or an expression. The next case, in contrast, shows an example in which imitation and the resulting translation actually led to the homogenization of practices – that is, to isopraxism.

Before we move to the next case, however, let us reflect further on the picture formed by the case of quality assurance. In our attempts to interpret that case, we have found it impossible to maintain DiMaggio and Powell's (1991) distinctions among coercive, normative, and mimetic mechanisms. Coercion (mostly legal) and normative pressure are two possible reasons or motives for imitation. The opposite of imitation is *invention*, and it is this distinction that attracts the attention of practitioners and theoreticians alike. In the example of the regional R&D centers mentioned by Czarniawska and Joerges (1996), the practitioners claimed that the center was their original invention, even though each region did the same thing. What is more, the historical split between the two schools in anthropology, diffusionists and evolutionists, run along the same lines (Czarniawska, 2001). While the former claimed that people imitate what others did, the latter claimed that human nature, being what it is, leads to parallel inventions. Even today, invention has a heroic aspect to it, whereas imitation is scorned. Thus there are many claims to invention and many protests against the attribution of imitation, although these differing points of view tend to differentiate actors from observers. Typically, what researchers (such as us) see as imitation, the actors prefer to see as invention.

Why would there be any difficulty in distinguishing between imitation and invention? Translation is the villain of the piece: anything moved from one place and one time to another will arrive in a different form; thus the points "same or not? " or "old or new?" are among those most debated in organi-

55

zational practice. The issue of "quality assurance" is an excellent example: Were they all doing the same thing or were they not?

No such qualms were attached to the matter of accreditation, although accreditation itself was a translation of quality assurance.

Accreditation of Clinical Chemical Laboratories

In 1989, a new law (1989: 164) on control through technical testing and measurement was introduced in Sweden. It granted all laboratories the possibility of being accredited by The Swedish Board for Technical Accreditation (SWEDAC). Previously, only laboratories that were appointed by the government were obliged to apply for accreditation. The new law was introduced as an adjustment to the prevailing EU directives that promoted an open mutual European market. The idea behind the directive is that a laboratory accredited according to the mutual EN 45,000 standard would acquire a quality mark that would be valid within the entire EU. Thus an accredited Swedish laboratory would be able to sell its services to other countries in the EU. The idea behind the law is the idea of a mutual market with mobile finances and products – an idea that is dependent upon a certain degree of harmonization among the countries that have entered the mutual market. The application of the EN standard is, however, voluntary which means that the law is not designed to force laboratories to submit to an accreditation process, but rather to offer the possibility of accreditation to those laboratories that wish to apply.

SWEDAC is connected with an EU project concerning the development of standards, as well as to specific interpretation documents, and thus the accreditation model is linked to European norms and standards (Stanton, 1995). When the new law (1989: 164) was introduced in Sweden, the EN 45,000 standard was translated into Swedish. The translation was literal, word for word, without any changes or modifications. SWEDAC, the only Swedish accrediting body, now has control of the Swedish EN 45,000 standard for voluntary accreditation of laboratories.

As the law was based on voluntary enrolment in the system, SWEDAC initially found it difficult to find a laboratory interested in accreditation. However, by the end of the 1980s the Head of the Medical Clinical Chemical Laboratory at the Sahlgrenska University Hospital in Gothenburg was looking for a way to improve the routines of the laboratory, and had heard about SWEDAC's initiative. After some discussions, the process began, and the Clinical Chemical Laboratory at the Sahlgrenska University Hospital obtained SWEDAC accreditation in 1992, to become the first Swedish laboratory accredited by the European standards.

Subsequently, accreditation became something of a trend in Sweden and other parts of Europe, and other laboratories followed suit. At first, this new fashion spread primarily through clinical chemical laboratories, but was later adopted by other medical laboratory specialties such as clinical physiology and Blood Central. The clinics that were engaged in the accreditation process shared a common feature: they all employed technical procedures and technical equipment. It is worth mentioning that although enrolment in the accreditation process is voluntary, the EN 45,000 standard is compulsory for those laboratories that have chosen to attain accreditation.

Accreditation in Lund

The management of the Clinical Chemical Laboratory applied to SWEDAC for accreditation in 1992. The reason for the application was given as prevention – in case of deregulation. If various hospital clinics had free choice of the laboratory they used, there was a certain risk that the Clinical Chemical Laboratory might lose some of the routine tests that could be performed at a lower cost by other, more specialized laboratories. A quality assurance program in form of accreditation would be a good selling feature for the laboratory. Some people even said that it was a matter of competition between the different big hospital laboratories.

The accreditation process was carried out between 1992 and 1994 and the laboratory finally received its accreditation stamp (the three crowns) in early 1995. The work with accreditation was going full speed during our research at the Clinical Chemical Laboratory. After SWEDAC had paid a visit to the laboratory to ensure that it was suitable, an accreditation group was formed comprising one doctor, two laboratory assistants responsible for quality work, two administrators, and the chief doctor who also was the head of the Clinic. The group delegated much of the work to the people on the shop floor. The laboratory assistants were actively involved in producing new routines and documents and putting them into use. They found this to be an exhausting but creative period, and claimed that it made them proud to be associated with a laboratory on its way towards accreditation, and, with it, a higher status.

The most important document produced was the quality manual. Every group of employees was involved in writing it. The manual contained a complete description of the Clinical Chemical Laboratory, including a description of its premises and complete job descriptions for all categories of staff. Thus the quality manual was not merely an abstract description of an average laboratory: it was an *exact description of this particular laboratory*.

Other new routines were, for example, handling deviations in log books placed by every workstation, signing lab answers in the computerized system, making lists on the education and competence of the staff, and making charts of the temperatures at different times in the refrigerators containing lab tubes. Other important changes were the calibration of all technical equipment, and a change from "pirate" glass to accredited glass, which was twice the price but more reliable. Even the physical facilities were affected by the accreditation standards. The lab had to build a reception area and install a security system with locked doors and pass cards for people who were allowed access to the lab. These requirements had to be met by all laboratories applying for SWEDAC accreditation. Thus accreditation changed forms that led to changes in practices; it also changed practices in a way that made them more similar to practices in other laboratories: thus isomorphism *and* isopraxism.

Internal audits were an important part of accreditation, and served as preparation for the external audit made by SWEDAC. Internal audits were performed in all sections of the Clinical Chemical Laboratory and were organized as follows: the two laboratory assistants in charge of accreditation at the laboratory assumed the roles of auditors and inspectors, conducting walkthroughs of the lab sections together with the manager, doctor, and engineer of each section. The auditors had a form which they followed and completed during the audits. Many questions where of the sort, "do you have X?" or "do you do Y?" All equipment, machinery, and technical tools, even a dishwasher, was required to have a user description or a manual. Somebody commented that a dishwasher manual seemed unnecessary as "everybody knows how to operate the thing"; nevertheless the auditors insisted. An interesting feature of the accreditation was that only procedures and techniques that were quantifiable were included in it. Manual and qualitative procedures were therefore omitted from the accreditation.

Isopraxism: imitation through copying

As we could see, all laboratories accredited by SWEDAC were becoming similar to each other – both in the way they were organized (forms) and work process (practices). Several translations were involved in the homogenization process, which led to such *isopraxism*. First, there was a translation that consisted of defining what can be accredited and what cannot. SWEDAC chooses practices that can be connected to the standard as fit for accreditation and excludes the ones that are not. Thus all qualitative processes such as diagnosis, estimation of a sample, or manual laboratory work were omitted from accreditation, as they could not be adjusted to the standard. What could not be standardized was not accredited; as a result, it could not be copied from one laboratory to another.

That copying was a central part of the accreditation idea could also be seen in the translation of the EN 45,000 standard among countries and languages. The translation process was monitored by the standardization organization of EU and by the Swedish counterpart, whose role it was to ensure that the Swedish version of the standard faithfully replicated the original. This was hardly as simple as mechanical copying, however. SWEDAC forbade the previously accredited laboratory – at Sahlgrenska in Gothenburg – from sharing its manual with the Laboratory in Lund. Thus the standardization was not done by copying one manual to another but by copying the local practice – adequately standardized – into the local manual. As the laboratory assistants engaged themselves in finding various solutions to practical problems revealed or created by accreditation, they were transforming both themselves and their work place, adjusting it to the accreditation requirements. By writing down all their work prescriptions in the manual, adjusted to the accreditation standard, and then working by the manual, the laboratory staff overtly adjusted and standardized their work process in accordance with the accreditation standard.

It has been pointed out that imitation or mimesis can be performed either by copying or by contact (Taussing, 1993; Czarniawska, 2002; Diedrich, 2004). In this case, it was both. Much of it was done by copying, but the standards were introduced into practice partly by the responsible laboratory assistants visiting all sections in the internal audit process. The translation, however, went mostly one way: practices and people were adjusted to the requirements of the standard and not the other way around. The connections between the standard and the practice were primarily cognitive;[3] the laboratory work was tied to the measures and requirements described by the standard. Yet there has been an emotional connection between the accreditation and its expected results, a feature that helped make the laboratory staff enthusiastic about the project.

Although this case made us aware of the translation that leads to isopraxism rather than to isonymism or isomorphism alone, a longitudinal study would provide richer insight into how the translation actually happens. The third case, the "chain-of-care" study, provided us with such a possibility.

Before moving to the third case, we would like to point out some of the most noteworthy connections between the first two cases. The medical laboratories can be seen as belonging to the organization field of technical laboratories, but as medical laboratories they also belong to the health care sector. As it turned out, being accredited as a medical laboratory has by no means saved the laboratories from the general quality assurance trend. Most laboratories, in spite of their accreditations, have been obliged to enroll in whatever quality assurance method or model is being tried out at their hospital at a given time. The idea and methods of quality assurance in the broader health care sector in Sweden have not been connected to EU directives or regulations, as is the case of the accreditation model for laborato-

---

[3] This distinction is purely textual. We take it for granted that each cognitive activity has an emotional undertone – that emotions are impossible without cognition. To be precise, we are speaking of connections that relied *primarily* on cognitive or emotional elements.

ries. Thus isopraxism does not fulfill the demands of isomorphism; the latter seems to proceed independently.

Also, the first two cases demonstrate that the difference between coercive and normative mechanisms of homogenization is a matter of degree. At least in Sweden, a widely accepted norm often becomes a law (Jönsson, 1995), whereas a law is expected to "normalize" a certain kind of behavior. The two cases differ however. In the case of quality assurance at Lund University Hospital, one occupational group (administrators, managers) tried to impose its norms on another group (doctors, nurses); whereas in the second case the norm developed within an occupational group (technical laboratories) and was willingly endorsed – probably for that reason.

Chain of Care in Gothenburg

The health care sector in Sweden is heterogeneous and consists of several different actors and activities, ranging from preventive care to emergency treatment. Despite its heterogeneity, the health care sector can be regarded as *one* organization field. Organization fields consist of organizations producing similar products or services and exist to the extent that they are institutionally defined (DiMaggio and Powell, 1991). Fields are kept together by a *system of relationships* in which central and peripheral positions are developed and *dominating organizations* form points of reference and models of activity (Sahlin-Andersson, 1996). Reforms implemented in the health care sector are often initiated by such dominating organizations. In Sweden, the Swedish National Board of Health and Welfare and the National Association of County Councils are the two most influential organizations in this regard. They adopt ideas, develop solutions, and act as distributors and carriers of these ideas. For example, The Swedish National Board of Health and Welfare has contributed to the distribution of ideas concerning quality by financing projects in which participants work with quality assurance. Another example is "process-and-flow" as an organizing principle, which has been a steady trend during the 1990s and which seems to live on. The idea of "chain of care" may be regarded as a manifestation of this trend in the health care sector.

Chain of care could be regarded as having been a fashionable idea in the health care sector in the mid-1990s. It is related to other general ideas such as quality and effectiveness, and was originally context-free. To exclude time- and space-bound features was actually necessary for the translation of the idea to local practice, where it could be regarded from a new perspective and given a different meaning.

One organization that has adopted the idea of chains of care is the National Institute of Working Life (NIWL). In the mid 1990s NIWL started a Healthcare program in order to support projects that focused on horizontal and patient oriented processes. The program managers wanted to avoid directions and control from above. Therefore they did not formulate the program as a means of goals achievement. Instead they emphasized the importance of stimulating local initiatives and experiences. The program was vaguely described and allowed for different interpretations. An invitation to participate in the program was distributed to health care organizations all around the country. More than 300 applications were submitted, many of which described projects that worked with chains of care. Eighteen projects were selected for inclusion in the program, which meant that they received financial support for three years. NIWL did not provide a specific definition of chains-of-care, but used it as a generic term for cooperative horizontal and patient-oriented processes. One of the 18 projects was the Högsbo project.

The patient's journey through the health care system

The aim of the Högsbo project was to develop a chain of care for elderly people. The project was located in one district of Gothenburg in which one-third of the citizens were older than 65 years. The Högsbo project originated from a quality-assurance project in the municipality health care for the elderly. There had been severe problems when older patients were transferred from one health care unit to another, e.g. when patients needed to be transported from their home institution to a hospital or the other way around. In the quality project, the participant organizations realized that they were limited by working merely from the municipality perspective. In order to improve the quality of care, they had to cooperate with other units and organizations; therefore, they redefined their problem from quality to cooperation. Thanks to the financial support from the Healthcare program, the original project members could expand the project to include other organizations. The chain of care was demarcated both geographically and by age – to concern elderly patients from the district of Högsbo. The idea of chain of care was well known among project participants even though it was seen as vague. One of the representatives of a participating organization described it as follows:

> I don't get this with "chain of care". Of course, it is very trendy. For me, a chain of care means that the cooperation between different units of care must be better – better for the patient. It means that people in different units need to understand better what the others do, so that the patient doesn't suffer from various mistaken perceptions (Chain-of-care coordinator at Sahlgrenska University Hospital).

Members of three local health care organizations participated in the project. They came from the local hospital, from primary care units, and from municipality-run care centres. Their activities were separated in space and time. The participants in the project had different occupational identities but they had in common the patients and their care. However the term "patient" had somewhat different meanings in the different contexts. In the hospital, the medical treatment of the patient was given priority. In the primary care unit, the medical treatment also dominated, but not to the same extent. In the municipal elderly care setting, the caring practice had priority. Thus, even if their activities were separated in space and time, the patient was an object that the participants of the project could use as a basis for their joint actions.

The first such joint action was to map the flow of patients. As a result, the journey of the patient through the health care system became abstracted from within the different organizations and illustrated with the help of a flow chart. The map described an ideal-typical chain of care, a description that obliterated (and objectified) the local conditions. This map proved to be highly useful for the participants in the project. It allowed them to identify elements of co-dependence among their various organizations in the chain of care – for example, in coordinated care planning. It also motivated them to read the two different laws regulating their work in order to find legal authority for cooperation. The description in the map supported the identification of units affected by the chain of care for elderly patients. Furthermore, it was used as a basis for the selection of chain-of-care coordinators to be included in a network. Thus, the description was also a way to identify the translators – the users of the idea who could contribute to the translation.

Activities in the chain of care

The Högsbo project was extended to include more units, but the participants of the project had no obvious meeting place. Their work places were geographically distant from each other and most of them had only a vague understanding of the activities in other units. The creation of their own network offered a context whereby the accounts of everyday work of the participants could be swapped. The form of the network meetings was standardized and the project managers defined the agenda. They decided, for example, that the chain-of-care coordinators should write "deviation reports" and that they should practice auscultation, by which they meant that they should "shadow" one another in their work.

The forms for deviation reports were standardized. On the one hand, it was important to make the reports simple and short, to ensure that the coordinators would be more willing to write them. Also, new participants in the project should be able to understand the procedure quickly and the coordinators should be able to transfer it to their colleagues. On the other hand, in order to provide information that enabled action to be taken to address the deviations, the description had to be sufficiently detailed. The chain-of-care coordinators, proceeding by trial and error, eventually developed a deviation-report form. Thus, the form was designed by people who used it in their everyday work setting.

The differences revealed in the deviation reports contributed to the identification of common problems. During the network meetings, these brief descriptions were complemented by more exhaustive narratives. For the participants, this storytelling was a way to mediate both their explicit and tacit knowledge about their work activities. The participants compared their routines and work situations, not with the purpose of finding a common strategy for how the action of care should be conducted, but to identify and clarify similarities and differences. The storytelling served as a substitute for contact during everyday work and facilitated interaction between the participants. Storytelling also facilitated the group process and the participants' understanding of each other's work situation. Thus, coordination was based on shared experiences and understandings mediated by narrative – not by what they saw, but by the stories that were told. They could start a story, leave it for awhile, and return to it in subsequent discussions.

Auscultation, an established practice in the health care sector, meant that the coordinators visited each other's work places and shadowed one another in their work for one day. This practice allowed participants to deepen their understanding of each other's organizations and work tasks. Thus, what for one person was an everyday work item, for the other was a learning situation. The face-to-face interaction guaranteed that the situation was experienced as "real", which also influenced the level of commitment in a group (Metiu, 2002). As one participant said:

> After all, we have watched each other during the auscultations. For me, this was the most important element of this project. I know now how things function in other places and I can even explain it to my colleagues (Chain-of-care coordinator at Sahlgrenska University Hospital).

A model of cooperation

The network meetings confronted participants from different social realms with each other, making it possible for them to reflect and communicate about differences and potential interdependencies among the organizations they represented. The storytelling and other comparisons contributed to the creation of cross-border knowledge among the participants in the Högsbo project. This knowledge was unique in relation to the knowledge of their colleagues, who had not participated in the project.

Soon after the establishment of the network the project, its managers became concerned about how to distribute information about the project to other healthcare organizations. They decided to produce a brochure describing how they worked on the project. They also invited politicians and managers of several healthcare organizations to a meeting to inform them of their experiences with the project. In both the brochure and the meeting the focus was to describe how the project unfolded rather than to discuss its results. The procedure of the project was objectified into what was called *a model of cooperation*.

In order to make it attractive, the model was packaged with help of stories and images. The packaging was carried out by rhetorical elements with the purpose of convincing an intended audience of politicians, managers, and other employees in the health care sector. The shared knowledge enabled participants in the project to combine their differences. The focus came to be *how* instead of *why*, enabling participants to create a common story. The model was a collective representation whereby different commitments and understandings were combined. This did not mean that they achieved consensus; rather the representation contained their multiple understandings and differing translations. As a consequence, the participants could retain their established occupational identities, while at the same time being identified as "chain-of-care coordinators".

The activities leading to objectification and packaging of the model, created a "we-relation" among the participants. They regarded themselves as originators of the model. The participants of the project became the "idea senders" who distributed the model of cooperation. By making presentations about the chain of care and of the project itself to an external audience, they also manifested their role as chain-of-care coordinators. As happened when the idea first came to Högsbo, time- and space-bounded features were once again excluded from the model. It was turned into an object that could travel in time and space carrying unchanged information. Because the content of the model consisted of activities that existed in established practice, it was easily transported to other organizations in the health care sector. Thus, the idea was packaged to appear as recognizable by using established practice and was unique in its combination of practices.

Isopraxism: imitation by contact

This third case demonstrates how practices might become similar to one another due to connections built among actions separated in time and space. In the Högsbo project, such a connection could be described as being simultaneously cognitive and emotional, which was made possible by imitation based primarily on contact.

The circulation of information and the mapping of patient flows achieved the *cognitive* connections. The participants received information and made observations providing them with input on, and an understanding of, the work process. Cognitive connections were also achieved by providing an image of the chain of care for elderly people. The image showed schematically how actions in the chain were connected. These actions did not require meetings between actors. Connections could have been made by referrals or by sending forms from one place to another. The constitution of the Swedish National Board of Health and Welfare that deals with information and coordinated health care planning was, in itself, a cognitive connection, contributing to stability of the project. Thus, the cognitive connections also permitted *coordination at a distance*.

The *emotional* connections were achieved in direct interactions. In the face-to-face encounters between chain-of-care coordinators, there could be a shared understanding concerning, for example, the patient, which contributed to the creation of an emotional connection between actions that were later performed independently. It may also be said that the encounters and the exchange of experiences increased loyalty among participants.

The participants of the project perceived themselves as representatives of a certain way of working, an object that they had constructed together. The emotional connections, on the one hand among the participants and on the other hand between the participants and the object of care, had the consequence of strengthening the willingness of the participants to connect their actions. There could have been resistance to the connecting of actions caused by a wish to retain separate traditions or by a threat to established professional norms. Instead, there was a strong willingness among the participants in the project to connect actions separated in space and time.

The imitation by contact and the resulting cognitive and emotional connections were enabled primarily by two elements of the Högsbo project. Firstly, auscultations enabled the participants in the project to make contact with each other's practice. The coordinators visited each other and "experienced" each other's practice. Secondly, the participants told stories providing examples of their own practices and translated their own stories and stories of the practices of others. This contact made copying easier but also more open-ended: words, actions, and symbols could be transformed into something else, i.e. reinterpreted and redesigned. Thus the achievement of isopraxism does not have to lead to isomorphism or to tight connections among actions. It allows a field to be structured by loose connections among actions that may be as sustainable and stable as tight connections (on the strength of weak ties, see Granovetter, 1973); additionally, they might be easier to achieve since they do not threaten established structures.

Isonymism, Isomorphism and Isopraxism: The Three Cases Compared

The origin of the ideas

In all three cases, the ideas were formulated in some kind of an "idea carrying" organization or organ like Spri or the EU rather than within the organizations that were meant to use them and translate them into action. The idea of using quality assurance in health care was adopted by Spri from the private sector and applied to the public sector like the idea of chain of care (a health sector variation on the "value chain" in marketing); whereas the idea of accreditation was obtained via the EU standardization organization, which in turn had received it through a circuitous route that took it from the USA to Canada to Australia to the EU. The ideas of quality assurance and chain of care were thus moved among sectors, whereas the idea of accreditation was moved among countries but within the same sector. The origins of the ideas are important, as they indicate what or whom the idea-carrying organizations were imitating. In the cases of quality assurance and the chain of care, the inspiration was sought from management models used in the private sector because the private sector, at that time (the mid-1990s) was seen as a good example of organizing and efficiency. The idea of the accreditation of laboratories, in its turn, was passed to the European standardization organ from the Australian one and carried with it the values of the European common market, i.e. free movements of people, finance, goods, and services. Thus, in all three cases, the translations are accomplished by interpreting the ideas in terms of "master ideas" (see Czarniawska and Joerges, 1996) concerning effective management and the power of markets.

Homogenizing and heterogenizing tendencies

The quality assurance idea has circulated within the health care sector in different forms and different practices. One reason for these variations is that, as the idea was moved from the private to the public sector, it became separated as a name, form, and practice. Quality assurance has therefore been open to reinterpretation in all three of these aspects. However, the law on compulsory quality assurance has enhanced the use of the name of the idea, whereas form and practice have remained more open for local translation. Thus the quality assurance case comprises mostly coercive but also normative pressures, as well as processes of isonymism, polymorphism, and polypraxism.

In the case of accreditation, the name, form, and practice are moved and translated together. Because the law on accreditation for laboratories is voluntary for the user, the idea has spread mainly among the laboratories themselves. Although the accreditation, as such, is voluntary, the SWEDAC model is compulsory for the laboratories that enroll in the accreditation

66

process. The accreditation case is thus the case of normative isonymism, isomorphism, and isopraxism.

The chain-of-care project was called different names at different times, including process, flow, cooperation, and chain of care. In the Högsbo project, the practitioners themselves established the practice of chain of care. As they found it to be successful, they "wrapped" the name and the practice into a new form, which, in its turn, could be dispersed in the field. The chain of care is thus a case of normative and mimetic polinymism, isopraxism, and isomorphism.

Both the idea of accreditation and chain of care have been accepted and promoted by the professionals in the practices where they were introduced. In the accreditation case the imitation was accomplished primarily through copying (of the EN 45,000 standard among countries and between SWEDAC's standards and the practices of laboratories applying for accreditation). But it also occurs by contact – between the internal auditors and the rest of the staff. In the chain-of-care case, the practices were imitated mainly through contact established among the participants in the project, but imitation also occurred by copying. Although practices in chain of care were imitated by copy and by contact, the form of this project is, as far as we could determine, an invention, making it conducive to ample use (or copy) of practices that are known to the field (auscultations, for example).

In contrast, the quality assurance idea was neither widely accepted nor promoted by the practitioners; in fact they did their best to decouple the quality assurance practice from the shop floor practice on the wards.

Polymorphism and isomorphism

In order to be sent or to travel in the organization field, ideas must be packaged into an object. In the case of quality assurance this has been a never-ending story; there was and still is no ready-made object – merely an expression associated with quality assurance. The idea carriers, picking from the shelf of existing models and methods, tried different variations at different times. As the models initially were designed for other use, they can be described as "second hand" without close fit. Because the idea has been translated into different models or forms in different practices at different times, it has created polymorphism rather than isomorphism.

Contrary to the quality assurance the accreditation arrived in a package "ready-to wear" (and to copy). As the standard has become not only ready-to-wear but also obligatory, it can be seen as a uniform worn by all accredited laboratories. Accreditation is always contained by the same form and thus isomorphism is the apt description of the phenomenon. In the chain-of-care case, we have yet another type of packaging, as the idea users designed the form of their invention themselves. This can be seen as a custom-made solution. When the new form is spread, it may well lead to isomorphism.

Translating the idea into a local practice

In the quality assurance case, the intention was to copy practices from industry. However there was a gap between what "they" do and the health care practices (probably because of unclear ideas as to what "they" actually do), and this made it difficult to translate the imported models and methods into local practice. As the name was connected to several different forms at different times, the practitioners did not really know what to do with it, other than to decouple it from the actual medical and ward practice. This does not mean, however, that nurses and doctors did not work with the quality assurance program; rather it means that the practice of quality assurance was not integrated into the medical or ward practices. The practice of the quality assurance was performed separately and thus nurses and doctors have been engaged in more administrative work due to implementation of new quality assurances models. As there is no uniform practice of quality assurance in health care, the result is best described as polypraxism.

In the accreditation case, standard and practice were matched on the basis of measurability and technology. In the implementation process, both the laboratory practice and the laboratory itself were transformed to fit the accreditation standard rather than the other way around. Because this process is repeated in all accredited laboratories, it leads to isopraxism.

In the chain-of-care project, the idea was taken from the idea carriers, but filled with local contents. The project demonstrates how the idea of quality assurance has been reinterpreted locally into a new practice, called cooperation, which is more practical both because it seems to be a better solution to problems at hand, and because the project financers were interested in cooperation. Thus, the users chose the idea for pragmatic reasons. The idea became adjusted to the practice, but adjustment occurs among different practices, leading to spontaneous isopraxism rather than to controlled isopraxism, as occurred in the accreditation case.

Three Cases, Three Ideas

The table below summarizes our comparison of the three cases.

Table 4.1. Three cases of translation.

	Quality assurance	Accreditation of laboratories	Chain of care
The idea travels	Among different fields	Within the same field	Among different fields
Name, form, and practice	Are separable	Arrive together	Are separable
Idea creators	Many	An international standardization organ	Many
Imitation through	Adopting the name	Copying	Contact; Invention
Package (form)	Second hand, and not a good fit	Ready-to-wear	Custom-made
The idea travels in the field by	Many different paths, back and forth between the promoter and the user of the idea	One way only – between the promoter and the user of the idea	Mostly from the users to the promoter and to other users
Produces similar or different; names, forms and/or practices	Isonymism, polymorphism and polypraxism	Isonymism isomorphism and isopraxism	Polynymism isopraxism and isomorphism
Translation from form to local practice	Decoupling between forms and local practices; administrative practice decoupled from shop floor practices	The local practice is transformed to fit the form; tight coupling between administrative and shop floor practices	Coordination of different practices; administrative practice becomes a part of the shop floor practices

In this chapter we have traced the three ideas – quality assurance, accreditation of medical laboratories, and chain of care – as they spread in the Swedish health care sector and materialized in the practices at which they were targeted. By using the Czarniawska and Joerges model of the "travels of ideas" (1996, p. 46), we have focused the series of translations through

69

which the ideas travel in time and space. All three ideas are related, although in different ways, to master ideas such as effective management and the power of markets. Such relatedness gives them legitimacy in the field. Two of the ideas are also directly linked, because the chain-of-care project had its origin in a former quality assurance project. We thus discovered the mechanism for how one idea (quality assurance) gets translated into another idea (chain of care) which, in turn, is translated into a practice and then objectified into a "new" form (model of cooperation) prior to being presented to other organizations in the field. Together the quality assurance and chain-of-care cases illustrate how ideas are linked in a continuous chain of translations, and how this continuous chain can be linked together in top-down (quality assurance) and bottom-up (chain-of-care) processes.

Furthermore, the detailed materials of the three cases reveal a much more complex and nuanced picture than the homogenizing effects predicted by the theory of institutional isomorphism. Our findings show that as well as producing sameness, ideas can travel by different paths, assume dissimilar names and forms, and even be transformed into dissimilar practices. We thus detected name, form, and practice as different expressions of an idea through which organizations can be homogenized or heterogenized.

Chapter 5

Lost and Found in the Translation of Strategic Plans and Websites[1]

Hokyu Hwang and David Suarez, Stanford University, USA

The global economy represents a worldwide marketplace with products, practices, and ideas that flow easily and quickly from one location to another. Some ideas and practices in the global economy become fashionable and then suddenly disappear while others maintain their popularity and diffuse broadly. Why some practices spread has been the subject of a number of diffusion studies (Fligstein, 1985; Davis, 1991; see Strang and Soule, 1998 for a review of this literature). A related line of research investigates why some practices become institutionalized, particularly when the benefits are ambiguous (for example, Edelman, 1990; Dobbin et al., 1993). In both lines of research, organizations play an important role as consumers, producers, and carriers of practices and ideas in the global economy.

An area of research that has received far less attention in studies of diffusion is how organizations appropriate and transform a given practice or idea. This stems partly from the theoretical and empirical orientation of diffusion models: "Formal models of diffusion ... are well posed to explain rises in the number of adopters but poorly equipped to account for almost anything else" (Strang and Macy, 2001: 148). Further, the appropriateness of certain ideas and practices differs according to an organization's position in a complex web of constituencies and institutional actors that often make inconsistent demands (Brunsson, 1989). Thus, an expanded flow of management discourse or the availability of organizational practices does not necessarily result in wholesale adoption of new management practices by organizations, but results in differential adoption among organizations.

Even when organizations adopt the same model, variation is common-

[1] Research support provided by the Center for Social Innovation at the Stanford Graduate School of Business, the William and Flora Hewlett Foundation, and the David and Lucile Packard Foundation. We would like to thank Woody Powell, John Meyer, Denise Gammal, Caroline Simard and participants at the Venice conference for comments on an earlier draft.

place. Decision-making within organizations is often "anarchic" due to problematic preferences, unclear technologies, and fluid participation (Cohen et al., 1972) and these internal processes often create divergent responses to the same adopted models. One source of divergence is familiarity. Some organizations are more facile at appropriating a certain idea directly though past experiences or indirectly through organizational members' learning in other settings. For example, if an executive director has extensive for-profit experience or has an MBA, s/he is likely to be well versed in the business language of management ideas and practices. On the other hand, she may not be as adept at dealing with the language or practices of grassroots, social movement organizations. Further, organizations may lack the resources or management skills to incorporate what is available to them even when familiarity and/or some necessity exist.

While taking theoretical cues from the new institutionalist literature (Meyer and Rowan, 1977; DiMaggio and Powell, 1983), we go deeper into the organizations that have adopted a set of practices and analyze how these practices materialize in various settings. As Sahlin-Andersson puts it, "In order to make sense of the fact that organizations simultaneously reveal a striking homogeneity and heterogeneity, we need to understand both how the 'diffusion' happens and how forms and practices are shaped and reshaped in various stages of this process" (Sahlin-Andersson, 1996: 70). In doing so, we employ the idea of translation (Czarniawska and Sévon, 1996). The concept of translation is a useful theoretical tool that is particularly well equipped to shed light on how and why certain practices are appropriated. Unlike the idea of diffusion, translation emphasizes specifically "transformation" and "transference." Translation implies that "a thing moved from one place to another cannot emerge unchanged" (see Czarniawska and Sévon in this volume). Translation thus suggests that the same idea can manifest itself very differently in practice in diverse organizations. Further, translation implies that organizations are not just passive adopters of practices, but are active interpreters and editors of external ideas and models. Therefore, rather than focusing on the diffusion of an idea or a practice itself, the relevant question is how an organization adapts and translates a practice to its particular context.

We begin with the observation that the practice of developing a strategic plan or a website for an organization has become common in many types of organizations and in a variety of areas throughout the world. This chapter sets out to understand how organizations adopt and translate these two practices. While we do not believe that these two practices are bundled together – many organizations adopt just one of these practices and many do not adopt either – we intentionally choose six nonprofit organizations that have both a website and a strategic plan. In this respect, we select "like-minded" organizations that are predisposed to adopting new practices in order to highlight how strategic plans and websites are translated and (re)constructed in different organizational settings.

We selected the six organizations from a broader study of the San Francisco Bay Area nonprofit sector involving interviews with leaders of 200 nonprofits (see also Powell et al. in this volume).[2] This region of Northern California encompasses the three urban centers of San Francisco, Oakland, and San Jose and as well as the surrounding suburbs and rural areas and is inhabited by a population of over 7 million. The quotes we present are drawn from interviews with executive directors of the organizations, and we complement the interview data with other documents and materials available publicly or obtained from the organizations.

In the following section we describe strategic plans and websites as artifacts that embody the modern ideology of organizations as bounded and purposive actors with identities and interests (Meyer et al., 1994) and present short descriptions of the organizations in our study.

Artifacts and Sites

Strategic plans

A strategic plan is a document that articulates a set of goals in various aspects of an organization, specifies action plans or items, and proposes in some cases a set of measures to track progress towards those specified goals in a given period of time. In this sense, a strategic plan portrays an organization as an actor with clear goals and with the capacity to achieve those goals. A strategic plan is formal to the extent that its goals and objectives are specified and to the extent that the plan provides indicators for gauging progress. Strategic plans vary in terms of scope depending on the number of organizational dimensions or aspects to which they apply. In practice, strategic plans vary widely with regard to both their formality and the scope of their contents.

Some goals purport to promote and strengthen an organization's internal capacity such as technological improvement and human resource management while others can be viewed as the organization's aspirations to move into a desired position or attempts to solidify its position in an organizational field. Still other objectives can fall into both categories. For example,

---

[2] Using data from the Internal Revenue Service, the United States taxation authority, digitized by the National Center for Charitable Statistics, we drew a random sample of 200 organizations out of the population of nearly 10,000 nonprofits in the ten-county San Francisco Bay Area. In the U.S., charitable organizations are classified as "not-for-profit" and are given tax-exempt status by the federal government providing they meet certain criteria. Operating charities and foundations are classified as 501(c)(3) nonprofits and are eligible to receive tax-deductible donations from individuals and organizations.

developing a new donor base can thrust an organization into a new location in its institutional environment *vis-à-vis* other organizations through establishing a relationship with a new constituency while strengthening the organization's financial health. Therefore, identities of organizations set the parameters for strategic planning and define appropriate goals on the basis of their current situations with an eye toward an imagined future.

Some organizations are more facile at articulating their aspirations in this particular manner while others frequently rely on consultants. Consultants can serve as planners, facilitators, or even authors for organizations. Differences in the role of consultants have implications for planning processes in which organizational members participate in varying degrees, resulting in divergent meanings and uses of strategic plans across organizational settings. Moreover, once in place, some organizations are more capable of implementing adopted plans and further translating their plans to adapt to changing internal and external conditions.

Websites

Strategic plans may or may not be intended explicitly for public consumption, but websites enable organizations to present themselves to a broad audience. In this respect, websites are "presentations of self" (Goffman, 1959) that reflect the identity of the organization. Research on social identity formation almost always emphasizes individuals or group of individuals, but organizations also negotiate their identities and their positions in the wider field of organizations. As an extreme example, Arthur Anderson, a well-known and now infamous organization, obligated its off-shot Anderson Consulting to change its name (now called Accenture) in 1999. Arthur Anderson wanted to promote its name and identity, and the organization dedicated considerable effort to protecting its brand. The names of organizations are an important component of identity, but websites are becoming increasingly relevant for marketing and for the presentation of self as an organization. While websites change from time to time to engage in various forms of face-work (Goffman, 1967) or identity work (Snow and Anderson, 1987), these modifications tend to be refinements, not wholesale transformations of image and mission.

Nonprofits also consider their potential audiences when they create or change their websites, and audiences can include individual donors, clients, foundations, members, and a variety of other stakeholders. A nonprofit can use a website to promote fundraisers, sell goods, and publish newsletters. It can create "chat rooms" for members to interact privately and provide a way for supporters to donate quickly and securely. The mission and identity of the nonprofit influence how the organization will appropriate a website and how different practices emerge in the websites.

Even when websites focus on the same activities, however, there is still variation in how organizations present themselves through their websites. For example, some organizations update their websites daily and go to great lengths to make information accurate while other organizations create a website and then almost never make changes. More than an issue of technical skill, some organizations may be unable to devote necessary resources to manage their websites; other organizations simply see their websites as a ceremonial statue, a standardized and unchanging representation of the organization. Moreover, variations in the environment of the organization, like relationships with constituents and donors, can also influence how a primary activity is represented on a website. In sum, how an organization translates a website is a dynamic process that involves several filters. While translation often occurs because the practice or "object" can have multiple meanings, translation also takes place as a result of variations in the translator.

Organizations studied

In this section, we briefly introduce the six organizations we investigate to illustrate the translation of strategic plans and websites across different organizational settings.

Companions for Seniors is a social services organization that trains volunteers and pairs them with seniors who need companionship. The organization recruits volunteers through local organizations and its own website, and seniors in need are identified through collaborations with other local social service agencies and hospitals that serve the elderly. The organization is heavily dependent on volunteers for service delivery and its five staff members concentrate on the recruitment and training of volunteers as well as on matching volunteers with seniors in need. Companions for Seniors used to be a local chapter of a national organization, but it recently became "independent" and is no longer financially supported by the national office. This change has caused the organization financial difficulties as it does not charge for its services and depends exclusively on contributions – individual donations make up half of its revenues, and the other half comes from corporations and foundations.

Family Aid is a health organization whose primary focus is on people struggling with infertility and on professionals working in the related areas – therapists, physicians, and attorneys. The organization carries out its work primarily through a telephone hotline, consultations, and semi-annual symposia. Staffing has been chaotic in the last few years. A full-time executive director left the organization due to financial pressures, and now volunteers run the organization. It receives few donations from corporations or foundations, and relies on income generated through program services and membership dues for 85% of its revenues. Family Aid is a regional chapter of a national organization, which provides support materials, information, and templates. Nevertheless, the relationship has been a very difficult and often antagonistic one. In the past this chapter was put on probation when its controversial proposals regarding reproductive cloning and gay and lesbian parental rights clashed with the national organization's positions.

East-West Theater is a dance production company whose main activities include the production of home season performances and touring engagements in the United States. In addition, through its academy, the organization offers dance classes and workshops. While ticket sales for performances at home and on the road generate a significant proportion of the organization's income, classes and workshops generate very little. Recently, government retrenchment has contributed to an increasing reliance on program service revenue. The executive director and artistic director are professionally trained – as a composer and a dancer, respectively. There is one employee with a business background and the other six part-time employees are all dancers. The organization has hired consultants – for example, contract grant writers – for various purposes to compensate for the lack of managerial skills.

Reproductive Choice for All is a pro-choice organization that coordinates a grassroots network of student groups scattered throughout the United States and Canada to promote abortion rights. The main mission is to advocate for changes in university-level curriculum through student activism in local communities. The national office supports grassroots student activism, organizes annual conferences, and coordinates internship programs. Due to the controversial nature of its cause, the organization does not pursue any funding from government or corporations and is entirely dependent on individual and foundation donations, which contribute over 90 percent of its revenue. Since the recent hiring of a new executive director, the organization has experienced a significant transformation with an almost complete turnover of staff and enforcement of a clear division of labor. The new director has extensive managerial experience, having served previously as the executive director of an organization with a staff of 115. The organization's active board of directors provides a number of services for the national office and is comprised mainly of students, physicians and other professionals.

Alliance for Children is an organization that unites agencies and institutions serving families and children in the region, but does not provide any direct services. At the most general level, Alliance for Children promotes social change and accomplishes this mission by bringing together a diverse set of stakeholders including children and families, nonprofits, local governments and politicians. It supports neighborhood-based agencies and organizations that provide information referral and other social services to families around the county. In short, this is a boundary spanning organization operating at the interface of these constituents. It relies primarily on donations and grants from a diverse array of corporations, foundations, government, and individuals. Alliance for Children has grown in the last 10 years under the current executive director's watch, employing 19 people and maintaining nearly $1,000,000 in yearly revenue. The executive director is experienced in social services and public policy, and the board of directors represents a variety of professions and backgrounds.

Food for the Needy is a human services organization whose volunteers deliver meals to senior citizens and people with disabilities in the community within which it is located. The organization chooses not to pursue government funding because it restricts serving meals to non-senior persons in the community. Food for the Needy charges its clients a small fee based on a sliding scale for the meals, but the majority of its revenue comes from individual, foundation, and corporate donations. The organization is highly dependent on its volunteers, as it only employs two part-time staff. Most volunteers are local residents and come from all walks of life: professionals, students, politicians, and even mothers with their babies deliver meals for the organization. The executive director says that she knows the community "like the back of her hand", which is of great help in finding volunteers and mobilizing resources.

Translation of Strategic Plans in Organizations

In all six organizations, consultants were involved in the development of strategic plans although their role differed from case to case. In two organizations (Family Aid and Companions for Seniors), consultants developed strategic plans with limited participation of stakeholders and staff. In East-West Theater, the organization's management team was actively involved in the process, even though the consultant was the main developer of the plan. The primary reason in all three organizations for hiring consultants was the lack of expertise or familiarity with strategic planning. In the remaining three organizations (Reproductive Choice for All, Alliance for Children, and Food for the Needy), consultants played a facilitative role at the outset while organizations themselves were the chief planners.

The differences in the role of consultants can be observed in the content and form of strategic plans. The three most comprehensive and formal plans were produced by the organizations who relied on the consultants for planning, while the other three showed less formal plans with varying degrees of comprehensiveness. In addition, the role of consultants and the interaction between the consultants and staff seem to influence the subsequent utilization of plans in organizations. While all three organizations that developed their own plans utilize and further appropriate them, albeit in different ways, only one of the three organizations whose plans were developed by consultants, East-West Theater, does so.

When consultants plan

Companions for Seniors sought professional expertise because of the previous experience: "... having somebody professional do it would be better than doing it internally, which is what we did before. They are experts. That's obviously what they do for a living, instead of us trying to make it up." The consultant was clearly in charge of producing the plan and the consultant's expertise was evident in the methodical "research" phase that included the collection and analyses of demographic data and the organization's own database of its programs, as well as interviews with various constituents, staff, and volunteers for the organization.

The organization's relationship with a larger national organization sets the parameter for the plan's goals, which are taken directly from the national organization's goals. The five-year strategic plan lays out the national organization's mission, philosophy, and operating principles in detail. The plan also includes objectives and success measures for five organizational goals selected from the national organization's eleven goals, followed by an appendix that presents basic organizational data on budget, staffing, and programs. In addition, the assumptions that guided the strategic plan and the SWOT (Strengths, Weaknesses, Opportunities, and Threats) analysis are included in the appendix as well. The espoused goals address two broad categories: outreach and organizational capacity building. Specific objectives are then framed under these five goals. Identification and targeting of "the truly isolated elderly" and the call for reaching out to ethnic elderly populations are squarely couched in the organization's mission of serving the elderly population. Measures to track progress toward these goals are also mission oriented, e.g. "75 percent of matched elders [should] meet isolation criteria by end of Fiscal Year 2005–2006."

While the plan is both formal in its presentation and comprehensive in its content, a close reading reveals a tension between this local chapter's aspirations derived from the national organization's goals and a self-diagnosed reality. In this sense, the plan has two separate parts. While the first part is nicely aligned with the national organization, the second part, particularly the SWOT analysis, is exclusively focused on this Bay Area affiliate. In the first part, the consultant seems to be adapting a template, probably provided by the parent organization in addition to the adapted goals. While the first part of the plan calls for expansion in services and outreach, the SWOT analysis in the second part refers to "unrealistic expectations for program expansion" and "setting unrealistic, unreachable goals" as weaknesses. In other words, the second part may be read as a critique of the first part.

The tension in the plan reflects the difficult transition this local affiliate is going through *vis-à-vis* the parent. This shift to an independent organization that "pulls its own weight" has led to stronger local engagement. Not only does the organization rely on volunteers for service delivery, but the organization has also begun to involve them in fundraising. The organization depends solely on donations for revenue; 50% come from individuals, with the other half coming from foundations and corporations. Also specific skills and profiles of board members and other volunteers have recently been identified and recruited. Board members used to be "friends," but now the organization recruits individuals with specific skill sets or backgrounds such as public relations skills or corporate backgrounds from the local business community that would help facilitate further local engagement. These organizational changes are not reflected in the strategic plan.

The consultant produced a highly stylized strategic plan, but the organization drifted away from it. The plan is less likely to be further appropriated and translated to serve as a meaningful organizational tool, particularly given the organization's changing relationship with the parent and the tension within the plan itself. Indeed, the executive director rarely referred to his strategic plan during the interview. When asked about the benefits of strategic planning, the executive director responded, oblivious to the contradictory assessments and the plan's split personality: "It helped us focus our planning ... and our deliverables."

Family Aid developed its current strategic plan when a consultant who was interested in the executive director position for the organization offered to develop a plan. The proposal, however, initially was met with hesitation, according to the interim, volunteer executive director: "Because we had done it before ... I knew how much work it was to do. And our board has been reluctant to put the work in, because it's so time-consuming." Reluctantly, the consultant was hired, and it was only the consultant who was involved in the development of the plan: "She has that skill, and it is really incredible. So she really jump-started a process that would have been very, very time-consuming and we may never have really been able to do it, it would have been like pulling teeth." The consultant conducted a "Needs Assessment" survey of a few board members and volunteers, but, curiously, without any input from the acting executive director. Based on the inputs collected through the survey and complemented by her observations of the organization, the consultant developed the plan.

Throughout the interview, the organization's acting executive director made a clear distinction between "professionals" – people who worked in business or the corporate environment – and "amateurs." Currently, volunteers are running the organization. The board of directors consists of professionals who work in related fields or are adoptive parents. The board is also comprised of "amateurs" who, the acting executive director elaborates, are "infertile people who have found a niche here." In the past, "professionals" managed the organization. For an organization that serves people with intimately personal issues, however, valued qualities for volunteers are personal (and sometimes professional) knowledge of particular medical and psychological problems and empathy for the people suffering from those problems. To these self-proclaimed "amateurs," strategic planning poses a daunting, time-consuming task. Indeed, there had been a strategic plan under the previous paid executive director – a "professional" who had corporate background. But since her resignation due to financial pressures, Family Aid's board of directors cancelled its annual board planning retreat.

There are four broad areas identified as goals in the strategic plan: services, outreach, organizational development, and fundraising. Each goal is elaborated with detailed action plans on specific elements. While the plan proposes various specific measures to "maintain, strengthen and expand existing services," and to "expand outreach to potential professional and regular membership and to improve publicity and marketing," the overall content of the plan illustrates the organization's insularity from the external environment. Given the specific nature of the issues concerning the organization, the organization may not necessarily have a broad appeal to the general public or engagement with the external environment. However, according to the plan, there are resources to be appropriated, and the organization currently does not take advantage of these opportunities. One obvious source is the national organization which provides useful resources to its affiliates. For instance, regarding board development, the consultant suggests:

> Develop an updated board "book" containing bylaws (including recruitment strategy and policy), business and strategic plans, minutes from recent meetings, policy decisions and educational articles. Examples of all these can be found in the existing board book. The national organization's "Developing a Chapter Management" is a useful document.

In fundraising, the plan proposes to develop sponsorships and partnerships with for-profit organizations in related fields to generate more revenues. In short, the strategic plan, as developed by an outsider, cries out for the need to link up and reach out to the external environment, starting with the parent organization and for-profits in related fields.

The reaction of the acting executive director to the plan suggests that this may not be an easy task:

> It is sometimes very strongly worded. I think the consultant became a little disenchanted, and some of that shines through in a negative tone that was quite painful upon first reading. It has taken some days to distance myself and realize it is not about me. It is not about me.

Her initial reaction was to take the strategic plan's critical tone personally, but eventually she saw its potential benefits. It remains to be seen whether the plan will have positive ripple effects through this volunteer-based organization whose board considered strategic planning time-consuming and in fact discontinued the annual board planning retreat. Further, the organization's prior planning experience suggests that it was not the absence of planning, but the lack of capacity and resources that hindered plan implementation. The executive director mentioned that she and her staff "would spend a lot of time talking and make a lot of what we thought were decisions, and then we would realize we cannot afford to hire people. Those decisions were fantasies. It was fun, but not realistic in any way." This may suggest that the strategic plan may have been dead on arrival.

East-West Theater's initial motivation for strategic planning was the opportunity for funding from the National Endowment for the Arts (NEA), a prominent federal agency that provides funding for arts organizations. The executive director – a classical music composer by training – admits to earlier doubts as to the benefits of strategic planning: "In the beginning we didn't have any motivation ... we didn't realize the benefits. Why do we need this?" Upon receiving an NEA grant, however, the organization hired a consultant to develop the East-West Theater's strategic plan.

This plan is a product of a year-long interaction between the consultant and the management team in which the latter took it as a learning opportunity and benefited immensely from the planning process. The consultant came to the office every two weeks to discuss a specific issue such as fundraising or the board of directors. The discussions were written down and later incorporated into the plan. During this process, the executive director's conception of strategic planning was transformed:

> We did not care about those things before. Sometimes we did not know where we wanted to go for the next two years, and now from that process, we learned how to think about a lot of things two years ahead ... the benefit is not the words on the paper – it is the process of making it clearer in our minds.

The strategic plan covers all organizational aspects, from artistic visions, philosophy, and programs, to marketing and development, as well as human resources and financial management. The plan even touches on facilities management and includes detailed job descriptions of key positions. In the plan, the organization's identity is defined as the cross-section of the West and the East, traditional and contemporary arts, and mainstream and ethnic America. As a result, the organization contributes a unique voice to American arts and explicitly models itself after established mainstream arts organizations: "The artistic director seeks to contribute her distinctive Chinese American dance technique to the field of professional dance, with the hope that one day it will become as mainstream as the Martha Graham technique or the Katherine Dunham technique." Further, as part of defining its role to fuse traditional Asian and Western culture, collaborations with other mainstream arts organizations figure prominently into the plan. At the same time, the plan, motivated by flagging government support for arts organizations and increasing competition for foundation funding, lays out development efforts to reach out to the corporate sector for funding and to develop and expand its ethnic donor base.

Given the organization's current capacity of 3 full-time staff, the plan and its ambitious goals serve as a long-term vision statement. For instance, securing "a low-cost, long-term (20 to 30 year) rental lease from an established studio" is planned under facilities management. The organization is in the business for the long haul, and its vision to grow into a mainstream arts organization like the Martha Graham Company is clearly embodied in the plan. The planning process, then, serves as an exercise for articulating the organization's identity and niche: "The most valuable outcome of our planning meetings was not only greater clarity about our identity, but also discovering our niche in American Arts." The lack of general managerial skills or knowledge has been overcome by learning the ropes "little by little," and it seems that strategic planning is another learning process. The plan is now updated internally, the executive director mentions. This suggests that strategic planning has been embraced by the organization as a useful process and is becoming a routine feature of organizational practice. Indeed, at the time of the interview, the organization was in the process of developing a plan for the next phase.

When organizations plan

In the case of **Reproductive Choice for All,** with the departure of the founding executive director, staff and the board of directors "needed a new strategic plan that reflected the new life phase of the organization". The board initiated a planning process and formed a strategic planning committee. A consultant was hired to help facilitate the process. The executive director describes the planning process from the beginning and emphasizes the competence of her board:

> I started on October 15th. Less than two weeks later there was a full weekend board meeting. At the meeting the board decided it was time to do another long-range plan. They wanted to complete it between the end of October and the board meeting in the beginning of April. So they assigned a committee to this process and hired a consultant to help the board facilitate the process. They sent out stakeholder surveys to all the student group leaders, all the student advisory council members, all of our funders, and they conducted 12 telephone interviews with seven of the funders and five select other important people and factored all that data into the development of the plan. And they did that all in less than six months.

Evident in this account is that the board initiated the planning process with the intent to usher in a new phase of the organization and had the capacity to push forward to produce the plan in a relatively short period of time. The process also highlights the organization's identity as the supporter of student groups.

Reproductive Choice for All's plan is divided into two parts. The first part deals with "strategic goals" mainly dealing with its programs. The second part deals with "organizational goals," laying out objectives in fundraising, communications and technology, and board and staff development. While the plan covers a broad array of issues, the plan does not specify measures to track progress in particular plan objectives. The only exception is the fundraising section, which proposes expanding private donations by at least $50,000 and increasing individual donations to over 30 percent of annual revenues. Enhancing and broadening ties to its pro-choice constituencies and medical institutions figure prominently in the plan. The goal of developing the organization's own grassroots network of student groups is particularly notable. Its organizational goals concern the rationalization of the organizational structure. For example, annual evaluation of job roles, staffing needs, salary, and benefits are proposed in the staff development section. These rationalization goals fit with the board's initial motivation for developing a plan that reflects a new, mature phase of the organization and also the arrival of a seasoned executive director.

It is difficult to overstate the role of the organization's extremely capable board in the planning process. The newly hired executive director, with her extensive managerial experience, was up to the task of dealing with a board comprised of overachieving students. Her own managerial knowledge allows her to appropriate the adopted plan to fit the capacity of the organization:

> We adopted that strategic plan of April 2002 and then in the winter of 2003 I went back to the executive committee, and I said the strategic plan is written so that all the goals are of equal importance. We had six staff people at that time, and I said, "There is no way we can do everything in the plan well. So you need to tell me what the priorities are, what you would like us to do really well, and what you're willing to have us attack in maintenance mode." So that led to another whole process of priority setting that has helped a lot.

For this organization, translation of the strategic plan is an on-going process. The plan is a living document that has been appropriated by the executive director to guide the organization with a limited staff.

In **Alliance for Children's case**, strategic planning is a taken-for-granted, routine exercise: "I think people generally feel that in order to be doing a good job as a nonprofit, you need a strategic plan. You have to. That's just part of doing business." The Alliance for Children produces strategic plans with the help of a facilitator and does so regularly (every three years). The executive director, senior staff, and the board of directors participate in planning, and a consultant who used to be a board member and is familiar with the organization serves as a facilitator. Although strategic planning is a regular part of the organization's activities, the executive director showed ambivalence about planning:

> Circumstances around us change so fast. Strategic planning is useful in knowing where we would like to go and sort of focusing our thoughts. But when you start trying to get into Step A, Step B, time-lining stuff, it doesn't turn out to fit the real world very well. And if you get too locked into following that, you miss other opportunities.

The executive director is well aware of both the benefits and the pitfalls of planning. She further elaborates the purpose of planning by comparing a plan to a baseball mitt:

> When my sons were learning how to play baseball, they'd tell them to get into this stance in the outfield with their legs spread and in a slight crouch. And their hands out, so they can move in any direction at any moment. And I think that that's what we need to do. So there's planning involved, because there are the rules of the game. You have to know the rules of the game. You need a mitt. You need to know something about catching, but when it comes right down to it, you have to be able to move on a moment's notice.

The purpose of planning, in the end, is to help the organization "move on a moment's notice" as circumstances change, and ultimately, to help fulfill its mission: "The bottom line is that we're going to all be on the same page, and we're going to continue to try to notice what the problems are that families are facing and figure out how to bring people together to address those issues." The Alliance for Children's plan, as the executive director indicates, is intentionally open-ended.

The open-ended nature of the process explains the plan's informal quality. There are six stated goals in the plan, falling into two broad categories: internal capacity building (e.g., fundraising, board and personnel development) and external relations (e.g., public relations and coordinating with other organizations it supports). No measures to track progress are found in the plan. Further, the strategic plan is underdeveloped and to a certain extent under-articulated. For example, although "Develop and communicate a clear public image" is stated as one of six goals for the plan, there is no section devoted to issues regarding public relations. It is particularly surprising that this is not addressed since public relations are identified as a key weakness in the SWOT analysis in the plan.

Nonetheless, the organization hired a for-profit marketing firm, as a result of strategic planning, to conduct a study of community members' perception of the Alliance for Children and to help build a better image. Two tasks for the firm were to develop the website and to help the organization better articulate its message. The planning process identified the perception of the organization and the visibility of the organization as two weaknesses. These findings were particularly problematic for the Alliance for Children, given that the organization works as the central hub of collaborating organizations. The utility of planning, then, was to identify and focus on the problem of visibility, but the specific course of action that was actually taken was never formally written into the document.

Food for the Needy's board of directors initiated strategic planning. The board proposed a planning retreat, created a strategic planning committee, and hired a local consultant familiar with the organization to facilitate the meeting at the retreat. According to the executive director, the primary motivation was to build solidarity within the board and organization:

> The main reason I think the board got together ... was just to build some camaraderie between board members because the organization felt very scattered. About six or seven board members met several times and ... the big decision was to have a retreat and get everybody together, and surprisingly every single member of the board gave up a day of work and came to that retreat.

The obvious outcome of this strategic planning retreat was increased solidarity as every board member sacrificed a day of work to participate. Substantively, moreover, a need to focus on outreach to respond to changes in the community was identified.

Food for the Needy's strategic plan looks more like a summary of the board retreat meeting during which the plan was developed; the plan is neither formal nor comprehensive. First, the plan does not indicate any specific time period covered although the proposed goals have time lines associated with them. The document summarizes accomplishments since the previous strategic planning meeting and identifies issues brought up at that meeting. In addition, the document identifies issues that have not been addressed since the previous planning meeting. These issues are then taken up as goals. There are two very specific goals and one general goal. The first goal is simply to increase the number of meals delivered. The second is to secure adequate office space that is in close proximity to a kitchen where meals are prepared. The third is "to review and increase corporate giving." Board members proposed a list of potential corporate donors – almost all local businesses such as retailers and banks. However, no target amount is provided with the list of potential donors or the proposed program to increase corporate donations.

To promote the organization's meal services, the plan proposes the formation of a committee to personally visit various sites listed in the plan. As with the list of potential corporate donors, this list of sites is almost exclusively local and includes organizations such as schools, churches, and senior centers. The plan also calls for the development of a "large postcard" for multiple uses such as mailing to new families moving into the community. Similar to the Alliance for Children, the planning process was more valued than the actual product of planning. Planning happens, but not regularly – more like when there is a need for a team building exercise. Moreover, a sense of community permeates every page of the plan. Goals are proposed and implemented, but it was the camaraderie among board or "family" members at the retreat that was valued more than the actual contents of the plan. The contents are more incidental by-products of group solidarity. In other words, the strategic plan is more valuable as a process that the Board went through to strengthen its in-group ties and understanding, thus playing out its localness, and less as a formal exercise with immediate strategic application.

"Living" plans vs. "dead" plans

While all six organizations adopt a strategic plan, Companions for Seniors and Family Aid are what in diffusion theory is called "passive adopters," and the other organizations are active translators, involved in sensemaking. This difference leads to the production of "dead" plans that are unlikely to be appropriated in the future for Companions for Seniors and Family Aid. In contrast, the other four organizations actively utilize the plans to benefit the organization and are therefore more likely to continue with planning, although each for different reasons. Active translation leads to different appropriation of strategic plans. East-West Theater's plan serves a long-term guide or vision in its efforts to join the mainstream arts world. Reproductive Choice for All's plan serves as a shorter-term organizational tool. Both Alliance for Children and Food for the Needy find the process of producing a plan more meaningful than the actual plan, but for different reasons. For Alliance for Children, strategic planning helps the organization to respond quickly to external opportunities on a moment's notice because planning helps everyone to be on the "same page". On the other hand, for Food for the Needy, strategic planning is a vehicle that enhances group solidarity.

Website Translations

All organizations used their websites for a variety of purposes, but differed in how they represent these activities and in what they prioritize. We identified three primary activities for the websites we analyze: *resource mobilization, network building, and program promotion.*

Resource mobilizing websites

The website for Companions for Seniors is focused particularly on fundraising, volunteering, and public relations. Every page of the website encourages visitors to donate money directly to the organization, and donors can use a credit card to give online. The website includes a specific page on different types of donations. Potential donors are encouraged to give through workplace giving campaigns and to participate in matching gift campaigns with their employers in addition to typical ways to donate. Visitors can use their credit cards to buy tickets for raffles and for other fundraising events. In addition, the website encourages volunteering and thanks corporate sponsors. According to the executive director the website serves as the primary tool for recruiting new volunteers to act as companions to seniors.

Food for the Needy also prioritizes fundraising activities and public relations on its website. Although visitors to the website cannot use a credit card to contribute, every page of the website underlines the value of donations. The website describes exactly how donations are used and specifies how long a client can be fed with different contribution amounts. The website offers the opportunity to leave a legacy donation or to give in the honor of other individuals. Several pages of the website are devoted to ways corporations can get involved with the organization, soliciting corporate donations, and to explaining why their contributions are necessary. Food for the Needy acknowledges corporate sponsors in a page devoted to them and lists hyperlinks to each organization for visitors who might want to learn more about the corporate sponsors.

Besides the common emphasis for their websites, Food for the Needy and Companions for Seniors are similar along a number of other dimensions. Both organizations rely on a large number of volunteers to carry out programs and provide services to the elderly and the needy at low or no cost. In spite of the fact that these two organizations have similar goals and prioritize the same activities on their websites, however, the websites are utilized in very different ways. Despite its website content, Food for the Needy virtually ignores its website, does not work to update it, and in reality mobilizes resources almost exclusively through interpersonal contact. By contrast, Companions for Seniors actively and successfully uses its website to recruit volunteers and board members, and increasingly uses the website to generate donations. Subtle differences in the goals of the two organizations and their stakeholders explain some of their differences.

Food for the Needy decided to develop a website in a strategic planning session in 1998. The executive director said, "Outreach has been one of the keys that came out of strategic planning – like establishing a website." Although "outreach" can have many meanings, in this case the executive director refers to maintaining a presence on the Internet. The executive director clarified, "There is a real feeling of community here, so frankly, if the organization had a problem financially I would pick up the phone and call ten people and say that I need a check from them for $50." The identity of the organization is "grassroots" and local, and the organization relies on face-to-face interactions for financial support and for volunteer recruitment instead of the website.

Food for the Needy operates in a small community. The executive director is from the community, and she knows the community well. The focus of the work is local, and "high-touch" contact with its community renders the website only marginally salient for fundraising and for recruiting volunteers. The same is true for public relations and interacting with donors. The executive director has a background in public relations and uses those skills in her daily work. Even though the organization solicits and acknowledges corporate donations through the website, in practice the fundraising and relationship building takes place through personal interactions. The executive director is a capable fundraiser, but does not apply her skills to the website. It is not so much a lack of technical capacity, but rather Food for the Needy simply does not exploit its website for fundraising and volunteer recruitment to the same extent as Companions for Seniors. For Food for the Needy, fundraising and recruiting volunteers on the website is more of a ceremonial activity than a practical, resource-seeking activity.

Companions for Seniors provides an interesting contrast. In the past, the organization successfully utilized the website to recruit new board members and to solicit individual donations. Recently, the organization changed its website substantially to reach and recognize a wider array of donors and sponsors, expanding its use of the website as a practical tool. The website gives a more prominent role to corporate sponsors – corporate "logos" of donors now appear on the homepage. The updated website also enables individuals to purchase raffle tickets online, and it has become the primary means to recruit new volunteers. The executive director hopes to further expand the use of the website for other purposes.

Why does Companions for Seniors more actively utilize its website for resource mobilization than Food for the Needy? Both organizations have the same mission and "core competencies" – they are both very good at recruiting volunteers and soliciting donations. Whereas Food for the Needy relies on interpersonal relationships rather than investing its resources in its website, Companions for Seniors does not have that luxury. Companions for Seniors does not operate in a small, tightly-knit community where the executive director can simply "pick up the phone" to get enough donations or volunteers. For them, the Internet presents an important opportunity to reach a wider audience to mobilize resources with limited staff.

Network-building websites

The Alliance for Children and Reproductive Choice for All focus on building a community of supports through their websites. The Alliance for Children attempts to develop a cohesive network of providers for children's services and links children and families to the services they need. According to the executive director, the website is intended to be a visual replication of the organization itself. The website posts a searchable database of service providers and directs visitors to local organizations that can provide assistance. Because the organization does not provide direct services, it uses the website primarily to bring families in need into contact with service providers.

The website for Reproductive Choice for All attempts to build a network of individuals dedicated to serving the cause of the organization. The website describes how to participate in local groups and promotes the annual conferences as a way to interact with members who are dispersed throughout the United States. In addition, the website has a secure, members-only section where the community may interact. This protected space also has a database where group leaders "report a consistent set of data to the national office so we know how many events they held and how many group members participated." Data of this nature help the central office coordinate new activities and plan future events. In addition to providing the secure section, the organization goes to great lengths to maintain the anonymity of donors and to protect the privacy of its members.

The Alliance for Children and Reproductive Choice for All both utilize their websites to maintain large and diffuse networks of individuals and organizations. The broad nature of their programs influences how they represent these activities on their websites. In both organizations the websites link individuals and organizations that do not often engage in face-to-face interactions. Although the mission, the goals, and the identities of the two organizations focus these organizations on network building, the network for Reproductive Choice for All may seem insular and opaque to non-members. On the other hand, the network for the Alliance for Children is completely transparent. This difference in the nature of their causes is reflected in the ways the two organizations organize and present their websites.

Members of Reproductive Choice for All communicate with each other constantly over email, and the executive director admits, "our whole network works on emails." The Internet is a key way for members to meet and stay in contact with each other, which is further facilitated by the website. The network is large and active, and requires smooth communications among members, but much of the work of the organization requires anonymity. Reproductive Choice for All makes significant efforts to insure confidentiality. The decision not to list sponsors on the website stems from controversy over the wider issue of abortion; they protect donors from unwanted publicity. The same is true for other aspects: the website never mentions staff, never mentions the board of directors, and never identifies members by name.

Like Reproductive Choice for All, the Alliance for Children's website encourages individuals to contribute and makes it easy through online giving. The organization hired consultants to help develop the website, but the executive director says, "We decided on content as a staff. We just went through what we thought the uses were, and they had a big staff planning session on it." The focus of the website is on community building, maintaining the network of organizations dedicated to protecting children, and on making all of the resources for clients completely transparent. The Alliance for Children wants its website to serve as a "one-stop shop" where all information on local services relevant to children can be found. The Alliance for Children thanks its sponsors, lists affiliated organizations and staff members, and offers free public access to its database. The executive director states the purpose of the website very clearly:

> The primary purpose is to link people together around children's issues, and make things happen for kids. The website is an electronic replication of that. So it's a way to link people together ... we created a website where everybody can get information.

Both organizations stand out in their focus on network building and in their ability to support and facilitate their networks via the website. Differences in identity and stakeholders influence variations in how the two nonprofits organize and present the websites to support and facilitate their networks. Reproductive Choice for All advocates for a sensitive cause, and it is situated in a context that necessitates high levels of anonymity and confidentiality. The Alliance for Children, on the other hand, advocates for a cause far less controversial than abortion. Consequently, the two organizations actively employ websites as organizational tools, but they vary in how they translate network building to the websites.

Program service websites

East-West Theater and Family Aid both feature program services and earned income activities on their websites. Family Aid's homepage provides a general overview of the organization and makes the case for its program services. Fees are charged for most of the program activities, and the website reflects this emphasis on generating revenue. The homepage also recruits members, advertising the organization's symposium and fee-based support groups such as adoption, surrogacy, and in-vitro fertilization.

The website for East-West Theater also focuses on its program services and other revenue generating activities. The homepage describes the dance company and its distinctive performance style. The website posts the touring schedule and explains where and how to purchase tickets for performances. The website also promotes an online gift shop and explains how to book the dance company for private performances. Finally, the organization features its after-school and other school-based programs. East-West Theater recently revised its website to make corporate sponsors more visible and to increase sales in its new gift shop. These changes are part of the organization's attempt to utilize the website "to sell home season and touring tickets, but to also promote the image of East-West Theater, to break into e-commerce, and to generate a stronger web presence". The website has become a central aspect of the organization's marketing strategy, and these changes are based on the notion that the Internet provides new opportunities for sales and for promoting the identity of the organization.

This level of capacity for translating program services onto the website is, at first glance, surprising because the executive director of East-West Theater had no experience managing a business before founding the organization and no background in technology. He admitted, "It takes a little while to become professional." Although this might suggest that the organization would be unlikely to translate program services skillfully onto the website, his comment indicates that business skills are desirable and helpful for the organization. In describing one of his employees, the executive director clarified, "She's from a business background, not from a nonprofit background, but I think we get advantages from that … it helps the organization a lot. I think business backgrounds are very good." Although the executive director does not have a business background, he is "professionalizing" the organization's management, and this managerial orientation is reflected in the way the organization has incorporated the websites as a revenue-generating strategy.

While East-West Theater views the Internet as an opportunity and actively uses the website to market its performances and other services as a revenue-generating strategy, Family Aid has been unable to translate business practices skillfully to the website. Although Family Aid also relies on program services, the organization has a totally different orientation toward marketing and the Internet. The executive director recognizes that similar organizations have been using the Internet to provide services and grow revenue, yet Family Aid has been slow to utilize its website in such a way.

In the past, the organization experienced difficulty professionalizing its staff:

> We have had people here who have been professionals, people who worked in the business sector and can really bring those skills to our organization. People like that … have been almost too good for what we do – the kind of day-to-day little office stuff. I call it "playing office", what you have to do

becomes rather boring to people like that. They want a bigger stage. And they talk sometimes about making us a bigger stage, but ultimately become frustrated and move on.

Affected by these experiences, the executive director has since been reluctant to hire individuals with a business orientation. Rather than viewing the Internet as an opportunity, the organization has been paralyzed in its efforts to develop an Internet-based marketing strategy. This is particularly problematic for Family Aid because it is clear that the Internet as a medium is having a negative impact on the organization. When asked how the recent economic downturn has affected Family Aid, the executive director replied:

Well, membership has dropped. And we believe that it's partly because of the fee to be a member. I believe the Internet has also had an impact on us … people can get advice or support via the Web twenty-four hours a day for free by chatting away, and we can't offer that. So I think the Web has been the impact more than anything.

This suggests that Family Aid is losing revenue to other organizations that are more skilled in utilizing the Internet to serve clients or that have different revenue structures to support their missions and services. The strategic plan calls for the organization to "expand electronic services: online membership applications, donations, registrations for volunteers and events, members-only chat room". Despite this plan, the organization has not been able to secure "in-house" capacity to develop program service revenue on the website, and the executive director's antipathy toward hiring professionals makes it difficult to acquire the necessary capability to implement these ideas.

Both organizations attempt to translate revenue generating activity onto the website, but only East-West Theater has been able to embrace the Internet as a new opportunity for sales and to appropriate the website for marketing and revenue generation. It is the orientation toward professionals, or the lack thereof, that influences organizational capacity to utilize the Internet for service provision and revenue generation.

The many faces of websites

All six of the organizations in this study have websites, but these organizations differ substantially in the content they emphasize and in the ways in which they present that content. These organizations are situated in different environments supported by diverse stakeholders, leading to differences in how they create websites to serve their missions and clients. Even when they employ similar strategies, there is a high degree of variation between organizations. Similarly, organizations that adopt the same practices often differ in the actual presentation of those activities on their website. While in some cases differences are related to organizational capacity, in other cases organizations use their websites for ceremonial purposes or as signals of legitimacy rather than for functional purposes. Further, variation occurs throughout the translation process in the commitment to or use of the website as well as in the way an organization's identity and activities are portrayed with varying skills and efficacy.

Polysemic Artifacts and Innovative Translators

The analyses of strategic plans and websites show that the same artifacts can materialize very differently in concrete organizational settings. In our text, we privilege the organizations over the artifacts as primary sources of variation – that is, the translator, over what is being translated. However, our descriptions of strategic plans and websites across six organizations show the protean qualities of these artifacts. Translation is an interactive process that involves both the translator and the translated. And during the process, both the translator and the translated are transformed. This implies that there are at least two sources for the polysemic nature of the translation process. While a thing or idea can be received and appropriated differently across settings, that thing or idea itself can contain multiple meanings. Moreover, an artifact with multiple meanings lends or manifests itself to more imaginative or innovative translation.

Finally, isomorphic changes can create diversity within similarities: all six organizations developed strategic plans and websites, but they appropriate these artifacts for different purposes and uses. Although the diffusion of a practice can create surface-level convergence among organizations, we find variation and diversity where most diffusion studies would find only isomorphism. In other words, while an idea or practice may diffuse widely, the translation of that idea or practice in concrete organizational settings and contexts ensures great variation in purpose and utilization. Diversity produced as a result of active translation by organizations, however, turns out to be somewhat bounded because the translation of these artifacts reflects organizational attempts to engage the wider world. As externally constructed "soft actors" (Meyer, 1994), organizations interpret, edit, and translate exogenous ideas to fit their perceived realities; and organizations do so in large part to confirm their externally derived identities and thereby further integrate themselves into the wider environment.

Chapter 6

Environment's Many Faces: On Organizing and Translating Objects in Stockholm

Petra Adolfsson, Göteborg University, Sweden

A focus on actions is a valuable perspective for understanding organizing as a process (Weick, 1979). But what actions should be studied? One way to choose is to let another element of organizing – objects – lead the way. And why objects? As Bruno Latour (1996a) says, for somebody who wants to be an important actor, it is essential to create lasting relations. Thus, it is not only people who are recruited into chains of associations and whole networks; as much durable material as possible is recruited as well. This chapter is a story about the environment becoming part of a city, and one of the ways in which this city is organized. I show how air and water are translated into digits, which are translated into reports – objects– that are part of the environment monitoring. Objects, in different shapes and forms, are crucial for such monitoring.[1]

Cities are interesting in many ways. As Rolf Solli and Barbara Czarniawska (2001) point out, there is something magnetic about the city: it is a place where you can find everything – including ideas. Thus environmental concern is an idea that was attracted by and incorporated into city management – the process of running the city. This general idea is, in turn, being translated in the local context into actions and objects. The focus of this chapter is on such objects and collective actions in the city and the ways in which they are connected to each other. The city is Stockholm, the capital of Sweden, often marketed as a "Clean City" because of its fresh air and pure water. How does one know, however, what air is fresh and which water is pure? What interpretations are made, by whom, and how are they used? In order to answer these questions I have followed the translation of air and

[1] The study was part of Managing Big Cities, a research program at GRI, Göteborg University. The Bank of Sweden Centennary Foundation has financed the program and my research has also been supported by *Adlerbertska Forskningsfonden* and the Department of Business Administration at Göteborg University.

water into information about air and water quality, and then into its uses in different situations in the city.

Air

Let me begin on the roofs of Stockholm.

On a roof in the middle of the city there is an air monitoring station that has been there for 40 years. It was the first such station in the city, but today it is a part of an automatic monitoring system run by SAN, an organization unit in the city administration. Analyzers and instruments, including computers at the stations, transmit average levels of different pollutants to the office hourly.

There is also a so-called passive monitoring – of sulphur dioxide and nitrogen dioxide – conducted by samplers mounted on a simple construction that can be placed on a tree or a drainpipe. The samplers are removed once a month, sent to a laboratory for analysis, and replaced with new samplers. This method is used continuously and on a project basis.

The staff members have their specific areas of competency and responsibility. There are several actions involved in the work related to air quality: buying and installing monitoring instruments; buying or creating the software that allows the instruments and computers to communicate with each other; collecting data and creating graphs and texts from the calculations; and, of course, maintaining the stations.

The automatic monitoring systems used by SAN are based on various technologies, like chemical processes. The systems include both well known standardized monitoring systems and, more recently, developed systems. Together, the instruments generate data on air quality, which are transferred to the database at the office at specific time intervals. Once this information has been stored in the database, it becomes available on the Internet the same day for all interested parties to study. Great effort is expended in tracing various types of errors, a task that requires the staff member to have experience with normal variation in different situations in order to recognize unusual variations. Some staff members work primarily with the computers, busying themselves with calculations of the collected data based on models and report production. They often focus on the relationship between air pollution levels and the limit values, which are based on the air indicators for health protection suggested by the European Community and the World Health Organization.

In the translation of the object "air", other objects are important: the instruments. The monitoring staff are busy maintaining the instruments and ensuring that there is no interruption in the monitoring process. Instruments permit the creation of inscriptions, which are easy to move and reproduce.

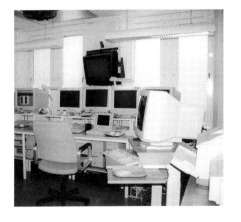 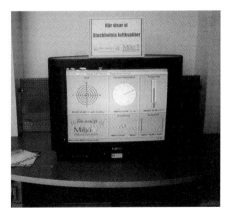

Air Quality Indicator nitrogen dioxide (NO₂)

for Stockholm County urban area.

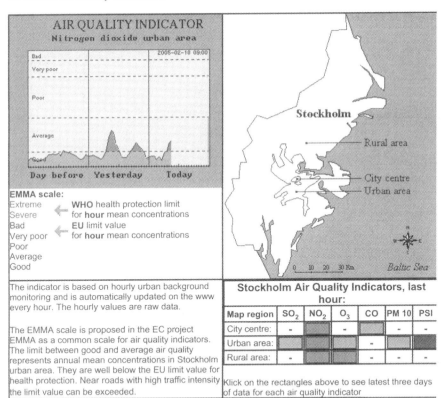

There are significant advantages to inscribing the air into figures, graphs, and other descriptors (Latour, 1990). Although mobile, inscriptions are immutable and their scale can be modified; they can be added, subtracted, multiplied. Also, the database makes it possible for actors all over the world

97

to print graphs of the Stockholm air quality situation just hours after the measurement is taken.

The use of instruments based on standardized methods is an example of ideas that have been materialized and are now spread globally by technology companies, resulting in hundreds of imitators worldwide. SAN is one of these imitators. This distribution of ideas is reinforced by authorities and standardizing organizations that have an impact on *how* actors act locally (see also Hedmo, Sahlin-Andersson and Wedlin in this volume). Nevertheless, the standardization of methods also gives the local actors room for local translations – *why* monitoring is conducted, for example, which can be for reasons other than legal ones. One could hardly market Stockholm as "clean" if standards were not followed, but it is also an argument for funding the air monitoring activities. A close cooperation with the university gives SAN access to valuable knowledge and to the possibility of trying new methods. The air quality monitoring is also known outside Sweden, and international visitors come to see if the system constructed from a combination of traditional and new methods is good enough to be imitated.

It is not only methods that are standardized, but also scales. Data presentations are made according to limit values set by, among others, the European Union. The legal texts say what to measure, how to measure it, and how to present the results. The legal vocabulary becomes the language of the monitoring field. This standardized way of creating, storing, and presenting data also makes the aggregation of data possible. Regional, national, or even international organizations can collect data from local contexts, translate it into large databases, repackage and present it to various geographical areas: a city, a country, the entire planet.

One of the most important advantages of inscriptions is that they can be part of texts – reports on air quality, for instance. Such reports can have many uses, some of them quite unusual.

> One of SAN's customers – the Energy Company – wanted as part of its long-term contract, a study of the effects of its activities on the city's air. The project was discussed by both parties and resulted in three subprojects, including three different studies and reports. The first report documented how the Company's heat supplying system had affected city air during the last three decades. The study included dispersion calculations based on data from the monitoring systems and from a database of emissions caused by such pollutants as industrial plants and traffic in the area. The customer also provided SAN with its own statistics of the emissions. Sulphur dioxide was an obvious focus for both parties, as it is one of the most common air pollutants traditionally related to heat production.
>
> After the report was delivered to the contact person, who also was a member of an environment unit at the Company, copies were distributed to other people in the company who might be interested. Around the same time, the

Company was sponsoring a public exhibition of a new building area in Stockholm. The project group was to decorate an apartment and to make its activity – heat production – visible and interesting to visitors by mounting pictures related to the environment. Having decided to avoid the usual photographs of beautiful landscapes, the project group was searching for pictures of a more abstract character. Somebody who had seen the SAN report suggested using its pictures. The texts obviously differed from those in the report, and alluded to the positive effect that the Energy Company's method of heat production has on air quality.

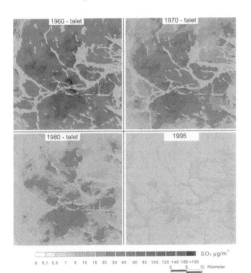 

Bild 2a. Totala svaveldioxidhalter under 60-, 70- och 80-talet samt 1995.
   Beräkningsrutorna är 500m x 500m.

Many visitors came to the apartment during the exhibition, and although their purpose was mainly to see the new housing area, one of the company representatives claimed that the pictures provided a good opportunity to propagate the importance of the quality of heat-producing systems.

The contact person at the Energy Company was a member of an environmental unit at the Company, used to dealing with air pollutants and other environmental issues. The staff at SAN and the contact person could easily agree on the aim and direction of the project; they could both relate to the report. There seemed to be no visible boundaries between them, and they came to a relatively stable, shared view on the measurement and presentation of the sulphur dioxide.

Actors interact around and negotiate about the air quality measures while the reports are being created. Such process might be facilitated by the *intermediaries* (Callon, 1991). Actors define one other in interactions, and intermediaries are all that pass between the actors, defining their relationship. Michel Callon mentions four such intermediaries: texts, technological artefacts, skilled humans, and money. In the daily activities at SAN, the instruments are one of the most important aspects of how the work is organized, but, as the above example demonstrates, it is the report that becomes an intermediary and defines the relationship between the parties. SAN can use the reports to exemplify what it is able to do with its models and databases. Reports enable SAN to present itself as a "good model builder".

The Energy Company can use the report to demonstrate that its heating production system has a positive effect on the environment by lowering the sulphur dioxide levels in the city. This evidence, provided by a neutral actor, gives the Company a useful, stable fact, allowing it to become the "environmentally friendly company". But a report can also be part of other activity, as when the illustrations of sulphur dioxide were transformed into colorful pictures in order to create good public relations. This does not mean that the report was not taken seriously. On the contrary, it was included in another practice, one aimed at creating attractive images of the Company.

Water

Air is not the only thing in Stockholm viewed as being "clean". As Czarniawska (1999) has shown, water is one of the areas in which the tradition of constant environmental improvements in Stockholm is especially visible. Is the translation of water quality similar to that of air quality?

> SWACO is a large, publicly owned water company in Stockholm. It supplies drinking water to one million people and treats the waste water for approximately the same number. Besides water supply and water treatment, the company is also involved in lake and watercourse restoration in the Stockholm area. Many of these lakes and watercourses are heavily polluted – the result of lack of water treatment in the past combined with today's surface water.
>
> Companies that run treatment plants are, according to law, also responsible for monitoring the effects of these activities. The company is, therefore, running a monitoring program of the Stockholm archipelago where samples are taken several times a year at different sampling points.
>
> Except for one point in the centre of Stockholm, sampling is done from a boat. The water samples are then transported by car to the company office where the laboratory is located. It is important to keep the bottles of water in order, and the bottles are labelled to indicate the depth at which the samples were taken. Bottles are marked with digits and using that number, the person who takes the samples records what the bottle contains.
> The laboratory staff distributes the water samples in various bottles, depending on the type of analysis to be done. The paper form that was completed during the sampling is then used to record the results of the analysis.
>
> The analytic processes follow standard methods, and the SWACO laboratory is accredited for several of these analyses. The results are subsequently

entered into a computer program designed to process water data. The data can then be used by staff members at SWACO – for writing reports based on these results, for example.

As a part of a large water program, the company also takes samples from the lakes and watercourses in the area. During the winter, when the lakes are frozen, the staff must walk on the ice and drill a hole in order to obtain these samples.

Water quality has been monitored in Stockholm for decades, and only a few new parameters have been added to the measuring process: tests for phosphorus, nitrogen, and several heavy metals, for example. Historical documents show that prior to the last century measurements were made in research projects that were often led by an important scientist, whose name legitimated the results. Influences from abroad were also important. Swedish scientists travelled to and studied in other European cities in order to learn more about water quality or drinking water systems. No such historical documents about air quality in Stockholm exist, however. In the beginning of the 20th century, there were debates in the national parliament about the air situation and debates in other countries have influenced the national discussion over the years. Today the European Union has a major influence in both areas – various directives and the monitoring organizations see to it that actions are taken in preparation for new limit values.

Thus the air and water in the city are translated, by standardized methods and limit values, into inscriptions – figures, graphs, and illustrations on air and water quality. For both SAN and SWACO, the instruments are a critical element in the organization of monitoring and interpreting air and water quality. People in these organizations are busy keeping the labels on the bottles and the instruments functioning according to a specific level of quality because the instruments and the data that they generate are the basis of all actions taken. The basis for SAN's and SWACO's legitimacy is an uninterrupted chain of humans and non-humans – including the air and water.

> Since the 1970s, a group of representatives from several local authorities have met regularly in order to improve the watercourses in Stockholm. SWACO is one of these parties. This work was extended in 1994, when Stockholm started a water program initiated by local politicians. The daily work was managed by several local administrations in Stockholm, led by the Environment and Health Protection Administration. The focus of the program was a survey of the lakes and watercourses in the Stockholm area, and undertaking actions aimed at restoring, at least to some degree, the water in lakes and watercourses. In 2000, the group of administrators that had been working for the last five years with the earlier program suggested a new program. Included was a description of the situation, actions that had been initiated or completed, and actions that were needed to improve the situation further.
>
> When the group had agreed upon a text, it was sent to the parent offices for consideration and then to the City Council. Everyone accepted the program. There was agreement among the political parties in Stockholm about the importance of the water program. A disagreement over the financial aspects arose, however, as some political parties wanted to increase the budget, while others opposed it.

Boundary Objects

For understanding the way in which the water program in Stockholm is organized, with cooperation between administrative units in their issuing of joint statements, the concept of *boundary objects* seems to be especially suitable. This concept was used by Susan L. Star and James Griesemer (1989) in their study of the creation of the first museum of natural history in California. They noticed that the stuffed animals that populated the museum were objects of science for scientists, objects of attraction for business people, and relics of the region for local patriots. Thus the idea of boundary objects: objects that are solid and can therefore maintain their identity when handled from different perspectives, but are also adaptable enough to be attractive to the representatives of those differing viewpoints.

In the case of the water program, it should be emphasized that the cooperation around lakes and watercourses in Stockholm existed for many years. The parties share a common goal, which, according to Star and Griesemer (1989), is a most important aspect of the emergence of boundary objects. In the case of Stockholm, the goal is to achieve good water quality in the area. And just as California once attracted scientists, amateurs, and sponsors to the state, the beauty of the Stockholm area with its lakes and watercourses represents a common goal uniting the representatives of different municipalities and political parties. Besides the program, there are other boundary objects in the water area: the database of water quality data, including the data that SWACO translated from water samples.

The monitoring data, together with recreation aspects, were used to categorize the lakes and watercourses in order to give priority to various measures. Because officials and politicians seem to agree on the produced text – the water program – it has become not only a boundary object but also an obligatory passage point (Callon, 1986) for people interested in water issues or issues that have an effect on the water in Stockholm.

A similar situation exists in the area of air quality, where cooperation among several municipalities has existed for over ten years based on a shared goal of lowering the air pollution levels in the area. The boundary objects are not only the program, but also databases, standards, and forms. In the case of SAN, the database with data from the automatic monitoring system is available on the Internet. In addition, an important input in the process of doing dispersion calculations, one of the calculation methods used at SAN to describe air quality, is an emission database. It is constructed by the municipalities that co-operate in the area of air quality monitoring in the region. SAN is assigned to run its monitoring stations and administrate the emission database, which contains data on point, area, and line sources of pollution. These sources can be industrial plants, petrol stations, or roads. Statistics are also important, as descriptions of the emissions must be as accurate as possible, including such details as chimney height and working hours. The results of calculations can be presented in color, where different colors represent different levels of air pollutants. The actors share the goal of providing detailed information on pollutants. The different municipalities can use the database in legal situations, but they also receive statistics that can be used as arguments in debates on fruitfulness of specific political actions. The database gives SAN a strong competitive advantage because its detailed data for a large area gives it a strong argument for recruiting local customers.

One important boundary object is standardized forms.[2] Standardized methods are important in both the air and water area[3] and standardized forms are vital elements in the process of collecting and analyzing water samples. They enable staff members to work at various places at different times. Samples can be taken one day and analyzed another day in the laboratory. The data can be entered into a database days or even weeks later.

Organizing the City

The calculations and illustrations of the measured data play a significant part in the creation of reports. These reports become intermediaries, defining the actors involved in their creation. But the results of air and water quality can also be boundary objects and can show similarities among different social worlds and practices. They can even demonstrate differences among them – especially differences in the ways they are transformed in various situations. The facts and figures presented in reports and on the Web can be incorporated into a number of actions undertaken in various practices in the city. Concepts and pictures are obtained from texts and illustrations presented in the reports and put into another context. In this way, the representation of the air and water is translated into a re-representation of the air and water. Actors in the city take the air and water quality information for facts. They have confidence in the way experts are creating the information. The contents of the reports are often taken for granted; they are black boxes. The information gives the actors in different contexts the possibility of being connected to the organization of Stockholm and the argument of being environmentally friendly. In this way, they contribute to the view of Stockholm as a clean and green city, as it has often been described in information material from the City Administration.

But even texts are less durable than inscriptions in such final medium as stone. Yet another, and perhaps more impressive way to present the results from the monitoring system, is to be found on The Royal Environmental Monument situated in the centre of Stockholm. Shining like the water around them, the two lighted obelisks gleam above Stockholm's harbor. They were erected in 1994 and were inagurated by His Majesty King Carl XVI Gustaf, well known for his great personal interest in environmental

---

[2] See Roth and Bowen (1999), on forms and labels in environmental fieldwork.
[3] See, e.g. Briers and Chua (2001), on the importance of following standardized work methods.

matters. One shows the state of the water in the city and the other the air – as wave-shaped pillars of colorful light. They were described as "the first informative object of art of Stockholm" in the newspaper. The inscription on the monuments says that the obelisks are "a reminder of our common responsibility for the present and future environment". And while the play of the light indicator is dependent on the electronic system that feeds it, the stone monument contains also metal plates with engravings showing the long-termed changes.

The story of air and water quality in Stockholm shows that air and water, through translations, acquire many faces in a big city. Environment is an object – like air and water. One also finds environment represented in the inscriptions. Environment appears as ideas like "sulphur dioxide levels" or "good environment". As an argument, environment is visualized in texts on "good environment" and in local debates it is claimed that it is a positive and worthy goal for the city and as a marketing element. The master-idea (Czarniawska and Joerges, 1996) of "good environment" is never questioned in this process of continuous translation of the local environment, the air and water.

Chapter 7

From "Nature" to "Economy" and "Culture": How Stockfish Travels and Constructs an Action Net

Tor Korneliussen, Bodø Graduate School of Business, Norway and Fabrizio Panozzo, University of Venice, Italy

This text has two starting points. One is a compelling story by Bruno Latour, "Circulating reference",[1] showing how samples of soil from the Amazon Forest become translated – and transformed – into a scientific paper. Latour shows the chain of translations step by step, and we borrowed his method in our study. The other starting point is a video called "Tørrfesk. Fra Lofot skrei[2] til stoccafisso[3]", conceived by the Norwegian anthropologist Helge A. Wold (Wold, 1987), who provides a commentary for it. It shows how cod caught in Lofoten becomes dried, and then exported to Italy, where it is a staple of legends, tradition, regional cuisine and, much as in Norway, local employment. The video was created by the museum at the University of Tromsø as part of an effort to document the historical roots of traditional industries.

The video gives a thorough description of the chain of translation from catch to consumption, and we decided to follow it, allowing it to be the guide in our investigations. For the reason of access we were studying a connection between Røst (a fishing village in Lofoten) and Sandrigo (a village near Vicenza), whereas the movie concentrates on analogous connection

---

[1] Latour, 1999: 24–79. Originally published in 1995 as "The 'Pedofil' of Boa Vista", *Common Knowledge* 4 (1): 145–187.
[2] Norwegian for cod.
[3] Italian for stockfish.

between Ballstad (another fishing village on Lofoten) and Badalucco (a village near Genoa).[4] The chain of translation is, however, quite similar.

We have also located a video produced in Italy in 1996, illustrating the cooperation between Sandrigo and Røst, made cooperatively by a Norwegian (Petter Johannesen, script, narration) and an Italian director (Massimo Magipinto). The two videos, and the relevant literature, were complemented by interviews conducted in Røst and Sandrigo.

Introducing Stockfish

cod

(species Gadus morhua), large and economically important marine fish of the family Gadidae, found on both sides of the North Atlantic. The cod, a cold-water fish, generally remains near the bottom, ranging from inshore regions to deep waters. It is valued for its edible flesh, the oil of its liver, and other products. A dark-spotted fish, with three dorsal fins, two anal fins, and a chin barbell, it varies in color from greenish or grayish to brown or blackish, though it may also be dull to bright red. It is usually caught at weights of up to about 11.5 kg (25 pounds) but can reach a maximum length and weight of more than 1.8 m (6 feet) and 91 kg (201 pounds). It is a voracious migratory fish, feeding largely on other fishes and various invertebrates.[5]

It is the *Gadus morhua*, and more specifically *Gadus morhua callarias* that we are going to follow in its translations and transformations (Arcangeli & Zanellato, 2002). A truly economic fish, if there was one. It has been involved in commerce and nutrition for centuries, and continues to do so, effortlessly joining tradition with innovation (Kurlansky, 1997). But not only these two: it also joins "nature" with "culture" in a way that is very instructive in present times, when the frontiers between the two are constantly abolished and re-established. The Norwegian video states at its very beginning:

Stockfish is a truly natural product. It has been produced for more than a thousand years. But it has also been a commercial good with a long tradition [our translation].

Here is the core of the dilemma: if it is "natural", then it has not been "produced" (natural things are usually found or discovered). If produced and

---

[4] Following localities have a "stockfish festival" in Italy: Ancona (mid-September), Badalucco (mid-September), Sandrigo (late September) and Somma Vesuviana (Naples, early October); information from Norwegian Trade Council in Milan, 25 February 2000. The total annual export of stockfish from Lofoten to Italy is relatively stable with a variation between 3,401 tons in 1992 and 4,049 tons in 1997.

[5] http://www.britannica.com/eb/article?eu=25006 [Accessed February 9, 2002].

natural, then nature must be one of the producers, as indeed is the case. Observe the trace of another received dichotomy: "But it has also been a commercial good" – economy and nature are separate realms, it seems. Even this dichotomy, together with the third one – economy versus culture – will dissolve as we proceed. Indeed, in the local language, stockfish is called "all-around-fish", but also "Lofoten's gold" – because of its quality and its price.[6]

Stockfish is Norway's oldest export article. Findings indicate that stockfish was exported from Norway before the Viking era, and that it formed an important part of the Vikings' staple diet. Cod meat has practically no fat (0.3 percent) and is about 18 percent protein; when dried, it contains 80 percent protein (Kurlansky, 1997).

One of the first records of Norwegian stockfish as an export article is from the 9th century, when the local chief Ottar brought stockfish with him to England (Borch and Korneliussen, 1995). Norwegian stockfish has probably been exported continually since the 12th century, and for a long time stockfish was the only export article. An Italian aristocrat, Pietro Querini, who was stranded on the Island of Røst in 1431 wrote "They have no other industry than fisheries. During the year they catch tremendous amounts of fish. The one that exists in large, yes, enormous amount is called stockfish. They dry stockfish in the wind and sun, using no salt, so it becomes dry as wood. Stockfish is a large and valuable trading commodity in the north" (Wold, 1991). The institutions created around this business have survived over a long period of time. We shall try to present the stockfish business as an action net (Czarniawska, 2004b), where the content, the form, and the connections between various actions are part of various types of institutions and institutionalized representations of "nature" and "culture".

First Station: Nature as a Supplier

The Norwegian video starts by explaining that the Lofoten islands are especially favorable for the production of stockfish because of their climate: in spite of its vicinity to the Northern Pole, " the winter climate is mild, stable and airy, air humidity is low: the cod reigns in its waters from January to April, but it can be caught all year round." More precisely, cod come to the Norwegian coast to spawn during the period between February and April. It needs to be added that "nature" is an unreliable supplier: there are years with few fish in the sea.

The picture shows a night view of Lofoten. A boat is moving in the dark. A close-up shows heavy ropes drawn by a mechanical pulley. A big net

---

[6] The Italian video is called "Stockfish – the treasure of the Lofoten" *(Stocafisso il tesoro delle Lofoten)*.

appears from the water – full of fish, which open their mouth, gasping for air. The commentary says "First class stockfish needs first class raw material", and the pictures show the fish bled immediately after the catch. A close-up (which should be forbidden for minors if not for the fact that it is minors who traditionally cut the tongue out) shows a young man cutting fish throats with a knife. The close-up moves to the steering cabin and changes into a panoramic view: another boat, another catch from afar. Sea-gulls encircle all boats: is it then that nature gets its pay?

It does not mean that the human and machine part of action is unimportant. The fishermen have the choice of gear with which to catch the fish, and the way the fish is handled after bringing it onboard. The choice of fishing gear has changed over time. For instance in 1900, 34.9 percent of the catch was caught by gill net, 62.3 percent by long line and 2.8 percent by hand line. In the 1950s purse seine[7] was introduced in Lofoten, but the use of this type of gear was prohibited in 1958 due to it being considered too efficient.[8] Maintenance of the cod stock during the time of cod spawning was then already an issue of great concern for the fishermen. In the early 1960s the "Danish seine" was introduced. In 1995 57 percent of the catch was caught by gill net, 20 percent by long line, 8 percent by hand line and 15 percent with Danish seine.

Back to the video: the boat arrives at a port. Fish is unloaded, put in containers, and unloaded in one of the 60 fish processing plants in Lofoten. The boat departs again.

The Lofoten fisheries are claimed to be the world's largest cod fishery in terms of catches and participation (Jentoft and Kristoffersen, 1987). The fishermen come to participate in the Lofoten fisheries from all places along the Norwegian coast from North to South. There are still fishermen in their seventies who have participated in the Lofoten season since they were fourteen years old (*ibid*). The fishermen are a heterogeneous group of coastal (inshore/mid-shore) fishermen. Also the boats vary – from 20-foot wooden boats to 100-foot steel boats. In the beginning of the 19th century there were about 30,000 fishermen participating in the Lofoten fisheries. By the late 1990s the number of fishermen had declined to about 4,000. About 20 percent of all Norwegian fishermen make an important part of their annual earnings from work in the Lofoten fisheries (*ibid*). Also those combining fishery and farming earned most of their cash income in the Lofoten season.

---

[7] A large net with sinkers on one edge and bouys on the other edge. This net hangs vertically in the water and is used to enclose fish when its ends are pulled together like a sack.

[8] Exhaustion due to over-fishing is a constant threat to cod, especially as such possibility was for a long time deemed impossible (Kurlansky, 1997). Recently, there has been a long and complicated debate about cod fishing in the Baltic Sea. The Swedish fishermen lobbied at the EU to stop cod fishing in the area (Pedersen, 2002; Tougarrd, 2002).

The coast of northern Norway used to be divided into a men's world and a women's world (Wold, 1986). The men went to Lofoten to fish, while the women stayed home running the villages. This, by the way, may be one of the reasons for the traditionally strong position of women in northern Norwegian society. Today, however, genders mix more in the production process.

Second Station: People and Machines Take Over

The Norwegian video shows the cleaning of the fish in great detail, including one man who is smoking while cleaning the fish. The cleaners are mostly young men, but also some women, and a young boy is given the ambitious task of removing "cod tongues" (a local delicacy) with a simple device consisting of a used wooden fish-packing crate with a nail sticking out of the top. The underside of the fish head is impaled on this nail in such a way that the cod tongue is on it. The boy then uses his knife to cut around the tongue and remove it.

The cleaned fish is rinsed and then the tails of two cods of somewhat equal size are bound together with a string. This must be a very demanding job, as people are working in cold wet places with thick rubber gloves, and the fish is very slippery and awkward to handle. A tractor brings the fish to the drying racks. Two fish bound at their tails are easily hung on a rung.

The workers in fish processing plants are often locals who for various reasons have chosen not to be fishermen: they may not have access to a boat or do not possess the appropriate skills. They may not enjoy work that often takes people away from their homes for parts of the year, or it may be due to more prosaic reasons, such as the tendency towards seasickness. Furthermore, as we said before, fishermen are men, while at least a certain percentage of the workers in fish factories are women.

The two types of wooden constructions used to dry cod are referred to as flat lofts and drying racks. Flat lofts demand use of greater area, while drying racks exploit heights. A flat loft is a two storey high wooden structure that is formed like a long rectangle. Across the long sides are lateral rungs from which the cod hangs to dry. Flat lofts have the advantage of easy access as it is relatively easy to hang the raw cod on it and to take down the dry cod.

In some places the conditions for drying fish are less advantageous, due to a lack of space for building flat lofts on or due to inadequate drying conditions. In such places it is necessary to build drying racks. These drying racks are several storeys high, and provide good circulation of air flow around the cod. These racks are made of lateral rungs attached to an A-frame structure. Its advantage is space efficiency, as it is possible to hang several layers of cod on them, without the problem of the upper rungs of cod dripping down over the cod hanging on the lower rungs and reducing the quality of the cod. The disadvantage of such a structure is that it is cumbersome and therefore labor intensive.

The lifespan of these drying racks is about 30 years. After such a time period under harsh weather conditions they often have to be rebuilt. If a drying rack falls down it could lead to large economic losses. It destroys the quality of the stockfish, can lead to human injuries and in the worst case, a loss of lives.

Third Station: Nature Gets to Work

Now, the Norwegian commentator says, "sun and wind of Lofoten get to work, in order to ennoble the fish". But nature, like any other worker, cannot be left unsupervised. The commentary tells the viewers that Italy is the main market for stockfish, and the picture shows two Italians controlling the racks. They are speaking about the fish color, and the – presumably – "Norwegian Italian" says: "Look how beautiful it is" (meaning quality, not aesthetic value, however appealing it is to a tourist). It might sound like a small talk, but the Italian importers have a long experience in importing stockfish, and are therefore good at evaluating the quality of the stockfish. In fact, the longest part of the Italian video is dedicated to the sorting process (Johannesen and Magipinto, 1996). If the importers find that the fish does not live up to the grading by the sorters, this could lead to complaints and, if worst came to worst, to importers changing exporters. A special Quality Assurance Manual has therefore been published, based on the Standard for Production (NBN 30-01) and the Branch Standard for Grading (NBS 30-01) (Fiskerinæringens Felles Kompetansestyre, 1990; Prosjekt Bransjestandard for Fisk, 1998).

Usually the Italian agents visit Røst some time in February, March or April to collect information about the current production of stockfish (Korneliussen and Pedersen, 2001). Potential importers often come along to be introduced to the exporters and to make some preliminary negotiations.

"'Stockfish dries in the wind and the sun without salt', wrote the Venetian Pietro Querini in 1432", as the Norwegian commentator informs the viewer. The climate is therefore very important. If it is too warm, the fish rots; if it is too cold, it freezes, which changes its consistency.

The workers are covering the racks with a net, to protect the fish from the birds. The commentary says that Røst, on the tip of Lofoten, counts as one of the best drying places. Drying preserves all the nutritional value of the fish. Stockfish becomes a kind of a concentrate of the fish.

The drying process varies from one year to another depending on the weather (nature is more moody than industrial workers). The hanging usually takes place from early March to the middle of April, as later the temperature in Lofoten is often too high for drying. The drying period is 2–3 months. In old times, it was forbidden in Lofoten to take fish off the rack before the 12th of July. The fish is hung with the gut incision away from rain, which means that the fish is hung with the belly facing North and the back facing South.

Stockfish was always the symbol of the possibility of making a living out of the sea in Norway. But it is not exactly that the sea presents its fruit on a platter: fishing is hard work, and good dried fish requires constant supervision. The Norwegian video shows a Norwegian worker controlling the fish with a poke; he separates the two tied fish at the other, non-tied end to ensure sufficient airflow. It is important that the fish does not come into contact with other fish or the board. This can cause hanging marks that can later lead to a reduction in sales value.

Fourth Station: The Production Continues, and the Commerce Makes an Appearance

In June the Italian agents come back to Røst together with their buyers to meet with the exporters that the agents are representing (Korneliussen and Pedersen, 2001). Further negotiations are undertaken and deals are made. The actual exports do not normally start before August. At this time the exporters know how much stockfish they have and which prices they would like to receive. They are therefore ready to negotiate with the agents to try to settle on contracts and prices.

The Norwegian video shows June. Fish is collected: the string joining the two cod is cut and the fish falls on the ground. A young boy is sitting on the top of the rack and is doing the cutting. A truck takes the "fallen fish" back to the processing plant and then brings it up to the stockfish loft for after-drying and sorting.

The stockfish is put in layers facilitating free circulation of air through the piles of fish. The biggest fish need most after-drying and are thus placed on the sides and the top of the piles. A completely dried stockfish contains between 14 and 16 percent water. The sorting, grading and discarding process starts while the after-drying is still in progress and thus the fish will dry some more and thus change a bit after the completion of the sorting. This has to be taken into consideration by the "vraker" (the sorter) during the sorting process. The vraker grades the fish according to 20 categories for *Lofotrund*, i.e. unprocessed cod caught in Lofoten. It is length, thickness, weight and qualitative properties that determine where the fish is assigned.

The sorting and grading takes place according to a business standard, called Sorting and Grading of Stockfish, NBS 30-01.[9]

A man and a woman sort fish or, to be more exact, the woman pushes the fish towards the man who does the sorting. "To sort fish is an occupation which one learns life long. The oldest sorter did it for 40 years now and claimed that he learned new things each time he sorted fish."

The sorter puts the fish into a machine that removes the top part of the spine in the neck of a cod. In some cases it is hard to know if a cod has the appropriate quality. If the wind has been too strong in the beginning of the drying process, the outer part of the fish has perhaps dried too fast, preventing the inner part of the flesh from drying in the appropriate way. Alternatively, if there has been too little wind, the drying may have taken too much time, giving the inner part of the cod lower quality. Removing the top part of the spine allows the sorter to both visually inspect and smell the inner part of the cod. There is the first, second and third sort of stockfish, and the first divides into many types. The best is Ragno, the leanest type, free from fault and over 60 cm. Another example is Bremer, plump type, hung early; yet another Hollander; Italiano grande; Italiano piccolo, etc. Names derive from various places in the long history of stockfish. The term "stockfish" itself comes from an observation that the dried fish is stiff like a rod, thus "stock".

As we said before, the Italian video dedicates a long time to the sorting process (with a marketing purpose in sight?). We learn from it that sorting and packing are supervised by a "king cod", a mutant cod whose head is shorter than that of a normal fish and resembles a human face. It is dried together with its head, and it hangs on a string, looking around.

Stockfish is then thrown into a big hole and comes one floor down, where it is weighed and put into a press. The press is a big box open sideways, which will be filled to a certain weight (25, 45 and 50 kg). It turns out that the box is also a press: it presses the fish up, reducing its volume to about one third, in the same way as occurs with a leaf put between the pages of a book. The pressed fish is held together by steel strings, forming a package. A package is hand sewn into a jute sack, which gets proper stamps before hand. Stamps are enormous metal circles and rectangles that say where it comes from (Røst, Ballstad, etc.), the brand of the producer, and the type such as "Ragno, Grand Premier". More stamps, in red: the brands "Lofoten Extra" and "Marca Sole", and the quality "WPrima" (inscriptions are in mixed languages). The Italian market for stockfish is highly segmented making a fine-grained product assortment system necessary. Packing is done by men and women; there are more women here than in other jobs in the industry.

---

[9] For a detailed historical description of *vrakers* occupation, see Hauan, 2000.

Fifth Station: Stockfish Hits the Road

Fish is exported by boat, usually from Lofoten to Trondheim, and from there to Italy. The frontier is at Chiasso, and this is where stockfish changes nationality or, as the commentary says, "the responsibility for the fish goes to the Italians". Historically seen, Italy has always been the biggest market for Norwegian stockfish (it needs to be added that the fact that Norway is outside the EU does not make things easier). Italians, so it goes, know how to appreciate the delicacies of the ocean. Thus, about 80 percent of Norwegian stockfish is sent to Italy – apparently since the 1400s.

An (Italian) man cuts open the sack with "Albistok, Albisol" on it. He cuts the steel strings with tongs. The fish is put into fresh water, and then taken out. A young man cuts them in two, longwise, and then puts them into pools of fresh water. Another bath, and yet another: the fish gets into and is brought up from the pools in a kind of a steel basket. The dried "stock" becomes a "fish" once more. This is also a final test of quality, because if the cod froze during drying, it will not expand into a "fish meat" but will remain "stocky".

Sixth Station: The Stockfish Starts Making Culture

The Norwegian video ends with the following point:

> Stockfish is not only food and workplaces. The production of stockfish teaches us a lot about history, life forms and identity.

Indeed. The Italian video completes the Norwegian one, explaining (and showing) how *bacalà alla vicentina* is made.

Norwegian stockfish has a number of clearly identifiable areas of consumption across Italy and each of them has its own particular way of preparing and cooking dried cod. One of the recipes that has attained a vast reputation across the country is *bacalà alla vicentina*, typical of the province of Vicenza and of Sandrigo, Røst's twin town, in particular. The origins of such a celebrated connection go back again to Pietro Querini. Allegedly, he found it hard to sell dried fish in Venice where there was a daily supply of fresh fish and turned instead to the inland market where the inhabitants of Vicenza looked upon stockfish as an alternative to the expensive fresh fish which, moreover, went bad quite soon. It is rather unlikely that an aristocrat like Pietro Querini was involved in the stockfish trade, but this is a story that is told in Venice and "inventing traditions" (Hobsbawm & Ranger, 1993; Czarniawska, 2004b) plays an important part in the action net we are describing here.

Central to the preparation of the actual dish is time, as it requires a sequence of operations that are largely devoted to the reconstitution of the dried cod as edible foodstuff, rather than to actual cooking. Much of this process takes place outside the kitchen and resembles a proper manufacturing process where other mechanical tools and natural elements are put to work. To make bacalà alla vicentina, the stockfish first needs to be pounded into tenderness. Various technologies are used in this initial phase. Some use a wooden rod or, when greater quantities need to be processed, the dried fish is passed trough a cogged roller. The original recipe would nevertheless require the cod to be carefully pounded with a power hammer. It is at this point that water re-enters the stage. The pounded cod is soaked in cool running water for at least three days, changing the water twice daily. Once it has fully softened and regained its "natural" texture, it is broken into medium sized pieces but not fragmented, and drowned in a hot skillet containing oil, onion, garlic, salt, and pepper.

To call it *alla vicentina*, one has to add rinsed, boned salted anchovy filets, parsley, and garlic, which have been pounded in a mortar with milk, flour and parmesan cheese. Large quantities of oil and milk must be poured until all the cod pieces are completely covered. To absorb the seasonings the bacalà has to cook slowly, on a very low flame, for about 4 hours. During this long cooking period, one should refrain from even stirring the fish and the saucepan should only be gently moved every now and then. The word in Venetian dialect that describes this phase of cooking is "pipare" (bubble like the smoke from a pipe): it emphasizes the slowness of the process and a kind of autonomy of the food that gains its final gastronomical identity almost without additional human intervention. But before the bacalà is finally served, time intervenes once again. To be appreciated at its best, bacalà alla vicentina (that should be firm, slightly chewy, and not at all fishy in flavor) has to rest in between 3 to 6 days. The overall preparation of the dish therefore takes between 7 to 10 days: bacalà alla vicentina is literally "slow food".

In 1987, the Brotherhood of Bacalà alla Vicentina was formed. Such gourmet or culinary brotherhood was not very common at the time in Italy, and the one established in Sandrigo was among the first to be founded in the Veneto Region. It soon entered a well developed national network of associations linking culinary traditions with history, culture and local developments. In fact, other gourmet associations from all over Italy took part in the solemn ceremony of "investiture" of the first "knights of the brotherhood" who were regaled – following the ritual tasting of bacalà – with the membership symbols: the silver velvet cloak, which represents the cod's scales, and the yellow cape which is the same color as polenta. The investiture takes place to the tunes of Mendelsohn's "Wedding March", apparently to symbolize the union between Sandrigo and Røst (Johannesen and Magipinto, 1996).

The general aims of the brotherhood were, and still are, to defend, preserve and promote the typical dish from Vicenza and, more generally, to favor the local gourmet culture and the tourism linked to it. The first activity was to identify and preserve the "true" recipe of the bacalà alla vicentina. Dozens of different ways of cooking it had been proposed in the past and virtually every restaurant, not to mention family, had its own. The brotherhood did not necessarily want to impose the one best way of cooking stockfish, but it nevertheless identified the "correct" way, the one that granted to bacalà the appellation alla vicentina. This was seen as instrumental to the identification of those restaurants where bacalà was still prepared in the good old way in order to draw a "Bacalà Route", connecting the restaurants certified by the brotherhood. The route now winds along the province of Vicenza and its restaurants, *trattorias*, and inns – in places quite different from each other in culture, setting, and price. What they have in common is the daily preparation of bacalà, according to historical rules. Each restauranteur will interpret this dish in a slightly different way, cooking it in his or her own way. The Sandrigo way, for example, differs from the vicentina in that it replaces garlic with onion and sometimes removes anchovies. One of the original concerns was the suspicion that very few restaurants still engaged in the time consuming, cost-ineffective process of bacalà preparation, which fuelled concerns that bacalà could disappear from culinary culture and, most of all, eating habits. The fashion for slow food came in handy (see e.g. Miele and Murdoch, 2002; Czarniawska, this volume).

The Brotherhood did not want to limit its role to the preservation and promotion of good cuisine. The celebration of food-and-wine connoisseurship was also seen as a way to support sustainable tourism in the region. The basic idea was to attract tourists visiting more traditional places such as the shore of the northern Adriatic, Lake Garda and the towns of Venice, Verona and Vicenza. In the words of Michele Benettazzo (chairman of Pro-Sandrigo), "if tourists have the opportunity to eat well, besides admiring our artistic and natural attractions, they are likely to come back even more gladly".

Action Nets Lead to Networks Lead to Identities

The chain of translation, as presented above, shows the crucial role of stockfish in developing, stabilizing, and providing with meaning the two communities. Different collective actions are connected to one another: fishing to drying, drying to sorting and grading, sorting and grading to packaging, packaging to transportation, transportation to retail selling and food preparation, food preparation to dancing and celebrating. Fish, people, machines, money, regulations, and standards are stabilizing the connections. But, above all, the actions, and the connections between them, are repeated. The travel of the cod, and its translations, takes about eight months each year. In order to produce and maintain a durable action net, and the resulting networks and identities, it had to be repeated great many times. It is this other temporal aspect, the history of the connections between Røst and Sandrigo that we explore presently. As the action net becomes stabilized and repeated, it starts producing new entities: networks and identities.

Creating Røst

Røst is a relatively small island located in the outskirts of the Lofoten archipelago in Northern Norway. The island has about 700 inhabitants. They live in a dense social network and have an intimate understanding of each other. The local industries consist of fisheries and several local services. Most of the activities in Røst are related to fishing, the production of fish, and the export of fish and fish products.

The annual production of fish and fish products in Røst accounts for about 300 million Norwegian kroner (approximately 35 million euro) per year. About 65 percent of their production of fish is exported as stockfish to the Italian market. In terms of value, the export of stockfish from Røst is about 25–30 percent of the stockfish that is annually imported to Italy. The stockfish produced in Røst has traditionally been exported by export companies located in Bergen. The first export of stockfish by a company located in Røst was done in 1962. Today, all the six producers of stockfish in Røst export their own stockfish.

The first alleged exporter and an importer of stockfish from Røst to Italy was the legendary Pietro Querini. During a trade voyage from Crete to Flanders his ship wrecked in the North Sea before Christmas in 1431, and stranded on a small island near Røst on January 6, 1432. After a while, the shipwrecked men noticed smoke coming from Røst and made contact. Out of crew of 47, 11 survived at Røst until the spring of 1432. When Querini and his men then left for Italy, they brought along 60 stockfish (Svendsen, 1916). It is possible that this was the start of the export of stockfish from Røst to Italy.

The first evidence of Røst's investments in a relationship with Italy can be found in 1932, when an obelisk was erected in Røst in memory of Querini and his crew some 500 years after Querini's shipwreck.[10] In 1982, 550 years after the wreck there was a new celebration of Querini's adventure. In this celebration the participants were served shell-fish and mussels, food that is

---

[10] A crisis in the relationships with Italy took place in 1935, when the exports were stopped because of the Ethiopian (Abyssinian) war. The sanctions were lifted in 1936 and the first Italian import office was established (Hauan, 200).

typically not eaten in this area, to commemorate how Querini and his men survived the first few days after their wreck.

The consumption of fish in Italy is increasing. It is now about 23 kilos per capita (Hauan, 2000). Recently, however, the consumption of stockfish has declined. The market size seems to have stabilized at about 3,700 thousand tons during the last few years (Korneliussen, 2000). A relatively high percentage of Italian families buy stockfish during a year, but there is a great variation in the frequency of buying. In 1994, 20 percent of the households had bought stockfish during the last year (*Eksportutvalget for fisk*/Bates MMR, 1994). Market research shows that in the areas of Veneto, Genoa, Naples, Calabria and Sicily, 63 percent of the inhabitants consume less stockfish than they did 15–20 years ago (Teigland and Mangseth, 1998) and most of the consumption is done by consumers older than 40 years. There are at least two reasons for this.

Firstly, as we have seen, it takes a great deal of time to prepare traditional stockfish dishes. Time is often a scarce resource in modern households. A large percentage of women work outside the home, and they prefer less time-consuming dishes. The contemporary Italian consumers mostly consume stockfish on weekends, during parties or in restaurants. It is an open question whether the producers and importers of stockfish will be able to develop new and more consumer-oriented stockfish dishes. On the other hand, the above mentioned fashion for "slow living" and especially "slow food" might relieve this problem, at least temporarily.

Secondly, stockfish has traditionally been sold in small local shops, and this pattern still continues, whereas the supermarket chains have to a large degree taken over the role of traditional small shops. Stockfish products have not (yet) adapted to this change in the distribution system of food products, and it is not clear whether the producers of stockfish will be able to adjust to this change in distribution.

Another problem is that in the last 20 years, the arctic cod stock has been seriously depleted. The fishermen went from free access fishing to a situation where each fishing boat is allowed only a small quota to catch. The following reduction in catch resulted in fewer landed fish and less work for the processors. As with most other coastal communities in northern Norway this led to the tendency for young people to move away from Røst. In the time period from 1981 to 1991 the population decreased by 22 percent, from 798 to 621 (Karsteinsen, 2001: 28). The decreasing size of the Italian market was followed by the increased intensity of competition for market share. This competition was so high that the Icelandic exporters withdrew from the stockfish market in the early 1990s.

A rationalist commendation of that time (see e.g. Heide and John, 1988: 24) suggested that exporters from Røst try to reduce their dependence on the Italian market by "engaging in bonding behavior with the market".

Accordingly such efforts should try to link actors in the market more closely to the community of Røst, in this way safeguarding the inhabitants of Røst. But the actual remedy to the perceived threat was the one that linked in an even more complex way the nature, the economy, and the culture in Røst.

While the market for stockfish decreased, an intensification of the competitive climate followed. This increased the feeling that people's jobs, their culture and their sense of identity were under pressure, which led to an upsurge of celebration of the historical roots of Røst, with particular focus on the stockfish trade and the adjacent cultural activity. The connections with Sandrigo were central to it.

One expression of this cultural energy, boasted by the stockfish trade, is the annual puffin-festival. This festival focuses on local culture, with sub-themes such as coastal culture and the rights of the coastal communities to use local resources. A T-shirt with a puffin slogan is produced and sold. Other popular T-shirts show slogans like *Røst – en perle ytterst i Lofoten* (Røst – A pearl furthest out in Lofoten) or *Det er liv laga* (We shall live on). The second slogan makes use of positive connotations with being a fisherman, and having the wit and ability to do well under all types of hardships and difficulties. The food served during the puffin-festival and other cultural arrangements is often Italian stockfish-based fare.

The local dance band is called The Puffins. One of the songs they perform is the football song for the local team. The daughter of the stockfish exporter, who learned Italian during her visit to an Italian importer family as a child, has translated it to Italian and sometimes performs this Italian version together with The Puffins during local celebrations. This action is very welcome in Italy, well renowned for its craze for football. One of the Italian importers has a picture of Røst's football team on his office wall.

Another expression of the importance of stockfish trade for local identity can be found in the recent project Artscape Nordland, where 33 sculptures by artists from 18 countries, were placed in the counties of Nordland, one sculpture in each county. As we can read in the book presenting *Artscape Nordland* (Jaukkuri, 1999: 6) "the sculptures are an invitation to experience, proposals for communication". Again, interestingly enough, the sculpture chosen to be placed in Røst was created by the only Italian artist within the project (*Il Nido* – The Nest – by Luciano Fabro).

The one hotel in Røst is named Havly (shelter from the sea), and the only eating place is named Querini Pub and Restaurant. This restaurant has recently started to offer Italian stockfish-dishes.[11]

---

[11] There is also a standing joke at Røst that Querini and his crew left a long lasting impact on Røst by fathering several children while stranded there. There is no actual proof of this, nonetheless this has turned into a longstanding cultural myth. A typical local way of pulling one's leg is to allude to the Italian blood of certain dark-haired Røst inhabitants.

Creating Sandrigo (and its province)

At the other extreme of the action net knotted by stockfish lies Sandrigo, a village with a population of about 6,000 inhabitants, which, in the last decade, actively sought and gained the title of "capital of the bacalà alla vicentina". Sandrigo is a typical village of the North East of Italy, the macro-region that in the last decade has constituted one of the most debated economic and social phenomenon nationwide. Much of the interest in the Northeast and particularly in its most important region, Veneto, is due to its rapid and multifaceted economic development. In the last decade, the fast growing regional economy produced a constant increase in per capita income that in turn stimulated political demands for greater autonomy from Rome and even separatist claims. More precisely, and of crucial importance for the purpose of our study, Sandrigo lies exactly at the center of the province of Vicenza, the third most industrialized province in Italy, extremely export oriented (in fact it exports as much as Portugal or Greece, according to official statistics). But this present condition of full employment, entrepreneurship and ever increasing wealth has a peculiar history.

Sandrigo is part of what has been called the "Third Italy" to distinguish it from the heavy industrialized economic triangle of Milan, Turin and Genoa (Bagnasco, 1977). Fifty years ago, more than 60 percent of the population in the province of Vicenza was made of land laborers who scraped a subsistence living and knew the reality of periodic starvation. Up until the early 1970s high unemployment rates in the province fuelled substantial emigration especially to the promised lands of Australia, South America and Northern Europe. By 1999 only 6 percent of the population worked in agriculture. Now the province of Vicenza regularly appears among the top of Italy's highest earners (€ 36,000 per capita income in 2000). It has one of the highest concentrations of small and medium-sized enterprises in Europe – one in six of the population is involved in a family business. The typical form of business organization – the "(industrial) districts", i.e. networks of small and specialized firms located in close proximity and embedded in local institutional structures became practically legendary (Brusco, 1982). These networks are noted for high trust, extensive specialization, mutual co-operation and the sharing of ideas, plants and even orders and premises. This symbiotic co-operation, however, is found alongside intense competition and innovation. Because of their economic success, such territories as Sandrigo are often seen as a "third way" to economic and social development, operating at the center of a fundamental historical transformation in society and economy (Sabel, 1989).

The explicit connection between this business success and stockfish is a recent one. As mentioned before, bacalà alla vicentina had been for centuries one of the most typical dishes in Sandrigo and its vicinity, but it was not until the late 1980s that its consumption became a "cultural" phenomenon

120

and the linkages with Norway and Røst in particular, were suddenly re-discovered or invented from scratch.

The connection was devised and put into practice in a relatively short period of time by a small network of key actors that included local promoters of Sandrigo's history and culture, Norwegian diplomats and stockfish traders. The locals gathered around the *Pro loco*, a private, nonprofit institution that operates in most Italian municipalities for the support of local culture and history and had always been particularly active in Sandrigo. Pro-Sandrigo was (and still is) chaired by Michele Benettazzo, the one person that is unanimously credited with having rediscovered bacalà alla vicentina and developed the close relationship with Røst.

The idea came about as part of a broader reflection on the identity of the village and of its province and on their potential attractiveness as tourist destinations. The Pro-Sandrigo had a pretty good record of initiatives aimed at making Sandrigo a more interesting and attractive place. In the 1970s, for instance, it promoted a festival of Venetian popular music which attracted widespread national interest for more that a decade. As a consecration of such a successful endeavor, the head office of the National Association of Pro loco was established in Sandrigo and Michele Benettazzo became its president. But by the mid-1980s the situation had significantly changed. The cultural and social life of the village had lost much of its intensity and the Pro loco found it difficult to perform its roles. The local economy was booming and the ethos of the entire province had quickly turned to the mundane imperatives of entrepreneurship, hard work and individual wealth. This meant a sheer break with the recent past of poverty and emigration but also a likely neglect of the cultural roots of the territory. An innovative idea was therefore needed to reposition Sandrigo within some virtuous circle of cultural, and not just economic, visibility. It was at this point that bacalà came about as the idea that could revamp the distinctiveness of the province as something more than just a huge business park. Additionally, the whole idea didn't require much conceptual work. The province of Vicenza was already known all over Italy for its association with stockfish. Therefore it appeared as pretty natural to take advantage of this "brand" to link further initiatives to it in order to call attention, curiosity, interest, and, eventually, to produce profitable touristic-economic consequences.

Creating connections

In March 1988, a meeting promoted by the Italian-Norwegian Chamber of Commerce and by the Norwegian Embassy was held at Savini restaurant in Milan: on that occasion the foundations for a number of promotional tourist initiatives were laid that particularly regard the Region of Veneto and Vicenza.

In 1989, fifteen years after the start of direct export from a Røst company, the then mayor of Røst, Arnfinn Ellingsen, was invited to Sandrigo by *Norske Tørrfisk Eksportørers Landsforening* (The National Organization of Norwegian Stockfish Exporters) to attend the newly established stockfish festival. The festival was placed within the broader program of the "Italian-Norwegian Week".

During the festival, stockfish is the absolute protagonist in Sandrigo. It is brought from Norway by the major exporters and representatives of the Røst local community, and then cooked by the best restaurateurs of the province, who hand out portions by the thousands in the huge pavilions that are put up in the main square of Sandrigo. The festival also includes historical parades, folk group performances, cabarets, slideshows and films about Norway.

In 1997, a delegation of nine people from Røst visited the stockfish festival and the "Norwegian days" in Sandrigo. During this occasion, to honor the people of Røst, a square in the town centre in Sandrigo was named Piazzetta Røst Isole Lofoten. Arnfinn Ellingsen was appointed an honorary member of the Brotherhood of Bacalà. He was presented with a medal and a diploma in a formal ceremony.

When the municipality of Røst was celebrating its 70th anniversary in 1998, a delegation of eighteen Italians visited Røst. A voluntary organization collected money in Røst for a bronze sculpture of a porpoise. The sculpture was placed on a small island in the entrance to the harbor of Røst, the one upon which Querini had allegedly stranded. This island was named Isola di Sandrigo, and symbolically donated as a gift to the town of Sandrigo. During the unveiling of the sculpture an opera singer from Røst performed the Italian anthem.

In the same year, a women's group NettNo, arranged for an Italian to come to Røst to give an Italian language course. Since then a study group has been created that meets weekly to maintain and develop their knowledge of the Italian language. This group is now working to create an exchange program for children and youth in Røst and Sandrigo. This is a follow-up of the appeal of the Mayor of Røst to look for new ways to strengthen the ties between Sandrigo and Røst, to learn more about each other, and create mutual solidarity and interest for culture and ways of living.

This appeal was made in 1999, when a delegation of 42 people from Røst took part in the stockfish festival. Among the delegates were the Mayor of Røst and the owners of the fish factories that produce and export stockfish. The mayor made a speech in Italian, in which he praised the good relationships between Italy and Norway in general, and between Sandrigo and Røst in particular. The speech was translated for him by the same daughter of a Norwegian exporter.

Epilogue

During the 1990s the population of Røst has stabilized and the trend of population decline has been somewhat reversed. This could have been one effect of the liberalization of the stockfish exports that took place in Norway in 1989. The inhabitants of Røst feel more optimistic and firmly believe in fisheries as a good and stable provider of work and income. The establishment of several new export companies after 1989, larger fish landings in the late 1990s, and greater focus on connections with Sandrigo and the stockfish trade as a way to develop and express cultural identity may have something to do with this new optimism. Sandrigo and the whole province of Vicenza is doing well, too.

As we were writing this chapter in summer 2003, the fishery in Lofoten was approaching the end of its season. As usual, there were voices of government officials and ocean researchers worrying that the cod stock was too small, whereas fishermen claimed that the stock was much bigger than the researchers believed. Factory owners worried about too much fish being caught too fast, the owners of various types of vessels complained about quotas being too small. Recently, several trailers have been robbed in the vicinity of Naples, and the Norwegian insurance companies are threatening to refuse to insure stockfish. There is always some dramatic story concerning the fishery of cod.

It needs to be added that the action net spun around the chain of translations of the cod that goes from Røst to Sandrigo, and similar action nets built around other chains is but a small and modest chapter in the history of the encounter between the people and cod. According to Kurlansky (1997), cod was the cornerstone of the welfare of Newfoundland, New England and, later, Iceland.

One could also say that the story of connections described here is not unique, either. Miele and Murdoch (2002) describing the Slow Food movement in Tuscany, emphasize three elements important for the creation of this phenomenon: "practical aesthetics" (tacit knowledge of local crafts and skills), "an ethics of local" (evaluation criteria that are local), and "local connectedness". What is striking in the Røst-Sandrigo story is that all this has been made *translocal*, almost against all odds, in the sense that the movement seems to be dependent on its "localness". It turns out that "localness" can travel!

On Doing Research in Complex Contexts

One of the reasons behind this text was our belief that the story of the "translated" cod, and the resulting welfare of the two communities, was interesting in its own right, and as a model to imitate. At the same time, we wanted to point out the necessity of a multi-perspective approach to study such complex phenomena (and which phenomena that we study are not complex?)

The traditional way of dealing with complexity of the social world in the social sciences goes through distinction and reduction. Both operations are unavoidable and necessary, but might produce unwarranted results. One is that complexity remains enigmatic, and is replaced by a complication of the research report. Hacking social reality in small bites and counting them afterwards resembles the early exercises in anatomy, which produced an inventory of body parts, but could not say much of their connections and coordination. The other is that analytical distinctions become reified into entities, which then are studied with complete seriousness by social scientists who do not remember that they invented them themselves.

One such set of distinctions, specific not only to social scientists but to the modern western culture as a whole, is the distinction between nature and culture, and between economics and politics. Our story shows how these distinctions have nothing to do with actual practices that weave all these supposedly separate realms seamlessly. This observation has been repeatedly made by sociologists of science and technology, represented in our text by Bruno Latour. The distinction between nature and culture, however, has important and negative consequences, visible precisely in the case of cod. We followed the chain of translations from "nature" to "culture", but it is not a chain, it is a loop, a circuit. Over-fishing has a long tradition, based on the assumption that "nature" will take care of itself and replenish the stock to supply "culture's" needs (Kurlansky, 1997). Kurlansky gave his fascinating book a subtitle "A biography of the fish that changed the world", thus attempting to attract attention to cod as a possible actor, and not just a thing taken from the bottom of the ocean to be eaten and sold. Luckily for cod, the idea that "nature" needs to be "cultivated" is, recently, bridging the gap created by nature-culture dichotomy – and by that we do not intend "fish farming", but a serious approach to cod – our fellow nature/culture being.

Another such set of distinctions, not so grand but much closer to home, is the traditional divisions within our own discipline, management. This chapter has been produced by people with background in two sub-disciplines: marketing and accounting. We could easily use the help of somebody in logistics (the section dedicated to transport is the shortest), finances and maritime law. We do not make a claim of presenting "a whole story" (which is still more complex), but, aided by organization theory that we have in common, we tried our best to show that all these perspectives must be combined if the ambition of rendering the complexity, and therefore furthering understanding, is still the one that steers research endeavors. This is a plea of relevance to researchers and management practitioners alike, we believe. Following a recommendation that comes from one perspective only ("diminish the dependence on Italians") makes sense within that perspective, but not in life and in business.

As to the process that we have been describing, our story corroborates the postulate that action nets create networks and identities, and not the other way around. Sandrigo and Røst connected their collective actions to one another, stabilized it in a formal relationship, and the stability of this net, due to repetition of the actions made new/old identities appear (see also Frenkel, this volume). This sequence is visible only when a temporal, historical approach is taken. Otherwise it is easy to take identities for granted and networks for fixed. Action nets have to be constantly produced and reproduced; they are fragile and require maintenance. The stabilizing elements – the cod, the liberal regulation, the "slow food" fashion – may all vanish. This process of construction and stabilization is at the core of management and organizing, and yet is given little attention.

PART II

*How Do Ideas Travel
And How Do They Land?*

Chapter 8

Fashion in Organizing

Barbara Czarniawska, Göteborg University, Sweden

FASHION IS CUSTOM IN THE GUISE
OF DEPARTURE FROM CUSTOM (SAPIR, 1931: 140)

Writing in 1995 about "Winds of organizational change: How ideas translate into objects and actions", Bernward Joerges and I have remarked that fashion was a phenomenon treated with disdain and neglect in contemporary social theory and organization studies. Part of the blame we attributed to critical theorists, who were prone to statements like the following by Joanne Finkelstein: "Fashionability allows individuals who follow the imperatives of fashion to abandon the responsibility to make history and shape culture" (1989: 144). However, we also apportioned blame to the masculine culture of the social sciences, where war, sport and technology were worth serious scrutiny and became a source of unproblematic metaphors; not so events and phenomena perceived as coming from feminine realms.

To us, a metaphorical, but above all a *literal* understanding of fashion seemed to be the key to comprehension of many puzzling developments in and between organizations. We wanted not only to redeem the importance of fashion, but also to frame it as the inseparable part of the "iron cage" of institutions, paradoxical as it may have sounded. It seemed to us that our postulate was about to be fulfilled. Eric Abrahamson, following the inspiration of Henry Mintzberg (1979), took up the issue of fashion in management (Abrahamson, 1991). Kjell-Arne Røvik (1996) argued convincingly for the need of fashion theory in studies of organizing. Indeed, fashion became soon fashionable in management and organization studies,[1] but was conceptualized in ways that considerably differed from our framing of it, to which I wish to return in this chapter.

---

[1] See e.g. the special issue of *Organization*, 2001, vol. 8 no. 1, *Management fads and fashions* edited by Sue Newell, Maxine Robertson and Jacky Swan.

Fashion in Organization Studies:
Moralized about, Made Mechanical and Manageable

To begin with, fashion has been portrayed as an irrational deviation from rational managerial behavior, as indicated by a frequent repetition of the alliteration "fads and fashions" (see Clark, 2004; and Sturdy, 2004, for reviews and critique). Because of the stubbornness of the phenomenon, however, a simple denigration of it to the status of deviant behavior did not solve the problem: it was too frequent and too persistent to be classified as pathology. This has been noticed already by Paul Nystrom (1928/1930) who set out to find "a rational explanation of fashions" (p. 193). Accordingly, managerial fashions (observe frequent use of plural noun, connoting symptom rather than a phenomenon by itself), have been "rationalized", for instance through their framing into the supply-and-demand model (Abrahamson, 1996a, b). A double and triple interpretative loops were constructed to show that there must be *something* in a fashion[2] – if not a promise of efficiency, than at least legitimacy, striving for which is highly rational in modernity. Further, the phenomenon has become tamed through its "division in stages" (see e.g. Gill & Whittle, 1993). In the same vain, it has been "set under control" through an assumption that there exist "fashion-setters" (Abrahamson, 1996a, b). Thus fashion could be explained: there was a market for it, as it was rationally (although not in a simple sense) demanded by managers and supplied by consultants (in another take, more conspiracy-minded, the suppliers controlled the demand). Division into stages (e.g. invention, dissemination, acceptance, disenchantment and decline) made fashion appear orderly and therefore predictable. Sequencing is a powerful heuristic for sensemaking, points out Weick (1995: 129), but sequencing as such is not enough to serve as a plot for a story. It is hard to expect that a fashion will decline before reaching its peak, and stating that it is usually the other way around does not ofer much added meaning. Furthermore, if fashion-setters can be distinguished before a fashion spreads, it must be manageable – controllable at its origins.

One could speculate that it is the Lutheran or Calvinist morality, many a time suspected to lurk behind theories of economics and management, which shapes the perception of management theorists. It well may be, but in terms of the history of science, the culprits are easier to pinpoint. It was Thorstein Veblen (1899/1994) who set up fashion as the way to promote "conspicuous consumption" and contrasted it to valuable productivity: "The leisure-class canon [fashion] demands strict and comprehensive futility; the instinct of workmanship demands purposeful action" (p. 159). He was not alone in his judgment; indeed, he expressed an opinion typical in his

---

[2] See e.g. Benders and van Veen's ingenious "interpretive viability", 2001.

times. Ada Heather Bigg, who espoused the Spencerian theory of fashion, wrote without hesitation:

> That fashion serves no useful end is indeed the confirmed opinion of a large number of thinking men and women (...) what they understand by the term is a series of frequently recurring changes undetermined by utility (...) It is this circumstance which puts a clear line of demarcation between the changes which go to make up Progress and those which constitute Fashion (1893/1973: 35).

And then she added, as a proof of her restraint: "Were we looking at the moral aspects of the matter, we should say that it was all silly, disgusting, and hateful, but, as it is the industrial aspects which claim our attention, adjectives can be spared" (p. 37).

Paul Nystrom, in search for the rational theory of fashion, adopted unhesitantly Veblen's insights, arriving at a "business rule (...) that a style, to succeed as a fashion, must have qualities that advertise either conspicuous leisure or conspicuous consumption for the user" (1928/1973: 204).[3] It has not occurred to him that conspicuous leisure might itself be a fashion, replaced in time by "conspicuous employment", so typical nowadays.

Consequently, the "trickle *down*" effect posited by Georg Simmel (1904), diverted all attention from the "trickle up" and especially "trickle across" effects (Partington, 1992: 150). Trickle-down effect echoes Herbert Spencer's "reverential imitation": for example, the modification of a costume introduced by a monarch, no matter how absurd, would spread down. According to Ada Bigg, reverential imitation was a thing of the past in 1893; but in such case, it certainly returned recently via celebrity cult, although it is doubtful whether the latter follows the "trickle down" effect. Also, the trickle-up effect is quite old: Freudenberger (1963/1973) gives examples of English gentlemen taking up peasants' jackets in the 17th century, and looking like "stage-coachmen, jockeys and pickpockets" in 1739. He also quotes Sombart as claiming that prostitutes and mistresses dictated women's fashion. In contrast, but in the same vein, J. C. Flügel wrote that "[i]n case of men's clothes especially (...) changes occur as much from below as from above" (1930/1973: 232). Finally, Simmel himself claimed that fashion – for both genders – is usually invented at the margins (in the *demimonde*), and only "legitimized" by its adoption by higher classes, from which it then "trickles down" to middle classes.

Many observations concerning fashion made a hundred years ago might be still valid, but not all, and the duty of organization theorists is to put

---

[3] Many of fashion's "rationalizers" attempted prediction: thus Edward Sapir (1931), in a very convincing reasoning demonstrated that lipstick is doomed to vanish soon whereas *rouge* will remain for ever between the US cosmetics.

them to test. Indeed, the importance of the above quoted studies of management lies in just that: in confirming that the diffusion curves do tend to be bell-shapen, and that one can distinguish innovators, early adopters, early and late majorities, and laggards (Rogers, 1962) if one so wishes. Further, now like before, there are several reasons that certain ideas, forms and practices spread more and quicker than others. As we mentioned in the introductory chapter, the inventions and innovations that are imitated are allegedly superior, in the first place on the grounds of their qualities (Gabriel Tarde [1890/1962] called these "logical reasons"; I would call them pragmatic). The other reason is their provenience in time and place (Tarde's "extra-logical" reasons; in today's parlance we would call them power-symbolic). It is impossible to tell the difference between the two at any given time, as the power-symbolic superiority tends to masquerade as a superiority of quality. The third type of superiority, according to Tarde, characterizes ideas that have many allies in other ideas – we would now say that such ideas are well anchored or that they do not threaten the institutionalized thought structure. This "power of associations" has been documented both by the old institutionalists like Rolland Warren who studied US city reforms in the 1970s (Warren et al., 1974) and by the actor-network theorists (Latour, 1986). Densely populated settings (big cities), social networks and organization fields facilitate and encourage imitation, etc.

It had been necessary to check whether these observations were valid in the present time and whether they were relevant in the field of management. Now that we know it, however, the time has come to move further and to try to grasp the specificity of management fashion, and the possible contribution that an understanding of management fashion can bring into the understanding of contemporary society (Clark, 2004 and Sturdy, 2004, seem to agree with my plea, although they phrase it differently).

In order to be able to do so, it is necessary to inspect the assumptions brought to the studies of fashion, often unintentionally. Is the moralizing tone justified? Needs fashion to be made orderly and manageable? Mechanisms, too, vary from simple to sophisticated. Many people and organizations would like to become trend-setters, but is it possible to plan and implement a fashion? In general, is it not high time to abandon the quest for determinist explanations of fashion and to allow for historical contingency in organizational dynamics?[4] I am not pleading for an "irrational" theory of fashion, but for a greater attention to the processes of rationality construction, which also change with times and places. One way to rescue

---

[4] Abrahamson and Fairchild (1999) try to do both, constructing an explanation that is deterministic *and* historically contingent; structurally-functionalist *and* psychodynamic. Such fusions are of course possible although rare; the usual divide lies in whether a theory promises prediction or interpretation.

the fashion from the old as well as new straight-jackets might pass through the field that treated it with greater respect than sociology or management: cultural theory.

Fashion in Cultural Theory[5]

Students of culture have repeatedly pointed out that fashion is a hybrid subject: it can be seen, and studied, as a *cultural phenomenon*, but also as a *production system* (Leopold, 1992: 102). A curious mirror-like symmetry characterizes studies of these two aspects in cultural theory and in organization theory. The former has spent much attention on fashion as a cultural phenomenon, but little on fashion as a production system (Leopold, 1992). In organization theory, fashion as a system of production is actually well researched, but its cultural aspect is treated sparingly.

Mazza & Alvarez (2000) have shown that, in contrast to earlier mechanical models of fashion production, the supposed consumers of managerial fashion are in fact its co-producers (Clark, 2004, corroborates their point). Nevertheless, they stop short of adopting the *circuit model of culture* (Richard Johnson, 1986/7), insisting on discerning "phases" (production, diffusion, legitimation) in what is obviously a circular process. Also, Mazza and Alvarez use *haute couture* and *prêt-à-porter* as metaphors, whereas treating them as analogies would reveal information that might be crucial for understanding managerial fashions. Contrary to popular belief, *prêt-à-porter* clothes originated not in France but in the USA during the Civil War ("ready-to-wear", Leopold, 1992). Consequently, initially they had nothing to do with high fashion. The two met only in the 1930s, where *prêt-à-porter* clothes and the US market became the saving line for French high fashion houses.[6] As to whether this encounter vitalized the ready-to-wear industry or hampered its technological potential by forcing it to imitate hand-sewing, opinions differ (Leopold, 1992; Steele, 1992). In management, this encounter has not yet taken place: ready-to-wear organizational prescriptions, originating in USA, proliferate in no connection, or a hostile one, with "high fashion" of university research as metaphorized by Mazza and Alvarez.

Ernst and Kieser (2002) and Kieser (2002) used fashion theories to explain the success of management consulting. Although Kieser (2002) mentions several of them, the final explanation relies heavily on Sombart's

---

[5] Although several theories I am quoting here are actually economic theories of fashion, they come from times when economy was still seen as a central facet of a culture.

[6] Nystrom (1928) sets this date earlier, seeing the encounter as resulting from the Chicago World's Fair in 1893.

(1902, quoted in Kieser, 2002) "marionette theory"[7]: "Consultants are able to create demand for their own services by creating management fashions, by stirring up managers' fear and greed, and by making managers dependent on them" (2002: 181). Sombart's theory is at present not well known to the Anglo-Saxon scholars[8], but the sentiment is widely shared by many critical researchers. As Latour (1996b) pointed out, framing people as puppets is characteristic for critical theory. Similarly, the followers of trickle-down theory tended to equate women's interest in fashionable clothes "with the fetishism and spectacularisation which create the 'illusion' of changed conditions of existence" (Partington, 1992: 149). Studying the postwar fashion in the UK, Angela Partington noticed, however, that "[i]n trying to impose certain standards of taste on consumers, the design profession and the marketing industries created the opportunity for the roles of 'good consumption' to be broken, inadvertently allowing consumers to produce unexpected meanings around fashion goods" (1992: 147). Partington concluded that English working-class women in the post-war period were able to articulate their own specific tastes (often subversive) by using the cultural codes of the mass-market fashion system. It is perhaps not too far-fetched to assume that contemporary managers are able to act similarly.

Let me then return to the early theoreticians of fashion as a cultural phenomenon to see which of their insights can be imported into organization theory. The travel starts with Veblen and Simmel's predecessor, Gabriel Tarde[9]:

> ... in our European societies (...) the extraordinary progress of fashion in all its forms, in dress, food and housing, in wants and ideas, in institutions and in arts, is making a single type of European based upon several hundreds of millions of examples (Tarde, 1890/1962: 16).

Tarde claimed that fashion was already a strong force in antiquity, although he admitted, in agreement with the later scholars of fashion from Braudel on (Wilson, 1985), that it was the 18th century that "inaugurated the reign of

---

[7] An allusion to Parisian puppets called Pandoras (*bambole* in Italian and "fashion babies" in English) which, dressed in the latest fashion, toured European capitals each month, the practice starting in the first half of the 18th century (Freudenberger, 1963).

[8] After early Marxist writings, he espoused the Nazi ideology at the end of his life and even before attributed first to the Jews and then to women (fashion!) the worst excesses of capitalism (*Luxury and capitalism*, 1922/1967).

[9] Veblen was 14 years younger and Simmel 15 years younger than Tarde (for more on Tarde, and its relevance for organization studies, see Latour, 2002 and Czarniawska, 2004c). Tarde often alluded to Herbert Spencer's *Ceremonial institutions* (vol. 2 part 4 of *The principles of sociology*, 1879), mostly in order to disagree.

fashion on a large scale" (Tarde, 1890/1962: 293 n. 2).[10] His explanation for changes of fashion were the same as for inventions, and he clearly saw its paradoxical character:

> In the case of industry and fine arts, it is for the pleasure of change, of *not doing* the usual thing, that the part of the public which is influenced by fashion adopts a new product to the neglect of some old one; then when the novelty has become acclimated and appreciated for its own sake the older product seeks a refuge in the cherished habits of the other part of the public which is partial to custom and which wishes to show in that way that it also *does not do* the same thing as the rest of the world (Tarde, 1890/1962: 293 n. 2).

In Tarde's view, fashion was contrasted to custom; but he did not discuss fashion as such, as it inevitably accompanied imitation in his writings, to the point that it is often joined by a hyphen: fashion-imitation (contrasted to custom-imitation).

As we know, after Tarde, Veblen and Simmel took up the topic of fashion and examined in it great detail. Due to their mode of referencing, or rather non-referencing, it is impossible to know whether they were aware of Tarde's work. But whereas for Veblen fashion was a negative phenomenon at the service of conspicuous consumption (1899), Simmel seemed to continue along Tarde's train of thought; he saw in fashion a democratic and democratizing phenomenon, intensifying with the progress of civilization. This was mostly because fashion connected together two opposing tendencies: equalization and individualization.

> Fashion is the imitation of a given example and satisfies the demand for social adaptation. ... A the same time, it satisfies in no less degree the need of differentiation, the tendency for dissimilarity, the desire for change and contrast (Simmel, 1904/1971: 296).

Simmel's theory was taken up by Herbert Blumer, who postulated that fashion is a *selection mechanism* that influences the market and distorts the demand and supply curves, both using and serving the economic competition (Blumer, 1969). Its important element is a *collective choice* among competing tastes, things, and ideas; it is oriented toward *finding* but also toward *creating* what is typical of a given time. One could add that fashion operates at institutional fringes. On the one hand, its variety is limited by the "iron cage" of existing institutions, which fashion actually reproduces; on the

---

[10] Although Freudenberger (1963), after Max von Boehn, places it around 1630, while Caroline A. Foley (1893) would also locate the beginnings of fashion in ancient Greece. Here, like in the case of fashion theoreticians, one is reminded of Merton's (1965/1985) dictum that there are no beginnings, only the patience of the researcher has an end.

other hand, fashion is engaged in a constant subversion of the existing institutional order, gnawing at its bars. This is the second paradox connected to fashion: its simultaneous unimportance and saliency.

The notion of translation helps to understand yet another paradox: fashion is created even as it is followed. It is the subsequent translations that simultaneously produce and reproduce variations in fashion: repetition creates and re-creates difference. Tarde has pointed out that this needs not be seen as a contradiction, merely as a difficulty: a difficulty consisting of discovering an original idea within an already dominating style (Tarde, 1902/1969: 157). This is why Lyotard (1979) insisted on differentiating between an invention and an innovation (Tarde, or at least his translators, treat them as synonymous): whereas an innovation remains within the already prevailing style, an invention changes such style.

Fashion stands for change. But as fashion is also repetitive, in a long-range perspective it stands for tradition as well. Indeed, as pointed out by Agnes Brook Young, fashion is not related to progress (although it stands for modernity):

> In a real sense, fashion is evolution without destination. The world generally considers that progress in material things consists in changes that make them more useful, or better looking, or less expensive. In the long run fashion never attains these objectives. Its idea is slow, continuous change, unhampered by the restrictions of either aesthetics or practicality (Young 1937/1973: 109).

Young's notion of "evolution without destination" is close in spirit to Tarde's "evolutionary diffusionism",[11] although she, too, quotes only Simmel. Fashion operates through dramatized "revolutions", but "… in a real sense, fashion is evolution." (ibid.) Tarde would agree: in his view, fashion first opposes custom, and then, if successful, becomes a custom itself, only to be opposed by the next fashion.

Fashion, then, transpires as a highly paradoxical process. Its constitutive paradoxes are invention *and* imitation, variation *and* uniformity, distance *and* interest, novelty *and* conservatism, unity *and* segregation, conformity *and* deviation, change *and* status quo, revolution *and* evolution. And it is indeed translation, side to side with negotiation, that is used to resolve these paradoxes in each practical action. As Simmel observed, "social institutions may be looked upon as the peace-treaties, in which the constant antagonism of both principles has been reduced externally to a form of cooperation" (1904/1971: 296). The predilection for military metaphors typical for social

---

[11] Tarde differed from diffusionists (an early school in anthropology opposing evolutionists) pointing out the variation inherent in each displacement, and from evolutionists pointing out the role of action, i.e. imitation. Thus he speaks of "evolution by association" (1893/1999: 41) à la Stephen Jay Gould, or "diffusion by transformation" (which is synonymous with translation).

sciences put negotiation early into focus of attention, but it was not until the arrival of Studies of Science and Technology and the linguistic turn that an obvious point could be made: in order to negotiate, the parties must at least believe that they are speaking about the same thing (see Rottenburg in this volume). Translation comes first. Fashion would not be able to proceed without constant translation, which permits it to appear in many different guises in different times and places.

I have already illustrated such understanding of fashion with the example of city management, excerpted from a study conducted in three European capitals, Stockholm, Warsaw and Rome (Czarniawska, 2002).[12] Fashion seemed there to be the main selection mechanism – indeed the steering wheel – of organizational forms and managerial practices. Fashionable were not only solutions, but even problems, in line with garbage can theory. Perhaps this was to be expected. Big cities, especially capitals, are laboratories of fashion (Freudenberger, 1963; Solli & Czarniawska, 2001). Big cities set examples, but they also collect experiences from their region or country and re-present it in further contacts. An innovation can either start in a capital or, initiated somewhere else, find its most extreme expression there. The duty of modernization in Europe resides in big cities.

Nor is the notion of a "fashionable city" a new one, although undoubtedly a modern one. Tarde quotes an author who studied cities of the old regime in France and who noted that it was fashionable in the 18th century to use secret ballots in municipal elections. Moreover, Angers adopted this mode of voting as early as the 16th century, justifying it by the example of Venice, Genoa, Milan, and Rome (Tarde, 1890/1962: 293). Therefore in what follows I shall use both contemporary and historical examples; of my own and others' studies.

Fashion and the City: Three Examples

Market making and unmaking: Fast tram in Rome

Fashion is an agency of collective choice, which influences the market and distorts the demand and supply curves, pointed out Herbert Blumer (1969). A good example of this was the project of introducing the fast tram in the center of Rome (Czarniawska, 2004a). The project was crammed with difficulties, but it did not deterred Rome authorities: at the time of the study, that is, in the late 1990s, a fast tram was "a must" in an European capital. Cities that previously eradicated their tram lines put them in anew; cities that had a quite satisfactory public transportation system (like Stockholm)

---

[12] The research program, *Managing the Big City: A 21st Century Challenge to Technology and Administration*, has been conducted at the Gothenburg Research Institute and financed by the Bank of Sweden's Tercennary Foundation. See also Adolfsson in this volume.

put in a line in the peripheries, just to have it. However, another trait of fashion is that it cannot exist without spectators and because of it, each if its element might have a symbolic value, especially when the stage is the capital of a country. The fashion for fast trams has created a great demand for fast trams; several companies, among them Siemens, could respond to this demand quickly and efficiently. FIAT, however, the jewel in the crown of Italian industry, was not producing fast tram cars at the time, specializing in metro cars (a previous urban fashion). Traffic authorities in Rome decided to use old tram cars until FIAT opened a new production line. The trams were not fast, but they were there, until the new cars were eventually produced by a national company.

This distortion of market laws was specific for Rome, but only its actual contents were unique. In a more general discussion about fast trams, it has been suggested that it is the transport technology producers, who present their newest ideas at "catwalks" of conferences and fairs, who are the actual trend setters. Urban transportation follows the fashion, much as the citizens would like to believe that it is their needs amended with efficiency considerations that shape its actual form.

Pattern recognition: IT city

Fashion is oriented towards finding tastes, things, ideas typical of a given time but also creating them: "No design works unless it embodies ideas that are held in common by the people for whom the object is intended" (Forty, 1986: 245). This is why fashion leaders might be actually seen as early adopters. Agnes Young has quoted in this context the saying of (Zachariah?) Chandler "Look where the people are going and lead them where they drive you" (1937/1973: 118). Simmel spoke thus of "the dude" (dandy): "He leads the way, but all travel the same road" (1904/1971: 305). It takes time, however, and trials and errors, to discover what this object or that direction is. It is not easy to aspire to a role of a trend-setter, which amounts to walking ahead without turning back to see whether you are followed, at least for some time. At the point in time when I finished my study of Stockholm, that is, in 1999, a fiber optic network was among the most important projects in the city. Two years later, my collaborator discovered that the broadband took its place (Dobers, 2001; 2002). The moderate enthusiasm of the citizens and the events of September 11, 2001 pushed the attention in yet different direction. Here is an article from *Biometric Technology Today*, March 2003:

> A futuristic city, where biometrics will be common place, is being established on the Singapore/Malaysia border in the Malaysian State of Johor. This waterside border crossing has been shown to attract about four times as much traffic as Kuala Lumpur International Airport, yet has no adequate facilities to deal with the flow of people and traffic (...)

The new city will be quite small at 300 acres and could be considered to be a large local area network (LAN). The domestic company that will design, coordinate and implement all the ICT technologies is **Waterside IT Solutions**. The company's ICT project director Shukor Ahmed told *Btt:* "The key is that everything from entertainment to the healthcare facilities will be connected. In such a set up, the internet and intranet will play a major part…" (p. 2)

This excerpt announces the key elements of the newest trend: firstly, a complete ICT "urban infrastructure"; secondly, biometrics as the key safety measure; thirdly, the special role that suburbs hosting airports or other crossings acquire as the protectors of big cities in the present focus on urban safety. Will this trend dominate? Future will tell.

Fashion's Janusian face: Radiant City 1930s/1960s/2000s

It would be wrong, however, to conclude from the previous example that fashion stands only for what is new, or for the future. Fashion, as Agnes Young pointed out, has no destination; it runs in what seems to be cycles, although their regularity might be in the eye of the beholder, especially one keen on periodization.

At any rate, Le Corbusier galvanized the world in the 1930s with his vision of a city cut into radiuses of highways that effortlessly transported Organization Men from their suburbs to the office in the City and back. By the 1960s, this vision stood not for fashion but for being old-fashioned, as the following quote from Jane Jacobs suggests:

> … it is understandable that men who were young in the 1920's were captivated by the vision of the freeway Radiant City, with the specious promise that it would be appropriate to an automobile age. At least it was then a new idea; (…) it was radical and exciting in the days when their minds were growing and their ideas forming. Some men tend to cling to old intellectual excitements, just as some belles, when they are old ladies, still cling to the fashions and coiffures of their exciting youth (Jane Jacobs, 1961: 371).

The idea should be dead by 2000s, but it is not. Sometimes it stands for the horrors of the past, like in the TV movie from 1996; sometimes it is revived in a new shape, as suggested in the following excerpt from an article "Radiant City Redux", written by Edward B. Driscoll, Jr:

> Having spent about twenty minutes cruising around on a Segway, that scooter-like device that's been hyped up and down the Internet and TV, I can safely say that it's a technological marvel. But what its designers want to do to the urban areas that it will operate in, is yet another attempt to build a utopian city, much like Le Corbusier's ill-conceived efforts, 70 years ago (16 April 2002, http://www.techcentralstation.com/041602A, accessed 04-08-22).

Investigations into the role of fashion in city management have shown that fashion (together with other processes like control or negotiation) introduces order and uniformity into what might seem an overwhelming variety of possibilities. In this sense, fashion helps people to come to grips with the present. At the same time, it "serves to detach the grip of the past in the moving world. By placing a premium on being in the mode and derogating what developments have been left behind, it frees actions for new movement" (Blumer, 1969/1973: 339). "Fashion always occupies the dividing-line between the past and the future, and consequently conveys a stronger feeling of the present, at least while it is at its height" (Simmel, 1904/1973: 303). One could read in Jacob's and Driscoll's referrals to the Radiant City a signal of an absence, of lack of a comparable fashion, which would make *their* present distinct.

Fashion also introduces some appearance of order and predictability into preparations for what is necessarily disorderly and uncertain: the future. Fashion, in its gradual emergence, attenuates the surprises of the next fashion, and tunes into the collective by making it known to itself, as reflected in the present fashion and in the rejection of past fashions. Additionally, like in the case of Radiant City, a specific fashion can become not a custom but an institution, thus helping to relate other fashions to it. This idea is somewhat different from the postulate of the supposedly cyclical character of fashion and therefore requires some attention.

Fashion Translated Through Time and Space

In the context of the present volume, an especially interesting aspect of fashion are the necessary translations that occur during the period of imitation. This acquires an additional interest when the "imitation wave" is very long, as in the case of City Manager reform, which, apparently, took 90 years to reach from Staunton, VA, to Rome, Italy.

> In 1908 the city officials of Staunton, Va., hired Mr C. E. Ashburner as a "general manager". They were disgusted with the inefficiency of the existing system and passed an ordinance giving the city manager all administrative power and responsibility. The plan worked, and in the fall of 1910 Lockport, N.Y., prepared a plan combining the commission form with the Staunton idea of a city manager. The next experiment was at Sumter, S.C., where in 1912 a new charter was adopted which embodied the Lockport idea. In Dayton, Ohio, after the usual expensive experience with wasteful political administration of the older type, the need for a new government became acute after the disastrous flood of 1913, and in 1914 a new charter was adopted which embodied the city manager plan. From this day on the idea spread rapidly to other American cities, large and small (Chapin, 1928: 340).

F. Stuart Chapin, a sociologist inspired by Tarde who reported this event, attempted to analyze the causes, or the motives and circumstances, that prevailed in cities that introduced the city manager plan. He found out that "the agent most likely to precipitate a change from the old type of government is dissatisfaction with the conventional (...) system, either because of the inefficiency and wastefulness of its operation, or because of this factor in combination with a crisis which crystallizes sentiment and forces a change (Chapin, 1928: 341). The problem with this explanation is that it fits practically all cases of public administration reform (see e.g. Brunsson and Olsen, 1993). Why City Manager Plan? Why then? Why there?

Chapin conducted a proper diffusion study, but did not pose himself the questions I am asking. His results looked as follows (p. 208):

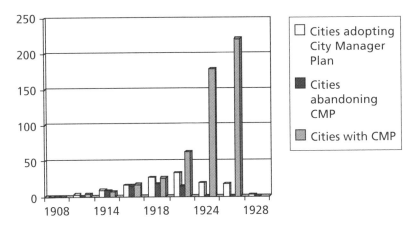

His explanation concerning the changes in time was inspired by Tarde and suggested

> ... the rhythmical character of imitation. It diffuses from central models enjoying prestige, it spreads by geometric progression in many directions, in some cases it is refracted by its media more considerably than in other cases, it reaches a point of saturation, and the old model declines before some new model which has set up a wave of counter-imitation (Chapin, 1928: 208).

Chapin's study and reasoning resembles the contemporary studies of diffusion (yet another fashion that returned after many decades) and population ecology. He also suggests various stages: spreading, saturation, counter-imitation, just like organization scholars do nowadays. Because of the short time horizon, the question of the persistence, or the cyclical character, of fashion, did not come into his picture. It is for us to ask, in which way the city manager plan reached the city of Rome in 1997, when the Italian Law n° 127 of 1997 (*Urgent measures for slimming of administrative activities*), introduced a function of the City Manager. Such City Manager was to be appointed with a fixed term contract and should not become a member of the bureaucratic structure. The appointment was to be made by the Mayor, who would also issue guidelines to City Manager. The latter's duty was to implement the programs and the objectives enacted by the governing bodies; to this purpose City Manager was to devise an Executive Management Plan. According to the Law, City Manager was to be ultimately responsible for the management of the city pursuing optimal levels of efficiency and effectiveness.

Fabrizio Panozzo, then unaware of the ancient roots of the reform, explained its occurrence within the contemporary circumstances:

> Within the Italian reform of municipal government, questioning the objectives and outcomes and calls for greater accountability acquired a meaning which is dependent on the institutional conditions generating them. (...) In the slow transition of Italian public administration, the new Latin of management has been translated into a kind of pragmatism infused with intellectual and moral appeals and hence used as an expressive rhetoric of transparency, impartiality and honesty, which is opposed to "old politics" and corruption and thus becomes "morally good". The ethos of the manager, the leading and accountable person, has gained widespread legitimacy (...) (Panozzo, 2001: 82, English in original).

This fascinating analogy suggests at present more questions than answers; the latter require a solid historical detection that, however, might bring a lot to understanding of fashion phenomenon, processes of imitation, and the role of translation. A mechanistic explanation would suggest that "the cycle of urban reforms" is about 70 years long (unlike the cycle of women's skirts that, according to Agnes Young, come back in 100 years time). It is likely, however, that further examples might change this period to anything between 70 and 10 years (Gill and Whittle, 1993, opt for 40 year-cycle of management fashion). A structural-functionalist explanation would suggest that big cities in the 1920s suffered from the same problems as big cities in the 1990s, and thus looked for the same solutions. But this elegant (if reductionist) explanation provokes further doubts: who and how decides what is "same" and what is "different"? Or is it so, as suggested by Solli, Demediuk and Sims in the present volume, that it is the aura of a name that is being exploited in order to relate to quite different problems, different solutions, and different circumstances? Else, could it be that problems recur, same names are applied, but actual solutions (actions and activities) are different, Zeitgeist-dependent? After all, as Robert Merton (1965/1985) pointed out, there are no "new ideas": all ideas circulate most of the time, at least in some places.

Last but not least there is a suggestion that what seems to be "cycles" of fashion results simply from forgetting. Chapin himself quotes a well-known dictum: "Men learn from history that men never learn from history", 1928: 2). Røvik (1996) spoke of "fading", but Karin Brunsson suggested that the process is much more active, in fact, an "organized oblivion" (1998). Røvik claimed that unfashionable prescriptions are stored in organizational "wardrobes" to be retrieved after a long enough time period. This is a convincing explanation for retro-fashions in the same place, but how did the Italian authorities find the key to the Stanton, VA's wardrobe?

A short look at the Web in August 2004 reveals 1,030,000 entries for "City Manager", most of them in the USA (one entry is from Italy, and one from Finland). Some of them speak of a rejection of city manager plan, some of adoption, most of the details of its practice: "Appointed by the City Council, the City Manager is the chief executive officer for City government. He and his staff coordinate and manage the activities of all City departments and offices, prepare the annual budget, oversee the implementation of all City programs, and provide administrative assistance and support to the City Council. The City Manager also appoints all department heads and certain other staff." (The City of Raleigh). The blog from City Hall in Eden Prairie, MN reads: "Hi, I am Scott Neal, your friendly City Manager." The fashion that seemed to be fading out in 1928 has actually stabilized into an institution that the Italian authorities decided to imitate – possibly, with help of an organization like ICMA – International City/County Association:

> ICMA is the professional and educational organization for chief appointed managers, administrators, and assistants in cities, towns, counties, and regional entities throughout the world. Since 1914, ICMA has provided technical and management assistance, training, and information resources to its members and the local government community. The management decisions made by ICMA's nearly 8,000 members affect more than 100 million individuals in thousands of communities – from small towns with populations of a few hundred to metropolitan areas serving several million (http://www2.icma.org, accessed 04-08-24).

Somebody, somewhere, found the City Manager plan sitting on some shelf in some US municipality, and many hastened to facilitate its return, probably around 1995. But why City Manager? Why in Rome? Why now? The Romans adopted the institution of the City Manager from the USA, but why the US municipalities went back to it? It has been severely criticized in the 1940s and the 1960s (Nalbandian, 1991).

Here again an analogy from clothing fashion might help: retro-shopping is a well-known way of looking for inspiration. The analogy certainly works in social sciences: thus Mary Douglas re-discovered Ludwik Fleck, Bruno Latour dusted off the shelf Abbott's *Flatland*, and Stephen Barley and Gideon Kunda retrieved E.P. Thompson. Fashionable items do not have to be created; they can be found, in anybody's wardrobe or at any flea market. They become translated into the idiom of the day, or rather the rhetorical code of the day, as Barthes (1967) pointed out, and circulated – with or without acknowledgment of their origin. Knowing this mechanism helps to understand time we live in: the fact that Tarde and Simmel seem to be replacing in status Durkheim and Weber says more about the era we live in than about these authors. The travels and the translations of City Management Plan, barely hinted at here, promise an opportunity of a detective work that might turn equally satisfying to the researcher-detective and her or his readers.

Studying Fashion in Management

Various examples of relating management to fashion and vice versa translate, in my view, into an imperative to study the *process* of fashion and not, as is more common, its results. Fashion plays its tricks, also, on fashion research: focusing on its products, scholars reach the conclusion that fashion is fickle and ephemeral. But in reaching this conclusion, they miss the stable character of the production process itself. Similarly, there is a need to acknowledge the simultaneous homogenization and heterogenization that accompanies fashion. Fashion means that many people do the same thing at the same time across space, but fashions mean that they will be doing something else soon. Given a longer time horizon, however, it is likely that they will be doing the same thing, but in another place, etc. As Røvik put it succinctly, fashion "is a stable social mechanism that continually produces change" (1996: 155).

The paradoxical character of fashion needs to be acknowledged in order to understand it. Fashion is an expression of conformism (social adaptation), and anticonformism (Simmel, 1904), therefore managers might follow it for opposite reasons. It helps to introduce order and uniformity into variety of possibilities, and through that helps to come to grips with the present and to unfasten the hold of the past in the shifting world (Blumer, 1969). At the same time, it introduces an appearance of predictability into the future: emerging gradually, it softens the surprises of the next fashion, makes a "time-collective" (Sellerberg, 1994) better known to itself by reflecting it in the present fashion and in the rejection of past fashions.

There is no doubt that there exist "fashion leaders" and "trend setters"; the point is, they are known only in the retrospect. As actor-network theory rightly postulates, people and organizations acquire "character" as a result of a successful performance, not as a result of good intentions (Czarniawska and Hernes, 2005). Therefore the convenient focus on the "trickle down" path must be complemented by tracing various kinds of "trickle up",[13] and, especially in the world of organizations, of "trickle across".

Therefore, as suggested at the outset of this chapter, students of management might learn a lot from students of culture in this endeavor (perhaps also the other way around, when it concerns fashion as production apparatus). It is important to admit that the world of management can learn from the world of fashion, by the way of analogy, not metaphor. Management is as fashion-prone as clothing industry, interior design, science and everything else. These lessons might be quite practical: after all, there are well established ways of sensible fashion-following in clothing. This does not mean that the analogy needs to be accepted on my word: indeed, there are all the reasons to inspect whether the analogy holds and to what degree. Elisabeth Wilson ends her book on fashion by pointing out that

> The pointlessness of fashion, what Veblen hated, is precisely what makes it valuable. It is in this marginalized area of the contingent, the decorative, the futile, that not simply a new aesthetic but a new cultural order may seed itself. Out of the cracks in the pavements of cities grow the weeds that begin to rot the fabric (1985: 245).

Is she right? The last sentence alludes to the saying "Sous le pavé la plage" by Arthur Cravan, an anarchist and poet (1887–1918). We who study cities know, however, that under pavement there is no sandbeach but the city's own garbage. Still, couldn't it be that Cravan's romantic idea inspired the city managers of Paris who recently constructed a beach at Seine? So, if Wilson is right, does her observation apply to managers? Do they also, while cultivating façades and futile practices, open cracks in the solid rationality of formal prescriptions? Or, the other way around, do they "seek to save their inner freedom all the more completely by sacrificing externals to enslavement by the general public?" (Simmel, 1904/1971: 313). Their "inner freedom" might express itself in frauds and political games, but fashion, and façades, deserve more respect and – curiosity.

In order to satisfy such curiosity, it is important to initiate processual studies of fashion, aiming at capturing how a fashion develops. Already Simmel (1904) criticized the history of fashions for its concentration on the development of their contents only: a critique that can be directed against studies of management fashions. It is important to report what is in fashion, but also to inquire: why this? why now? Therefore, studies of fashion need to be firmly *situated*: what was the previous fashion? what is the accessible repertoire at the time? (what are the contents of the contemporary garbage can?)

---

[13] It can be best seen at present in the enormous influence of sportswear on design: anoraks in gold lamé by Versace, Reeboks in rhinestone-studded velvet by Ozbeck, and bumbags in quilted leather by Chanel (Rumbold, 1992).

what is happening elsewhere at the same time? As Edward Sapir had said: "Fashion is emphatically a historical concept. A specific fashion is utterly unintelligible if lifted out of its place in a sequence of forms" (1931: 140). Remembering this might help to redefine fashion – from a deviant irrationality on the part of erring managers, to the key to pattern recognition, permitting a better understanding of the dynamics of management – across time and space.

Chapter 9

Something New, Something Old, Something Borrowed: The Cross-National Translation of the "Family Friendly Organization" in Israel

Michal Frenkel, The Hebrew University of Jerusalem, Israel[1]

This chapter focuses on the interrelations between the spread in time (from "old" into "new") and space (from "global" into "local") of the "Family Friendly Organization" (FFO),[2] a fashionable and somewhat fluid set of organizational ideas and practices assembled by employers to help their employees balance their work and family obligations.

In an age of changing workforce demographics, such as increases in female labor force participation and dual-earner and single-parent households, and when family working hours are lengthening, organizational stakeholders across the industrial world have argued in favor of work-family practices, such as workplace crèches or subsidized childcare, maternity/parental and other family leaves, flexible work arrangements, and other family support services. Such practices, these advocates have argued, do not only ameliorate employees' work-life balance (especially among women) and answer legal requirements for affirmative action policies, but they are also held to improve organizational performance.[3]

This latter rationale, known as "the business case for work-family policies" (Kelly, 1999; Glass, 2000; Litvin, 2002) has made the FFO a popular

[1] The Author wishes to thank the HR managers interviewed for this study for their cooperation and Yehouda Shenhav, Michael Shalev, Alexandra Kalev and the participants of this volume for helpful discussions, comments and suggestions. This study was supported by grants from the Israeli Foundation Trustees (2003–2004) and the Levi Eshkol Institute at the Hebrew University of Jerusalem (2002).
[2] Also known as the "family responsive workplace".
[3] See Rapoport et al., 1996; Hochschild, 1997; Galinsky, 2001; Rapoport, 2002.

organizational practice. In 1997, more than half of the Fortune 500 CEO's announced their support for FF practices (Kelly, 1999), concurring that they lead to lower worker turnover, create a larger pool of potential employees for in-demand professions, reduce absenteeism, promote more efficient usage of recourses and time, improve organizational flexibility, create a diversified workforce, and accrue greater public legitimacy to the firm.

Embraced by feminist organizations, multinational consultancies, business journals, and international organizations such as the ILO and the EU, the FFO gained popularity and traveled across cultural and national boundaries (den-Dulk, 2001; Appelbaum et al., forthcoming). Yet, despite the accelerating spread of FFO practices around the glob, studies of FFO adoption still focus first and foremost on the diffusion of US' practices, disregarding the complicated history of such practices in other parts of the world and the translation they undergo when traveling from one social context to the other. This process of translation is especially crucial given the growing literature emphasizing the wide differences in state level work-family policies (Sainsbury, 1994; Esping-Andersen, 1999; O'Connor et al., 1999) and in the cultural conceptualizations of work-family issues (Pfau-Effinger, 2000; Lewis, 2001). Thus, in the context of the liberal welfare regime in the US, the idea that employers should be involved in helping their workers deal with the provision of family care was presented as a new one in contrast to the notion that work and family are separate and largely unrelated spheres of life (Kelly, 1999). In other industrialized societies however, this was not the case. Many of the family friendly practices had actually already been implemented by a large number of organizations sometimes even as early as the beginning of the 20th century. This was the case especially in countries with social-democratic welfare regimes (Esping-Andersen, 1999). In these societies, however, rather than being related to gender equity or a "business case", the implementation of FF practices was either attributed to the logic of "welfare capitalism" or resulted from state enforcement. Nevertheless, even in those societies in which current FF practices are "old news", firms today make sure to present their commitment to family friendliness in their organizational vision and Internet home pages as an expression of managerial innovativeness.

"Management fashion", argue Czarniawska and Sevón following Blumer (see the introduction to this volume), "help to come to grips with the present. At the same time, [the concept] 'serves to detach the grip of the past in the moving world. By placing a premium on being in the mode and derogating what developments have left behind, it frees actions for new movement", (Blumer, 1969: 289). Students of management fashions thus argue that the "newness" of practices constitutes at least part of the explanation for their wide dissemination (Abrahamson, 1996b, c; Abrahamson and Fairchild, 1999).

148

This chapter, however, focuses on "oldness" and its role in the legitimization and propagation of management fashions. Based on a close analysis of the way HR managers have translated the FFO model in the context of the social-democratic welfare regime of Israel,[4] I show that the fashion for FFOs has not been adopted across the world as a prêt-à-porter garment. Instead, it has been deconstructed, cut up and re-sewed into its local and contemporary shape.

During the translation process, new practices have been put forward as the organization's way of distinguishing itself from the "old". However, at the same time "old" practices are also represented as "new". Furthermore, in order to deal with diverse organizational stakeholders, new practices are submitted as a direct continuation of traditional mechanisms. This resembles the process known in the fashion world as "customizing" and as "vintage" fashion.

Following Latour (1986), I stress the importance of the ways in which actors actively interpret the past and reconceptualize the "old", and show how this interpretation becomes "energy" that allows the translated object to spread in time and space.

On Fashion and Time Horizons:
The Old, the New and the Vintage Product

It has been pointed out that many management models, after being apparently legitimized and institutionalized, subsequently undergo a period of deinstitutionalization during which they are marginalized, at least until they reemerge under a different name and in a different interpretive framework (Røvik, 1996). Fashion setters – mostly management consultancy firms – develop new models of management, to create further demand for their services (Abrahamson and Fairchild, 1999; Ernst and Kieser, 2002; Kieser, 2002). As well as offering an attempt to understand the rapid spread of management models and ideas, the concept of fashion thus conceived focuses attention on one point in time: the present. New fashions are said to replace old ones, but the role of the old in the spread of the new is hardly discussed.

But old fashions do not just disappear. As findings reported for instance by Abrahamson (1996b) and Strang and Macy (2001) show, new management fashions are often formed out of the ashes of older ones.

The lack of theoretical development of the deep interrelations between present and past, and old and new in the analysis of fashion may be attributable to the long-standing schism in organization studies between static and dynamic explanations of organizational behavior. While students of organi-

---

[4] Some would say, "the *formerly* social-democratic regime of Israel".

zational change constantly look at new phenomena and provide explanations for organizational transformations, researchers of organizational inertia tend to examine consistent phenomena, overlooking or underplaying organizational changes.

Another possible explanation is rooted in Simmel's writings, still very much an inspiration to researchers of fashion. For Simmel, fashion is a prototype of a "social form", a stable structure that emerges from the plurality of social facts. Even though the content and the social meaning attributed to it in the process of its adoption may change, the structure itself remains the same. It is not the content of any particular fashion that is important, but rather the fact that something is recognized as being fashionable. According to Simmel "(f)ashions are always class fashions, by the fact that the fashions of higher strata of society distinguish themselves from those of the lower strata, and are abandoned by the former at the moment when the latter begin to appropriate them" (Simmel, 1905/1997: 189). Changes in content are significant only in that "they give to fashions of today an individual stamp compared with those of yesterday" (ibid.). From this point of view, then, the "old" is important only to the extent to which it is different from the "new".

Yet, as Czarniawska has pointed out earlier in this volume following Agnes Young, it would be wrong to conclude that fashion stands only for what is new, or for the future. "Fashion has no destination; it runs in what seems to be cycles, although their regularity might be in the eye of the beholder, especially one keen on periodization". One way to make sense of these cycles and to theorize how the "past" or the "old," and recollections of them, might affect the adoption and translation of management fashions, is grounded in Latour's theory of translation (1987). He points out that new scientific paradigms and theories, for instance, are not adopted for their reflection of an objective truth, but rather become "objective" as they travel across social contexts and recruit allies. Moreover, in contrast to diffusion approach (including the diffusion of management fashions), the translation approach assumes that organizational actors themselves have an active role in the displacement of everything. According to Latour, temporal and spatial dissemination – of claims, orders, artifacts, goods – lies in the hands of identifiable people, each of whom may act in many different ways, such as letting the token drop, modifying it, deflecting or betraying it, adding to it, or appropriating it (Latour, 1986: 267). He is also concerned with the way that different actors *actively interpret* the past, and how this interpretation becomes "energy" that enables the displacement of the translated object. A study of the translation of management fashions from this perspective, therefore, should first ask how and with what rationale actors interpret their past. In the light of this interpretation, it should then go on to clarify why they choose to invest the "new" fashion with enough energy to keep it mov-

150

ing. In this regard Latour deploys the metaphor of rugby players, who ensure the continued movement of the ball as they pass it to one another; the ball itself, of course, has no energy of its own.

In that respect, one might argue that old practices, organizational memory and history might be viewed as non-human "actants"[5] playing a role in displacing management fashions. Old practices can be recruited as allies to push for the investment of energy in new ones. Organizational memory might work for or against specific practices and general systems of justifications.[6]

In what follows I first reconstruct the story of the emergence and global dissemination of the FFO as a US management fashion, following its evolution in contemporary work-family literature. I then move on to the Israeli case to study in detail the way old practices, organizational memories and recollections of the past affect the translation of these professional practices in Israeli organizations.

Between Two Paradigms:
Managerialism and Welfare in the spread of FFO

Something new: The managerialist paradigm

As a management fashion the Family Friendly Organization emerged in the late 1980s in the US as an organizational response to affirmative action legislation (Kelly and Dobbin, 1998; 1999; Kelly, 2003) and the unique structure of the US gender segregation regime (Chang, 2000).

According to Chang, the US is characterized by a gender segregation regime that she calls formal-egalitarian, which is characterized by a formal commitment to gender equality in the labor market. This commitment often takes the form of equal pay and anti-discrimination laws, but is most strongly evidenced by laws governing market outcomes, such as affirmative action or government quotas. State-sponsored services that help provide women with access to paid work (such as childcare) are either non-existent or only available to a small subgroup of women, usually on a means-tested basis. In this type of regime, women workers are treated as individuals rather than as mothers or potential mothers and are therefore expected to manage the complexities involved in combining work and child rearing without the help of the state (Chang, 2000: 1664).

In their research into the spreading of the organizational maternity leave

---

[5] Latour borrowed the term "actant" from narratologist Algirdas Greimas. Greimas replaced the traditional narratological term "character" with the term "actant": "that which accomplishes or undergoes an act" (Greimas & Courtés, 1982: 5), because it can be applied not only to human beings but also to animals, objects, or concepts.

[6] For a somewhat similar analysis at a macro level see Dobbin, 1993.

in the USA, Kelly and Dobbin (1998; 1999) point to the central role played by legal interpretations of the law against discrimination. Although the law is foggy and does not explicitly define discrimination or explicate the efforts that must be taken to prevent it, courts generally rule that organizations offering maternity leave to their female workers have made a sufficient effort to prevent gender discrimination. Maternity leave, along with setting up crèches or providing organizational assistance in finding care solutions for children and other dependents, has thus been identified in the US setting as the organizational response to the problem of promoting gender equity.

Parallel to their spread as responses to legal requirements, however, the FFO practices were also embraced by feminist and pro-family organizations, policy and research institutes and management consultancy firms, who provided the energy for the its broad dissemination.[7] These various actors have not just passed the FFO ball along from hand to hand as is; rather, they invest it with new energies and translate it so as to ensure its continued passage (Latour, 1986). In order to promote the agenda around which they are organized, these actors have been working since the early 1980s to present the FFO as the solution to a range of contemporary problems: the rise of dual career families and the lengthening of the family working week; the increased importance of business trips that keep workers away from their dependents; and organizations' reliance on workers from ever more diverse communities who bring with them an increasingly diverse set of knowledge and skills.

As noted above, as part of the effort to spread the FFO model, a "business case" for family friendliness was also developed. It recognized the contribution of work-family practices not only to the workers' well-being, but also to the organization's improved business performance.[8] This framing of the FFO also meant that new allies could be recruited who would influence its continued diffusion.

Indeed, the abstraction that accompanied the institutionalization of the fashion for FFOs, and the way the fashion setters detached the model from the specific US institutional context of its development, allowed international organizations such as the International Labor Organization (ILO) to adopt the US agenda without adapting it, and to encourage its dissemination

---

[7] For an example of the ways in which feminist and other grassroots organizations helped developing the FFO as a management fashion see Rapoport et al., 1996; Rapoport, 2002.

[8] The emphasis placed on the business case spurred criticism from feminist circles, who claimed that by making that argument, feminist activists were failing to sharpen the organizations' social commitment, and were thus preventing deeper social change that could make the organization gentler and kinder, and open the way to a withdrawal from uncompromising capitalist models. In response, researchers have developed the dual agenda (Rapoport et al., 1996), which emphasizes the tight mutual relations between the critical feminist agenda and commercial success.

around the world. For instance, the organization's homepage (www.ilo.org) includes suggestions for workers' unions and employers who wish to promote organizational family friendly policies.[9] The standards and recommendations promoted by the ILO are identical to those developed in the US setting, and they recommend their sweeping implementation in every social context. All the while the link between family friendliness and gender equity is stressed, as are the business advantages that will accrue to adopting organizations. In this instance, the emphasis is on changing specific organizational practices, and not altering patterns of work or legislation (though the ILO does deal with such issues elsewhere). Discussions of FFOs in the ILO's website present them as universal, and not as the outcome of a specific institutional context. Similarly, beyond the strong European tradition of dealing with work-family issues at the state level, the EU has also adopted the "US-managerial" interpretation of the family friendliness model, pushing states as well as employers to allow for work-family reconciliation as a means to achieving gender equity (den-Dulk, 2001).

Institutional theorists of globalization often see international organizations as a central mechanism in promoting the diffusion of ideas and practices (Berkovitch, 1999; Meyer, 2002), it is thus unsurprising that the ILO, and in particular the adoption of the FFO model as an international standard, should be involved in the worldwide diffusion of the FFO fashion. Indeed, an initial survey of evidence from around the world would suggest that the idea of family friendliness has found many allies in most industrialized countries. For example, US-style institutions have been set up in Canada for promoting work-family balance. In a preliminary Internet search, similar institutions were also found in England, Austria, Germany, Australia, New Zealand, India and Japan. Organizational practices associated with the FFO model have also been found in organizations across the globe.[10] The Internet sites of many leading European companies, such as BMW and Nestle, proudly display declarations that they are FFOs. Furthermore, as in the US, women's organizations and publications, as well as business magazines around the world, award commendations to organizations that are especially family friendly.[11]

---

[9] See *Promoting Gender Equality – A Resource Kit for Trade Unions*, http://www.ilo.org/public/english/employment/gems/advance/trade.htm.

[10] For examples, see Van Doorne-Huiskes et al., 1999; Van der Lippe and Van Dijk, 2002; Wood et al., 2003.

[11] Treating the FFO as a management fashion does not assume that the model is being opportunistically used to establish the power of fashion setters and leaders, as would seem to be the case in other contexts (Abrahamson, 1991). Most of the bodies involved in advancing the FFO do so out of what is termed a dual agenda: an attempt to simultaneously advance deep social change that will allow men and women, and society in general, to better cope with the sometimes contradictory demands of the market work and family work (Rapoport et al., 1996; Williams, 2000).

The few comparative studies of the adoption of FFO practices outside the US support the notion of the translation of global ideas: although they travel, such ideas do not reach their destinations intact. Den Dulk (2001), for instance, whose comparative research on the adoption of work-family practices in the service sector in four European countries (Holland, Italy, Britain and Sweden) is the most comprehensive to date, shows that the rate at which practices are adopted can be predicted by the kind of welfare regime in each state.

Another equally interesting finding is presented by Wood et al. (2003), who studied the extent of diffusion of different FFO practices in England. Their most singular contribution is that there is no statistical link between the adoption of FF practices and the existence of Affirmative Action or official diversity policies. Their research hints at, but does not develop, the claim that during the translation process a gap is inserted between the idea behind fashionable practices, and the objects grouped around that idea in a fashionable model. In other words, it suggests that the welfare regime, organizational traditions, and the history of discussions about work-family relations in any social context, state or organizational, will bring about the customizing of the FFO such that it will preserve its fashionable characteristics and continue to give the organization its desired legitimacy, but at the same time will adapt itself to the fundamental world views concerning work-family relations in the various communities that surround the organization.

These findings teach us that the process of translating a management fashion in different social contexts is not only based on its innovativeness and ability to offer solutions to contemporary problems, but is also deeply embedded in a local context and tightly linked to meanings given by various actors to the specific practices included within the model. These meanings rely to a great extent on the old paradigm of work-family relations that characterizes the translating society.

Something old: The welfare paradigm

Unlike in the US, in other industrial societies family friendliness is, to some extent, "old news". Organizational practices designed to meet the needs of the worker's family were already widespread in the US and elsewhere by the end of the 19th century as part of welfare capitalism, but they were not presented at the time as a tool for the promotion of gender equity, nor as managerial practices with a clear business rationale behind them. The relevant model for advocates of welfare capitalism was that of the male breadwinner solely responsible for financially supporting his family (Pfau-Effinger, 2004). The employer's paternalistic responsibility for his worker's welfare therefore included concern for his family, and was aimed at preventing industrial problems and ensuring a basic standard of living. Many western countries – particularly those with strong trade union tradition, such as the Scandinavian states, France, Australia, New Zealand and Israel – preserved this tradition, and even expanded on it. Organizations in these states kept on supporting workers' families as part of collective bargaining mechanisms, while the state took responsibility for promoting gender equity by legislating concrete provisions for maternity/parental leave, leave to care for sick family members, and subsidies for childcare. The business logic behind the implementation of such practices, known today as work-family/FF practices, was not emphasized at that time, and they were perceived either as part of the organizational welfare system or simply as meeting the demands of the law. In any case, they were certainly not held to be constitutive of a distinct management model. The global spread of the managerialist FFO paradigm should therefore be understood in light of this "old" welfare paradigm.

Something borrowed? FFO in Israel

Israel provides a laboratory case for studying the translation process of the FFO fashion in the era of global economy. Historically, a combination of pro-natalism, a tight labor market that required large numbers of women to join the workforce, and the presence of strong trade unions led to the development of particularly extended organizational work-family practices that were institutionalized through collective agreements at the organizational and state level (Izraeli and Tabory, 1988; Fogiel-Bijawi, 1997).

Employers' engagement with work-family issues has largely followed the logic of welfare capitalism rather than that of equal opportunities. Thus, for example, summer camps for workers' children organized or subsidized by the employer have been conceptualized as part of the general concern for the welfare of the (male or female) employee, and not as a way of attaining a healthy work-family balance. Similarly, employers, particularly in the public sector, have subsidized workers' children's higher education, after school activities, family vacations, holiday and family birthday gifts, and other such family-related expenses as (sometimes tax-free) work benefits. In many cases these benefits have been seen as union achievements, and their contribution to organizational performance, beyond peaceful labor relations, have not been discussed or weighed against their financial cost (Izraeli, 1993; 1995; 2003).

This situation changed drastically with Israel's entry into the "new economy": the weakening of the welfare state and trade unions, and reduced protection for local industry drove Israeli employers to withdraw from their traditional system of labor relations and to emphasize their commitment to efficient management solely measured in terms of organizational performance. The constant increase of the rate of women in the workforce, together with increased exposure to US management ideas, make Israel an excellent site for observing the widespread adoption of the US model of the FFO.

155

The Study

This text is based on 30 interviews with Human Resources managers of companies in Israel, both local firms and subsidiaries of US multi-nationals. Because exposure to the new economy may influence the way organizations translate elements of management fashions, firms from four industries with different levels of global exposure were sampled: the computing industry, which embodies the new economy and is most significantly affected by it in terms of the flexibility of employment arrangements and the movement of technology and people across national borders; the pharmaceutical industry, which also markets highly developed technologies to a global market, while at the same time displaying many of the features of an old economy organization, especially long-term employment; banking, which in the Israeli case both provides and purchases globally-based services, though without being exposed to global competition; and the food industry, considered a traditional industry, especially because of its patterns of labor and organization.

The different levels of exposure to the new economy also lead to differing proportions of local companies and branches of multi-nationals in each industry. This proportion is reflected in the number of firms sampled in each category.[12] In their answers, HR managers referred to the reasons for adopting or rejecting specific FFO practices, to the sources of their knowledge about them, and their contribution to the organization and the general philosophy that guides the organization in questions of work and family.

Customizing of desire and belief: FFOs in the Israeli computing industry

As mentioned, until the 1980s at the organizational level, work-family issues were identified with the unions and workers' committees. Matters related to the worker's family were dealt with by in-house welfare staff, and were seen as pertaining to the discipline of social work rather than management. The organizational attempt to "come to grips with the present or to detach itself from the grasp of the past in a moving world" was initially expressed through rejecting existing work-family policies, perceived as archaic and inappropriate for the new economy. For example, Rivka, the first HR manager of a successful Israeli hi-tech firm (hi-tech glo 9) founded in the early 1980s, claimed:

[12]

	Computers	Pharmaceutics	Banking	Food	Total
Local	5 – (hi-tech loc)	4 (pharma loc)	6 (bank loc)	5 (food loc)	20
Subsidiaries	5 – (hi-tech glo)	3 (pharma glo)	1 (bank glo)	1 (food glo)	10
Total	10	7	7	6	30

With us, everything was done on an individual basis, we all came from organizations which had strong unions' that saw to subsidies, summer camps, gifts for the family, and things like that. We wanted to distance ourselves from that model. We thought it was a mistake to impose policy from above. Decisions were made on an individual basis.

According to Rivka, the company she worked for was consciously attempting to change its organizational and management patterns from those associated with the "old economy" to ones more suited to the "new". This program included an effort to adopt US management models, perceived as more appropriate to the new organizational environment. In order to mould her firm's HR policy, Rivka read professional literature from the US and found out what HR departments in the US were doing. Nonetheless, the interpretation that shaped organizational policy on work-family issues was not rooted in the US model of the FFO, which had started to develop at around that time, but rather in the rejection of what Rivka saw to be the traditional Israeli model, and on the basis of organizational memory (which in this case rested on the company founders' experience in other organizations). Two frameworks of meaning common in Israeli society can be found in Rivka's words and actions: identifying work-family policies with demands made by workers' unions, and not with organizational needs or the business case; and seeing family needs as pertinent to all workers, unrelated directly to questions of gender equity.

Twenty-five years later, most of the hi-tech companies who participated in this research presented formal and wide-ranging FF policies in such a way as to testify to their innovativeness in the field of management and HR, and to show how they respond to the challenges of the times. However, a closer look at the justifications given by HR managers for their actions, and a thorough examination of the practices that have been adopted or rejected, show that even among those organizations that see themselves as global, whether they are listed in Israel or the US, FF fashions are locally customized, and old ideas and practices are incorporated in the new management model.

The aspiration to resemble successful companies, or identification with them given the belief that what works for them will work for the adopting company, are seen as powerful motives for imitating and adopting fashionable models (Sevón, 1996). Organizations identified with the new economy, especially in the computing industry, tend to see themselves as part of a global industry that is less subject to local rules and traditions. Global markets, frequent traveling, relocations, contact with the world via the Internet, direct communication with colleagues around the globe, and the large number of cross-national acquisitions and mergers all make it significantly easier to observe other firms and to translate their practices. Even the very innovativeness of organizations would seem to weaken their affinity to local management traditions and makes possible the full adoption of fashionable models.

Indeed, from the interviews with HR managers in large hi-tech firms in Israel the pattern of imitation of belief with the FFO model can be clearly discerned. All hi-tech HR managers who were interviewed presented their organization as family friendly and emphasized the contribution of such policies to the organization's business performance, especially in terms of retaining employees' loyalty and productivity. They all pointed out that most of the practices they implemented were relatively new and had been adopted in the light of professional literature and current best practice in large hi-tech firms in Israel and especially the US. Some of them highlighted the distance between the union practices characteristic of Israeli society in the past and the logic employed by their organization. The clearest example of this can be found in comments made by the Human Resources VP of a large Israeli hi-tech firm with branches in other countries, including the US:

> We heard that a company similar to ours in the US had been sued for gender discrimination and lost a lot of money and prestige, and because everything that happens in America eventually gets to Israel, we decided to look into the situation in our firm. We found that it wasn't so bad, but decided to check what other companies like ours are doing in America to reduce discrimination. We found that they are really occupied with the subject of family friendliness, so we are now trying to gauge how we match up to those standards, and what else we can do to position ourselves at the forefront. So that when someone comes to visit us or goes into our website it will be obvious to him that he is dealing with an advanced, global company (hi-tech loc 3).

This VP creates a clear affinity between contemporary problems, particularly the issue of gender equity, and work-family practices, and explicitly presents the policies being examined by his company as part of a process of imitating successful and fashionable models.

Hi-tech loc 3 was one of the first employers to set up a crèche for employees' children within the organization (as opposed to the more common practice of subsidizing childcare in public kindergartens), forming part of a very small group in Israel. In interview, the VP stressed the difference between the "old" practice and the "new" one implemented by his organization: "The aim was to set up a place that would meet the special requirements of the people who work for us. Unlike public kindergartens that are open until 4 or 5 and force the mother to rush out to pick up her child before they lock up, our crèche was more flexible and allowed parents to see their children even if their work day looked like it was going to be a long one." At the same time, he pointed out that the main reason for setting up the crèche was symbolic: "We wanted to signal to potential employees that we are on the front line. That we are also innovative about this issue. The aim is to attract new employees and keep the current ones." It should be noted that most firms in the US have also chosen to provide untaxed subsidies for childcare in the private sector rather than establishing on-site crèches. Both practices are perceived in the US context as reflecting organizational commitment to work-family issues, though the organizational memory that associates child-care subsidies with the "old economy" largely shaped the way the professional model was translated in Israel. Other Israeli hi-tech firms indicated that in recent years they had examined the idea of establishing a crèche at the workplace, but rejected it for budgetary reasons.

Through his comments, the VP testifies to a process of imitation of desire. He studied companies "like ours", even though his company is Israeli and the models to be imitated were designed in the US' context, and despite recognizing the cultural and institutional variance within which the company and its branches operate.

The old paradigm had a different effect on the translation of FFO practices in a large Israeli subsidiary of an US computer giant. The US Head-Quarter goes to great lengths to define the firm as an FFO, and even appointed a work-life manager to the Israeli daughter company:

> In America they did satisfaction surveys among the firm's employees and got very low results. In their interviews before leaving, employees repeatedly complained that the firm was not family friendly. They work long hours and there is no consideration for them. It was also proving difficult to recruit new workers, especially women, who we know are more loyal to the organization and stay for longer. So they decided to tackle the issue at the headquarter level in America, and now we get very high family friendly scores. There was an order from above to implement those things here too, though of course it fits the way we see things … We are constantly looking at ourselves with regard the recruitment and promotion of women and really go out of our way to enable that at every level. Both engineers and production workers. We even changed the shift structure so that mothers with young children could reduce their working hours until the child is 6 years old, like in the rest of Israel. At first the production managers said it was impossible, but we checked the whole process and showed them that it requires a small effort, but that it is both possible and worthwhile.

Here too the US model that links family friendliness to questions of gender equity is unquestioningly accepted, but the organizational perception that the local subsidiary must be attentive and responsive to local employment norms led the company to adopt the very same practice (subsidizing child-care) that had been rejected by a different Israeli hi-tech firm precisely because of its localism:

> … I get all my instructions from America and go there to meet with the work-life managers at the US headquarters, and in Europe. We exchange informa-

tion but ultimately the company understands that you've got to adapt to the local context. In America, for example, they've got crèches in the factories. We didn't think there was any point in doing something like that because there is good public childcare, so we came to an arrangement with a local kindergarten that we help and develop, and in return they give us longer work hours for the employees who want that (hi-tech glo 7).

An attempt to fit the FFO model to what is perceived as local tradition can also be seen in the actions of another daughter company of an US hi-tech firm. During his interview, the VP from hi-tech glo 6, a daughter company active in Israel for 30 years, constantly stressed the influence of the US firm's management patterns on the Israeli branch. However, he pointed out, "We do not take everything they do for granted just because it's written in English". The organization offers many benefits in the work-family field, and, he says, is perceived as a leader in that area. However, in response to a direct question about the connection between FF and issues of gender equity, he firmly replied that "in America, more than here, I think there are more feminist elements that get in on the act in one way or another and that upsets the balance somewhat. We are here, and that issue isn't a factor, and I think we treat all those things like workers, and that's where it ends" (hi-tech glo 6).

This declaration highlights the VP's awareness of the cultural and institutional contexts within which the FFO model works in the USA, as well as his conscious decision not to adopt the model because he sees it as inappropriate for the local setting. This kind of argument was made in a similar way by other local subsidiary outside the computing industry. Replying to direct questions, HR managers demonstrated awareness of the gendered context of work-family issues in US organizations that are held up as models to be imitated, and chose to "edit" the model so as to fit what they see as the "local context".

The hi-tech companies that identify themselves as global firms standing at the forefront of the "new economy" all presented the adoption of the FFO fashion as part of their integration in the global economy and as their way of dealing with contemporary problems. However, the ways in which they choose to translate and edit the model rest largely on their interpretations of pre-existing organizational traditions and what they see as "old", as opposed to their definition of the "new". Nonetheless, the role of the "old" in the adoption of management fashions does not only boil down to defining the past; in established organizations, be they local firms or daughter companies of multi-nationals, the translation of the FF management fashion can largely be seen as the reframing of old and acknowledged practices.

Vintage FFO: Bringing in the business case and presenting the old as new

As mentioned, many of the organizational practices that were formulated by and developed within welfare capitalism are identical in their form, if not in their justifications, to those that were established as part of the management model of the FFO. In fact, the establishment of the FFO can be seen as a process of translation, in which historical practices, or practices implemented outside the US that seemed relevant in improving the work-family balance, were brought together under a single umbrella. At the same time, they take on an interpretive framework that argues for their contribution to the organization's business success and the promotion of equal opportunities for women. Practices such as subsidizing kindergartens or other educational frameworks for children, financially supporting summer camps, medical care, and even caring for families in need, were all implemented as part of welfare capitalism in many organizations in the US, Europe and Israel with no connection whatsoever to gender equity. However, as part of turning them into a management fashion, fashion setters in the US set about defining them as new practices that are responsive to new organizational problems, especially emphasizing their business contribution and the rationality that their implementation conveys.

A close inspection of the pattern of translation of the FFO fashion in Israeli organizations shows that they too, like the US fashion setters, strove to present old and familiar practices as new and fashionable, while emphasizing their direct contribution to business performance. However, while the business case was widely embraced, this was not the case with the gender equity argument. Unlike Israeli hi-tech firms who occasionally made references to gender issues in discussing work-family practices, organizations in other sectors were much less likely to highlight changes in their needs with regard increased women's labor, or considerations of promoting gender equality of opportunities.

Asked whether their organization sees itself as family friendly, all of the interviewees from older companies, and most of the interviewees from relatively newer firms, confirmed that it does. They all recruited the rhetoric of the business case that not only highlights the contribution of FF practices to the organization's performance, but also the rational cost-efficiency considerations that the organization employs when deciding on their implementation. When the organization takes care of his family needs, argued all of the subjects with slight variations, the employee can give his all to the organization and increase his productivity.

> We fully believe that the employee's family is part of our family. The employee's ability to function, his ability to work, to contribute to us, is directly influenced by his family situation, by the encouragement or lack thereof that

he receives from his family.[13] From his internal peace as a human being... so that is an integral part of our ability to maintain the system (hi-tech glo 6).

Another interviewee, who works for a local hi-tech company, claimed: "Every person has three or four circles in his life: work, family and personal. In order for him to invest the maximum in the work circle, it's up to me to try and help him attain quiet and satisfaction in the two other circles" (Hi-tech loc 5). A similar picture emerges from policy declarations made by a large pharmaceutical firm: "When we have a good relationship not only with the employee but also with his family, his feelings and relationship with the organization are much better and stronger... We think that [the family's] relationship with the organization and feelings of belonging are a significant tool in increasing motivation ..." (pharma loc 1). The same interviewee went on to point out that in leaving interviews, whether after the worker's resignation or because he was fired, employees say that separating from the employer will be even harder for their family than for themselves.

This business-case rhetoric is often contrasted to another, more morally based rhetoric, that views FFO practices as an expression of the organization's human and social obligations. Feminist criticism, for instance frequently states that the significance of the business case in presentations of FFO practices actually has a boomerang effect, in that it does not force organizations to recognize their moral and social commitment to the issue of gender equity. As long as the only consideration is a business one, we shall never see organizations working towards a better world, says Glass (2000). To get a feeling of this "other" rhetoric, which was perhaps characteristic of the justifications that organizations used to offer for their moral activities in the family realm in the "old" times, here are some comments made by the Human Resources VP at a large food company (food loc 1): "In the Jewish faith we are commanded to care for the family and enlarge it. I think it is our role to encourage our employees to set up families and educate their children. It's also, but not only, a business consideration." Even though sentiments such as these are expressed only rarely by other interviewees, we can hypothesize that this rhetoric, which presents activities in the family sphere as part of a commitment to the nation, would have been more common in the past (Izraeli, 1993).

Despite the fact that in many organizations the practices presented as part of the new model were actually old, interviewees insisted on emphasizing that they are not just simple benefits but rather practices that contribute to the firm and its employees in ways that have been measured and confirmed by research. "Research in the US has shown that when you involve the employee's family in company activities his loyalty increases", said the HR

---

[13] The gendered language is historically accurate.

manager of pharma loc 2 in justifying the wide range of leisure activities her company puts on for employees' families, for example. "During recession, like now, when you are not worried about workers leaving and it is easy to recruit new staff, we are cutting back on such activities, both because there are fewer resources and because it is less necessary."

Family friendliness as a way of recruiting the best employees also comes across in the words of the Human Resources VP at bank loc 2:

> It's what ties the worker to the bank and us to our employees. Because we believe that it's better for the bank as a firm... Four years ago the CEO set as a target that the bank should not only be the customers' first choice, but also the employees'. That you don't come here because you have to, because you can't find anything better, but rather, that it will be your first choice.

According to this Human Resources VP, most of the practices currently presented as FF have been implemented by the organization for years, most of them before he even came to the job 15 years ago, and yet he links those practices to a four year old organizational vision.

In response to specific questions about the history of long-standing practices, such as summer camps for the employees' children, and about the role of the strong and active workers' union in running or subsidizing the camps, the same VP answered: "It's ancient history. I don't remember what the reason was for doing it in the first place. I know that today it's examined on its own right and we find out how it contributes to advancing the bank's aims. If in the past the main aim was to get the child to identify with the bank, today we have realized that it's not economical. The bank's employees are spread out around the country so we subsidize summer camps in order that the parents can keep on working without the children getting under their feet." The summer camps cost a lot of money, he said, but that the bank cannot cancel them for fear of the employees' reactions.

The reliance on contemporary research and the business case rhetoric is characteristic of advocates of the FFO in USA and beyond, which testifies to its influence on organizations' activities. However, the practices presented as part of a fashionable management model are mostly old and institutionalized practices that do not necessarily sit well with the FFO model as it appears in the literature. Thus, the practices spontaneously mentioned by most of the managers when asked to name the activities that define their organization as "family friendly" related to gifts for the employee's family at festivals or special family occasions (birth of a child, birthdays, wedding, etc.). Further practices included subsidizing family holidays, special events for employees' children over national holidays, social and cultural activities, subsidizing children's higher education (and sometimes that of the employee's partner), and so on. These practices are indeed aimed at the employees' family, but do not purport to assist them in caring for their family or to improve women's chances of equality in the labor market, as one would expect from the way that the model has developed over recent years. Presenting old practices in a new and fashionable manner legitimizes the model, which is perceived as compatible with established traditions, and at the same time strengthens the organization's image as up to date in its response to contemporary problems.

Putting forward old practices as part of a new and fashionable model also allows organizations to detach themselves from the old economy, and mainly from perceptions that they are controlled by workers' committees. The older the firm, and the broader and more institutionalized the activities of its workers' union, the higher the chance of finding traditional work-family practices. However, with the weakening of workers' unions and their declining legitimacy in Israeli society, most of the interviewees tended to deny that the union had a role to play in this context. "Decisions are made by management alone in line with professional considerations about their contribution to the organization's performativity. The workers' union is sometimes involved in funding activities, but not in decision making", said the Human Resources VP of an Israeli bank, for instance (bank loc 1). The VP of another Israeli bank said that "Maybe the committees had more influence on our policy about such matters in the past, but now we act according to research and professional advice" (bank loc 2).

Another anecdote that shows the vintage of the old in the new comes from the job definition of the employee responsible for work-life balance in hi-tech glo 8. In the USA, the appointment of an employee responsible for work-family issues is seen as an expression of the firm's commitment to take such matters seriously. However, a suitable term in Hebrew to describe the work-life manager's position has not yet been found, and so she is defined in Hebrew as the "welfare manager", a term for those who used to take care of family problems in the traditional welfare capitalism setting.

An additional indication of the way that old practices define the range of possibilities for the adoption of new ones can be found in a practice that has not been taken up by any of the firms operating in Israel, namely job sharing. Common in USA, this practice allows two workers (usually women) to share a single job, and it gives a part-time employee the chance to hold an interesting and responsible position that could not usually be carried out on a part-time basis. Even Israeli daughter companies of US firms that have implemented job sharing in the States have not even considered introducing it to Israel. Despite the growing tendency to refrain from appointing part-time positions, previously a popular practice in Israel, all the interviewees said they would prefer to allow an employee to reduce her hours for a limited period in order to care for her family rather than divide the job between two people. A traditional practice is unequivocally preferred over an unfamiliar and novel one.

However, the representation of old practices as new, and especially the overemphasis of business considerations, is liable to conceal certain dangers. In older industries with strong workers' unions, employees at least partially base their identification with the firm on their feeling that it helps care for their families' day to day problems. Under such conditions, the translation of old practices into a new language could alienate the workers and promote industrial unrest. New practices directly taken from foreign models might also arouse discomfort, especially when they take the place of institutionalized practices that are widely taken for granted. In order to preserve their alliances with various powers both within and outside the organization, and to ensure their support for new practices, some organizations endeavor to promote the new as an improved extension of the old.

Recruiting allies: Presenting the new as old

The strong tradition by which the organization's support for the worker's family is taken for granted makes it very difficult to rescind established FF practices. Interviewees from both old and new, and local and global firms all said that the decision to annul an existing practice, or not to provide a benefit common in their respective industrial sector, is problematic and liable to meet with serious resistance. In food loc 1, for instance, the VP was considering the possibility of canceling childcare subsidies for women employees. Traditionally, the subsidy was only awarded to women, but recently, and with the support of the workers' committee, the firm's male employees had been saying that this constitutes discrimination, and that the benefit should be provided to all employees, a demand that would of course drastically increase its cost. In order to solve the problem, the VP wishes to withdraw the subsidy altogether, but has encountered widespread resistance from the workers. Likewise, the Human Resources manager of the Israeli branch of an US bank described how difficult it is to decide not to give employees a benefit awarded throughout the banking sector: "I suppose it filters out the potential employees who turn to us. It you think these things are important, you just won't want to work here" (bank glo 6).

One of the solutions to this difficulty is to present new practices as a functionally equivalent substitute for old ones. This, for instance, is how food loc 2 replaced its FF system: it had included daycare subsidies and cultural activities for the employees and their families, but it was switched with a welfare package awarded to all employees regardless of their marital and parental status. The new package could be used to pay for a wide range of activities, including family events that had previously been subsidized. Thus the organization somewhat reduced its commitment to the employee's family as a value in and of itself, as most of the budget was aimed at activities solely for the employee and not so much for the family. Nonetheless, by including subsidies for employees' children's higher education in the new welfare package, the firm's management could present a new practice as old, thus sidestepping the struggles involved in promoting new practices.

Possible Social Consequences of FFO Translation

Researchers of management fashions tend to emphasize the importance of innovativeness as one of the main factors behind the migration and subsequent translation of management models to broader social contexts. Sociological work on fashions, and particularly management fashions, emphasizes their role in detaching the past from the present and focusing on the contemporary. Through the example of the translation of the FFO in Israeli society, this chapter has tried to emphasize the importance of the past, embodied in organizational memory and management traditions, in explaining how management fashions are translated as they travel between social contexts.

This insight is particularly meaningful in relation to work-family practices. Feminist criticism has shown that the use of work-family practices, especially in the US context, often entails significant punishment in terms of the employee's salary and promotion prospects (Glass, 2004). The strong identification of US FFO practices with gender issues might explain this pattern of punishment. To a large extent, and accompanied by the protests of many feminist advocates of the FFO fashion, the family is mainly seen as a "problem" to be dealt with by working mothers, and not as pertaining to working fathers or society in general. The influence of the welfare capitalist tradition – which sees care for the family as part of the organization's social responsibility – on the translation of the FFO model may slightly loosen the link between family and womanhood, and by extension reduce the punishment that often accompanies the use of such practices. The work-family field is one of the only areas in which US firms are trying to learn from European cases (Gornick and Meyers, 2003). Understanding the ways that "old" management traditions influence the shaping of "new" fashions might allow for their increased sophistication in the sphere of family friendliness, and could lessen the price women are required to pay when they make use of family friendly practices.

Chapter 10

Articulating Agendas and Traveling Principles in the Layering of New Strands of Academic Freedom in Contemporary Singapore

Kris Olds, Department of Geography, University of Wisconsin-Madison, USA

Our vision, in shorthand notation, is to become the Boston of the East. Boston is not just MIT or Harvard. The greater Boston area boasts of over 200 universities, colleges, research institutes and thousands of companies. It is a focal point of creative energy; a hive of intellectual, research, commercial and social activity. We want to create an oasis of talent in Singapore: a knowledge hub, an "ideas-exchange", a confluence of people and idea streams, an incubator for inspiration.

We will be doing so through a two-pronged approach. The more visible one to most of you is our strategy of attracting top foreign universities to Singapore. We have had some success in this. INSEAD and Chicago Graduate School of Business have set up branch campuses here. They will take in their first students this year. Our universities have also actively formed partnerships with top foreign universities. NUS, NTU and MIT are collaborating in the field of postgraduate engineering education and research through the Singapore-MIT Alliance. NUH and Johns Hopkins University are conducting joint PhD and Masters programmes in clinical research. The youngest of the fold, Singapore Management University is working with the Wharton School of the University of Pennsylvania to set up the Wharton-SMU Research Centre.

The other strategy is to develop our local universities into world-class institutions. We have a firm foundation to build on. Our two "older" universities, the National University of Singapore and the Nanyang Technological University, have well-deserved reputations in education and research in the region and beyond. NUS has been ranked 2nd in academic reputation among comprehensive universities in Asia while NTU has been ranked 3rd in Asia among science and technological universities.[1]

Singapore, a small Southeast Asian city-state, is known worldwide for its economic development trajectory over the last three decades. The transition from neglected colonial outpost, to an uncertain independence, to post-colonial "air-conditioned nation" (George, 2000), has provided ample fodder for triumphalist sagas (e.g., Lee, 2000), relatively even-handed and incisive analyses (e.g., Rodan, 1989; Chua, 1997; Kong and Yeoh, 2002), and caustic critiques (e.g., Tremewan, 1994; Lingle, 1996).

Regardless of one's views on forceful forms of modernist planning and social engineering undertaken by the Singaporean state (as guided by the continually ruling People's Action Party [PAP]), a structural change is underway in Singapore's economy. The shift from manufacturing based export-platform status to global city/knowledge hub status is occurring. Statecraft is also being used to shape this restructuring process, in part through the though the targeting of select industrial sectors (as delineated by the Singapore Economic Development Board, http://www.sedb.gov.sg):

- Biomedical Sciences
- Chemicals
- Education Services
- Engineering and Environmental Services
- Infocommunications and Media
- Logistics and Transport Engineering
- Professional Services
- Shared Services [support functions]

A discursive reframing is also underway as Singapore, once controversially deemed as "Disneyland with the Death Penalty" (by William Gibson in 1993), seeks to become legibly known, in selective (mainly western) business and academic circles, as a cosmopolitan and especially creative space, a vibrant and diverse global city integrating into the lattice under girding the global network economy.

In the context of an awareness of Singapore's evolving developmental objectives, this chapter focuses on one increasingly high profile aspect of the planned structural transformation – the creation from 1997 to the present of opportunities for the provision of new foreign-led or foreign-linked "education services", especially higher education services, in Singaporean space.

---

[1] Source: extracts from an address by RADM (NS) Teo Chee Hean, Minister for Education and Second Minister for Defence at the Alumni International Singapore (AIS) Lecture on 7 Jan 2000 at the NUSS Guild Hall @ 6.35 pm, available at http://www.moe.gov.sg/speeches/2000/sp10012000.htm, accessed 19 March 2005.

The Singaporean state has sought to achieve this goal, as noted in the extract from Rear Admiral Teo's speech, by opening up its territory (and its society) to the presence of foreign institutions of higher education. The opening up of territory is selective, this said, for fashion and imitation have led to the targeting of "world class" institutions, when at all possible. These world class institutions are identified in the types of benchmarking surveys noted by Hedmo, Sahlin-Andersson and Wedlin in this volume, and in discursive fields associated with academia and international business (both capitalists and the business media). In addition, alumni networks and citation indices have been used to delineate the terrain of suitable universities. Singapore is unapologetically in search of university brands equivalent to Gucci and Mercedes: Northern Territory University and the University of Oklahoma need not come knocking.[2]

Singapore's attempts to become the "Boston of the East", a global knowledge-based hub associated with innovation, creativity, informed debate, and significant university-industry linkages, has generated rapid impacts. Universities including Duke, Johns Hopkins, Chicago, Cornell, and Carnegie Mellon have established campuses, set up formal joint ventures, research labs, and joint degrees, all since the "World Class University" (WCU) programme was launched in 1997.

The formation of these global networks facilitates, and is dependent upon, flows of information, people, technologies, and concepts. In the case of Singapore's emerging "global schoolhouse", foreign universities and the Singaporean state have enabled their developmental agendas to articulate, and elements of each agenda have been sutured together, though on a bilateral Singapore to university basis. This is clearly a development process *in formation*, and global assemblages are being created. Assemblages can be thought of as:

> secondary matrices from within which apparatuses emerge and become stabilized or transformed. Assemblages stand in a dependent but contingent and unpredictable relationship to the grander problematizations. In terms of scale they fall between problematization and apparatuses, and function differently from either one. They are a distinctive type of experimental matrix of heterogeneous elements, techniques and concepts. They are not yet an experimental system in which controlled variation can be produced, measured, and observed. They are comparatively effervescent, disappearing in years or decades rather than centuries. Consequently, the temporality of assemblages

---

[2] I worked at the National University of Singapore from 1997 to 2001. I can still recall a disgruntled Charles Darwin University (then called Northern Territory University) representative complaining to some of us that NUS had a "Gucci complex", for he had great difficulty in establishing student and faculty exchange ties between the two universities. A University of Oklahoma geography professor also stated the same viewpoint after it was recommended that we turn down an Oklahoma overture.

is qualitatively different from that of either problematizations or apparatuses (Rabinow, 2003: 56).

In turn, the denatured notion of assemblage makes much more room for *space*. Assemblages will function quite differently, according to local circumstance, not because they are an overarching structure adapting its rules to the particular situation but because these manifestations are what the assemblage consists of (Ong and Collier, 2005).

The chapter highlights select aspects of how this development process is unfolding (see Olds and Thrift, 2005a, 2005b, and Ong, 2005 for more details). Key historical, policy and institutional matters are discussed so as to lay a context for an analysis of how some of the western (mainly US) universities reaching out across space into Singapore have sought to carry along the principle of "academic freedom" with them. I pay particular attention to how the principle of academic freedom has been *translated*, to date, during the articulation of developmental agendas. In the process the meaning and significance of academic freedom has been altered, and indeed splintered or layered in uncertain and contingent ways. This is, perhaps, not surprising given that the globalization of higher education, and the stretching of institutional fabrics across space, is designed to unsettle institutional and pedagogical practices. It is also not surprising given that academic freedom in Singapore has been viewed with disdain, for the most part, since independence.[3] What is worthy of investigation, though, is the governance process, including the technologies of government that are shaping the translation/ transformation process, and the opportunities and tensions that are emerging in association with this relatively unique global assemblage.

Assembling Singapore

As noted above, Singapore, a Southeast Asian city-state with a population of 4.4 million (of whom about 750,000 are foreigners), is a *celebrated case* with respect to economic development. Independent since 1965, the city-state has seen considerable growth in virtually all of the typical indicators associated with economic development. Table 1 provides highlights of but a few of these indicators over the last two decades:

---

[3] In part because of efforts to wrest control of the universities from expatriates, and move a post-colonial developmental agenda forward in very difficult circumstances.

Table 10.1. Key Economic Indicators on Singapore, 1985–2003.

Item	1985	1990	1995	1999	2000	2001	2002	2003
Population (million)	2.74	3.05	3.53	3.95	4.02	4.13	4.17	4.19
Labor Force (thousand)	1,288	1,563	1,749	1,976	2,192	2,120	2,129	2,150
Employed	1,235	1,537	1,702	1,886	2,095	2,047	2,017	2,034
Agriculture	9	4	3	4	4	5	5	4
Manufacturing	314	445	404	396	435	384	368	365
Mining	3	1	1	1	1	1	1	1
Other	909	1,087	1,295	1,485	1,655	1,657	1,644	1,664
Unemployment rate (%)	4.1	2.0	2.0	3.5	3.1	3.3	4.4	4.7
Structure of Output (% of GDP at current prices)								
Agriculture	1.0	0.4	0.2	0.1	0.1	0.1	0.1	0.1
Industry	34.5	33.0	33.3	32.9	34.1	31.8	33.1	32.7
Services	68.8	67.8	65.3	67.8	64.3	68.3	67.5	66.4
Growth of Output (annual change, %)								
GDP	14.6	9.0	8.0	6.9	9.7	−1.9	2.2	1.1
Agriculture	−8.1	−7.6	−3.1	−1.8	−4.9	−5.9	−5.8	−0.4
Industry	−0.2	9.4	9.8	6.6	11.1	−9.1	3.5	0.2
Services	14.5	10.3	7.4	6.3	7.9	2.5	1.4	1.1
Trade (as a % of GDP)	n/a	49.5	63.9	n/a	n/a	77.1	78.0	n/a
Per Capita GDP (at current prices in $US)	6,872	12,110	23,806	20,891	23,043	20,775	21,206	22,070

Source: http://www.adb.org; accessed on 20 March 2005; http://www.worldbank.org, accessed 20 March 2005; http://www.singstat.gov.sg/keystats/hist/gdp.html, accessed 22 March 2005.

Economic growth and structural change has been fueled by Western and Japanese transnational corporations who use Singapore as a regional head-quarters, and/or export platforms. As Peter Dicken (2003: 61) points out, Singapore has the highest percentage share of inward foreign direct investment as a share of GDP of any other country in the world. The Singaporean economy is effectively dominated by foreign firms, leading to dependency upon investors and traders in the United States (Singapore is the US' 11th largest trading partner, while the US is the largest source for investment, closely followed by Japan and the Netherlands). The dependency of Singapore on American and European investors provided some of the underlying structural pressure to draw in American and European universities, especially those with strong engineering, science, and business programs.

The development process in Singapore has been guided by an "authoritarian" (sometimes deemed "soft-authoritarian") government that has been controlled by the PAP continually since 1959. The PAP, under the leadership of Lee Kuan Yew (Prime Minister, 1959–1990), Goh Chock Tong (Prime Minister, 1990–2004), and Lee Kuan Yew's son Lee Hsien Loong (Prime Minister, 2004 to present) has developed and used the state apparatus to achieve a wide range of social, cultural, political and economic objectives (Chua, 1997; Kong and Yeoh, 2002). The state form is typically characterized as a "developmental state", guided by an elite bureaucracy, focused on medium-to long term economic objectives, and frequently prone to eclectic and effective forms of social control in the stated interests of national development (Wade, 1990; Weiss, 1998; Woo-Cummings, 1999). In the case of Singapore, the powers and capacities of the nation-state (in material and discursive senses) are used to transform society and space, all with the aim of embedding the city-state within the evolving lattice of network relations that propel the world economy (Olds and Yeung, 2004). Existing space and social formations were and are being purged, razed, flattened, cleansed, restructured, re-engineered: in their place "world class" infrastructure/education/legal/financial/healthcare systems are developed, maintained and constantly refashioned. As the noted urbanist Rem Koolhaus (1995: 1011) put it in a typically overstated but thought provoking manner:

> Almost all of Singapore is less than 30 years old; the city represents the ideological production of the past three decades in its pure form, uncontaminated by surviving contextual remnants. It is managed by a regime that has excluded accident and randomness: even its nature is entirely remade. It is pure intention: if there is chaos, it is authored chaos; if it is ugly, it is designed ugliness; if it is absurd, it is willed absurdity. Singapore represents a unique ecology of the contemporary.

The generic characteristics of the post-colonial developmental state, in conjunction with the specific personalities involved (most notably the erudite albeit driven Lee Kuan Yew), and the small geographic scale of Singapore, fueled a series of controversies about the governance of higher education systems and academic freedom in the post independence era. These include, in the 1960s and 1970s, the Enright affair and forceful political involvement in university governance (cf. Puccetti, 1972). The 1980s witnessed the forced dissolution of the University Academic Staff Association when the government merged the University of Singapore with Nanyang University to establish a more ethnically pluralist anchor institution of higher education (Wong, 2005). More recently, in the mid-1990s, the National University of Singapore was unsettled by a series of controversies including the Chee Soon Juan affair, and the Christopher Lingle affair.[4]

Clearly the discourse if not the principle and practice of academic freedom has existed in Singapore (how could it not given the cosmopolitan and crossroads nature of the place) for several decades. However, university life is highly politicized given the relative status accorded to academics (Clammer, 2001), the city-state character of Singapore (Wong, 2005), and the nature of the long-ruling PAP. In such a context the activities of faculty and students have been and continue to be governed in a relatively intense fashion.

The 1965 to 1995 era was noteworthy in that the governance of academic freedom was framed with respect to intra-national political dynamics, and the posited existence of "Asian values", an argument, made forcefully in the 1980s and first half of the 1990s. The Asian values argument, as put forward by Singaporean leaders and other thinkers (e.g., Mahbubani, 2002), recommended that "Asians" approach human rights from a communitarian perspective, with rights best interpreted as being culturally specific and a matter of national sovereignty. If "community" and family is perceived to take precedence over the individual (in this case a faculty member or a student), if collective conceptions of rights are perceived to minimize tensions between diverse segments of a population (e.g., an ethnically diverse population in a city-state situated in a turbulent region), and if this approach to social control is alleged to play a key role in economic success, then arguments about the rationale and indeed existence of academic freedom (as practiced in the West) were and will be inevitable.[5]

---

[4] D.J. Enright was a British expatriate faculty member who was involved in a major controversy regarding his depictions of "local culture" (see Lee, 1966; Enright, 1969). Christopher Lingle was an American lecturer at NUS who was sued by Lee Kuan Yew for defamation of character after he felt that Lingle's statements about "compliant judiciary" in an *International Herald Tribune* article were directed at Singapore, the PAP, and especially Lee Kuan Yew (see Lingle, 1996; Lee, 2000: 154–155). Chee Soon Juan, an opposition party leader with the Singapore Democratic Party, was fired from his job as a lecturer with the National University of Singapore in 1992 for "misuse" of his research funds, and was subsequently sued by his department head (a Member of Parliament for the PAP) with regard to how Chee had framed the dispute process.

[5] This said, most of the historic texts and rulings on academic freedom actually note the collective societal benefit that is derived via an active and free market of ideas and debate.

Assembling the Global Schoolhouse

The above discussion sets the context for the articulation process whereby:

- The Singaporean state adjusts to structural economic change at the global, regional and national levels, in part through the reframing of higher education policy;
- western universities adjust to emerging fashions in higher education, including the establishment of exchange programs, and overseas presences (though mechanisms like joint-ventures and campuses), especially in Pacific Asia.

Singapore, even more than most countries (given its limited geographic scale), is faced with the realities and myths associated with economic crises. Given the relatively small population, and lack of natural resources, economic crises always generate a series of material cum discursive shifts in statecraft. The mid-1980s crisis, for example, led to the emergence of a "twin-engine" strategy of higher valued-added manufacturing and exportable services, as well as a regionalization drive (ERC, 2002a). Much of the mid-1980s to mid-1990s was spent devising and implementing a series of related development policies and programs (these are outlined in Chui, Ho, and Lui, 1997).

Five to seven years later, the Asian economic crisis of 1997/98, and concern about China's booming manufacturing capacity, spurred on a considerable rethinking of socio-economic development strategy. In the midst of the crisis a series of rapid adjustments were made (including wage cuts, benefit cuts, tax-cuts, reductions in rentals on industrial properties). These adjustments merged with the service-oriented agenda, and the trope of the "knowledge-based economy" (KBE) that began quickly circulating at both the global and regional (i.e., Pacific Asian) scales in the 1990s. As Coe and Kelly (2000) demonstrate in the Singaporean case, this phrase first surfaced in a speech by Prime Minister Goh in 1994. By 1998 the phrase was gaining some currency. By 1999 it was in wholesale circulation, having "seemingly entered the common vocabulary of all Ministers, bureaucrats and media commentators in Singapore" (Coe and Kelly, 2000: 418; also see Coe and Kelly, 2002).

It is in this context that the strategy emerged to further develop Singapore's knowledge-based economy via hitherto unexplored regulatory shifts. A particular conception of the KBE was developed, one that elevated principles of life-long learning, creativity, innovation, competition, and talent. A series of linked higher education reforms were then initiated, including:

- Comprehensive and integrated reviews of university governance and funding systems
- Greater autonomy for universities, though linked to a need for greater "accountability"
- The diversification of financial resources for universities, including private endowments designed to draw in corporate and private (alumni) monies.

The nature and outcome of these reforms is discussed in Ho and Gopinathan (1999) and Lee and Gopinathan (2003). In examining these articles, and Ministry of Education and Ministry of Trade and Industry reports, it is clear that key aspects of these reforms were designed to create a "vibrant university sector". This is certainly conveyed in RADM (NS) Teo Chee Hean's 2000 speech above, as well as in Dr. Tony Tan's[6] (2002) speech in association with a University of Chicago Graduate School of Business graduation ceremony in the Raffles Hotel:

> Going forward, we should aim to develop a vibrant university sector with three key characteristics. First, a strong university sector should feature broad international representation, with the presence of top international universities in Singapore. This will anchor our internationalisation efforts, and build stronger networks for R&D. Our people will benefit from having the global orientation characteristic of a highly competent and capable workforce.
>
> We have made good strides in the form of the World Class Universities programme, which has considerably extended our international fraternity and EDB has informed me that there will be more exciting collaborations to come.
>
> Second, we should strive to encourage healthy competition among institutions, both local and foreign. Presently, there is some limited competition amongst our three local universities, and with the presence of World Class Universities like the University of Chicago Graduate School of Business, universities in Singapore will be kept on their toes. Within a competitive education ecosystem, universities will need to entrench their strengths and carve out new niches of excellence by improving their quality of teaching and research to attract funding, faculty and students.
>
> Third, we need to intensify a pervasive entrepreneurial climate within our university sector. The role of world-class universities with strong research capabilities and the ability to take research to the market is critical in a knowledge-based economy; Silicon Valley and Boston's Route 128 are convincing success stories. Thus, we must strengthen the links between industry and academia to seed new ideas and nurture an entrepreneurial environment. Our research efforts will pay off in the form of new value propositions and the commercialisation of products and services.

---

[6] Dr. Tony Tan Keng Yam was Deputy Prime Minister and Minister of Defense in 2002. He has played a key role in drawing in foreign (especially elite North American) universities.

A focus on creating a vibrant university sector, and diversifying Singapore's economic base, and reworking its image in select discursive fields, led to the 1997 launch, by the EDB, of the "World Class Universities" (WCU) programme. This program was designed to attract "at least ten World Class Universities (WCU) to Singapore within ten years" via a variety of linkage mechanisms (from joint ventures to autonomous campuses). The WCUs are placed at the apex of a three tiered university system.[7]

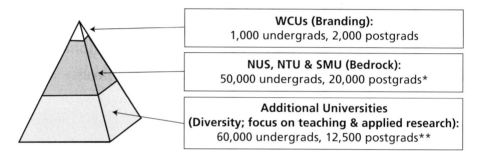

WCUs (Branding):
1,000 undergrads, 2,000 postgrads

NUS, NTU & SMU (Bedrock):
50,000 undergrads, 20,000 postgrads*

**Additional Universities
(Diversity; focus on teaching & applied research):**
60,000 undergrads, 12,500 postgrads**

* The figures respresent organic growth. Currently, NUS, NTU and SMU enrol approximately 37,000 undergraduates and 15,000 postgraduates.
** These would be new students. Of the total, an estimated 50,000 would be international students (40,000 undergrads, 10,000 postgrads).

Figure 10.1. Idealized Three-tier University System in Singapore. (Source: ERC, 2002b)

Since establishing the WCU Programme in 1997, a large number of Singapore-foreign university connections have been formed (Table 2).

---

[7] Significantly, much of this educational strategy was concerned with institutions associated with the "cultural circuit of capital", including the field of business and management that is discussed in Chapter 11.

Table 10.2. Substantial Singapore-Foreign University Initiatives (1998–2005).

	Initiatives (by date of establishment)
Johns Hopkins University (JHU)	Three medical divisions of JHU were established in January 1998: Johns Hopkins Singapore Biomedical Center, Johns Hopkins Singapore Affiliated Programs, and Johns Hopkins – National University Hospital International Medical Centre. These institutions facilitate collaborative research and education with Singapore's academic and medical communities. In July 2003, these joined to become the JHU Division of Biomedical Sciences in Singapore (DJHS). DJHS operates in partnership with Singapore's Agency for Science Technology and Research (A*STAR), which provides core grant funding. Ten to twelve JHU Medical School faculty will supervise research labs and coordinate graduate training with medical faculty at the National University of Singapore. Web link: www.hopkins.edu.sg JHU's Peabody Institute collaborated with the National University of Singapore to create the Yong Siew Toh Conservatory of Music (YSTCM). The Conservatory enrolled its first class in August 2003, and will offer numerous student and faculty exchanges. It is part of a strategy to position Singapore as an "Asian renaissance city of the 21st century for the arts and culture." Web link: http://music.nus.edu.sg/
Massachusetts Institute of Technology (MIT)	The Singapore – MIT Alliance (SMA) was established in November 1998 with the National University of Singapore (NUS) and Nanyang Technological University (NTU). Programs focus on advanced engineering and applied computing, with Singapore-based students participating in video-conference classes and exchanges to MIT. Six hundred students received Singapore degrees (Masters or Ph.D.) and MIT certificates in the Alliance's first phase. Phase II (2005–2010) adds specializations and will allow students to receive MIT Master's degrees. Web link: http://web.mit.edu/sma/
Georgia Institute of Technology (GIT)	The Logistics Institute – Asia Pacific (TLI-AP) was established in February 1999 as a collaboration between NUS and the Georgia Institute of Technology. It trains engineers in specialized areas of global logistics, with emphasis on information and decision technologies. TLI-AP also facilitates research, and the acquisition of dual degrees and professional/executive education. Web link: http://www.tliap.nus.edu.sg/
University of Pennsylvania (Penn)	Singapore Management University (SMU) was officially incorporated in January 2000. Wharton School faculty from the University of Pennsylvania (Penn) provided intellectual leadership in the formation of SMU's organizational structure and curriculum, and will formally continue to do so until 2007. The Wharton-SMU Research Center was also established at SMU, with emphasis on "technopreneurship", knowledge transfer, technology-based industries, and e-commerce in the Asian context. SMU has grown from 306 students in 2000 to more than 3,000 in 2004, with eventual enrollment of 9,000 (6,000 undergraduates and 3,000 graduates) planned. A new US$650 million campus will open in Singapore's downtown in August 2005. Web link: http://www.smu.edu.sg/

INSEAD	INSEAD, the prominent global business school in France, established second campus in Singapore in January 2000. A US$ 40 million its building was built to enable Singapore-based faculty, and European campus visiting faculty, to offer full- and part-time courses, as well as executive seminars and an EMBA program. European and Asian campuses are "fully integrated", with student exchanges integral to the MBA program. The Singapore campus enrolls approximately 250 MBA students and employs 34 permanent faculty. INSEAD announced its Singapore campus broke even in 2003, and recently expanded its physical facilities. In addition, it launched a commercial research institute (InnovAsia) to monitor and disseminate regional emergent technologies. Web links: http://www.insead.edu/campuses/asia_campus/index.htm and www.inseadinnovasia.com
University of Chicago	The University of Chicago Graduate School of Business (GSB) established a dedicated Singapore campus in July 2000 to offer its Executive MBA to a maximum of 84 students per program. The curriculum is identical to the Executive MBA Programs in Chicago, and faculty are flown in from Chicago to teach on it. Web link: http://gsb.uchicago.edu/
Technische Universiteit Eindhoven (TU/e)	The Design Technology Institute (DTI), jointly administered by National University of Singapore (NUS) and Technische Universiteit Eindhoven (TU/e), was launched in May 2002. The courses and projects offered by DTI seek to balance basic engineering concepts with product design and development. Joint degrees of Master of Technological Design (a TU/e specialty) and Ph.D. (from NUS) are offered. TU/e has strong links to Philips Electronics, both in the Netherlands and in Singapore. Web link: http://www.dti.nus.edu.sg/
Technische Universität München (TUM)	The National University of Singapore (NUS) and the Technische Universität München (TUM) established a Joint Master's degree in Industrial Chemistry in January 2002. A new Joint Masters in Industrial Ecology began in 2004, with programs in Integrated Circuit Design and Industrial Health Technology to launch in 2005. These programs, along with executive training and contract research, are now operated by the German Institute of Science and Technology (GIST), the first private German university with operations abroad. Singapore's Nanyang Technological University is also a partner. Web link: http://www.gist-singapore.com/
Carnegie Mellon University (CMU)	Carnegie Mellon University (CMU) signed a Memorandum of Understanding with Singapore Management University in January 2003 to collaborate on the development of a School of Information Systems (SIS). The School will be SMU's fourth since its establishment in 2000. The 5-year partnership includes the design of undergraduate and graduate/professional programs, delivery of research and graduate training, and faculty development. Web link: http://www.sis.smu.edu.sg
Shanghai Jiao Tong University	Shanghai Jiao Tong University (SJTU) formed a partnership with the Nanyang Technological University Business School in October 2002. Two hundred students have completed MBA degrees at SJTU's Singapore campus. SJTU is considering adding graduate programs in IT and bio-, chemical-, and ocean engineering. No website available.

Stanford University	Stanford University and Nanyang Technological University (NTU) signed an official Memorandum of Understanding, in February 2003, to offer joint graduate programs in environmental engineering. The Stanford Singapore Partnership graduated its first class of 18 in July 2004. The program combines distance education with student and faculty exchanges, and results in an NTU degree. Web link: http://www.ntu.edu.sg/CEE/ssp/
Cornell University	Nanyang Business School (NBS), the International Hotel Management School (Singapore), and Cornell University's School of Hotel Administration agreed in May 2003 to establish the Cornell-Nanyang Institute of Hospitality Management. Courses leading to joint degrees will begin in July 2006, with 50 students annually dividing their time between Cornell and Singapore. The Institute will also facilitate research on the Asian hospitality industry. Cornell will supply faculty in residence at NTU. Web link: http://www.hotelschool.cornell.edu/
Duke University	Duke University Medical Center and the National University of Singapore signed a Memorandum of Understanding in June 2003 to establish a graduate medical school in Singapore. Singapore's Cabinet approved the partnership in January 2005, and the program will accept its first cohort of 50 students in 2007. Web link: http://medschool.duke.edu/
Karolinska Institutet (KI)	Stockholm-based Karolinska Institutet (KI) and the National University of Singapore signed an agreement in July 2003 to operate joint programs in stem-cell research, tissue engineering and bio-engineering. A joint Ph.D. program in genetic and molecular epidemiology currently enrolls 18 students in its second year. KI plans to establish research labs at NUS soon. Web link: http://info.ki.se/index_en.html
Indian Institute of Technology (IIT)	The multi-sited Indian Institute of Technology (IIT) gave in principle approval, in May 2003, to the idea of establishing a Singapore campus. The IIT campuses involved include Bombay, Chennai, New Delhi, Kharagpur, Kanpur, and Roorkie. The exact modality of presence being negotiated in conjunction with the Singapore Economic Development Board. In January 2005, IIT Bombay and Nanyang Technological University agreed to closer teaching and research ties in bio- and molecular engineering, infrastructural engineering, and information/communication technologies. No website available.
Waseda University	Waseda University and NTU's Nanyang Business School announced a double masters program in Management of Technology in November 2004. The program will include faculty visits from Waseda and study trips to Japan, and will offer MBA degrees. Its first student intake is planned for July 2006. Weblink: www.nbs.ntu.edu.sg
University of New South Wales	Australia's University of New South Wales will open a branch campus in Singapore in 2007, with plans to enroll up to 15,000 students by 2020 (70% non-Singaporean). The university will conduct research and offer a full range of courses with a focus on science and technology. Weblink: http://www.unsw.edu.au/international/int/unswasia.html
Warwick University	Warwick University is in negotiations to open a Singapore branch campus with a research focus. Singaporean authorities have guaranteed they will not pursue another stand-alone private university in the near future. Warwick University is currently conducting a £400,000 feasibility study on the issue. No dedicated website.

The remaining part of this chapter is allocated to a select aspect of how critically important principles and practices associated with "world class" universities (especially American universities) travels, and more importantly how these principles and practices get translated in the process. The focus is on the principles and practices of academic freedom.

Academic Freedom

Academic freedom, like all forms of freedom, is a social construct. As Louis Menand (1996: 3) notes, in a text on academic freedom that was published by the University of Chicago Press:

> Coercion is natural; freedom is artificial. Freedoms are socially engineered spaces in which parties engaged in specified pursuits enjoy protection from parties who would otherwise naturally seek to interfere in these pursuits. One person's freedom is therefore another person's restriction: we would not have even the concept of freedom if the reality of coercion were not already present. Since freedoms are socially constructed and socially maintained, their borders are constantly patrolled, and on both sides.

Academic freedom is a social construct that has traveled far, been translated and debated about across time and space, and practiced and governed at a range of scales. The voluminous literature on academic freedom (e.g. Hofstadter, 1955; Metzger, 1955; Schrecker, 1988; Hansen, 1997) highlights some key historical and conceptual facts worthy of note given the *assemblage* focus of this chapter.

The origins of academic freedom have been traced back to the Middle Ages and debates about the relationship (a mainly negative one) between scientific inquiry and religious doctrine (Metzger, 1955). Pushes forward included the establishment of the University of Leiden in 1575 in the search for freedom and more enlightened forms of government in the State of Holland. Yet the contested cases over the knowledge produced by Copernicus or Galileo in the 16th and 17th centuries, or the tight 17th and 18th century era controls over faculty and administrators in universities such as Harvard or Oxford, corroborate the point that academic freedom was, for the most part, extremely limited in the West (as it would have been in the rest of the world), by design (Stone, 1995).

In the West, the direct and indirect effects of the Enlightenment, Darwinism, industrialization, urbanization, and of abolitionist, suffragist and pacifist movements destabilized intellectual contexts, laid some of the critical foundations for the institutionalization of the principles that shape the variants of academic freedom that now exist in many parts of the world (Metzger, 1955; Stone, 1995).

German universities, in particular, acted as model spaces of new forms of academic freedom. There were three key aspects of this (following Metzger, 1955, Chapter III):

- *Lehrfreiheit:* academics should be free to conduct research on any topic and publish or speak about their findings without fear of reproach from both church and state. This freedom also applies to the teaching process;
- *Lernfreiheit:* minimal administrative coercions such that students should be free to determine their own course of studies; and,
- *Freiheit der Wissenschaft:* academic self-government with respect to internal university affairs.

German universities increasingly became research intensive, hence the structural pressures for more transparent and institutionalized forms of academic freedom.

It is noteworthy that Johns Hopkins University, one of the first WCUs to establish a commercial presence in Singapore, was the first university to be established in the United States on the basis of the German model (Metzger, 1955). The condition of academic freedom has played a key role in the link between Johns Hopkins, the production of knowledge, and creativity via scholars such as Thorstein Veblen and John Dewey (later one of the most eloquent spokespersons of the principle of academic freedom; Storr, 1966), and institutions such as the Peabody Institute, the School of Medicine, and the School of International Advanced Studies.

Over the course of the 20th century, the principle of academic freedom has traveled far, mutated into a plethora of forms, and become institutionalized in a myriad of different ways. The traveling process has actually been facilitated by, in many contexts, controversies associated with the control of professorial activities. For example, the 1894 Richard T. Ely case at the University of Wisconsin-Madison has been identified as a key event in the reframing of the rights of responsibilities of academics and the institutions they work for. Ely, a Johns Hopkins professor of political economy, moved to Madison in 1892. Two years later an ex-officio member of the University of Wisconsin-Madison's Board of Regents (the governing body) attacked Ely for "supporting labor union strikes, organizing boycotts of nonunion businesses, and teaching socialism and other 'dangerous' theories" (Hansen, 1997, p. 3). After much consideration and debate, the Board of Regents (1894) issued this statement:

> In all lines of investigation ... the investigator should be absolutely free to follow the paths of truth, wherever they may lead. Whatever may be the limitations which trammel inquiry elsewhere, we believe the great State University of Wisconsin should ever encourage that continual and fearless sifting and winnowing by which alone the truth can be found.

These words were inscribed on a plaque located close to my office, and are continually referred to by faculty and students on the University of Wisconsin-Madison campus, and in innumerable books and reports. Thus the discourse of academic freedom needs to be associated with an array of performances for the principle to exert any hold or effect.

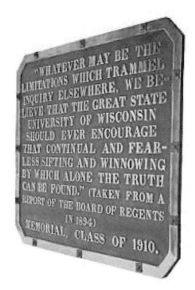

Figure 10.2. Plaque outside Bascom Hall, University of Wisconsin-Madison. Source: University of Wisconsin-Madison.

Given the contested time-space travels of academic freedom there are innumerable definitions of the concept. Some of these definitions have been developed at the university scale, some at the national scale (e.g., by the Canadian Association of University Teachers), and some at the supranational scale (e.g., by UNESCO or the NGO Human Rights Watch).

The American Association of University Professors (AUPP)[8] developed one of the most commonly referred to definitions of academic freedom in 1940:

> a. Teachers are entitled to full freedom in research and in the publication of the results, subject to the adequate performance of their other academic duties; but research for pecuniary return should be based upon an understanding with the authorities of the institution.

---

[8] The AUPP was formed when Arthur O. Lovejoy (the Berlin born Johns Hopkins University philosopher) and John Dewey (the noted philosopher and educationalist who was based at both Johns Hopkins and the University of Chicago), organized a meeting about academic freedom in 1915 (Metzer, 1955; Menand, 1996).

b. Teachers are entitled to freedom in the classroom in discussing their subject, but they should be careful not to introduce into their teaching controversial matter which has no relation to their subject. Limitations of academic freedom because of religious or other aims of the institution should be clearly stated in writing at the time of the appointment.

c. College and university teachers are citizens, members of a learned profession, and officers of an educational institution. When they speak or write as citizens, they should be free from institutional censorship or discipline, but their special position in the community imposes special obligations. As scholars and educational officers, they should remember that the public may judge their profession and their institution by their utterances. Hence they should at all times be accurate, should exercise appropriate restraint, should show respect for the opinions of others, and should make every effort to indicate that they are not speaking for the institution (http://www.aaup.org/statements/Redbook/1940stat.htm, accessed 21 March 2005).

The freedom *to* inquire, discover, publish, teach, and even participate in political activities, is linked to the notion that academics, students, and academic institutions are also supposed to be free *from* the undesired control and authority of government, business, and the church. In addition, all academics are also held to be responsible (the AAUP uses the phrase "duties correlative with rights") to ethical standards, professional standards, and codes of practice associated with relevant disciplines and research approaches.

Obviously the AUPP approach to academic freedom is a distinctively American one, though the Germanic origins (and Johns Hopkins and Chicago influences) are starkly evident. The definition has served as a model (and anti-model for some) for higher education communities in many parts of the world as they struggle over the rationale and practice of academic freedom. Regardless of your views on the legitimacy and utility of the concept, it is undeniably powerful concept. In the United States, for example, the AUPP statement has been endorsed by over 180 scholarly and professional organizations, including all of the US universities with presences in Singapore.

New Strands of Academic Freedom in Contemporary Singapore

As noted above, the target universities of Singapore's WCU programme are primarily American and European universities, though Australian universities are thought to play a key role in the bottom tier of the three-tier pyramid (see Figure 1).

Singapore has played an important role in courting select universities in R&D rich contexts (e.g., Boston) via the powers and capacities of the developmental state (e.g., targeted financial subsidies), along with doses of bureaucratic persistence and persuasion. Persuasion has been required because of the risks involved in stretching the institutional fabrics of universities across space. Institutions of higher education are only now seriously considering the establishment of "commercial presences" (in the parlance of WTO speak) in foreign countries. Equally important, universities have flat hierarchies compared to private firms, and university administrators cannot force faculty to conduct their research, teaching, and service activities in 12–24 hours flying time away from home base.

Given the relatively flat hierarchies associated with Western universities, the Singaporean state devised an intensive courting process, one that relies upon demonstrating commitment to the unique needs and concerns of academe. As Tan Chek Ming, Director EDB Services Development, put it "Every faculty member has to agree. All you need is one person to disagree and the whole deal will be thrown out of alignment." In this context,

> EDB team members act as tour guides, flying in faculty staff for a look-see trip to Singapore. The usual highlight is a meeting between the dons and senior Cabinet Ministers, namely Deputy Prime Minister Tony Tan, who oversees university education, Education Minister Teo Chee Hean, and Trade and Industry Minister George Yeo.
>
> These meetings are important, stresses Mr Tan, as they send a strong signal to the visitors of the political will and commitment in drawing reputable universities to Singapore. Team members also double up as property agents, scouting around for suitable premises in Singapore to locate the foreign university. They also help look into the legal and financial aspects of setting up shop in Singapore (Nirmala, 2001).

This approach has achieved results, though obviously Western universities were concurrently seeking to establish presences in other parts of the world (most notably Pacific Asia) at the same time (Olds and Thrift, 2005a, 2005b). Yet it is noteworthy that one of the main concerns of the courted foreign universities was academic freedom. As two key EDB officials in charge of the WCU programme put it in a *Straits Times* article (Nirmala, 2001):

> But the No. 1 question, say Mr Tan and Mr Kua, is the issue of freedom of expression in Singapore. This issue is a big concern to academics who value the space to air their views. Inevitably, the name of Dr Christopher Lingle crops up during discussions. He was an American lecturer who taught European politics at the National University of Singapore. In his article, published in the *International Herald Tribune* in 1994, he referred to the judiciary in some Asian countries as being "compliant". When the Singapore police

investigated him on charges of contempt of court and criminal defamation, he fled the country in the same year. "The fact that he fled Singapore has stuck in the minds of many academics", says Mr Tan. EDB officers clear the air by telling academics that they are free to publish factual and accurate material. "I tell them if you are going to be doing bona fide work, why should you be afraid?", says Mr Tan.

This quote highlights the *first* method of assuaging concerns: addressing the issue "head-on" in negotiations with Western universities, including in negotiation sessions with senior Government of Singapore politicians and EDB officials. The Singaporean state did not seek to shy away from the issue; instead it sought to (a) discredit the academics associated with previous high profile (in the Western press) controversies, while (b) laying out its principles for the practice of teaching and research in Singapore. "Out of bounds" (OB) markers were clearly delineated (e.g., see the quotes from INSEAD's dean, and the first president (an American) of Singapore Management University, in Olds and Thrift, 2005: 282–283) in exploratory conversations. Mutual understandings of the issues were then built up during the intense decision-making and planning phases. These OB markers focused on issues related to inter-ethnic relations in Singapore, the involvement of faculty in Singaporean politics, and the desire to ensure Singapore-based foreign faculty did not generate any tensions between the 77% ethnic Chinese city-state and its larger Muslim neighbours (Indonesia and Malaysia).

Of course, negotiation sessions also enabled representatives of Western universities to convey their understandings of the codes of practices that their faculty operate in, and seek affirmation that they would be able to practice their craft in Singapore space. For example, Robert Hamada, then dean of the University of Chicago's Graduate School of Business, was asked about the issue of academic freedom in an interview with a journalist with the *Asian Wall Street Journal*. The journalist, Richard Borsuk (1999), had this to say:

> Although Singapore has in the past placed restrictions on some media and constraints on political expression, Dr. Hamada said Singapore authorities have guaranteed full academic freedom to the university. He said he gave a statement of the University of Chicago's policy on academic freedom to Singapore authorities, who "agreed they could live with that". That gave us some comfort on that issue.
>
> If "something really unexpected happens" that's against academic freedom, "we will have a faculty committee formed in Chicago to decide what to do", Dr. Hamada said.

In this case, Dr. Hamada was referring to The University of Chicago policy on academic freedom, as set out in the Statutes of the University, enacted by the Board of Trustees. Statute 18's most relevant section begins:

> The basic policies of The University of Chicago include complete freedom of research and the unrestricted dissemination of information ... The normal method of dissemination of the results of academic work is through publication in scholarly or other public media.

In the Chicago case it is also important to note that all faculty are based in the United States though they fly in on short-term residency for teaching/research purposes. Consequently, the deterritorialized nature of the faculty base *vis a vis* the University of Chicago's campus in Singapore unsettles traditional notions of the need for the institutionalization of academic freedom.

Regardless of which party is expressing views on the issue of academic freedom, it is important to note that a large number of the agreements are verbally constituted, and require mutual equivalencies with respect to the agreements that are made, as well as more than a modicum of trust.

The *second* method of mitigating concern about academic freedom in Singapore, especially when joint ventures or joint degrees are involved, involves Singaporean institutions (including local universities) and western universities incorporating reference to guarantees of academic freedom in the Memorandums of Understandings (MOUs) and Agreements that are signed.[9]

Over a dozen MOUs and Agreements have been signed or renewed between various arms of the Singaporean state, and foreign universities. For example, in 2003 Cornell University's School of Hotel Administration, Nanyang Business School (NBS), the International Hotel Management School (Singapore), agreed to establish the Cornell-Nanyang Institute of Hospitality Management. Concerns about academic freedom were expressed on behalf of Cornell and a potential resolution was met via the contract that was signed between itself and Nanyang Technological University. As David W. Butler (2004), Dean of Cornell's School of Hotel administration put it in a 29 September 2004 memorandum to the Cornell University Faculty Senate:

> The principles of non-discrimination and academic freedom are clearly spelled out in the contract. As mentioned earlier, oversight is through the two committees to the Deans of the respective institutions. If an issue cannot be resolved, there is a provision for resolution through international arbitration. New York State law will apply in all legal proceedings. Nanyang University and their Business School have a variety of educational initiatives with other American universities. Cornell's counsel's office has engaged in due diligence

---

9 The main differences between these two inter-party documents is that an Agreement is "legally binding if there is the intention to create legal relations", while a MOU is "usually a document which records the understanding of the parties on a proposed project and is therefore not legally binding" (Ministry of Education, memo, no date, available at: http://www.moe.gov.sg/corporate/pdf/MOE-Educational-18dft.pdf, accessed 21 March 2005).

with MIT, Carnegie-Mellon, and Duke to assess their satisfaction with Nanyang. All information received was positive.

Contracts and MOUs have enabled agendas to articulate through formation of pliable networks, and mutually coherent understandings of academic freedom, though on a bilateral (foreign university to Singaporean institution) basis.

The *third* and most recent form of governance regarding academic freedom relates to the new University of New South Wales campus that was announced in April 2004. The broad-spectrum (in terms of disciplines) campus is expected to be open by 2007. Initial discussions, as reported by Australian newspapers, suggest that academic freedom will exist, as will a "students union", though the principle of academic freedom will only apply while faculty and students (and presumably administrators) are geographically situated *on* the 10 hectare campus. As O'Keefe (2004) notes:

> The UNSW council [in Sydney] will govern the satellite campus and UNSW's academic board will approve all programs.
>
> International students studying in the notoriously strict nation would be guaranteed freedom of speech and association on campus, but once outside, they would be subject to Singaporean laws.
>
> Professor Ingleson said Singaporean society was becoming more open and young Singaporeans are much more critical of their government than their parents' generation. "But there are rules and regulations that are tighter than here and in the public space you have to be aware of those", he said.

This variant of academic freedom will obviously firm up over the course of the planning and implementation process (given that the campus has yet to open), though initial discussions about academic freedom in the UNSW case point to another unique arrangement; one inscribed in what are likely to be private MOUs, agreements, or contracts.

Sights/Sites of Academic Freedom(s) in Contemporary Singapore

The emergence of a complex of Western university campuses, programs, and joint ventures in Singaporean space, and substantial local university reforms (Lee and Gopinathan, 2003) is obviously designed to further the developmental objectives of the Singaporean state and the long-ruling PAP. As noted above these objectives include those of both a material and non-material nature:

- The diversification of the city-state's labour market, and services sector
- The generation of economic spillovers

- The generation of opportunities for competition and synergy between foreign providers of education services, and indigenous institutions of higher education including the National University of Singapore, and Nanyang Technological University
- The discursive reshaping of Singapore's status to that of a "global knowledge hub", a space associated with knowledge production, innovation, R&D activities, significant university-business linkages
- The discursive reshaping of Singapore's status as a conducive base for professional expatriate residence; a base affording opportunities to attend lectures, seminars, workshops, short-term courses, etc.
- The discursive reshaping of Singaporean space in benchmarking venues, especially the *Financial Times*, the *Times Higher Education Supplement*, and disciplinary-specific discursive fields.

Yet despite the influx of a significant number of American and European universities in response to the emergence of these new socio-economic development objectives, the concept of academic freedom, one of the underlying foundations of world class university governance systems, has received remarkably limited discussion and debate. The discussions and negotiations about the nature of academic freedom *vis à vis* Singapore's global schoolhouse have been engaged with in a circumscribed and opaque manner. Deliberations have primarily taken the form of closed negotiation sessions between senior administrators representing foreign universities, and officials and politicians representing the Singaporean state. The agreements that have been made are verbal for the most part, though they have also been selectively inscribed in the confidential Memorandum of Understandings (MOUs) and Agreements that have been signed between the Government of Singapore or local universities and the foreign universities in question. Strands of the concept have been brought over by the foreign universities, reworked during negotiations, and constituted in verbal and sometimes confidential textual form. The development of a series of *case-by-case* conceptualizations of academic freedom is hybridizing in effect. Through verbal agreements of unique forms, and through MOUs and Agreements of unique forms, foreign universities and the Singaporean state have splintered academic freedom in unique ways, unsettling previous notions of academic freedom in quite significant and hitherto unexamined ways.

In addition, these agreements have not generated any ripple effects, to date, vis a vis the emergence of substantive discussion of the future of academic freedom in local universities. Research has failed to identify any policy statements regarding academic freedom by Singapore's Ministry of Education (the main governing body for institutions of higher education). No Singaporean officials or politicians have ever spoken, in an official manner, about what academic freedom means, if anything, since Lee Kuan Yew's

24 November 1966 speech titled "Academic freedom and social responsibility" (Lee, 1966). Moreover, in this new era of reform, the modern day Singaporean equivalents of Johns Hopkins' Daniel Coit Gilman, or Chicago's William Rainey Harper (Shih Choon Fong of NUS; Su Guaning of NTU; Howard O. Hunter of SMU) have not formally spoken about academic freedom; this despite the fact that the NUS president (Shih Choon Fong) spent approximately 30 years in the USA (including most of his career at Brown University), and Singapore Management University's president (Howard O. Hunter) is a US lawyer and has written about academic freedom in the United States. The lack of interest in pursuing this theme is also evident in that university handbooks and manuals of Singaporean institutions of higher education do not contain policy statements about academic freedom, nor have they established committees or boards that are tasked with enacting academic freedom.

The structural pressures to create a "Boston of the East" are immense, and the Government of Singapore has sunk enormous resources into generating complex of active universities and affiliated institutions. Moreover, as was the case in Germany in the 1880s, and the United States in the 1900s, the emphasis on research inevitably brings to the fore the issue of academic freedom. But these are early days in the most recent higher education reform era of Singapore's history, and the governance process regarding the ideal and *realpolitik* of academic freedom (or academic freedoms, to be more precise) in Singapore is only now coming into view.

Chapter 11

Fields of Imitation: The Global Expansion of Management Education

Tina Hedmo, Kerstin Sahlin-Andersson, and Linda Wedlin,
Uppsala University, Sweden

Organization Fields Shape Organizational Development, But How Do They Emerge?

Questions as to how and why organizations become increasingly similar over time have attracted much attention from organizational scholars over the past few decades. Theories of organization fields have been developed to capture the operation of such homogenizing processes among organizations. According to the now classic definition formulated by DiMaggio and Powell, an organization field consists of "those organizations that, in the aggregate, constitute a recognized area of institutional life: key suppliers, resource and product consumers, regulatory agencies, and other organizations that produce similar services or products" (1983: 148). DiMaggio and Powell (1983), DiMaggio (1983), and later others (e.g., DiMaggio, 1987; Leblebici *et al.*, 1991; Sahlin-Andersson, 1996; Greenwood *et al.*, 2002; Lawrence *et al.*, 2002) have shown that once such a field is established, processes of structuration lead to isomorphic pressures, so that with time, organizations in a field tend to become increasingly similar. Imitation is one mechanism whereby isomorphism occurs within fields; other such mechanisms include coercive and normative forces (DiMaggio and Powell, 1983).

How then do organizations become part of a field and how do fields emerge in the first place? In this chapter we use results from studies of the development of management education to show how such organization fields can be formed. We assert that a field is formed through multiple and intertwined processes of imitation. By this token, imitation is a more central process in field formation than previous studies of organization fields have assumed; imitation not only develops in organization fields but is actually central to the formation of such fields. Imitation is thus the basic means whereby fields develop and become recognized as a particular area of institutional life. We find that the organization field of management education is composed of organizations that imitate, are imitated by, and promote the imitation of one another. To highlight the importance of imitation to the emergence of organization fields, we refer to such fields as fields of imitation.

Management education has expanded dramatically over recent decades. Global ideas as to what management education is and should be have evolved concurrently with this expansion. Management education encompasses a diverse mix of schools and programs: business school and university-based business programs; full-time, part-time, and distance-learning MBA (MBA stands for Master of Business Administration) programs; and executive management training programs – to name but a few. However, with this expansion all programs have increasingly come to be regarded as comparable and as belonging to the same category. In other words, what we are witnessing is the emergence of an organization field of management education. Why have so many educational providers embarked on this same path? Why and how have certain forms of management education developed and spread? We will use insights derived from earlier theoretical developments regarding imitation to make sense of this development and its dynamics. We will especially build on theories of imitation as translation (Czarniawska and Sevón, 1996).

This chapter is based on four sets of research studies.[1] The first traces the historical development of management education in Europe and elsewhere, building on field material from secondary sources such as guidebooks and directories of business schools and MBA programs. This material was compared with and complemented by findings reported in previous studies (Locke, 1989; Engwall, 1992; Daniel, 1998; Engwall and Zamagni, 1998; Moon, 2002). We combined these results with those from studies of three salient categories of actors and activities involved in developing management education, namely media and media rankings, professional organizations and accreditation, and business school deans. The second study analyzes the development of media coverage of management education, with a special focus on the development of European media rankings. The third study tracks the emergence of a European system of management education accreditation, while the fourth presents the results of a survey of the deans of business schools, asking for their reactions to the emergent accreditation and ranking systems.

The chapter continues as follows: First, we briefly review theories of organization fields and discuss how such fields have been shown to lead to

---

[1] These studies have been presented in Hedmo (2004), Wedlin (2006), and Sahlin-Andersson and Hedmo (2000).

the increased interaction and homogenization of their members. Second, we review theories of imitation as translation, and distinguish between three modes of imitation, each involving different constellations of actors, activities, and dynamics. We then turn to our empirical material, illustrating the expansion of management education and how this field has evolved via the three modes and intertwined processes of imitation. These modes of imitation form a field of imitation, leading not only to further imitation, but also to the shaping of a global organization field of management education.

Organization fields

Field models have been developed in the social sciences as ways of exploring and explaining the interplay between actors, meanings, and activities. There are many variants of such field models, building on various theories and taking inspiration from a range of disciplines. Kurt Lewin (1936, 1951), who first brought the concept into the social sciences, built his social psychological conceptualization on a combination of insights from gestalt theory and theoretical physics. By this he sought to embrace the complexity of the real world, and he defined fields to be the "totality of coexisting facts which are conceived of as mutually interdependent" (Lewin, 1951: 240).[2] Physics inspired him to develop a topological model – a spatial view – as a way of depicting this mutual interdependence and to enable him to analyze "everything that affects behaviour at a given time" (1951: 241).

Warren (1967) introduced the concept interorganizational field, building on Lewin's work. Warren defined interorganizational field as follows: "The concept of interoganizational field is based on the observation that interaction between two organizations is affected, in part at least, by the nature of the organizational pattern or network in which they find themselves" (Warren, 1967: 397). With his use of the field concept to study interrelationships between community-level planning organizations in three cities, the field concept became associated with a spatial territory and also with the notion of field as in field study. Moreover, even though the definition clearly displays a topological view of relationships, the relationships considered are restricted to intrafield interaction, so that field can be regarded as synonomous with a network. Bourdieu's (1977) version of the field concept incorporates further aspects of fields and draws on other sources of inspiration, although his work also partly builds on Lewin's and clearly resembles his in some respects. Bourdieu (1977, 1984) emphasized that it is the common belief in and upholding of the importance of certain activities that holds a field together. A coherent pattern of action and meaning thus develops, even without any single actor intentionally striving for coherence or conformity. However, while actors in the field may uphold a shared defini-

---

[2] See Mohr (2005) and Martin (2003) for extended reviews of this theoretical development.

tion of certain activities, they may struggle over how these activities should be understood, assessed, and developed. Moreover, the field is a system of relationships in which dominant actors occupy central positions; more peripheral actors continuously seek greater influence and more central positions, challenging central actors and dominant understandings in the field. When the concept was brought into the new-institutional theoretical fold (primarily through the works of DiMaggio, 1983, and DiMaggio and Powell, 1983), it came to be associated with Weberian notions of rationalization, the iron cage, and spheres of value. DiMaggio and Powell emphasized that organizations may have a great deal in common and may develop in similar ways without ever being in contact with one another. Thus, any analysis of organizational and institutional change should not focus only on interactions between organizations, but should acknowledge that organizations also change through cultural and normative forces and through changes in identities and positions.

Even if the field concept has drawn on many different sources and has been interpreted in various ways over the years, the various related field theories are approximately coherent. "Field theory is a more or less coherent approach in the social sciences whose essence is the explanation of regularities in individual action by recourse to position vis-à-vis others. Position in the field indicates the potential for a force exerted on the person, but a force that impinges 'from the inside' as opposed to external compulsion" (Martin, 2003: 1). Individual actions should thus be understood to be dependent on the characteristics of the field and on the positions that individual actors occupy vis-à-vis others, rather than caused by individual mechanisms. Thus, field theories teach us that to understand how individual actors and activities develop we need to study the relational positions and meanings that make up the field.

Such a relational approach has been emphasized by Scott et al. (2000). Their approach can be described in organizational theory terms as follows: organization fields "incorporate both organization sets – individual organizations and their exchange partners and competitors – and organization populations – aggregates of organizations exhibiting similar forms and providing similar or related services" (Scott et al., 2000: 13). DiMaggio and Powell (1983: 148) made a similar point when noting that "the field idea comprehends the importance of both connectedness and structural equivalence." The identities of actors guide their actions, but are at the same time shaped and reshaped as activities and events unfold (see also March and Olsen, 1998).

Fields should primarily be understood as analytical constructs (DiMaggio, 1983). However, fields are also clearly "out there" as they shape both the identities and activities of actors. Moreover, fields should not be seen as static. As much as a field shapes involved actors and activities, these actors and activities reshape the field. DiMaggio (1983) characterized this, inspired by Giddens, in terms of processes of structuration. Once a field is created we can expect to witness the following among the organizations in it: increased interaction, increased information load, the emergence of a structure of domination and a pattern of coalition, and the development of a common ideology and mutual awareness (DiMaggio, 1983: 150). With structuration follow isomorphic pressures, so that organizations in the field tend to become increasingly similar to each other as they are subject to coercive control and to normative and mimetic pressures (DiMaggio and Powell, 1983). This does not necessarily mean, however, that people in the field develop common interests or that conflict disappears.

While structuration describes the forces and outcomes of field formation, the question remains as to how fields are recognized in the first place. How do fields emerge? What are the means whereby increased interaction and mutual recognition among actors arise? We suggest that at least one important way in which fields emerge is through processes of imitation. Imitation thus not only is a mechanism that increases isomorphic pressures once fields are formed, but also drives structuration processes as well. Imitation not only follows on the formation of fields, but also paves the way for the formation of fields and actually forms fields. To understand these dynamics we need to look closer at processes of imitation, in particular at how these are related to processes of identity formation.

Imitation as translation

Imitation is a basic social mechanism tying people together (Tarde, 1902/1969). Actors tend to imitate those they want to resemble (Sevón, 1996). As certain models, actors, or practices become widely known, these shape the wishes, ideals, and desires of others, thus providing the impetus for further imitation. Thus, perceived identity shapes imitation: one imitates those one relates to and those with whom one identifies. The process of imitation involves both self-identification and recognition of what one would like to become (Sevón, 1996). The opposite is also true, however, in that imitation shapes identity. Imitation constructs new relationships, references, and identifications and opens new avenues for comparison and for creating new identities. In this way fashions and trends largely form through processes of imitation (DiMaggio and Powell, 1983; Tolbert and Zucker, 1983; Czarniawska and Joerges, 1996; Sahlin-Andersson, 2001; Sahlin-Andersson and Engwall, 2002). Furthermore, because imitation is shaped by and shapes identity, the motives, dynamics, and consequences of imitation may differ between places and over time.

Imitation is an active process, and can be distinguished from diffusion insofar as the latter is defined as a phenomenon whereby a certain model, idea, or practice, once created, spreads next to a number of *passive* recipients or trend followers. In contrast, imitation has been conceptualized as a *performative* process (Sevón, 1996; Sahlin-Andersson and Sevón, 2003). The results of imitation may thus turn out to be quite different from the imitated model. This phenomenon has been variedly called recombination (Westney, 1987), accretion (Rottenburg, 1996), translation (Czarniawska and Sevón, 1996), editing (Sahlin-Andersson, 1996) and hybridization (Boyer *et al.*, 1998; Djelic, 1998). This points to the importance of understanding how ideas are translated, shaped, and changed through processes of imitation. What is being transferred from one setting to another is not an idea or a practice as such, but rather accounts and materializations of a certain idea or practice. Such accounts undergo translation as they spread, resulting in local versions of models and ideas in different local contexts (Czarniawska and Joerges, 1996). Both those seeking to be imitated and those imitating translate ideas and practices to fit their own wishes and the specific circumstances in which they operate.

Most commonly, ideas and practices circulate in the form of written presentations or oral communications that are formulated and shaped differently in different contexts; for this reason we find the concept of editing to be particularly fitting (Sahlin-Andersson, 1996). Through editing, an idea or an account of a practice may be formulated more clearly and made more explicit; however, the editing process may also change not only the form of the idea or account but also its focus, content, and meaning. Even small reformulations of an idea, which may accrue as the idea is transferred from one context to another, may fundamentally change its meaning or focus. Thus, it is only after the fact that one can distinguish revolutionary or fundamental shifts from less substantial "semantic" type changes arising from editing. Furthermore, while some aspects of an idea may remain stable as the idea circulates, other aspects may be transformed. Though labels often remain the same as they diffuse easily between settings, this does not necessarily mean that the attendant technologies, and practices necessarily remain the same as the idea spreads from one context to another (see Solli *et al.* in this volume). Even in a globalized world, differences between continents, countries, sectors, and industries have an impact on how widely disseminated knowledge is translated and applied in the local context. Models bearing the same label may acquire different local "flavors" as they are adopted and developed in different settings.

Even though these studies point out that imitators combine ideas from various sources in various ways depending on the situation (Westney, 1987; Rottenburg, 1996), imitation still seems to be understood primarily in terms of individual relationships, in which a single actor imitates one or several models. Our studies suggest, however, that greater emphasis should be placed on the complex webs of imitation processes, on how several imitation and translation processes may be interconnected, and on how one process of imitation may lead to another. In the next section we develop a framework for analyzing and exploring such intertwined modes of imitation.

Three modes of imitation

A first mode of imitation is one in which a central model inspires imitation. This can be called the *broadcasting mode* (March, 1999: 137). In this mode, imitation is based on a specific model or core set of ideas, picked up by actors in various settings and incorporated into local practices. Such imitation will most likely lead to the homogenization of practices and to further emphasis on a single central model that becomes a prototype to be imitated. Even if the dynamics of this mode resemble those of diffusion, in which a strong central idea or model drives imitation, imitation in the broadcasting mode is driven by the active participation, initiatives, and motives of those doing the imitating. Both those imitated and those imitating are active shapers of the process.

March (1999: 199) distinguished between the broadcasting mode and a *chain mode of imitation*. While broadcasting, by definition, originates in one place and spreads all around, in chain imitation an idea is imitated, and then this imitation is in turn imitated, and so on. This is, in fact, the main mode of imitation described by Tarde (1890/1962). The one who is imitating may in fact have no knowledge of the "origin" of the model; thus we can sometimes only discern after the fact that the imitation is part of a larger trend or development. Stressing that imitation may not originate from only one source or model, this mode of imitation highlights even further the active role of those involved in imitation.

The third mode of imitation is one in which the relationships between those being imitated and those imitating are *mediated by other organizations and actors*. Imitation does not always proceed from those imitated to those imitating. Many persons and organizations act as carriers and/or mediators (Sahlin-Andersson and Engwall, 2002). The usual diffusion perspective, according to which the diffusion of ideas takes place via more or less automatic processes, and according to which the main explanation for the success of an idea is its original strength, has likely helped deflect the attention of scholars from the actual carriers of ideas. Attention has instead been directed toward the local settings where new practices are found and where ideas are received. A carrier's identity has often been reduced (usually with the carrier's cooperation) to an entity that only reports on what is going on in various places, but is itself neither an activating entity nor an actor with influence. For example, researchers, media, expert committees, and international organizations are presumed to report on actions and events occurring elsewhere, but without taking any action or pursuing any interests in such events (such assumptions are demonstrated and analyzed, but also questioned, by Finnemore, 1996; Barnett and Finnemore, 1999; and Sahlin-Andersson, 2000).

If such carriers were only passive mediators "passing on" ideas and models to others, there would be little point in paying attention to them. John Meyer (1994, 1996) has used the term "Others" (inspired by G.H. Mead, 1934) to capture such organizations with their specific features and activities, thereby distinguishing them from "Actors," who are assumed to pursue their own interests and policies and are held responsible for their actions. Even though "Others" may present themselves as neutral mediators, they engage in activities that are crucial for the circulation and translation of ideas. Such "Other" organizations not only mediate ideas; they also influence and shape the activities that take place under their auspices, as they "discuss, interpret, advise, suggest, codify, and sometimes pronounce and legislate [and] develop, promulgate, and certify some ideas as proper reforms, and ignore or stigmatize other ideas" (Meyer, 1996: 244). To analyze how these "Others" translate and mediate ideas, Sahlin-Andersson (1996: 2000) conceptualizes them as editors. These editors not only report on and transmit ideas and experiences, but also formulate and reformulate and thus frame and reshape them in the process. Moreover, they teach (Finnemore, 1996) – more or less directly – other organizations how to act in order to be acknowledged as legitimate.

The three modes of imitation – broadcasting, chain, and mediated – should be understood as ideal types: though we will find one or more of them when we study processes of imitation, they will not always appear in their pure, ideal forms. These three ideal types are also used in analytical frameworks in imitation studies, and depending on which framework a particular study uses, one particular mode of imitation may be singled out for identification and emphasis. It appears to us that studies most often describe the broadcasting or chain modes of imitation; the mediated imitation mode, focusing on the web of imitated and imitating "Actors" and "Others" who create, modify, or circulate models and ideas to be imitated, has received less attention. In practice, these three modes exist together. Using the imitation field concept we can construct a framework that allows us to depict all three modes of imitation and how they interconnect. Furthermore, such a framework helps us explore how imitation processes both arise from and lead to changed identities on the part of actors, thus changing the meanings and implications of their activities.

A Global Expansion of Management Education

The growth and spread of management education has virtually exploded around the world over the last few decades. Though quite a few business schools and management education programs were founded in the United States and Europe in the late nineteenth and early twentieth centuries, it is only since the 1950s that university- and non-university-based programs in business studies have proliferated (Engwall, 1992; Crainer and Dearlove, 1998). If the turn of the previous century saw the birth of management education, the 1980s saw its boom, not only in Europe and the United States, but also elsewhere around the world.

A salient feature of this management education boom is the expansion of MBA programs, and their spread around the world. The MBA has its roots in the United States, where the first such program was offered by the Tuck School of Dartmouth in 1900 (Crainer and Dearlove, 1998; Daniel, 1998). In Europe, the first MBA program appeared with the founding of the *Institute Européen d'Administration des Affaires* (INSEAD) in 1958. In 2000, it was reported that about 2,200 MBA programs were being offered by 1,150 universities, business schools, and management colleges in 126 countries around the world (www.mbainfo.com 2003-10-13). Various specialized MBA programs have been established. A search form at www.mbainfo.com lists 68 specialized program categories, including arts management, church administration, e-commerce, health management, international business, luxury brand management, non-profit organizations, and sports management. A number of different formats are also available, such as full-time, distance-learning, one-year, and module-structured MBA programs. However, the simple fact that all these programs share the "MBA" label and are listed on the same search form indicates that they are regarded as comparable and as belonging to the same management education category.

Management education is thus expanding in all regions and countries. With this expansion, the ideals and practices of management education have come to be discussed, though not always practiced, in similar ways around the globe. Even though attempts to start programs and schools may resemble each other, and this may initially suggest homogenization, closer examination reveals differences between both the attempts and their results. Indeed, as is true of globalization processes more generally, the flow of ideas around the world may just as easily lead to increased variation and difference as to greater uniformity (Christensen and Lægreid, 2001; Sahlin-Andersson and Engwall, 2002). In fact, in-depth studies of the development of management education in Europe show that this proliferation has been followed by clear differentiation, with a central elite – a group of programs attracting increasing attention and prestige – and a group of followers that appear to be more peripheral and less influential (Hedmo, 2004; Wedlin, 2006).

Broadcasting becoming a chain: European translations of U.S. models

Bearing in mind that imitation is such a basic social form, it should come as no surprise that management educators imitate one another. Indeed, even cursory observation reveals that education providers not only resemble each other, but also often refer to each other as important inspirations and models. Business schools imitate other business schools; providers of MBA programs imitate other programs, and so on. Apart from references to specific business schools and management education programs, we also find frequent references to models on the basis of which schools and programs are compared, and from which management education providers draw inspiration and ideas for further development and imitation. Hence, it appears that the above described expansion has evolved through imitation. A look back at the course of management education development in Europe will explore this imitation.

Interest in U.S. business schools as the main sources of management education grew steadily in Europe throughout the 1960s and 1970s, and a number of business schools were set up in various European countries, mainly in the western part of the continent. By 1990, even such traditional universities as Cambridge and Oxford in the United Kingdom had established business or management schools. Business schools and programs have also been set up in France (e.g., INSEAD), Italy (e.g., the *Scuola di Direzione Aziendale dell'Università Commerciale Luigi Bocconi*, or SDA Bocconi), and Spain (e.g., the *Instituto de Estudios Superiores de la Empresa*, or IESE). In addition, a range of MBA programs, as mentioned in the introduction, have been initiated.

The expansion of management education in Europe since the 1950s exemplifies one particular track of imitation, namely, a shared reference to a U.S. model of management education and a traceable imitation of U.S. business schools and programs. Though it is questionable whether there really is a single "U.S. model" of business school and management education, the perception that there is one has been important in shaping European management education, as this purported "U.S. model" has been broadcasted across Europe.

This broadcasting has occurred by several channels. One such channel is what could be described as personal travels: individual scholars have visited U.S. schools, bringing back ideas on how to develop and expand their teaching and educational programs. This might not occur as part of any general or explicit plan, but simply represent an effect of the mobility of researchers – imitation being a basic mode of behavior, it is difficult not to imitate. Our studies also reveal a second, more strategic and planned form of imitation; it is driven by clearly articulated motives on the part of schools to become more like other schools, and to develop their reputations and the reputations of their scholars and students.

The first business schools formed in Europe were constructed via such imitative processes, and this pattern has repeated itself over the years, with some variation. The early European examples, however, indicate that not only U.S., but also early European schools constituted prototypes that were broadcasted across Europe. For instance, the Stockholm School of Economics was formed as a replica of German and British schools, and was thus partly modeled on the older European traditions of *Handelshochschulen* and "schools of economics." However, the main broadcasted model after the Second World War was the U.S. management education model in which business schools and MBA programs were emphasized. It spread via efforts to rebuild Europe after the War, with financial support from the Marshall plan and from U.S. organizations such as the Ford Foundation (Engwall and Zamagni, 1998; Hedmo, 2004). The trend toward greater proliferation of management education was thus partly driven by international organizations promoting U.S. ideals and models. Included in these efforts were the establishment of INSEAD, clearly formed as a U.S.-style business school, and the MBA program at IESE that was explicitly set up as a Spanish version of the Harvard MBA program. New units were also established on the initiative of Chambers of Commerce and/or wealthy businessmen. In addition, existing universities were being transformed through intentional processes of imitation. These efforts provide clear examples of the imitation of the U.S. management education model as well as obvious attempts to spread this model to other parts of the world. In these cases, explicit reference was made to the model imitated – through using the same or similar names or through formal agreements – in hopes of sharing the reputation of the model.

Our data clearly show that imitation can be motivated by the desire to become like the model being imitated, i.e., the model imitated forms a prototype for the imitating organizations. This process, in which a single model is being imitated, we called broadcasting – from one source to a whole set of potential adopters. However, there is more than one model that is being imitated, and the imitated models are clearly unstable themselves. Hence, the imitation often changes from broadcasting to chain-like processes, in which one entity initially imitates a model; the imitating entity is then imitated in turn, and so on.

The expansion of management education in Europe displays patterns similar to other processes of Americanization (Djelic, 1998) and imitation (Westney, 1987; Sahlin-Andersson, 1996; Sevón, 1996). Models were only partly imitated and were moreover clearly subject to editing. The MBA program is one component of the U.S. management education model that has perhaps been imitated most frequently in Europe. The proliferation of the MBA program provides an example of a label that has spread, taking different forms as it has spread across the continent. The MBA has become a

200

label for success, and schools have started offering these programs so as to become legitimate members of the evolving international or global field of management education.

Even though the newly founded MBA programs in Europe all came to adopt the same label, this proliferation also led to variation since new programs and schools were embedded in different local contexts. For instance, in some contexts schools and programs were incorporated into national systems of higher education, while in others the prevailing rules, norms, and values hindered this development. Moreover, as the MBA label became popular in Europe, many scholars and schools began to imitate not just U.S. schools and MBA programs, but also the most established and reputable European programs. While most full-time U.S. MBA programs are two years long, the MBA programs developed in Europe are often set up as one-year programs. One-year MBA programs, offered, for example, by INSEAD and IMD, have become models for most European MBA programs developed since the early 1990s, such as the programs at Oxford and Cambridge Universities. Thus some schools imitated and translated a U.S. model, and other schools imitated this translated model – broadcasting was thus followed by chain-like imitation. These chains of translation resulted in European MBA programs displaying considerable variation, which arose partly from national differences, partly from variation in the models imitated, and partly from the timing and procedures of the start of programs (Sahlin-Andersson and Hedmo, 2000; Mazza *et al.*, 2005). Because the label "MBA" was used for all these programs, despite their great differences in format, institutional framing, and support, all have been compared with each other and all have been subject to the widespread expectation that use of a shared label should signify a certain level of common content.

Mediators of imitation

In addition to schools and individual scholars, a number of observers and mediators of ideas and experiences, such as researchers, experts, international organizations, consultants, and publicists, have been active in processes of imitation. Parallel to, and interwoven with the broadcasting and chain-like imitation of U.S. models, these actors have formulated and pursued more or less global templates for management programs; in so doing, they have played important roles in processes of imitation, and in making the management education field global (Wedlin, 2006). We will especially emphasize the important role played by assessing and evaluating organizations, such as accreditation bodies and the media: they have produced and provided information and comparisons, reported on and proposed initiatives for change, and formed arenas for the exchange of experience, ideas, and ideals. Hence, to explain why business schools and management education programs have proliferated so rapidly and extensively, and to determine how their ideas are being picked up, processed, and distributed by these mediators (i.e., assessing and evaluating bodies), we also need to analyze in more detail how, and under what conditions, these mediators develop, act, and interact.

In 1997, the Brussels-based organization, the European Foundation for Management Development (efmd), launched a European accreditation system for the providers of management education. This system was the first such scheme covering business schools and other providers of management education from various countries in Europe, and was intended to establish a European standard for evaluating and assessing the quality of European management education. Also in the late 1990s, European management education providers witnessed the expansion and proliferation of ranking lists of MBA programs and business schools in international business newspapers and news magazines. In January 1999, for example, the London-based *Financial Times* published the first international ranking of European and U.S. MBA programs (*Financial Times*, 1999-01-25). Let us review these two important developments and investigate their roles in translating management education and in forming a global field of management education.

Accreditation

In the 1990s, when the number and variety of business schools and competing management education programs increased dramatically in Europe, the issue of accreditation was raised in efmd – a professional organization in the field of European management education. The idea of developing a European accreditation program for European business schools and management education programs was initially met with a lack of enthusiasm on the part of most efmd members. This was largely due to skepticism about the possibility of developing a uniform system for quality evaluation within the fragmented area of management education in Europe. However, when it became known in the mid 1990s that the main U.S. accreditation organization for management education, the Association to Advance Collegiate Schools of Business (AACSB-International), was planning to start accrediting European business schools on the basis of U.S. standards, attitudes changed. Efmd members then found it important to react and respond to the AACSB strategy, and to "defend and promote European values" by constructing a consistent European system (interview, efmd board member, 2000-11-08). Efmd also had organizational motives for launching this program. It was, for example, seen as a way for the organization to boost its financial profile and reputation in the management education market in Europe and elsewhere. The efmd strategy was also related to the expansion of the European Single Market, and political arguments for creating a common area in higher education more generally. Accordingly, in 1997 efmd launched the European Quality Improvement System (EQUIS) to be a European equivalent to the U.S. accreditation system (efmd, 1998).

To deal with resistance and diversity in Europe, EQUIS was formed and prepared in cooperation with European national accreditation organizations within an independent unit called European Quality Link (EQUAL).[3] Even though the AACSB accreditation system was severely criticized by most efmd members, the European accreditation scheme was formed partly in imitation of this U.S. model, and partly in imitation of the various schemes and standards of EQUAL members – albeit, national translations of the U.S. model. To handle the diversity of European management education organizations and programs, and to "guarantee" the system's continuing success throughout Europe, EQUIS was equipped with a "flexible approach" which allowed for the continuous development and refinement of the accreditation scheme. Also incorporated in EQUIS was the "European dimension" of management education – the international dimension, and connections with the business world (interviews, EQUAL project manager, 1999-10-05; EQUIS director, 1999-06-16).

After an initial period of doubt on the part of European management education providers, EQUIS accreditation spread widely in Europe and elsewhere. By June 2004, 73 management education units had been awarded accreditation after undergoing the EQUIS quality assessment process, and many more schools had announced interest in undergoing the assessment. Through this development, schools were looking at and imitating other schools; as well, they were imitating the model captured by the published accreditation criteria – at least for the self-evaluation and presentation undertaken during the accreditation process.

Rankings

Arguments and reactions similar to those that arose in response to the initiation of accreditation can be identified as we trace the development of media rankings of business schools and MBA programs. The development of these rankings is linked to the general expansion of management education, and to a specific increase in media interest in it. Moon (2002) shows that the coverage of management education increased significantly, in both the popular and academic business press, in the early 1990s; of particular media interest was the MBA label that had spread and became institutionalized around the world. Efforts by newspapers to launch business education sections and rankings of schools were intended to attract young, business-

---

[3] The core members of EQUAL were the Association of Business Schools (ABS) and the Association of MBAs (AMBA) in the United Kingdom, *Associacion Espanola de Representantes de Escuelas de Direccion de Empresas* (AEEDE) in Spain, *Associazione per la Formazione alla Direzione Aziendale* (ASFOR) in Italy, *Chapitre des Ecoles de Management* in France, and efmd (efmd, 1994).

school-trained managers to become readers and subscribers. As more news-papers increased their coverage of management education issues, competi-tion between newspapers led to the publication of more, and more extend-ed rankings of business schools and MBA programs; in turn this led to the imitation of ranking lists among newspapers.

The decision by the *Financial Times* to produce an international ranking list in 1999 was also a reaction to the proliferation of ranking lists in U.S. media, and to increasing press coverage of business schools in the United States. European business schools feared the dominance of U.S. schools would become too great, as U.S. ranking lists grew in importance outside the United States. They lobbied the *Financial Times* to initiate an international ranking list that featured schools outside North America. The rankings thus arose in reaction to a perceived U.S. dominance, but have also provided a way for European schools to be compared with these U.S. schools and to belong to the same perceived "top league".

Results from a survey of European business school deans suggest that some of the international rankings have introduced a more "European" approach to management education:

> International media tend to use Anglo-Saxon criteria. With their inclusion of European schools and universities they have found it indispensable to alter their criteria in order to take into account the specific characteristics of other education systems.
>
> (Survey comment, European business school dean)

International rankings have redefined positions in the field and have includ-ed European schools in these lists to a greater extent than before. In this way they have mediated and edited business school models and ranking criteria into a business school template that they find better fits the characteristics of European schools. Despite the fact that quite a few ranking lists have included more European schools and more "European" criteria, the opinion seems to persist that rankings in general promote and continue to support an "American model" of education:

> It is questionable whether rankings can be based on criteria uniformly applied to all schools irrespective of their strategy and philosophy. The cur-rent rankings rely on a very specific (North American) model of what and how business schools should be set up to do [sic]. This model itself is very questionable.
>
> (Survey comment, European business school dean)

An interesting feature of the development of both accreditation and rankings is that these systems have developed partly in reaction to existing evaluation systems, and also in reaction to a U.S. model of management education and to the perceived dominance of this model even in Europe. There is an endeavor to enhance the specifically European perspectives inherent in both the accreditation and the ranking procedures. If we look at how these systems are set up, however, it is clear that they are largely influenced by U.S. models and have themselves been formed through processes of imitation and editing. Through making international comparisons between programs and schools, these assessments have been fundamental in forming the identities and roles of business schools and other management education providers in the emerging global field of management education, as we will explore next.

Shaping the field

The development of rankings and accreditation is not simply a response to the proliferation of management education programs and schools in Europe, and thus to the global expansion of management education; it has also helped drive and shape this expansion and the imitation processes operative between and among schools and individuals. Ranking and accreditation systems do so by providing assessments, comparisons, and evaluations, and by constructing templates that providers and observers of management education can follow. Such templates have also been constructed through processes of imitation: the accreditation and ranking bodies created such templates by imitating and editing other ranking and accreditation criteria, themselves formulated in cooperation with prestigious business schools. They are thus mediating bodies involved in processes of imitation, and through the assessment templates they issue they are framing others' motives for as well as procedures of imitation.

Rankings and accreditation provide a means of distinguishing serious from less serious, or "good" from "bad" business schools in this evolving field – a desire expressed by business schools themselves. This point can be illustrated by a quotation from the Director of Manchester Business School, cited in a *Financial Times* interview: "It takes a lot of time and money and it is a pain at times, but it is a necessary condition for being in the MBA market. It does provide a minimum kitemark"; furthermore, "it puts us on an elite list and gets us into the game" (*Financial Times*, 2000-09-08).

The importance of international rankings and accreditation lies primarily in their ability not just to define any group, but to acknowledge conformity to an abstract notion of "the business school" – that is, to qualify an educational provider as an "international business school" and as part of the business school "community."[4] Rankings and accreditation are hence closely linked to a business school template, formed around the notion of what a

---

[4] Here we are discussing a business school template rather than a management education template. Again, while management education includes a broad range of programs and education providers, the template frames these simply as business schools.

business school is and what it should do. Business school identities and imitation processes are increasingly formed around this template and the notion of being a part of the business school field. The template also in itself becomes a prototype for schools to imitate.

A central component of this template and prototype is the MBA program. Having an MBA program is considered a core feature of a business school, and is believed to be necessary to be a "true" business school and a member of the top group. This is enhanced by international rankings, whose lists focus mainly on full-time MBA and sometimes also on executive MBA programs, and is supported by the accreditation procedures, which use business school model assumptions in making their evaluations. The strength of the template and the central role of the MBA partly explain why the number of MBA programs on offer is still increasing. There are, for example, recently developed MBA programs at the Copenhagen Business School and the Stockholm School of Economics. These were developed as strategic initiatives to strengthen the international profile of the schools, so they will be considered full-fledged business schools and be eligible to participate in the rankings. Rankings and accreditation thus contribute to the forming and circulation of a template for business schools, and thus to establishing criteria for what is included in a good business school.

Rankings and accreditation have also themselves become important features of this template. To be considered part of the top group, and to adhere to the template, it is important for business schools to have the quality label and certificate of accreditation, and to be highly rated in the published rankings. Results from our survey of European business school deans indicate that business schools consider international accreditation and rankings to be the most important sources of reputation and status, even more important than, for example, national quality labels, alliances, or participation in professional networks (Wedlin, 2006). Staying outside the rankings is not considered an option, at least not "if you want to run a major MBA school in the international market" (director of a European business school).

The growing importance of rankings and accreditation for reputation and status in the field has led to the continued expansion of MBA programs, as noted above; it has also led to increasing interest in and attention to how the business school is presented to the public, for example, in the media. Along with the pressure to submit information, the desire has grown within the schools themselves to structure the information issued to the media more carefully, and to strive to increase press coverage of their schools and programs. External relations functions, such as PR departments, media offices, and press officers, have recently been set up and developed in almost all top business schools. Business schools' PR efforts and attempts to attract media attention suggest that they are actively participating in constructing and diffusing a template as to what proper and "good" business schools should be like, and how they should present their work; in so doing, they are helping to form the template of "a good international business school." This shows the importance of properly presenting the business school and its activities to an audience. Furthermore, the active editing of this self-presentation by schools helps form presentation models for others to imitate.

As is true of most actors, be they individuals or organizations, providers of management education strive to be well regarded – they strive for recognition, respect, and reputation. This is nothing new. What is new, however, is the wide audience that is now aware of such reputations and the large group of schools that is now being observed and compared by the same or overlapping audiences. Accreditation and rankings have led schools to dedicate greater energy to presenting themselves. Moreover, such self-presentations are shaped in relation to the accreditation and ranking templates. Again, ranking and accreditation bodies both mediate and motivate imitation by issuing editing rules according to which such presentations are performed or read, and by actively participating in forming the templates that frame the perception and comparison of schools. Thus, they structure the emerging field in terms of who is in and who is out, who is central and who is peripheral, and what counts as good management education. In this way, by framing and driving imitation they are active mediators of imitation; in other words, they are central to forming and developing a field of imitation and, in turn, an organization field.

An Analysis of Fields of Imitation

Management education has proliferated because schools imitate each other. As in all areas of life, in management education the actors are formed and reformed through processes of imitation. Not only do education providers imitate, but so do students and their future employers. Also, rankers and accreditation bodies imitate each other; they also imitate prestigious schools and their self-presentation. Management education providers imitate the templates that are shaped by the rankers and accreditation bodies, and they imitate the self-presentation of other schools that are themselves produced in response to the assessment criteria established by the rankers and accreditation bodies. Through these entangled processes of imitation, the demand and supply of management education have both expanded, forming a more or less coherent pattern. Not all schools are similar, not all students request the same type of education, and not all employers look for similar abilities; through such processes of imitation, however, at least some elements have become recognizable across various settings. Through such imitation, a field has formed, developing further through comparison, reaction, further imitation, and structuration. We have given a brief account of such entangled processes of imitation through which this field of management education develop.

Based on this account of how imitation processes occur, we now return to some of the remaining questions about imitation processes asked in the introduction. We have seen how imitation takes different forms, but little has been said about what motivates this imitation. Why do people and organizations imitate? Who are the active participants in these processes of imitation, and what are they imitating? First we summarize our findings about what motivates imitation, then we explore the issue of who imitates whom, and what it is that is being imitated.

Motivation for imitation

We have shown that schools, individual scholars, and mediators have imitated other schools, programs, presentations, and templates which they wish to resemble and be associated with. The main motivation for this imitation is to become similar to others, and to become even more similar to the most prestigious, leading organizations in the field. This is the common imitation story. However, our study uncovered another motive for imitation: imitation may also be motivated by a desire to distinguish oneself from others, to be different. As explained by Czarniawska (2004), building on Tarde (1890/1962), the processes of identity formation and of imitation both involve a process of alterity construction – the formation of perceptions of being different. As important as the question "Who am I like?" is the question "How am I different?"

This dialectic of resemblance and difference is especially clear as we trace the establishment of accreditation and ranking systems in Europe. These processes have clearly been evolving through the imitation, not only of schools and management education programs, but also of other ranking and accreditation schemes. The *Financial Times* imitated its U.S. counterparts, while efmd modeled its accreditation scheme after that of the AACSB. However, in these cases the motive was not primarily to become similar to another entity; instead, we found that even if the regulatory bodies sought to attain a similar standing in the field and a similar ability to influence the development of the field, they still formed their schemes in reaction to their U.S. counterparts. What motivated their imitation was an emphasis on building and strengthening a uniquely European identity. Imitation, in these cases, not only aimed to treat the U.S. models as prototypes but also as templates with which the imitators knew they would be compared, and from which they sought to distinguish themselves. Moreover, these bodies pursued regulation and imitation as ways of hindering the increasing flow of U.S. models to Europe. The regulatory bodies pursued their regulations as a way of providing translation frames for European schools that were imitating U.S. schools, but that were at the same time also comparing themselves with them.

Even if the motive for imitation in these latter cases arose in reaction to and out of a desire to distinguish oneself from the prevailing model, ongoing developments show that this imitation paved the way for further comparisons and imitations across the Atlantic. European accreditation bodies and rankers could not stop their U.S. counterparts from having an impact on the European management education field. Instead, these modes of assessment became an institutional part of the European management education field (see Hedmo *et al.*, 2006). With the emergence of the field and the emphasis on the international dimensions of management education in Europe, comparisons between schools and between rankers and accreditation organizations have become commonplace. Hence, we find that the pattern of who imitates whom has partly developed as the field of management education has evolved. We will expand somewhat on the question of who is imitating whom in the next section.

Who imitates whom?

We have explored the many actors involved in the intertwined processes of imitation, stressing that imitation presumes actors who imitate, and have illustrated how models, prototypes, and templates are being formed through such imitation. The early imitation processes that contributed to the formation of a field of management education in Europe were partly driven by individual scholars, partly by schools, and partly by expert groups having the mandate to establish business schools as part of a program to modernize and rationalize European economies after the Second World War. Later imitation processes provided examples of imitation in which schools – or rather their leaders – decided to set up or develop MBA programs in an effort to gain a more central position in the field or to strategically develop the school as part of the field.

The more recent processes of imitation, occurring since accreditation bodies and rankers entered the field and become important regulators and mediators of models, have meant that assessment templates have diffused, motivating representatives of schools to still further imitation. The formation of a more or less global market for management education has also broadened the audience for management education presentations to include students and other stakeholders all over the world (at least management education providers hope that they are appealing to such a global market).

The entrance of rankers, accreditation bodies, and other observers and scrutinizers into the field was followed not only by more imitation but also by an enhanced emphasis on self-presentation. In this emergent field it has followed that management education providers not only imitate other management education providers, but also the templates and models issued by assessing and evaluating bodies, i.e., the rankers, media, and accreditation bodies. Clearly, all these are edited models that largely emphasize self-presentation. Hence, as the field has emerged – in the sense that the education providers and related organizations came to form a recognized institutional area (DiMaggio and Powell, 1983) – we find that greater emphasis is placed on such self-presentation, and we can expect to find yet more imitation of such self-presentations and more general imitation at a distance through mediated models and templates.

Schools compete for students and resources and they compete for recognition and status. The competition for status is nothing new: the history of universities is a history of competition for these attributes, and such competition is an inevitable component of market competition. With the development of global management education, however, competition for recognition has been further emphasized and structured. This is partly related to the marketization of the field of management education, and those education providers perceived as prestigious and "good" can be assumed to attract more students than not-so-prestigious providers can. Rankings and accreditation have emphasized and disseminated such self-presentation.

Conclusions: The Role of Editing in Fields of Imitation

Our analysis of the development of the global field of management education, with a special focus on Europe, has been used to show the dynamics at play as an organization field is formed. We have shown how a field is formed through intertwined processes of imitation, and we have distinguished between three modes of imitation: broadcasting, chain, and mediated imitation. These three modes are interconnected, and our studies show how they have reinforced and driven each other. Moreover, with imitation followed the emergence of common templates, categorizations, and identities, so that the imitation processes collectively led to the formation of an organization field. Our examples and analysis have particularly stressed the interrelations between these intertwined processes and modes of imitation. These have formed into a field of imitation in which one process of imitation leads to further imitation. These processes of imitation involve direct contact among organizations as well as imitation of more diffused models and meanings. We have pointed to the importance of the complex webs of numerous actors who are involved as a field is formed. Within this field of imitation, various models, prototypes, and templates developed that together led organizations to define themselves in terms of a common category, thus forming the basis of an organization field. To understand how an organization field is formed, we have thus argued for the need to investigate and understand not just the organizations imitating or being imitated, but the actors and organizations that create, modify, circulate, and promote the ideas, templates, and models used for imitation.

We have shown how broadcasting processes – meaning the promotion and imitation of a specific model – formed the starting point for the imitation and translation of a U.S. model of management education in Europe. Our analysis shows that these processes of imitation led to further interaction among management education providers. Educational providers do not simply act in isolation, but rather learn from, imitate, react to, and present their ideas to each other. With these interactions followed chains of imitation in which ideas traveled from one educational provider to the next, without any clear reference to one central model or organization.

As management education organizations continued to develop and imitate each other, the notion of management education spread even further. The imitation led both to similarity and variation. The spread of MBA programs provides a specific illustration of this. As the MBA spread and became a well-known form of management training, it was translated to suit different settings and a variety of MBA programs emerged. Concurrently, expectations arose that this well-known and widespread label should designate a certain shared content and equivalence in the degree granted. Hence, the spread of the MBA has not led directly to homogenization; rather, a recognized category was formed, which in turn led to a quest for order and distinction. Rankings and accreditation in turn arose as ways to distinguish serious from less serious, or "good" from "bad" management education. Thus, a number of mediating bodies, primarily accreditation and ranking organizations, were formed and in turn mediated the processes and models of imitation, providing the impetus for further imitation. Mediated imitation also shifted the focus towards self-presentation, and led to imitation of the models and templates promoted through these organizations, which have been particularly important in shaping recent developments in, and perceptions of, the global field of management education.

The importance of editors and how they form templates and prototypes outside the local context of schools and beyond interactions between these schools has been emphasized. We have shown how accreditation and ranking bodies have developed into important mediators and editors of management education. These have been formed through imitating other monitoring bodies in adjacent and overlapping fields. We have also shown that these bodies have formulated templates on the basis of which educational programs and schools can be compared, monitored, and assessed. In addition, the rules set by the monitoring bodies regulate what is considered to be good and appropriate self-presentation; as well, they frame and structure how the audience views the self-presentation and performance of schools. In this way, the emergence of an organization field is found to follow a combined logic of individual actors searching for reputation, status, recognition, and respect as well as following individual actors' rule-following logic.

The analysis suggests that mediating modes of imitation have become increasingly important in these times of globalization, and that this development is related to the expansion of monitoring organizations in contemporary society. Our analysis thus emphasizes the crucial importance of monitoring organizations, such as accreditation bodies and media, and other transnational regulatory and monitoring organizations in forming organization fields. This suggests a need for more empirical research into the routine activity of such transnational bodies and into their interrelations with actors in other transnational fields.

Chapter 12

Globalizing Webs: Translation of Public Sector e-Modernization

Hans Krause Hansen and Dorte Salskov-Iversen,
Copenhagen Business School, Denmark

The new information and communication technologies (ICTs) have become an indispensable ingredient in any thinking about governance and public management modernization anywhere in the world.[1] Few government institutions – from the local to the international levels – today question the potential of e-modernization. E-modernization is widely believed to improve the quality of life for public employees and citizens, purportedly by leading to reductions in costs and time, and by opening up new channels of communication between managers and employees, between the governing and the governed.[2] Proposing e-modernization as a panacea for curing the diseases of modern state organizations is clearly an idea that is traveling worldwide, and it is intrinsically related to conceptions of proper governance and innovative and efficient management. Such conceptions defy any simple definition, but they are unthinkable without implicit assumptions of power and authority relations.

Drawing on theories of governmentality and actor-network, this chapter sets out to investigate processes of translation and authority construction involved in organizational change and managerial innovation through e-modernization. More specifically, our analysis will focus on two state institutions, one in Mexico and one in Denmark, as well as on a Sweden-based transnational network, all of them engaged in the promotion and adaptation of e-modernization. Our concern is with how these organizations translate

---

[1] See e.g. Fountain, 2001.

[2] In a similar vein, an increasing number of private companies and civil society organizations around the world are currently adapting ICTs as part of their managerial, organizational or mobilization strategies, giving rise to conceptions such as the "networked business model" and "citizen networks". See Deibert, 2000 and Castells, 2001.

ideas of e-modernization into crosscutting organizational arrangements premised on interconnectedness and alignment. We refer to these arrangements as globalizing webs. It is our contention that organizations increasingly depend on the creation of such globalizing webs, as they facilitate the construction of political authority.

Exploring how organizations and the people who inhabit them relate to ideas such as e-modernization and transform them into governance and managerial practices is of course highly complex. Reformers may appropriate new ideas in a variety of ways (Newton, 1996; Hansen et al., 2001), such as through formal management education, international conferences and professional networks, evaluation practices and benchmarking exercises, financial, business and popular media including new software, or through best-selling management books purchased in airport lounges. What is spreading is not new practices, but accounts of such practices, which are in turn translated into social practices in local contexts through editing processes (Sahlin-Andersson, 2001: 54) – or repertoires that are appropriated by local actors as frameworks for action. In the process of local translation, they provide for a certain element of homogeneity and give rise to new or subtly different practices (Czarniawska and Sevón, 1996).

The links through which particular global meanings and conceptions of statecraft, governance and management are generated, diffused, appropriated and edited in local settings have been conceptualized under a wide variety of headings, including political networks, knowledge networks, epistemic communities and transnational discourse communities (e.g. Haas, 1992; Hansen et al., 2002; Stone, 2003). For the purpose of this study, the latter is of particular interest: the notion of transnational discourse community presupposes shared meanings and interests among state professionals, consultants and researchers operating within the field of public administration. This chapter tries a different track by exploring the journey of managerial ideas – epitomized by e-modernization – as globalizing webs. Analytically, the formation of globalizing webs does not presuppose a set of shared meanings and interests taking shape of a community.

Globalizing webs are not fixed or completed organizational entities, but orderings or arrangements in process. Neither do they require a meta-narrative of globalization and management to be subscribed to by different actors, although transboundary processes are a distinctive feature of them. The conception of globalizing webs is predicated on the idea that any social, political or economic ordering in time and space is created from a complex network of localized social and technical practices and devices (Barry, 2001: 12). These practices and devices make it possible to link calculations and action in one place with calculations and actions in another place. Such linkages involve processes of translation. Precisely because the term translation by definition implies a movement from place to place, the study of globalizing webs provides a glimpse of how ideas travel, what makes possible the creation of alignment and association between the different nodes in the webs, and by implication, how the authority of the different nodes is constructed.

Conceptualizing globalizing webs as relying on translation implies an attention to language. Here we draw on the literature based on Foucault. According to Miller and Rose (1990: 6), all government depends on the creation of a language "that claims both to grasp the nature of that reality represented, and literally to represent it in a form amenable to political deliberation, argument and scheming." In this account, language is not viewed as concrete text and intertextuality, but rather as a kind of intellectual and conceptual machinery that makes reality thinkable in such a way that one can act upon it (see also Rottenburg, in this volume). Language creates a linkage between aspirations and the means to fulfill them. In this vein, translation is what happens when general political rationales, often taking a problematizing and programmatic form, are transformed into activities and linkages within a given or specific problem area by means of a variety of governmental mechanisms and technologies. Further, it is precisely these activities and linkages that carry the potential for creating loose associations and networks across time and space:

> To the extent that actors have come to understand their situation according to a similar language and logic, to construe their goals and their fate as in some way inextricable, they are assembled into mobile and loosely affiliated networks ... [such networks] are made between those who are separated spatially and temporarily, and between events in spheres that remain formally distinct and autonomous. When each can translate the values of others into its own ambitions, judgments and conduct, a network has been composed that enables rule "at a distance" (Rose and Miller, 1992: 184).

The conception of rule at a distance has both a social and a geographical form and is based on two important assumptions. First, it draws on Latour's conception of power as something that is not possessed, but comes out as an effect of association. In other words, power is relational, and the power of an entity depends on its capacity to successfully enroll and mobilize others in the pursuit of its goals (Latour, 1986). Second, it is based on the assumption that (neo) liberal rule, because it carries the twin project of creating and preserving the private (in the broad sense of the term) while shaping the conduct of privacy, is bound to authorize entities beyond the state. In other words, for the state to govern at a distance in both social and geographical senses it must operate through the decisions and self-responsibility of non-state actors – their autonomy must be authorized. This, in turn, requires translation processes and governmental technologies that ally the objectives of government with the projects and autonomy of such actors.

The following study of a globalizing web provides an insight into how the journey and translation of the idea of e-modernization is contingent upon the formation of loose alignments such as the one that spans our three field sites, and how this idea, in the process of being translated, constructs and re-constructs relations of authority between state and non-state organizational forms. The first section unfolds the empirical grounding on which our conceptual thinking rests, and sets out to illustrate the dynamics of one such configuration of globalizing webs. We analyze how programmatic elements of the e-modernization vision are being appropriated for varying purposes and invested with particular meanings as they are being fed into a wide variety of organizational activities in our three cases – the Federal Government of Mexico, the City of Næstved in Denmark and the Stockholm Challenge. Even if the nodes constituting this web and the particular manifestations of the e-modernization vision across the localities that are connected via these webs bear very few if any similarities with each other, each of the nodes relies on the formation of a globalizing web for their authority. In the second section of the chapter, we put these empirical observations into perspective, elaborating and discussing the implications of globalizing webs for relations of authority.

The Formation of a Globalizing Web[3]

The first two studies explore a Mexican and a Danish state institution respectively. In both cases the engagement in the Stockholm Challenge is an integrated element of their compliance with, and an enactment of e-modernization, just as it can be seen to further their own schemes. The third study maps the history, rationale, activities and relations of the Stockholm Challenge. It describes the dynamics that inscribe this organization with the authority to bring others into alignment, even if this alignment is invariably a loose and indeterminate one, premised on our crosscutting globalizing webs.

Mexican state institutions

Upon his presidential inauguration in December 2000, ex-Coca-Cola executive Vicente Fox proposed an ambitious national programme. The prime objective of the project was to build out the country's Internet infrastructure and get its approximately 100 million citizens online. At the time, the ini-

---

[3] The following accounts are based on interviews with officers at the eMNSGC in Mexico City in November 2003, the City of Næstved in February and October 2004, and The Stockholm Challenge in January 2004 as well as on policy documents issued by these and related authorities. This research was funded by MODINET, a major Danish research programme (www.modinet.dk), running from 2002–2005.

tiative, dubbed E-Mexico, was by no means exceptional for developing economies. Similar large-scale e-modernization programmes were being fostered in Latin America, in Asia and Eastern Europe.

Today, if you try to access one of the innumerable and expanding government-operated portals in Mexico, you will most probably run into the comprehensive e-Mexico Portal – www.e-mexico.gob.mx – which is the online manifestation of the e-Mexico National System (eMNS). A public policy instrument of the e-Mexico initiative, the eMNS was established in 2001, with a specific view to fostering the transition of Mexico "towards the Information and Knowledge Society, integrating the efforts of different public and private actors in this task, and attracting the rest of the Mexicans" (SCT 2003: 1). A special task force and coordination unit with approximately 20 officers and specialists – the e-Mexico National System General Coordination (eMNSGC) – was established and placed under the auspices of a central federal government institution, the Secretary of Communication and Transportation. In formal terms, the eMNS is an integral part of the Fox administration's National Development Plan (2000–2006), which continues the efforts towards deregulation and simplification, now subsumed under the heading of Innovation. One of the main priorities of the new administration has been to further improve the quality and efficiency of government services, and to fundamentally change the government-citizen relationship through the creation of a digital space. The e-government model that is supposed to shape this space in the future is, according to eMNSGC officers, infused by total quality management ideas, the ideals of lean and inclusive government, and the conception of open, ethical and responsible government. It is supposed to create proactive, flexible and reliable government, in particular by enhancing on-line citizen services and aligning local, state, regional and federal services.

These programmatic claims about the role of e-modernization are clearly anchored in particular problematizations of Mexico's past and an attempt to establish the inevitability of innovation. Public administration in Mexico has historically been known as formalistic and inefficient, characterized by the absence of transparency and administrative accountability (Hansen, 1998; 2002). A large number of forms – *trámites* – and complex filing and renewal procedures have not only made business activity a difficult affair, but also made citizen confidence in government very difficult. After Mexico became a member of the OECD in 1994, the Ernesto Zedillo administration (1994–2000) launched an ambitious programme of administrative and regulatory reform. Its aim was to diminish bureaucratic red tape through simplification of administrative procedures, to reduce regulatory formalities, to instigate reforms of the legislative frameworks, and to get rid of what has been publicly characterized as the "disease of forms" – tramitis (Kossick, 2003). Tramitis had given rise to vast networks of middlemen and corrupt exchanges as people, generally unaware of how, when, and where to submit forms, saw no other way than to bribe their way through the system. During the Zedillo administration, however, there were few experiments with e-government as a tool to get rid of tramitis, and they were mostly found in local and regional governments. A predecessor of the full-scale national e-strategy under President Fox, the experience from the small state of Colima is cited by Federal officers as one of the important sources of inspiration for what later became the e-Mexico National System (eMNS).

Against the backdrop of the above narrative of governmental mismanagement, and operating with limited financial resources from the government, the eMNSGC has since its creation initiated a number of highly complex and interlinked activities. Overall, these activities reflect a concern with the low levels of Internet access and lack of computer familiarity among Mexicans. First, eMNSGC has set out to enhance connectivity through the development and expansion of a Digital Community Centers (DCCs) network to non-connected communities, with a specific view to connecting all Mexicans to themselves, and to the rest of the world (SCT 2003: 1). An e-Mexico satellite network was launched in June 2003, providing connectivity to 3,200 DCCs covering all municipal heads in Mexico. Agreements have been made with institutions specialized in distance training and with certified programmes to educate so-called facilitators whose task is to induce and help citizens to use the DCC equipment on location. The capacity to "appropriate" information and knowledge technologies is an important aspect of the programme: across the country, local communities are expected to identify and communicate its own needs, in order to assure "that the e-Mexico National System is responding to their needs and develops digital services according to each community" (SCT 2003: 4). Moreover, a so-called Virtual Private Network is being established between all the dependencies of the Federal Public Administration in the country, with a specific view to enhancing processes of "digital sharing" and "effective communication Government to Government, Government to Citizen and Government to Business" (SCT 2003: 3).

Second, e-Mexico National System has developed integrated service platforms on-line – i.e. portals – for citizens. The design of the service platforms is informed by the following "core values": Top-down design, bottom-up implementation; national coverage; private and public participation; privacy and security usage; reliable services; integration of Mexican social and ethical values, and community-based operations. These platforms address six areas and sets of objectives: (i) e-Learning, to provide new tools for accessing knowledge, education and training; (ii) e-Health, to increase the general welfare by providing the Mexican population with health information, obviating the obstacles to the access to the health services; (iii) e-Economy, to accelerate the development of the digital economy in micro, small and medium sized businesses, and to stimulate a "digital services culture, using digital sharing processes and promoting value chains and synergies that can drive the country to the New Economy" (SCT 2003: 2); (iv) e-Government, to allow all Mexicans at the municipal, local, regional and federal levels "to exercise their right to be informed" and to get "access to the services provided by the different government levels. Also, the State, by means of the different government instances, reassumes its duty of assuring all the population their access to the information related to the public administration"; (v) e-Communities with shared interests, such as indigenous people, migrants, women, handicapped and senior citizens communities among others; and finally, (vi) other e-Services, such as emergency and security services, employment, etc.

One of the key concepts in the philosophy of e-Mexico is the digital sharing process. Digital sharing is not only evaluated in terms of its content, i.e. to what degree it improves the quality of government and the social and economic well being among Mexicans. It is also seen as an important component in the process of connecting Mexico to the wider world. In a broader sense, the digital sharing process is knowledge sharing. Such practices of knowledge sharing are expected to contribute to changing social problems into opportunities, and to converting people's needs into services. The knowledge sharing of the e-MNSG embraces a variety of actors and includes the formal assistance that e-Mexico receives from international agencies, academic institutions, and corporate sponsored IT training programs provided by key IT actors such as Microsoft and Intel (Islas and Gutierrez, 2003). Further, knowledge sharing comprises initiating activities and assuming leading roles in arrangements such as the Latin American Digital Cities Network, engagement in formalized multilateral organizations such as the World Bank and the UN, as well as participation in the World Summit of the Information Society. The e-MNSG, the task force and coordinating unit, also collaborates with officials and specialists from countries such as Korea, Singapore, Malaysia, Sweden, England and Namibia. Relations with Asian countries are viewed as particularly useful: "Their working culture is slightly different from ours – it does our up-and-coming guys good to see how hard and how long hours these people work."

Importantly however, digital sharing is also defined as learning from international best practices and award programmes. When we accessed the e-Mexico Portal in May 2004, its news section on the front page contained the following message: *e-México: Finalista en Stockholm Challenge*. One more mouse click and the following details popped up:

> This year, the e-Mexico Portal has been selected as finalist in the e-government category and will be competing with other prominent cases. This symbolizes the progress in the use of better technologies in government. On the other hand, it also positions the portal as a unique government project in

Latin America, with its focus on the citizen and its high social impact (http://www.e-mexico.gob.mx/wb2/eMex/eMex_Premio_Stockholm, accessed on 7 May 2004, our translation).

While surfing the e-Mexico Portal's news section, we also discovered that another governmental web portal, organized under the eMNSGC, had been selected for the Stockholm race, namely the Citizens Portal. The screen reads:

The Federal Government's Citizen Portal (www.gob.mx) has received international recognition by being selected as a finalist in the e-government category of the Stockholm Challenge 2003-4. In this way, e-Mexico and gob.mx will represent our country in the award, to which more than 900 projects from 107 countries had been submitte ... among the criteria for selecting the finalist stand out innovation, necessity (relevance), accessibility, transferability and, in particular, the promotion of democracy ... it is an honor that the Citizens Portal has been chosen as one of the 24 finalists ... the award jury, which is international and composed of experts from all over the world, has after a thorough process chosen the finalists of what is an important award in the realm of the Internet ... (http://www.e-mexico.gob.mx/wb2/eMex/ eMex_eGobierno_Finalista_en_Estocolmo#, accessed on 7 May 2004, our translation).

Thus, while founding its mission, visions and organizational rationale on the perception of Mexican public administration as being in a process of fundamental and necessary innovation, the eMNSGC insists on the potential societal advantages of getting Mexico e-modernized. Providing information about the international recognition of Mexican state institutions in the realm of e-government is an important ingredient of the language of change and innovation that has characterized Mexico since the 1990s. From another perspective, it also demonstrates how Mexican state institutions depend on the clout of international entities to certify the efforts being made. In this respect, the submission of the e-Mexico Portal to the Stockholm Challenge competition speaks for itself: it suggests that the Mexican government considers international orientation and authorization of its e-modernization a strategic resource. At a more general level, it indicates awareness of how government organizations increasingly rely on the creation of globalizing webs that facilitate the construction of their political authority, both at home and abroad.

The City of Næstved

The City of Næstved, a provincial Danish city located on Southern Zealand with app. 47,000 inhabitants,[4] has for a number of years been particularly attentive to e-modernization as a vehicle for implementing Information Society. In contrast to the Mexican study, e-modernization in Næstved is not primarily cast as a panacea for curing bureaucratic diseases such as governmental corruption, or re-creating citizens' confidence in the state. In Næstved, the case for e-modernization is argued with reference to its benign implications for learning and knowledge production and knowledge sharing. Knowledge sharing was also articulated in Mexico, but subsumed under an overall and all-embracing state innovation project.

On closer inspection, it turns out that the City of Næstved is strongly engaged in e-projects and collaborative e-efforts both in Denmark and abroad. The engagement in globalizing webs commits members of the municipality to contributing to creating and showcasing best/good practices, identifying new ways and exchanging knowledge. One compelling example is Næstved's submission of e-governance projects to the Stockholm Challenge 2004. Another is its membership of Telecities, a major European network of cities "committed to leadership in the Information and Knowledge Society". These activities indicate that the global orientation of Næstved's activities is important. The accounts we heard stressed that, in Næstved, the particular constellation of senior officers and politicians over the last 10 years, is the key to the strategic role that transnational networking has played as a vehicle for e-modernization. A special responsibility rests with the Chief Officer who must ensure that the international activities the city engages in are communicated and translated to relevant units and committees in the organization. If networking is to be invested with meaning, to be a vehicle of knowledge sharing, benchmarking and thus steering, politicians and employees must relate to it and take ownership of the rationalities and practices that constitute the common, if diffuse, denominator of the network activities.

A recent survey of the 79 biggest Danish local governments suggests that only a third of the respondents consider international engagement of consequence for their daily business (Salskov-Iversen, 2005). The rest readily accepts that internationalization is an important factor with major implications also for sub-national government, but sees it essentially as a top-down phenomenon, not something that a local government can or should relate to proactively. The pros and cons revolve around two discourses: the pros draw on a knowledge society discourse, stressing the strategic implications of reaching out, of learning, of networking, while the cons draw on a discourse

---

[4] As per December 1st 2004, before the implementation of a major local government reform, redrawing the boundaries of most Danish municipalities.

which stresses concerns about it's-a-waste-of-tax-earners' money. Næstved clearly belongs to the one third of local governments that consider international orientation a strategic resource. These are the grounds given by Næstved for submitting projects to the Stockholm Challenge and, more generally, being internationally networked:

> Because we have something to share with other organizations. And because, no matter whether you are nominated or not, by the time you have submitted a project, you have become so much more knowledgeable about your own organization. Everytime we do this, we bring the project before the relevant political committee, to engage them and demonstrate to them how we work with this tool, to create political ownership of the process. The Danish cultural institution known as the Jante Law[5] is a real killer when it comes to using excellence as an organizational driver. In Næstved we insist that our politicians go abroad once in a while and project the municipality and experience that by international standards we are doing a good job, and bring back valuable new ideas. It's quite amazing what you can get from spending 895 DKR on a Virgin ticket (interview with Næstved senior officer, February 2004).

Clearly, Næstved's submission of projects to the Stockholm Challenge is brought into play differently in this locality than in the Mexican case. For Næstved, the Challenge initiative may not in itself seem so consequential, partly because Næstved was not nominated. But, when put into context, Næstved's submission tells two other stories: first, it is indicative of a certain mindset on the part of the leading politicians and officers, an awareness of the dynamics of translation in transnational networking. Second, its organizational implications become more far-reaching when you realize that engaging in the Challenge is not an isolated phenomenon, that it flows from Næstved's involvement in other transnational networks (some of whom, as we shall see, owe their beginnings to the Stockholm Challenge), notably Telecities, since November 2004 a sub-network of Eurocities (www.eurocities.org).

Næstved's membership of Telecities was a result of its gradual recognition of the limits of e-modernization experience and knowledge in Denmark. In 1997–98, when Næstved opened its Service Centre, the municipality worked together with four other Danish state institutions to explore and generate innovative e-government. In 1998–99 the city realized that the outcome of these efforts did not justify the investment, and that it needed a platform from where it could contribute to the development of either national or European information and communication technology standards. Næstved's

---

[5] The "Jante Law" ten commandments begin with "Thou shall not believe thou *art* something". Jante is a fictive Danish town in the 1933 novel by Axel Sandemose, *A Fugitive Crosses His Tracks*, published in English by Alfred A. Knopf in 1936.

subsequent participation in a project designed to create a common Danish framework for e-administrative solutions was also found too narrow in its scope and potential. Næstved then seriously began to target a European platform, applying for EU project funds. The city succeeded in getting funds, and got involved in Telecities. Telecities has ever since proved an important vehicle for tapping into the sort of rich and diverse network that the city had been looking for, and which is today the main plank of its international activities. And it has over the years steadily increased Næstved's engagement in and appetite for web entrepreneurship – the latest example being its bid for fame and exposure through the Stockholm and Dubai Challenges (a sister award).

The sustainability, and by implication, perceived value, of these global activities is a key concern: Næstved and other state institutions can cite examples of contacts and networks that somehow faded out, or never really got off the ground, and, in so doing, discredited the authors of the initiatives. A critical factor, then, is successfully to connect these initiatives, channels and fora to specific people in the organization. The knowledge that is appropriated must be ploughed back into the organization where it matters, not least to test Næstved's own approaches, to feed hands-on experience from its frontline service back into the web, and to identify partnerships that can help develop the city. If this is not carefully attended to, the global engagement cannot as readily, if at all, be mobilized as a source of legitimacy and authority when specific actions and initiatives are being introduced and implemented in the organization.

Despite the effort that Næstved's senior officers and leading politicians put into connecting and involving the practitioners and councillors to e.g. the Telecities activities, the city's international engagement is not uncontested. Among the proponents, this is a cause of concern, because it suggests an inherent hesitance, or even inability, in certain parts of the world of local government, to embrace knowledge society. The role of civil servants, also in local government, is changing towards a more active engagement in problem identification and solving as well as development, not only by way of managing but also by way of networking across institutional and geographical borders and with more emphasis on learning and innovation. Interestingly, in Næstved, this argument is put forward with reference to the OECD and its writings on the correlation between a competent public sector and a strong economy: the public sector must be proactive, innovative, efficient and effective, and to that end it needs to reach out, not only to citizens but also other actors and sectors, to partner and to network. The implication is that traditional administrative traditions and hierarchical systems do not sit easily with the sort of learning mode that underpins the vision of the knowledge society:

Getting permission to consult best practice in Dublin rather than in Fladså can be quite a challenge. Benchmarking, and international benchmarking, may be a fad, but in my opinion it can be a highly effective technology if you get your criteria for comparing and evaluating right, and, importantly, if you accept that there may be room for improvement in your own organization. In its recent report on Learning Regions, the OECD discusses the correlation between success, failure and learning. We could learn a lot from this report. For a municipality, relevant sparring partners and relevant knowledge are not necessarily to be found in the neighboring authorities – what matters are the issues and the parameters according to which these issues are being approached (senior officer, Næstved, February 2004).

In Telecities, Næstved is currently involved in a Charter of e-rights project, an area of high priority in Næstved. The City is concerned that formulating the principles guiding e-privacy should not be left to IT experts or "reactive" public servants. The vision is to provide a free-of-charge e-account for all citizens with their personal data, a daunting task that cuts right across the entire public sector and requires input from many types of actors. The city of Næstved has furthermore committed itself to implementing the e-Europe 2005 Action Plan, which is all about using technology to transform society. Also here is Telecities, and Næstved's chairing of a working group on e-security, e-inclusion and continuous learning, used as a vehicle for driving the city's e-government vision. The strategic framework for the 2004 Telecities programme is the Knowledge-based City. Næstved is taking part in a benchmarking project, co-led by Deloitte, on how cities use technology to develop their local communities.

Næstved's mayor also participates in COR (Committee of the Regions), one of the platforms that reinforces the city's transnational connectedness: "Here you meet some of the same people, the same politicians", a Næstved officer says, just as in The Global Cities Dialogue, a forum that has in part emerged from the Stockholm Challenge network (as has Telecities) and that focuses on the political level rather than on the hands-on and how-to-do-it level (as does Telecities). Næstved is not a member of the Global Cities Dialogue,[6] but is on its steering committee, as an observer, on behalf of Telecities[7]. Together, all these networks with their overlapping membership and regular interface work to strengthen the voice of local city governments in e-Europe; and to inscribe those who are active and visible in these circuits in their respective local contexts.

---

[6] The City has, however, formally decided to apply for membership at some point in the not too distant future.

[7] Some cities are members both places, and then there are Eris@ (the European Regional Information Society Association) and ELANET (which operates under the umbrella of the CEMR, the council of European Municipalities and Regions focusing on the deployment of Information Society at the regional and local level), sister networks of Telecities.

We have now seen how two very different public sector organizations use the Stockholm Challenge as an integrated part of their efforts to e-modernize their respective organizations and the way they service their respective citizens. In both cases, e-modernization is part of a wider narrative on knowledge society, which concerns the demands and opportunities that public sector organizations and their environments are facing, and in both cases we see how this story is translated into specific organizational activities and arrangements. We have also seen that the two organizations clearly do not constitute a community or share a particular destiny – they are as far apart as one can possibly imagine: the translation of e-modernization follows local dynamics and logics. However, they both avail themselves of the same globalizing web – a kind of non-fixed and incomplete organizational arrangement – and in the process, they also engage socially with professionals and e-enthusiasts from far-flung corners of the world. In the next section we will turn our attention to the Stockholm Challenge, to see what it is that this kind of organization can offer those who enroll, and its own reasons for playing the role as a node and thus facilitating the globalizing web in the first place.

Stockholm Challenge

The Stockholm Challenge owes its beginnings in 1994 to the European Commission and the Bangemann Report as well as to Sweden and the City of Stockholm, each of whom, at different stages of its life, have used the Challenge as a vehicle for promoting particular agendas. The EU used it as one of many initiatives[8] designed to instill and disseminate an information society culture across Europe. Thus, from 1994–96 the competition went under the title of the Bangemann Challenge, and was limited to eliciting best practice in Europe. From 1997–1999 it was continued as the Global Bangemann Challenge, in a larger international format. In 1999 the City of Stockholm, which had hosted the competition since its inception as part of its efforts to carve out a name for itself in the EU, took over entirely and the Stockholm Challenge Award was born. From 1999 and up till 2004 the

---

[8] Over the years, the EU has, in similar vein, spawned or indirectly supported several other fora in order to stimulate and advance new information and communication technologies across Europe, including the eEurope initiative (launched by the European Commission in December 1999 with the objective of bringing Europe on-line) and the related eEurope Awards (funded by the Commission and aiming at highlighting best practices, disseminating and sharing new concepts and ideas in the areas of eGovernment and eHealth); ELANET and Eris@ (see note 7); and IntelCities, a research and technological development project, led by the Cities of Manchester and Siena, bringing together eighteen European cities, twenty ICT companies (including Nokia and Cisco) and thirty-six research groups – the project is part of the European Union's Sixth Framework Programme, with a 6.8 m Euro budget from the EU's Information Society Technologies programme.

Challenge has thus been an integrated part of the City of Stockholm's continued efforts to consolidate its steadily growing reputation as a high technology hub[9], just as the Challenge also has acquired a reputation in its own right as a prestigious and authoritative "clearing house for the best and brightest ideas in the area of municipal information technology" (Stockholm Challenge 2002).

As an award programme for pioneering e-modernization projects world wide, the Challenge has established 6 different categories: e-government, culture, health, education, environment and e-business. Five people in a small office in central Stockholm manage the Award programme. It runs yearly and is open to already operating projects from the public, private and academic sectors. A 20–30-person jury composed of acknowledged ICT experts, in the beginning mostly from the US but in recent years from all over the world, chooses the finalists. The finalists are showcased at the annual Final Events, which also include seminars, workshops and other networking activities. Importantly, the winners of the award do not receive any monetary prices. But even if all finalists cannot get an award, "everybody is a winner".

The media effect of participation is receiving particular emphasis by the Stockholm Challenge. In the FAQ section, 'Why meet the Challenge?' is answered in the following way:

> The Stockholm Challenge gives projects the opportunity to participate in a fantastic networking activity where IT entrepreneurs and enthusiasts from all over the world meet and showcase their best solutions. Through exposure to media, politicians and venture capitalists, the Stockholm Challenge gives excellent promotional opportunities for entrepreneurs, universities, cities, regions and countries[10].

For participants, submitting a project to the annual award programme is thus believed to serve several purposes: a learning experience, a driver for organizational development and an important instance of external communication. And the reputation factor is important. Winners consider Stockholm Challenge as one of the most prestigious award rallies.[11] Some of the entries are clearly 'accomplished performers', 'beacons' and 'pathfinders', appearing in several both national and transnational best practice and

---

[9] For a discussion of city image construction in Stockholm, Warsaw and Rome, see Czarniawska, 2002; for a discussion of Stockholm as an ICT city and the origins of the Stockholm Challenge, see Dobers, 2002, 2003.

[10] http://www.challenge.stockholm.se/faq_right.asp, January 17, 2003.

[11] For example, after the Citizen Portal of the Mexican Federal Government turned out as the 2004 winner of the category of e-government on 13 May 2004, it was established on the portal that the government had received an important international recognition "considered the Nobel of the Internet", see www.gob.mx.

benchmarking/ranking schemes, i.e. organizations/institutions for whom participation is a very strategic choice. Examples include Singapore, Hong Kong, the City of Phoenix, the City of Seattle, Barcelona, and, yes, Stockholm.

In the spring of 2004, the parenthood of the Stockholm Challenge changed again – in the future it will no longer be run by the City of Stockholm. The team in the City of Stockholm Economic Development Agency who had run the Challenge since 1997 summed up the development as follows:

> In Bangemann's time, only cities could submit projects. This changed after two years when the City of Stockholm took over. At the time, Stockholm realized that an important step towards success in ICT was sharing and accessing knowledge in international networks. The Stockholm Challenge was one of the tools to make Stockholm known as an ICT city, now that's done. We have achieved the reputation factor. These days we don't run the Challenge for Stockholm, we don't do it for the City of Stockholm, there are other networks working for Stockholm. Still, we are doing all this for the tax payers' money – at this point, we don't have to run the Challenge ourselves any longer, and that's why we have externalized the running of it to a partnership, with ourselves as one of the four partners, i.e. the new IT University and two major Stockholm-based companies, one of them is a very important regional actor … and these days much organizational innovation in Stockholm is based on the public-private partnership model. So this development is almost what could be expected.
>
> The IT University will be the new home of the Stockholm Challenge, we, i.e. the City of Stockholm, will still host the annual award event. Even though the plans have not been signed yet, the IT University will prefer the Challenge to focus more on the 3rd world, and more on technology, less on 'best practice' and the broader organizational implications of applying ICTs. ICT is central to the IT University, for them it is a way to renew their research agenda.[12]

What we get here is a glimpse of the dynamics that keep a loose and unstable assemblage like the Challenge afloat, and by implication, the dynamics that maintain its governmental capacity: namely the continuous negotiation and adjustment of its rationale, organization, anchorage and membership so as to ensure that it can accommodate whatever configuration of persons, organizations and objectives that constitute it at any given point of time. The latest sequel of its history thus reflects a gradual departure from its original orientation, namely e-modernization in the EU and the remainder of the OECD world, in recent years with a clear predominance of entries from the

---

[12] Interview with the Stockholm Challenge in Stockholm, January 2004.

English speaking world,[13] towards an "ICT for Development" orientation, focusing on the potential of ICT in boosting development in the developing countries and connecting them to the developed world. It should be noted, though, that both orientations are embedded in an e-modernization discourse, which has a certain utopian streak to it (Fountain, 2001; Wittel, 2001):

> The Stockholm Challenge is unique since it provides room for both technically advanced and simple solutions, each of which is judged according to its specific context. This enables projects from both developing and industrial countries to compete on equal terms. Through the Challenge, a large number of very inspiring initiatives from all over the world have been made known. Over the years the Stockholm Challenge has accumulated more than 2,500 projects from all parts of the world. Many contacts have been made between pioneers in different countries all over the world. By highlighting some of the best projects, the Stockholm Challenge helps bring out new models for the information society of tomorrow. The experience of the Stockholm Challenge demonstrates that imaginative and generous ways are possible. In the Challenge you meet the forerunners of "digital democracy" (http://www.challenge.stockholm.se/about April 21, 2004).

Still, there are indications that its new developing world orientation causes some sadness to the outgoing management of the Challenge because, even if there will be some overlap, invariably, it will become a different network, brought together by a somewhat different set of objectives and world views. And according to our respondents, in a network like the Challenge, it is the "people" thing that is crucial for its operation. What the people in the Challenge have shared so far captures the "spirit of the challenge", which is all about one purpose: "Doing something good for the world".

Meanwhile, the former owners of the challenge are busy shifting their energy into other fora, some of which they have co-launched themselves. Firstly, the Challenge has spawned a number of "baby challenges", addressing either particular regional or professional themes, e.g. the Global Junior Challenge (education), the Chile Challenge, the Dubai Challenge. The Challenge is also the co-founder of two other e-networks, Telecities and the Global Cities Dialogue, both of which are committed to promoting e-modernization. Similarly, the EU has conceived and co-initiated a whole raft of different e-fora (see note 8). So, while there is clearly a sense in which the people who used to inhabit the Challenge are now moving on, as long as they continue to be involved in activities related to the development and pro-

---

[13] In 2002, the number of participating projects was 517, with 71 from the USA, 49 from Australia, 41 from India, 40 from Sweden, 30 from Canada, 25 from Italy, 19 from the UK, 15 from the United Arab Emirates, 11 from Bulgaria and 11 from Spain.

motion of e-modernization, the chances are that they will meet the very people they used to meet via the Challenge. In other words, once they have joined this globalizing web with overlapping memberships, they are on the eCircuit, and they have, literally, joined a world wide web of people dedicated to the eCause.

Globalizing Webs in Perspective

There is no doubt that the Mexican and Danish state institutions share a particular relationship to e-modernization, one that is based on broad and programmatic representations of the advent and challenges of the knowledge/information society. In organizational and societal contexts, such representations are translated and edited for specific purposes, such as internal organizational reengineering and modifications of public sector relations with citizens. While our two state institutions are translating more or less coherent conceptions of e-modernization into organizational practices, they also contribute to the formation of a globalizing web, which provides them with symbolic resources to be capitalized on.

Globalizing webs provide linkages to forces, actors and entities that act beyond the national purview of each actor. Our two state institutions have latched onto some of the international and transnational actors who elicit, share and co-produce knowledge about how best to govern, and e-modernization is certainly a vision on offer. In this sense, translation is what happens when actors like our state institutions are able to count upon a particular way of thinking and acting from other actors, such as transnational actors. The very diversity of the actors enrolled clearly suggests that membership is not in any way conditioned on being concerned about the same issues. What does matter, though, is that the problems, challenges, missions and opportunities faced by these actors can be envisioned and articulated in broadly similar ways, albeit without the goal coherence of strategic alliances. So, what we have here is a kind of fluid organizational arrangement, one that that brings "persons, organizations, entities and locales which remain differentiated by space, time and formal boundaries … into a loose and approximate, and always mobile and indeterminate alignment" (Miller and Rose, 1990: 10). By calling such indeterminate alignments globalizing webs, we assume that any social and political ordering is created from complex networks of localized social and technical practices which link calculations and actions in one place with calculations and actions in another place.

That these webs are globalizing may seem a trivial observation, but it is not. First, as we have seen, globalizing webs articulate a discourse of knowledge, which offers a view of why and how to make the world manageable in a context of globalization (Higgott et al., 2000). Second, globalizing webs challenge conventional distinctions between the inside and the outside of the nation-state. Their existence endorses the view that states are not unified but disaggregated actors.[14] In fact, they connect state institutions across this distinction, across local and national levels of state and relate them to a host of very different actors, including non-state actors and hybrids, indeterminable organizational forms that do not match conventional distinctions between the public and private, such as the Stockholm Challenge, which is organized as a partnership. In other words, globalizing webs can be seen as one organizational instantiation of how social processes are increasingly unhindered by territorial and jurisdictional barriers and enhance the spread of transborder practices in economic, political and social domains (Higgott et al., 2000). Third, globalizing webs also have an important technological dimension, as they incorporate and deploy the new information and communication technologies across the boundaries of persons, households, institutions, and public and private spaces. In this way they disrupt and reconfigure the boundedness of states, which has been central to modern political imagination (Barry, 2001: 20). We would argue that it is the relative indeterminacy, incoherence, mobility, alignment, combined with the intensive use of new information and communication technologies, which make our globalizing webs distinctive from the more focused political networks, knowledge networks, epistemic communities and transnational discourse communities referred to in much recent research.

The Stockholm Challenge is one of the many nodes in the globalizing web of e-modernization that brings together otherwise very different state institutions, such as eMexico and the City of Næstved, around a common cause, namely to further the creation of a knowledge/information society for everyone through e-modernization. Thus, while the fairly general and wide-ranging vision of e-modernization establishes a certain frame for action, a certain direction, it also offers those who eventually engage in it a globalizing web with a multitude of takes and positions to be harnessed in ways that are consonant with the particular aspirations and agendas of the entities in question. Viewed as a node in the globalizing web of e-modernization, the Stockholm Challenge reflects not only how e-modernization is at the heart of many governments' reform programmes, but also how the adaptation of e-modernization to the existing governance architecture to a large extent is being facilitated by entities from outside traditional government, including the private sector, and not least, by transnational organizational forms such as the Stockholm Challenge.

---

[14] For a discussion of the "disaggregation of the state", and "a disaggregated world order", see Slaughter, 2004.

In this chapter, authority has been understood as relational and as something that has to be made.[15] This position stands somewhat in contrast to the more conventional theories of power and authority that emphasize control over resources and sovereignty (e.g. Lukes, 1986), and it is controversial insofar as it implies that the accumulation of wealth (business), the control over territories, the physical means of violence (the state) and the existence of delegated power (ministers, judges) are irrelevant for the construction of authority. However, our point here is not to support the claim that power cannot be possessed or accumulated, nor to underestimate the importance of coercive power, but rather to illustrate how the effectiveness at enrolling others to one's project can be a very important, if not decisive, factor in the construction of authority: "Those who exercise the greatest power are those who enroll many others with more resources than themselves, and, more importantly, those who enroll others who are even better at enrolling others than themselves" (Braithwaite and Drahos, 2000: 482).

Both Mexican and Danish state institutions rely not only on their legal and institutional status as state entities, but also on the chain of actors that make up the globalizing webs. When tapping into and using the symbolic resources of the globalizing web, for example by submitting projects for award rallies, the Mexican and Danish state institutions also recognize purportedly non-political actors such as the Stockholm Challenge. For one thing, by showcasing best practice, by benchmarking and by celebrating excellence in the field of e-modernization backed by specialized and recognized expertise, the hybrid organizational form of Stockholm Challenge shapes, moulds and globalizes a particular understanding of what e-modernization might mean. In the course things, it is being recognized as an authority – an authority, which in the last instance, however, does not count on the same legal and constitutional backcloth as state institutions. It is only based on its certification and promotion of excellence, and on the recognition, legitimacy and prestige it has already gained in the field of e-modernization (Hansen and Salskov-Iversen, 2005).

An organizational form such as the Stockholm Challenge is clearly not in the same league as the OECD, or other heavyweight organizations. But it belongs to a big and steadily growing category of transnational organizational forms operating in the shadow of or entirely outside traditional government, fiercely competing for attention and recognition as an authoritative voice in a particular field. Their role is to offer expertise and knowledge, fora for knowledge sharing and new ideas, and their authority depends on the translation of their offers for its effects.

---

[15] For a similar view, see Latour, 1986; Rose and Miller, 1992; Law and Hetherington, 2000, and Flyvbjerg, 2001.

In other words, the authority of Stockholm Challenge and similar crea-
tures is the consequence of the actions of a chain of agents each of whom
translates, or better transforms a given set of ideas or pieces of knowledge
in accordance with their own intentions and projects. To the extent that
organizational forms such as the Stockholm Challenge manage to enroll,
enlist and align social actors to its purposes, they will gain authority.
However, any process of enrolment will always entail the probability that
competing organizations are doing a better work, or that social actors will
resist or have other objectives than those stipulated by the authority in question. If authority relies on the translation of ideas and the successful enrolment and subscription to these ideas, it will always be imperfect and can
always fade away.

As a final remark, we would like to emphasize that the idea of e-modernization and the closely related practices of global web entrepreneurship
(which is of course not restricted to the field of e-modernization) seems both
to subscribe to and reinforce a particular governance and management
modality. As we indicated in our introduction, (neo) liberal rule is bound to
authorize entities beyond the state. In other words, for the state to govern at
a distance in both social and spatial senses it must operate through the decisions, self-responsibility and self-management of non-state actors or hybrid
organizational forms. In this process, the expertise and voice of organizational forms beyond the state, such as the Stockholm Challenge, may
become authorized. This, in turn, requires translation processes and governmental technologies – both in state and non-state actors, or hybrids –
that ally the objectives of government with the projects and autonomy of
such actors. The globalizing web is one such governmental technology: once
connected, it provides a means to translate ideas with a view to construct
authority and manage organizational reform and societal modernization.

Chapter 13

Close Encounters: The Circulation and Reception of Managerial Practices in the San Francisco Bay Area Nonprofit Community[1]

Walter W. Powell, Denise L. Gammal and Caroline Simard, Stanford University, USA

The processes through which ideas and practices travel have long been of keen interest. Relatively few empirical analyses of diffusion processes, however, consider that the things that are adopted may hold very different meanings for diverse recipients. Indeed, passionate adopters may well interpret and transform objects in a manner that their originators never imagined (Westney, 1987). This chapter attends to the various ways that management ideas circulate across organizations, illuminating the differential reception of ideas. We draw on the concepts of circulation and translation (Czarniawska and Joerges, 1996; Czarniawska and Sevón, 1996; Sahlin-Andersson and Engwall, 2002), and give less weight to the idea of diffusion (Rogers, 1983). Diffusion implies a central broadcast point and wide reception with rather passive receivers, whereas translation implies a more relational and active process of reception. The concepts of circulation and translation recognize that ideas follow various routes and networks, and emphasize the possibility that ideas may be edited in the process of travel.

Stakeholders and managers often search for new ideas that will elevate or distinguish their organizations. The leaders of nonprofit organizations in the United States currently face a convergence of powerful external and internal

[1] Research support provided by the Center for Social Innovation at the Stanford Graduate School of Business, the William and Flora Hewlett Foundation, and the David and Lucile Packard Foundation. We are grateful to Eva Boxenbaum, Greg Dees, Hokyu Hwang, David Suarez, and participants at the Venice conference for comments on an earlier draft. Marc Schneiberg offered useful questions, as did audience members at a seminar at the Stockholm Center for Organizational Research.

pressures that have magnified the appeal of "new" management ideas and practices.[2] First, due to federal and state government cutbacks and retrenchment, there is increased unmet social need. Nonprofits are increasingly called upon to provide social services that are no longer delivered by federal or state governments (Abramson et al., 1999; Salamon, 2002). Second, as government provision declines, both for-profit and nonprofit organizations compete for the markets associated with the provision of social services. In mixed industries, such as health care, daycare, and other human services, where competition between nonprofits and for-profits is strong, increased convergence in organizational behavior has occurred (Mauser, 1998; Schlesinger, 1998; Weisbrod, 1998). Third, the economic downturn of the early 2000s put new pressures on the sector in a double blow: more individuals sought assistance from nonprofits, while shrinking government budgets and foundation endowments increased competition for funding. Finally, governance scandals across all sectors have generated questions about accountability and how best to achieve organizational goals and measure their outcomes.

The United States has the most developed nonprofit sector of any nation. The sector presently employs some twelve million employees, and in 2003, approximately 100 million Americans volunteered, donated to, or worked in the nonprofit sector (Light, 2004). Most employment is concentrated in health care, education, and social services; with volunteers added, religion becomes the most active area (Salamon, 2002). The scale and scope of the sector are due, in large part, to three distinctive factors. The origins of voluntary associations date back to the colonial era, and predate the formation of the U.S. federal government (Hall, forthcoming). Two, federal and state governments rely to a considerable extent on nonprofit organizations to provide public services, a practice Salamon (1987) termed third-party government. Three, the ethnic and religious diversity of the U.S. contributes to considerable organizational heterogeneity (Weisbrod, 1988).

The current amalgamation of social, political, and economic pressures has created a climate ripe for the circulation of ideas and practices across sector boundaries. Both the number of providers of new ideas and the volume of talk have greatly increased. Management consultants, funders, and the news

---

[2] Pressures on nonprofits to become more "business-like" are by no means new in the United States; such challenges have appeared frequently throughout the sector's history (Hall, 1997; 2006). In the early decades of the 20th century, the movement for scientific charity was led by progressives who sought to rationalize the delivery of social services (Lubove, 1965; Mohr and Duquenne, 1997). During the 1920s, champions of scientific management pressed for the adoption of engineering principles in schools, prisons, and social services (Callahan, 1962; Tyack, 1974). In the 1970s and 1980s, leading for-profit consulting firms persuaded many large, national nonprofit organizations to develop strategic plans to modernize their operations (DiMaggio and Powell, 1983; Mintzberg, 1994; McKenna, 2005).

media have pressed nonprofit organizations to become more "accountable" and "efficient" in order to "create value" (Letts et al., 1997; Porter and Kramer, 1999; Dees et al., 2001; Morino Institute, 2001). A new generation of donors and nonprofit leaders, including both "social entrepreneurs" and "venture philanthropists," are eager not only to share their wealth but also their management expertise with the social sector. Many key funders have become vocal proponents of a social return on investment, accountability, and outcome measurement. Ideas about efficiency, scalability, and performance measures, common to the realm of for-profit management, are currently popular in nonprofit circles. The aim of such efforts is well intentioned, to aid nonprofits in delivering services more effectively and spending money more wisely. Whether such efforts are novel or efficacious is the subject of much debate (Katz, 2004).

Nonprofits are not, however, equally exposed to these new ideas and practices. The transfer of business practices is mediated through divergent patterns of interaction, and shaped by key organizational characteristics. While external events and actors may pressure nonprofits to adopt new ideas and practices, internal pressures such as financial crises or the desire to grow also spur some managers to actively seek ways to change and enhance their organizations. And the increasing professionalization of the nonprofit labor force – itself a response to external demands – renders nonprofit executives much more active seekers and consumers of new methods of organizing.

Using data from the Internal Revenue Service, the U.S. taxation authority, provided by the National Center for Charitable Statistics, we drew a random sample of 200 organizations out of the nearly 10,000 nonprofits operating in the ten-county San Francisco Bay Area of Northern California. This region has a population of more than seven million, including the three urban centers of San Francisco, Oakland, and San Jose, as well as the surrounding suburban and rural areas. The organizations in our sample range from small, "minimalist" organizations to very large, diversified enterprises with multi-million dollar budgets. All quotes presented below are drawn from interviews with the executive directors.

In the next section, we present our ideas about the transfer of organizational methods and efforts at the emulation of organization practices. Drawing from our material from detailed interviews with the executive directors of 200 organizations,[3] we develop a range of ideal types that match specific organizational characteristics with patterns of exposure to managerial ideas. We then present five cases that illuminate these ideal types. We turn next to comparisons across the cases, abstracting from them to develop more general arguments about processes of emulation and resistance. We conclude with a summary and discussion of the implications of our work.

---

[3] For a more detailed description of the study, see Hwang and Suarez in this volume.

The Transfer of Managerial Practices

What factors determine the popularity and influence of managerial practices and the receptiveness of different organizations toward such ideas? Early statements in new-institutional analysis suggested that tension and contestation between sources of authority and expertise and organizations were not uncommon. Meyer and Rowan (1977) drew on Goffman's (1967) imagery of the contrast between front and back stage activities to argue that internal features of organizations were often loosely coupled with the more conformist or ceremonial poses that organizations adopted toward the external environment. DiMaggio and Powell (1983) noted that normative, coercive, and mimetic influences rarely occurred in isolation; rather these forces comingled, and often generated muddled organizational responses. Scott (1987) and Powell (1991) observed that divergent external pressures often triggered internal conflict within organizations.

Research designs that capture multiple external influences and their resulting cross-cutting and contradictory internal effects are by no means easy to develop, however. As commentators have noted, most empirical institutional analyses opted, quite sensibly, to focus on a single mechanism of institutionalization or to analyze the spatial diffusion of a specific practice (Mizruchi and Fein, 1999; Schneiberg and Clemens, 2005). Such research strategies, however, resulted in portraits of organizations and nation states as rather pliant or conformist. In response to this overly static imagery, scholars have turned attention to the dynamics of institutional change. Friedland and Alford (1991) were an important influence here, stressing that much of modern life is characterized by the rival institutional logics of the family, market, polity, and church. These logics serve as organizing principles, spelling out vocabularies of motives, courses of action, and conceptions of identity. This insight led a number of researchers to examine the processes by which a dominant logic erodes and is challenged by an alternative that is eventually triumphant. Davis et al. (1994) analyzed the dismantling of the conglomerate corporate form and its replacement by a leaner and more focused form. Scott et al. (2000) captured the transition in health care from a professional era of doctors and patients to a business model of health care providers and customers. Thornton (2004) studied the transition from family to market capitalism in college book publishing and the attendant decline of editorial power and the rise in the influence of marketing departments.

Perhaps the most extensive study of the borrowing of organizational practices is Westney's (1987) analysis of Meiji Japan's deliberate emulation of Western organizational models between 1868 and 1912. This remarkable societal transformation saw Japan model its navy on the British, its police on the French, the banking system on the American model, and its post office on the British. Standard accounts of this modernization process have characterized the Meiji adoptions through the metaphors of either the "rational shopper" or the "clever little copier" but Westney carefully documented that even the most assiduous efforts at emulation often result in alterations of the original patterns in order to adjust them to the new context. For example, Japan first modeled its army on the French, but then shifted to the German; the educational system cycled through a series of exemplars, first the French, then the American, and finally the German system. Moreover, while the Japanese were emulating and adapting, Westney notes that all the major Western powers were going through a period of extensive organization building on their own, thus the models the Japanese emissaries took back home quickly became dated pictures of their original sources.

These various excellent studies all draw on rich longitudinal data sets, taking a long view that affords insight into how a dominant logic is replaced by an alternative one. Viewed in this perspective, institutional change might appear to be inexorable. In contrast, micro-level ethnographic studies of institutionalization processes offer vivid portraits of fluidity and tension, highlighting a more conflictual and interpretive account of institutional dynamics (Elsbach, 1994; Alexander, 1996; Phillips and Hardy, 1997; Oakes et al. 1998; Creed et al., 2002). These studies emphasize contestation and struggle over the symbols that provide legitimating accounts of organizational activities. Both perspectives are deeply rooted in their respective research designs, and the choice of "thinner" over-time quantitative data or "thicker" short-term qualitative observations can color the interpretations that are advanced. Recognition of how much methodological preferences can shape analytical accounts has not been widespread, however. Too often, these different perspectives are posed as "theory contests" or "family squabbles" and the critical analytical differences glossed over (see, for example, Hirsch and Lounsbury, 1997).

A line of research advanced by Nordic management scholars focuses on processes of translation and circulation (Czarniawska and Sevón, 1996; Sahlin-Andersson and Engwall, 2002). Using a metaphor of travel, these scholars stress that the transfer of ideas is highly interactive, with diverse means of transportation carrying ideas from one setting to another. In this process of travel, ideas are frequently edited, translated, and cobbled together from various sources for idiosyncratic use. Moreover, Sahlin-Andersson and Engwall (2002) point out that management itself is a rather diffuse concept, one not tied to a specific content or meaning. Rather, management is a process dependent upon where, how, and by whom managerial activities are conducted. Such openness affords entry by all manner of practitioners, and thus the expansion of management knowledge in recent times has led to rapid growth in models, procedures, and purported solutions, as well as a proliferation of management consultants, publications, professional schools, and researchers. The management field is rife with ideas and tools that diverse carriers can package and circulate. We draw on these ideas to develop an analytical framework to study the transfer of managerial practices within and across sectors.

Our goal is to account for the differential receptivity or resistance by nonprofits to pressures for greater accountability and the adoption of business-like practices. We highlight the ways in which various influences and tools are linked to specific types of carriers and receivers. For example, when organizations belong to professional associations and sector organizing groups, there are strong normative pressures to consider certain practices. Thus, executive directors we have interviewed frequently mention professional intermediaries, such as nonprofit capacity-building groups or trade associations, as being a fertile source of new management ideas and practices.[4] One such intermediary that provides support and training for the sector advertises upcoming seminars on strategic restructuring, best practice, and effective meetings on its website, promoting a specific image of what it means to be well-managed.[5] Not all nonprofits are equally exposed to and influenced by management professionals, however. Community-based volunteer organizations, for example, may be unlikely to belong to a professional nonprofit association and therefore less likely to experience such normative influences.

Demands to implement specific ideas can sometimes be imposed. For example, our interviews reveal frequent instances of management practices dictated as a *sine qua non* condition for fiscal support. Diverse funders – government, foundations, venture philanthropists, and others – push ardently for the pursuit of specific practices. Such practices might include independent financial audits, accounting methods, strategic plans, or outcome measurements, to name but a few. Nonetheless, even when coerced, nonprofits can translate requirements in variable ways. Again, depending on nonprofits' need for a specific source of funding and the realm of activity in which they operate, nonprofits are more or less likely to be receptive to such demands.

In the course of more than 200 interviews with the directors of San Francisco Bay Area nonprofits, we found vivid examples of "encounters" between organizations, steeped in an expressive logic of volunteerism, participation, and charity, and forces, both internal and external to the organization, that call for economies of scale, a focus on income generation, and a more instrumental logic. Our sampling strategy was based on a random

---

[4] Scott (2003) suggests that intermediaries, ranging from government agencies to international organizations to labor unions to securities analysts, play a powerful role in shaping the transfer of ideas. See also Hedmo *et al.* in this volume.

[5] See www.cen.org, Center for Excellence in Nonprofits.

sample of the Bay Area operating charities population, but for our purposes in this chapter, we focus on five revealing cases drawn from our interviews that illustrate key dimensions of these encounters. We use these particular organizations and their experiences to develop illustrations of divergent organizational responses to contact with managerial ideas. Put differently, the views, positions, and influences captured by each case represent an ideal type, in the Weberian sense.[6] We specify key criteria by which the organizations and their contacts with external parties differ.

Four elements constitute the dimensions on which our ideal types vary. One feature is the *carrier* of the idea. Individual carriers can range from the passionate originator of an idea, to a convert or disciple who transplants the idea, to a consultant who adapts the idea to a specific context in return for compensation. The *context* in which practices travel is a second element. Some circumstances have a coercive aspect, as when a funder stipulates a consultant must be engaged if financial support is to be obtained. The venue of consulting lends itself to reception, as both the expert and client are bound together in common endeavor. Professional training, executive education, and conferences are sites where managers are both exposed to and searching for new ideas, and are subject to common normative influences as members of a field. Finally, professional journals, the Internet, the business press, and the op-ed pages of local newspapers are venues where ideas are promulgated and given a diffuse notion of legitimacy.

Aside from the carriers and the context, the *object* itself is, of course, important. The degree of tangibility of an artifact, its codification, portability, and fit with existing practices can render a new management tool more or less accessible. A fourth factor is the temporal and experiential nature of *contact*, which shapes adoption and translation. Encounters that are one-shot events have less impact than enduring repeated exchanges. Contacts with originators or their apostles are more direct and vivid than indirect exposure through professional consultants that have re-packaged or translated an idea.

An organization's mission is critical as well, as mission provides an interpretive lens through which practices are assessed. For example, a small, consensus-driven, all-volunteer nonprofit may resist developing a formal organizational chart because of its egalitarian culture, yet readily agree to institute annual independent financial audits as a condition for receiving government funding. An organization highly dependent on foundation grant money may be under more pressure to implement outcome measurement tools than an organization that relies solely on membership dues or individ-

---

[6] By ideal type, we mean a set of experiences that accurately capture a coherent and distinctive encounter. An ideal type is a typification, not an ideal in the sense of exemplary or a statistical average.

ual donations. Depending on the set of influences and the mediating organizational characteristics, managerial practices will be rejected, instituted, or translated in divergent ways.

These four dimensions combine to shape differential patterns of receptivity and resistance to managerial practices on the part of nonprofit organizations. We draw on these combinatorial patterns to develop a continuum that captures a range of possible responses to managerial ideas. We locate our types on this continuum, characterizing the organizations in the following manner:

– The enthusiastic adopter, an organization that actively seeks out new business models and best practices;

– The converted innocent, that wakes up to discover its *modus operandi* has undergone a marked transformation;

– The engaged translator, an organization intent on putting its own stamp on new business tools;

– The reluctant conformer, an organization forced to consider new practices, only to find itself rebuffed by the very proponents that urged the effort;

– The active resistor, determined to remain distinctive and willing to reject and fashionable ideas in order to hew to its historical mission.

Translation at Work

To explore divergent patterns of reception and resistance, we present examples that reflect the above ideal types.

The enthusiastic adopter

The "Bay Academy" has an annual budget of $15 million, educates a student body of 800, and employs 120 staff.[7] It is one of the largest nonprofit independent schools in the Bay Area and charges tuition of $17,000 per child. The private school field is highly competitive, and Bay Academy needs to maintain near full enrollment to cover its expenses. This earned income represents more than 80 percent of the school's total revenues. According to the head of school, the economic downturn has had little impact on enrollment at Bay Academy: "We lost some people to other schools or, most likely, to geographic relocation ... But we're still able to recruit new people to replace them, so it's not so much that the business is suffering but that the community is changing." Besides a high tuition price and a full enrollment, the school relies on a steady supply of individual gifts, especially from its board. Board members are expected to make significant financial contributions: "They have to give a lot of money. They shouldn't accept a position

---

[7] All names have been changed to preserve the confidentiality of participants in our study.

on the board if they're not prepared to do that." These individual gifts, the tuition rate, as well as more than 8,000 volunteer hours each year from parents, put this school in a stable and enviable financial situation.

The school's staff includes a number of positions designated as "senior management": assistant principals, a chief financial officer (CFO), a director of fundraising, and a director of information technology. Most managers have an education background, with the exception of the CFO (business) and the IT director (engineering). Bay Academy's twenty board members are an equal mix of non-working, well-to-do parents and professionals from the business, accounting, and legal fields.

Encounters. The Bay Academy was exposed to new ideas through its leader, an educator by training: "This is my first appointment as head of a school, and it's the first private school in which I've ever worked." Her lack of leadership experience prompted her to search for tools that would help her succeed in her new environment. Ten years into the job, she has become a veteran administrator who continuously seeks and adopts business ideas. She emphasizes that teachers are often ill prepared to run a school: "I think that for the future of the profession, more and more education leaders should be doing whatever business training they can … We should all do more business training." The head cites an important experience in her professional development while attending an executive education program at the Stanford Graduate School of Business: "I attended a program on leading and managing. It was mostly for-profit managers. This was during the big dot-com year in '98, so I was sitting there with lots of really interesting people, executives from Dell and HP, etc. It was very, very valuable."

The Bay Academy regularly hires consulting firms to bring in fresh ideas and convert them into practice: "We always seem to have a consultant hanging around somewhere." The school hired a national consulting firm specializing in the management of independent schools to develop the school's board training program. The school has found the consultant's input useful to establish a common language for the board and the staff; the consultant "has everyone speaking the same language about board work." The school used another large national consulting firm for fundraising. This firm's self-described mission as fundraising consultants is to help nonprofits' bottom-lines and improve their competitiveness for scarce dollars. Again, the head of school found the encounter quite positive: "It was quite useful in terms of thinking a little bit outside the box in the way we were doing fundraising." The school administration wholeheartedly implements the recommendations brought in from these consultants, and is a firm believer in the practices they carry.

Reception. The ongoing search for management tools has resulted in an abundance of business artifacts that are in regular use at the school. The organization produces a strategic plan, a technology plan, an emergency plan, an annual report, and an organizational chart, to name but a few. The school is an ardent proponent of business strategy and planning. Bay Academy views these practices as crucial to their credibility and reputation. Their strategic plan is used both as a tool for decision-making and as a marketing document for fundraising: "We can go to fundraisers and say, 'These are our goals.' Then you can measure your success as a funder. If you don't have a strategic plan, you're either doing the same old thing or you're floundering a bit." The school uses these business practices to signal its legitimacy to clients and donors. The head repeatedly emphasized that she "would not trust a nonprofit that does not feature business practices."

As someone who is a firm believer in the "best practices," the head also acts as a proselytizer to others in her field. Serving on the board of an international organization for independent schools, she often promotes management practices to a wider audience in her field through presentations and discussions. She developed a lengthy power-point presentation summarizing and promoting many of the concepts she has adopted, including BHAG (Big Hairy Audacious Goal), visionary companies, core values, change-based organizational models, and team building. These concepts were first encountered at the Stanford executive education program. Now the head of school carries these business ideas to other schools.

As the leader of a nonprofit operating in a competitive, elite environment, the head of school is also acutely aware of the non-profit field's desire for more accountability in the wake of recent corporate and nonprofit scandals in the United States: "I think people are becoming much more critical of the product they're buying in the nonprofit environment. Families say to us, 'Tell us what we're getting for the tuition.' They're asking for more accountability." The school also complies with expectations of accountability in order to compete for scarce donors, as foundations demand more evaluations and shift their funding patterns.

The Bay Academy was an early believer in outcome measurement. "We have every kind of measurement. We have language test scores, baccalaureate scores, advanced placement test scores, etc." The school is currently working to develop a comprehensive evaluation database: "We try to track some longitudinal studies on individual students, so you take Student X, track the score from third grade to grade 12 in every domain that they have taken a test and see if you can identify any trends. They you can add different things in, like who was the teacher that particular year, or how big was the class size. We are just building that." Such a longitudinal student achievement database would represent the implementation of one of the most comprehensive educational accountability practices, a further accomplishment for the elite independent school.

The Bay Academy seeks recognition not only as an excellent educational institution, but also for its management practices as well. The organization readily implements new workplace regulations that other nonprofits are unaware of or lack the resources to implement, including regulatory standards for ergonomics in the office, sexual harassment policies, and wage requirements. To stay ahead of the times, the school hired a full-time human relations director:

> I've had to hire an HR director who knows all this stuff. The school never used to have HR directors and business managers ... We had an ergonomic audit and we had to buy this and that for people's necks, arms, backs, ankles, whatever. You just have to keep ahead of that, make sure everybody's workstation is conforming to the rules. Every year there are new regulations and things you have to post to be legally appropriate. We put in a non-harassment policy, whistle blowing, and a fraud policy.

In sum, the Bay Academy is an active adopter, ardently searching for and implementing new ideas that enhance its reputation as state-of-the-art. The executive director is passionate about these efforts and in turn actively urges that other nonprofit leaders follow a comparable strategy.

The converted innocent

"Kids Place," a small, two-year preschool serving about 100 families, encountered new management ideas and practices in the last few years largely by chance. This contact resulted in an organizational transformation that has increased the viability of the school and changed it for the better in many ways. The preschool operates on a budget of $275,000 per year, quite small as preschools go, with more than 90 percent of its budget based on tuition revenues. The remainder of its income is derived from an annual fundraising event. The 30-year-old nonprofit is located in a relatively small rural community.

Until recently, a small board comprised of mothers of children attending the school governed Kids Place. The organization is managed by the executive director and by a part-time financial administrator with four teachers in the classroom. The executive director, who was previously a teacher at the school, noted the typical disservice the childhood development field does to its teachers: "Take a good teacher and turn her into a director, which they have no idea how to do, none." The director spent four years before she felt comfortable in the executive role. During this time, she sought out an introductory management class, driving several hours away to attend the University of California at Davis, to learn how to deal with supervising people who were just recently peers, board relations, and basic organizational processes. The director actively sought out ideas that might help her respond and grow in the executive position she was thrust into. Her openness to new ideas prepared her well for the transformation that was to come.

Encounters. The introduction of new managerial practices at this pre-school came through a transformation of its board of directors, a change that was not deliberate but by chance. This transition has been both blessing and curse, pushing the staff at times to take on practices with which they are not comfortable. The mother of a new student at the school who was from a different background than the other, all female, directors, joined the board. She had recently moved up from Silicon Valley and was "very business-oriented." According to the executive director, the new board member "was a full-time career person, not a full-time mom, and really took the board in a totally different direction." She became the board president in her second year. While this new board member brought many new ideas about board governance and operations to the organization, the shift was not without conflict. The director recalls: "It was a pretty hard transition in the beginning for all of us to see the 'corporateness' come in ... yet, when I look at the alternative of where we were just before then, I'm really glad. I think it is still very difficult for staff, at times ... but I think the new board has ensured our future in a way that a full parent board couldn't have done."

Coinciding with the arrival of the new board chair was a grant from a large Bay Area foundation as part of its board excellence program. The twin effects of board reorganization and foundation support signal the receptivity of Kids Place to new programs. While Kids Place sought this grant, it came with many strings attached. This foundation has a very strong vision of how to achieve board excellence. The funds are not allocated directly to the nonprofit but are handled by a county-wide intermediary agency that hires a consultant to work with the grant recipient. Together the consultant, director, and new board leadership worked on planning, structure, and board recruitment. The grant had the added effect of introducing the nonprofit to the intermediary organization and to the professional development and volunteer training it offers.

Reception. Kids Place is a very different organization today from the volunteer-governed organization of just a few years ago. Perhaps the most notable, catalytic change at Kid's Place has been the professionalization of the board. Members of the board now include executives from Hewlett Packard and Agilent, who do not have children at the school; alumni parents, whose children are no longer at the school; and, for the first time, men. This new board was "invested in policies that distinguish between the parent hat and board hat, policies so that things aren't decided arbitrarily, and targeting who comes onto the board." Second, the transformed board introduced new operational ideas leading to the creation of a reserve fund, now totaling more than $70,000, which is a difficult concept for teachers who wonder why their wages are not increasing when there is enough money for reserves. Another decision that exemplified the more long-term strategy of a reformed board was the purchase of the property Kids Place had rented for the past decade, with an arrangement to pay it off in a mere seven years.

In a typical two-year pre-school, governed by parents who volunteer, the entire board turns over every two to three years, so this case illustrates the impact of placing four or five new people with different mindsets on a small seven-person board. The experience changed the organization, but not without tension. While agreeing that the new board members have "done really great things for the school," the executive director is quick to point out that she has also learned to push back to adapt ideas for her context when corporate ideas do not fit the vision or infrastructure of a small nonprofit: "I've learned how to speak up and say, 'Wait a minute! We're not Agilent; we're a staff of *five*.'" The preschool has absorbed various professional practices, and now has a board dominated by managers rather than parents.

As a result of its positive encounter with the intermediary, the new board president, vice-president and executive director jointly attended the agency's seminar, entitled 'Boardroom Dancing,' on the relationships between boards and directors. All new board members are now required to attend the 'Boardroom 101' training. This straightforward adoption, where the staff or board members directly import the off-the-shelf ideas of an external consultant through a group training session, reduces negotiation over meaning in the implementation of board member training. One upshot of this transformation is careful scrutiny of the preschool's finances, and this focus has led to a key decision about the ownership of its facility. Clearly these efforts have helped institutionalize and formalize the activities of Kids Place. Board professionalization occurred by chance and was the vehicle through which new ideas were introduced, their meaning negotiated, and the results implemented.

The engaged translator

"Family Care" is a $1.5 million per year human services organization, created in 1979 to provide support for the families of patients suffering from life-threatening illnesses. The organization relies almost completely on donations from individuals, corporations, and foundations, with three-fourths of their income being raised through annual fundraising and the rest from interest on their endowment.

The current director joined the organization in 1994 and found an array of problems, including poor records for fundraising, little systematic effort at fundraising, and a mounting deficit of $70,000. The director was relatively inexperienced in the nonprofit sector, having worked in only two nonprofits over a period of a few years. She brought significantly more experience from having owned and run a small business, observing that: "Running a small business is pretty much like running a nonprofit." She encountered a supportive, semi-professionalized board comprised of local business owners, devoted volunteers and mid- to senior-level corporate employees, who were eager for improvement.

Encounters. The executive director was keen to experiment with new practices. Her prior experiences with boards or managers at other organizations that were risk averse led her to view the challenges at Family Care as a fertile opportunity to develop new ideas. The lack of internal processes and a worrisome financial situation created a sympathetic board, ready to listen to new ideas:

> They gave me the possibility of doing a lot of things that I had been thinking about all these years but couldn't really implement ... They were facing a $70,000-a-year deficit. When I realized that the deficit was caused by a three quarter million dollar mortgage, I said, "Instead of making up that deficit – let's pay off the mortgage." And we did. So I think that gave me a very long honeymoon period where people were really willing to listen to new ideas.

In turn, initial successes fueled an appetite for more. When the director proposed different fundraising practices employed by other nonprofits, the board quickly embraced them. Family Care purposively sought ideas it could adapt to its purpose. The director introduced fundraising strategies common to the field, such as an annual giving program and the development of corporate and foundation relations, which she encountered in her previous nonprofit experience. The organization hired "Smith Consulting," a consulting firm that had advised numerous other human service nonprofits on capital campaigns. The consultants provided advice on how to organize the campaign, and staff to handle many of the functions. They worked with director, staff, board members, and donors to adapt their campaign template to Family Care. In their ongoing interactions, Family Care needed to impress upon the consultants a fuller understanding of its culture and the attention to detail it wanted in work with donors. Often the director would step in, suggesting when an approach was not appropriate to Family Care's culture. She would either impose her own ideas of what was useful on the consultant or they would work together to develop a suitable application. Some of the client's interpretations or changes were adopted by the consultant, creating a "new" version of the template to be carried to the next client organization. The joint work on fundraising was a lengthy, interactive, collaborative process in which staff from both organizations worked closely together over a period of one year. Family Care raised almost double the original campaign goal of $10 million.

The director also sought new ideas through networking with colleagues in the field. She joined a popular monthly nonprofit managers' roundtable organized by a local non-profit intermediary to provide small, active groups for networking and the exchange of ideas. Through this intermediary, she received a scholarship to a Harvard University executive program designed for nonprofit leaders. She studied with a professor who is an expert on how to improve communication between executive directors and board members to facilitate more effective board governance. He contends that few boards systematically follow institutional performance indicators, and he developed a "dashboard" tool to help organizations gauge and represent their operational status. Like automotive dashboards, the template provides an at-a-glance view into how an organization is doing. This professor writes that: "Metaphorically, visually, and substantively, dashboards are an unsurpassed means for trustees to learn what to watch. Even more importantly, the very construction and continuous refinement of the dashboard requires, as no other exercise quite does, that the board and staff collectively and collaboratively discover what matters most." The executive director returned with high praise for the experience and was particularly intrigued by the dashboard concept, which the board and staff of Family Care adopted but revised extensively for their own purposes. They now prepare and distribute a dashboard prior to each board meeting.

Reception. The various ideas Family Care encountered around fundraising and fiscal management were largely intangible concepts that required active translation in order to be turned into new processes at the organization. The executive director acted as the primary carrier, importing new ideas for the organization to consider, and she led the translation of ideas into action. She built a new management team, saying: "It's the job of the leadership to create the common language. I actually prefer people to be newer to the field that I train ... someone younger and more open to my vision of doing things." She then actively worked with them and the board to institute new processes. Having laid the groundwork for a fundraising program, they collaborated closely with Smith Consulting to translate the organization's capital campaign template to their culture and mission, succeeding in raising nearly $20 million to renovate the facility and build an endowment capable of providing annual revenue and stability for the future.

In a similar vein, the executive director's encounter with a well-known carrier who specializes in nonprofit governance led her to introduce a new idea, the instantiation of which would provide a useful tool for future board meetings. The designer of the dashboard concept recommends that the creation of a dashboard start with an "extended discussion among trustees and senior staff ... about the critical success factors–the most essential areas of performance." The Family Care board and staff worked together, looking at the goals and indicators outlined in Family Care's strategic plan to create a dashboard suited to their organization's aspirations. The dashboard is not a fixed tool, but one that could be translated by each organization that implements it.

This director is not only comfortable fine-tuning ideas to specific internal uses, she seems to prefer intangible ideas to fixed templates, and she picks staff and consultants who will work with her to mold ideas into processes for Family Care. As a result of the success of these previous encounters, this year the board gave approval for the director to leave the nonprofit roundtable and join an international organization that bills itself as "the largest leadership development organization for chief executives, providing businesses with the tools to outperform both the competition and themselves."

The reluctant conformer

"Family Resource Center" is a nonprofit organization that provides services to children with special needs and their families. Founded through a parent-led grassroots effort in 1976, the organization has grown to an annual budget of nearly $2 million. The director is the mother of a child with disabilities. She was part of the grassroots effort to create the nonprofit and transitioned from volunteer to employee, eventually stepping into the role of director in 1995. The common bond shared by all 30 employees is having a child who has been a beneficiary of the organization's services. The seven members of the board are advocates for the community that Family Resource Center serves. At least half of the board members must be parents of children with special needs.

The organization relies on state government funding for 53 percent of its budget, and draws the rest of its support from foundation, corporate, and individual donors. The nonprofit tries to pursue a balanced funding model that combines government and philanthropic support. The economic downturn has significantly hurt this organization, forcing a 25 percent cut in expenses: "There is an awful lot of talk now about agencies going under." In the search for scarce funding, the organization has to continually balance the tension between fitting their mission to funders' interests while retaining their core values and programs: "For a while we were really good at redefining programs so they always looked new ... repackaging them so that they had something that would meet what the funder wanted, but were not different from what the community was expecting." The economic downturn has made such repackaging much more difficult.

Encounters. Family Resource Center is simultaneously under strong pressure from funders to adopt certain practices, and proactively searching for ideas to ensure the agency's long-term survival. The pressing financial shortfall leaves many nonprofits in a weak position. Nevertheless, the long-standing

248

relationship between service provider and funder can have the effect of binding both together, possibly in unexpected ways. Family Resource Center is willing to implement tedious evaluation practices in exchange for $15,000 from a dominant funder that provides a mere two percent of the nonprofit's budget. This funder is a nationally known, federated agency that collects monies from individual donors, primarily through workplace giving programs, then redistributes the funds to nonprofits, assuring donors that the recipients meet high accountability standards.

"Accountability" is interpreted by this funder as fiscal oversight through the adoption of strict accounting standards. The organization distributes a seventy-page audit guide to member agencies, including a list of management practices nonprofits must adopt in exchange for funding. Grant recipients must implement generally accepted accounting principles and open their doors to an independent, external audit process designed in accordance with professional guidelines. The resulting process is highly codified and fixed, leaving little room for negotiation and translation. The grant recipient is under coercive pressure to adopt this professionally sanctioned interpretation of fiscal accountability: "When you are [funded by this organization], there is a very vigorous administrative overview that they do every three to four years … It's horrendous. I mean, you have to share your strategic plan, you have to answer all these questions, you have to go before a review committee with your board members, a couple of key staff people, and yourself. Then they do a site visit where they go through the agency. It's a really long process …"

Nevertheless, the organization has a long history with this funder, and is willing to comply with its requirements. The CEO justifies the organization's compliance with these oversight practices by stressing the loyalty and trust that has characterized this relationship over the years: "It means a lot, even though we get a very minimal amount … We had been grassroots until 1984 when we became [funded by them]. They were our first funding source, and that gave us the credibility to be able to go out and ask for local and federal monies. That really launched us, so we're very loyal to them … If you can pass [their evaluation], you can pass anything!" The organization is willing to comply with stringent demands from this funder not so much for the amount of money but for the stamp of approval that a grant from it provides. Family Resource Center is loyal to the grantmaker for providing it with this legitimacy and the staff regularly works with the funder to appear jointly before donor groups.

Besides pressure from this external stakeholder, Family Resource Center was urged by its board of directors to design and implement a business plan. The director first tried to use a fixed template, in the form of software for business planning. But software is an impersonal, highly codified medium: "One of my staff members had gotten me Biz Ink [software], and I had gone through that, but except for the general outlines, it was for-profit and had all those market analyses and everything. I thought, I don't know how to do this; I don't know how to translate this and make sense of this." This rigid template was rejected because the director was not versed enough in for-profit language to modify the template to fit her organizational context. She turned to a consultant from the for-profit sector to help her implement the idea in her organization. "So I said 'John, I have to do this business plan. Will you help me?' And he said, 'Oh sure, there's only four key elements. You do an executive summary, you do a market analysis, you do a budget for the next three years, and where you're going to go. And I'll help you with that. Piece of cake.'" The consultant jointly designed the plan with organizational staff.

The director refers to instances where the staff stepped in and (re)negotiated the meaning of the idea to better reflect their organizational mission. For example, the consultant suggested changing the service delivery model of the agency:

> When we looked at the core competency, his suggestion was that we just become a business answering the phone and [responding to] questions. And we said, "No, no, no – that's not who we are." Our whole credibility is the fact that people know us because we've interacted with them for so long. So that was where I disagreed. We needed to look at how the programs fit with our mission.

The collaborative negotiation with the consultant allowed for a deeper application of the idea to the organization's context and brought the staff firmly behind the project.

Reception. The Family Resource Center board, which had pushed for the plan in the first place, did not, once finished, seem to see the plan as anything more than window dressing: "The board never liked the business plan. It was almost too much for them to assimilate; [their attitude was] 'just do it and then we'll look at it.' And then I did it and it was like, 'Oh, okay. That's okay.' But where do we go from here?" The champions of a specific idea may not, in the end, be fluent in its use or agree with the end product. The board's vision of how a specific idea would be adopted may not be represented in what the organization ends up with after meeting with the carrier. Or, it may be, that unlike the staff who had felt they had a tremendous stake in the plan's development and implementation, the board simply did not see it as anything other than an artifact the organization needed to have on the shelf for an external audience.

The active resistor

"Art in the Park" is a 70-year-old arts organization with a long history of providing free artistic events in the Bay Area community. A philanthropist from a prominent family started the group, and family members remain very involved in governance to this day. The board of directors has always been chaired by a member of this family, and it includes several descendants of the founder. While mature, the administration remains small with seven full-time employees and an annual operating budget of $1 million. Seventy-five percent of the revenue is derived from individual donations and corporate or foundation grants with the remainder from local government. Unlike many arts organizations, Art in the Park does not rely on ticket sales or other revenue generating strategies: "Our only revenue is contributed income. We don't do sales of any kind." Despite heavy reliance on donations, Art in the Park has been financially stable for some time.

The twenty-four board members are closely affiliated with one another, as they also serve in board and executive positions with many of the most recognizable for-profit, nonprofit, and philanthropic organizations in the Bay Area. The professional backgrounds of board members – including members of the founding family – are decidedly for-profit, with most holding senior management positions at companies such as banks or high technology and accounting firms. With such affiliations, one might expect the rampant transfer of management practices, yet this is not the case. Despite the large number of board members with corporate experience and the small non-profit staff, Art in the Park is in the unusual position of resisting pressures to adopt certain managerial practices.

The organization's staff is deeply rooted in the arts world. The director, who joined the organization in 2000 and is herself an artist, explains: "Most of the people who work in this organization have had experience in non-profits or in arts organizations. Our director of operations has worked in theatre and dance; our director of finance and business worked for a contemporary arts museum. Our associate director of development is a performing artist."

Encounter. Despite attendance rates in the tens of thousands at its free events, the organization does not charge admission. This is not because the organization is unaware of the considerable opportunities for income generation. The director explains how ideas involving generating more income, ranging from ticket to t-shirt sales, have been routinely brought to their attention, but are quickly dismissed by the board and staff: "There have been ideas floating about – selling alcohol or whatever. We have evaluated those proposals, and based upon a lot of factors, we determined that it would not be a good course of action for the organization. There are a lot of ideas people have about how you could make money at the events, but for our organization the intent is to keep it as pure and true to the original vision as possible."

While the organization is frequently exposed to proposals to earn income, the staff and board deem those ideas inconsistent with the mission to provide free arts programs. The director emphasizes the delicacy of staying true to that non-commercial vision while raising funds and recognizing the contributions of those who help make free admission possible: "We do what we can to accommodate our corporate sponsors, but we don't want to start slapping logos all over the park to make money. It's a balance between providing some exposure and some benefits, but also we rely really heavily on the community to preserve its nature. People would not be happy if there was a huge Pepsi sign on the stage or a logo everywhere you turned."

Reception. The first and most important factor that acts as a shield from the pressures to adopt revenue-generating practices is a strong commitment from the board of directors and the staff to remain tied to the organization's original mission statement to make high quality art accessible to all: "It's always been a very small organization and particularly with the family being involved for so many years. We still have [the member of a well-known San Francisco family] as our board chairman, and he's a descendant of the founder, so there's always going to be family involvement, both financially and in terms of the administration of the organization." Much like a small, family-run business, the leadership of the governing board remains firmly in family hands to protect the legacy of the founder.

Thus, the organization considers any possible change in programming or administration in light of its original mission. With the passing of an older generation of the family on the board and the arrival of younger members, the organization re-visited its mission statement to ensure that its artistic program would adequately reflect the Bay Area community:

> Our program was predominantly classical for many, many years. We're [now] trying to present a very broad array that serves the Bay Area community and its diversity. The organization is very solid right now in terms of being clearly defined by its mission and redefining what its mission means in the world we live in today versus 1938.

The founding family's considerable financial generosity and involvement in the administration of the organization affords it the ability to resist pressures to embrace current models of income generation that are becoming the norm in many arts nonprofits. Art in the Park is remarkably free from the usual economic pressures bedeviling nonprofits. The connection of board members affords it access to support from high-profile donors in foundations and corporations, securing a strong financial footing. Undeterred by the economic downturn, the organization recently embarked on an ambitious $20 million combined capital and endowment campaign. The organization has ample support from volunteers as well, averaging thousands of volunteer hours per year. Since a staff of seven cannot run high attendance arts events without considerable assistance, the organization relies on volunteers to ensure the smooth running of its programs. "We have about 400 volunteers that work throughout the season … We had 3,215 volunteer hours last year."

Art in the Park is an example of an active resistor to the transfer of business practices. The organization is able to forego commercial ventures because of a commitment to an historical mission and a stable supply of capital and volunteers. Family members on the board protect the original vision of their ancestor by providing the organization with ample funds and turning down proposals deemed inappropriate.

Processes of Emulation and Resistance

These cases illustrate the multitude of ways in which organizations may encounter, interact with, and respond to ideas about new practices. The range of responses is conditioned by a host of factors, including key characteristics of the respective organizations, the nature of the carriers that expose the organization to new ideas, and selective aspects of the encounter itself.

The first case, the Bay Academy, illustrates how adoption can turn into a cumulative process. Initial exposure to managerial practices at an executive program, attended by top managers of high-profile corporations, triggered an enthusiasm for organizational change that increased the likelihood of subsequent adoption. Thus, the Bay Academy engaged numerous consultants in change efforts, created job titles that were comparable to the private sector, and became an ardent user of strategic planning processes. This imitation effect created numerous lines of communication and multiple networks for contact between the school and various proponents of business methods. All this exposure was transformative in a second sense as well, as the Bay Academy's director acquired fluency with business practices and passionately championed these ideas whenever she could in meetings with administrators from other schools and other nonprofits.

At the other end of the continuum, Art in the Park consistently turns down numerous proposals that would generate considerable income for the organization. Concessions, "voluntary" donations as a substitute for ticket sales, and sales of clothing or other mementos have become ubiquitous at cultural events. The administration and board of Art in the Park know this, yet they rebuff overtures to pursue these widely accepted activities. Here the strong corporate background of the board acts as a barrier to these entrepreneurial ventures rather than as a carrier of managerial ideas. When business people put on their "arts hat" and serve on this board, they recalibrate their thinking and want Art in the Park to be everything a business is not – pure not practical, stubborn in its commitment rather than pragmatic, and unsullied by external demands. To be sure, the sound financial and volunteer base of Art in the Park enables it to resist bowing to financial exigencies. But other nonprofits in comparable circumstances have found the pursuit of entrepreneurial opportunities irresistible. Art in the Park's finances afford it the opportunity to be selective, but the organization's intense commitment to its founding mission inoculates the organization, causing it to reject commercial engagement that would taint its purity.

The Bay Academy and Art in the Park react to the ideas they encounter in opposite ways, placing them at the two ends of the continuum. What accounts for this difference? On the surface, both are in stable financial condition with highly credentialed staff and board members. The Bay Academy, however, is supported by tuition fees, which represent earned income secured in a competitive private school market, while Art in the Park relies on the patronage of its influential donors. Generous patronage is contingent on holding true to the organization's founding mission, hence resistance is necessary. At the Bay Academy, seductive carriers of business models and a director's enthusiasm for continuous organizational renewal render the school an avid adopter.

In between the two extremes of our continuum we find the most active examples of translation. Wholesale adoption or resistance lends little room for refashioning ideas. But in the space between these poles, much reconstruction, experimentation, and contestation is underway. Long ago, Alchian (1950) noted that a good deal of innovation results from imperfect attempts to imitate others. DiMaggio and Powell (1983) observed that many efforts at modeling oneself after exemplary organizations fall short because of the lack of an appropriate surrounding infrastructure. Westney (1987) took this line of argument further, suggesting that such departures may not be unwitting but represent selective emulation. For example, the British model of the postal system was adopted in the 19th century by both Japan and India, but the British practice of having women in charge of smaller branch offices was viewed as inappropriate and rejected by both countries (Westney, 1987: 27). In the 1980s and 1990s, U.S. automakers were eager to adopt Japanese production methods, but did not embrace the less hierarchical managerial structures of the Japanese, or the markedly lower salaries of top Japanese auto executives.

Family Care is an active translator, borrowing freely from its surrounding environment, but rarely whole cloth. While the director imported ideas from previous experience, selected consultants, and executive education programs, she edited them for local use. Such borrowed tools are often amended in light of local problems and demands (Sahlin-Andersson, 1996). The executive director recounted a narrative in which she helped a nonprofit become more professional, and was supported by a board of directors eager to resolve pressing financial and organizational problems. Operational disarray provided the opportunity to draw on external sources of ideas, but these practices were fine-tuned to fit the unusual context of a provider of services to the families of gravely ill patients. The director selected proven ideas from the nonprofit world that could be customized to address specific features of her organization.

These three positions – adopter, translator, and resistor – serve as anchors for our continuum of ideal types. Figure 1 portrays this continuum graphically, locating the organizations in terms of both their receptivity to adopting new managerial practices and their potential bandwidth for translating these practices. A spectrum of possible responses, we suggest, are positioned along the continuum, with actual location determined by the specifics of the interactions between the carriers, the ideas, and the organizations. We place two additional responses to either side of center to demonstrate further the variety of potential reception.

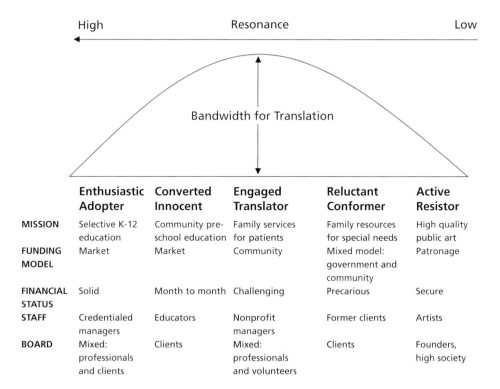

	Enthusiastic Adopter	Converted Innocent	Engaged Translator	Reluctant Conformer	Active Resistor
MISSION	Selective K-12 education	Community preschool education	Family services for patients	Family resources for special needs	High quality public art
FUNDING MODEL	Market	Market	Community	Mixed model: government and community	Patronage
FINANCIAL STATUS	Solid	Month to month	Challenging	Precarious	Secure
STAFF	Credentialed managers	Educators	Nonprofit managers	Former clients	Artists
BOARD	Mixed: professionals and clients	Clients	Mixed: professionals and volunteers	Clients	Founders, high society

Figure 13.1. Ideal types, arrayed by degree of resonance, and latitude for, translation of "new" managerial practices.

We label Kids Place a "converted innocent," in order to capture both the extent of its transformation as well as its organic commitment to children and its pre-school mission. Here the carrier came from the corporate world, but was also the parent of a child at the school and a board member. This engaged parent helped a small organization staffed by teachers to incorporate several business practices and to adapt others to fit the context. The timing of her intervention coincided with a grant from another activist – a foundation that has been campaigning for more effective nonprofit boards. The grant brought in a nonprofit consultant, and led to participation in the "Boardroom Dancing" program. Note that all of the carriers of organizational transformation come from "within," either committed to the organization or from the nonprofit community. Critics of attempts to refashion the nonprofit sector with models from business frequently observe that business practices either do not fit well or lack the necessary supportive surrounding environment (Sievers, 2001). In this case, even though the ideas at first seemed foreign, the supportive elements for interpretation were in place. Particularly important was the program for training board members, which served as a type of incubator, fostering the professional development of nonprofit governance. Such "organization-creating organizations" play a vital role in the creation and transformation of organizational populations (Stinchcombe, 1965).

Family Resource Center is an example of an organization trying to adjust to contemporary expectations. The board and staff recognize the diverse pressures on nonprofits in this period of financial distress. Reliant on government funding and loyal to a crucial nonprofit intermediary, the organization understood that fiscal transparency and business planning had become fashionable. In some respects, this case reminds us of a colonial model, in which an imperial power imposed variants of its own organizational practices, with little regard for whether those practices were suited to local circumstances. In such circumstances, the colony often resists this imposition. Even though the business plan was edited for the local context, when the plan was eventually presented to the board, there was little enthusiasm for it. The organization and board went through the motions of conformity, but its lack of enthusiasm for the exercise led to a decision not to implement the plan.

For the adopter, personal contact with exemplary models that provided accessible, fixed packages led to a warm and fast embrace of new business practices. The innocent converted much more gradually, taking on some ideas completely and tweaking others in incremental steps urged by a committed insider and nonprofit intermediaries. The adopter eagerly sought out business ideas, while the innocent had neither the time nor inclination to search, but encountered business models through the arrival of a new parent at the school. At the translator, a nonprofit manager emulated successful nonprofit models but selectively choose processes and tools that were malleable and could be changed to function in her organization's setting. The conformer tried to implement business ideas, but these packages were forced on the organization without any supportive structures, and the exercise proved useless and exasperating. The resistor is quite knowledgeable about business opportunities, yet its financial stability and its passion for free art immunizes the organization against the growing commercialism of the arts sector.

In terms of consequences, the adopter has become a searcher who seeks out new business practices and implements them, and in turn proselytizes their use widely. The converted innocent case is an example of a "frozen accident," where the chance arrival of a new board member triggered a subsequent awakening of a sleepy nonprofit. The sea change this organization experienced allowed it to move from operating on a month-to-month basis and to take a more long-term view. These interactions resulted in exposure to many more business practices, some of which have been unwelcome in such a small organization. The translator is clearly a *bricoleur*, borrowing from friendly sources that do not mind appropriation and extensive repackaging. The conformer experienced considerable tension from a key visible funder and a board that felt the organization needed to be more businesslike. But the new tools were not the right ones for the job, and resulted in bewilderment. Lastly, the resistor is by no means an organization with its head in the sand, immune to contemporary ideas. Indeed, it is keenly aware of commercial opportunities and their possible corrosive effects, thus the organization intentionally buffers itself from such influences.

Thus, opportunities for translation are unequally distributed across types of organizations. Nonprofit organizations with strong, clear missions are concerned with fidelity. This steadfast view makes them less interested in tinkering, whether they are organizations that resist new fashions or actively try many things off-the-shelf. Put colloquially, true believers are rarely engaged translators. This was the case with the ideal types we labeled adopter and resistor. In contrast, organizations are much more likely to experiment when located in positions where competing ideas are circulating and the grasp of authority is attenuated. The cases we dubbed converted innocent, translator, and reluctant conformer were in interstitial positions, where multiple, overlapping interests were at work. Consequently, we suggest that the bandwidth of experimentation, that is, the range of alternative practices that can be tried out, was much wider for these organizations. In these settings, even relatively fixed or highly codified managerial tools could be re-designed or deployed for alternative uses.

Our case analyses also point to an unusual feature of translation that appears endemic to the nonprofit sector in the United States. Most nonprofit organizations in the U.S. are relatively small, and their financial circumstances unstable. In our larger sample of operating charities in the Bay Area, more than 70% of the organizations had annual expenses of less than $500,000 in the year 2000. With respect to many key organizational features, these organizations resemble small businesses, particularly family-run firms. Both family firms and operating charities depend on the considerable expenditure of time, energy, and passion by a few key individuals. Yet relatively little formal transfer of ideas occurs from small businesses to the non-profit world. Instead, the dominant models and practices in circulation are drawn from the world of big corporations, business schools, consulting firms, or large foundations. There seems to be an odd fit between the worlds of large-scale enterprise and small, grass-roots charity. In some circumstances, this lack of comparability affords room for re-assembly and *bricolage*, but often the more dominant and prestigious world of large organizations serves as either an exemplary model or direct provider for their smaller brethren, dampening possibilities for appropriation that might better serve the needs of nonprofits.

Chapter 14

Code-Switching, or Why a Metacode Is Good to Have

Richard Rottenburg, Martin-Luther-University, Germany

The notion of *translation* as introduced by Michel Serres and applied by most contributors to this volume is one way of avoiding the old controversy about reality – the question if there is one reality or many equivalent realities. It assumes, in effect, an endless number of realities – shifting seamlessly along the time and space dimension. To take an example, fish specialists know that "the same" fish is never the same in different waters. Thus although the interlocutors agree to use the term "cod" for a creature that can be described by a common set of certain traits, everybody knows that the actual fish is different, and also that if an actual object-fish is displaced, it will change accordingly.

Not everybody is prepared to accept such a solution, as the constant accusations against politicians for their double-talk indicate. The argument that the building as talked about on Thursday in the city council became translated into a tunnel in a press conference on Friday does not convince. In other words, there are political necessities for and obstacles to smooth translation and translations are often contested. There are at least two fields of practice where this is evident: management and anthropology. As most of the contributions in this book deal with the former, I will concentrate on the latter, assuming that it offers reflection useful for all kinds of field studies, including management studies.[1]

One or Many Realities?

One can begin by asking relatively simple and easily answerable questions. Under what conditions do different interlocutors draw on the one reality argument? Under what conditions do they stress that there are many realities? When, where and by whom is an appeal to *one* reality problematized by interpreting this appeal to "naked reality" as an expression of the inter-

---

[1] The argument of this chapter is taken from my monograph on translations in the global organizational field of development cooperation, which focuses on the construction of objectivity criteria; see Rottenburg, 2002.

ests and the culture of the appellant? Conversely, when, where and by whom is an appeal to one reality questioned, by arguing that there are multiple realities? And when, finally, is the argument that there are many realties attributed to cultural delusion – by making reference to the universal reality on which all human representations are based?

Each of these questions can be answered to everyone's satisfaction, but not together and at the same time. They cannot be reduced to a common denominator, and they cannot be applied to themselves. What is denied in one operation is taken for granted in questioning just that operation. To establish their own critique, commentators are obliged to draw on arguments they denied their opponent. Approaching this dilemma from a different angle will allow asking more precise questions that have a better chance at being answered fruitfully.

The assumption of one describable reality presupposes in turn one *metacode* in which this reality can be described without distorting it. The assumption of the existence of such a metacode means that all other existing codes must be cultural codes (in the language of this book, one could say that it assumes existence of a global code, which at no place is a local code[2]). The assumption of one describable reality could not be maintained without differentiating between the one universal metacode and many particular cultural codes, since different cultural codes are each a basis for their own version of reality. Those, on the other hand, who argue that there are many realities are also reduced to drawing on a single metacode in order to formulate their argument of many realities, thus undermining their own argument. Does this mean that there must be one reality?

Instead of trying to resolve this paradox or letting oneself be paralyzed by it (Luhmann, 1991), my suggestion is to explore how and under what conditions a shift between metacode and cultural codes takes place in practice. I will not find an answer to the question of existence of one or many realities, but we may find an answer to the question of why the assumption of one reality is sometimes necessary in order to permit many realities to exist.

Representational vs. Performative Idiom

The critics of the idea of a *representational idiom*, who wish to replace it with the notion of a *performative idiom*, are paradoxical in that they need to draw on a code of representation in order to make the switch (Fish, 1989: 467; Luhmann, 1991). Otherwise, it is impossible to argue that the performative idiom is *better* than the idiom of representation. This is not to say that the other side is in better shape. The claim that a statement can be ver-

---

[2] Those who reject such an assumption point out that the "global code" is, in fact, a local code at such places as Brussels or the United Nations building.

ified as to be a correct or incorrect representation of reality assumes preconditions that vary culturally and historically and cannot be easily consolidated (Daston, 2001).

Before any statement can be verified, it must first be recognized as a statement, meaning that it must be communicable. Communicability means that a statement must be formulated in a recognizable code, which has its own rules. These rules set limits on a statement, which are independent of the referent of that statement. (English grammar does not change with the topic of a sentence). At the same time, the only way a communicable statement can draw attention to itself is by its partial lack of plausibility, i.e. by its lack of conformity. This is because a self-evident statement does not provide any information (for the difference between information and meaning, see Eco, 1989), and there will be no incentive to pay attention to such a statement or to challenge it.

These two cultural preconditions of the verifiability of a statement – its communicability and its lack of self-evidence – in turn have preconditions. The parties arguing about the validity of a statement need to agree at least on which areas of epistemology are pertinent to the controversy. Otherwise they would not even be able to initiate the dispute, as their arguments will never coincide. They must additionally share the ontological conviction that they are arguing about the same thing, which they both consider in principle to be within reach.

In brief, when two or more parties argue about the definition of a problem and its solution, they need to agree on, and limit themselves to, statements that they can verify. This means that they must agree – conditionally – on truth criteria and on definitions of reality, and these must be considered valid – in principle – for the purpose and the duration of their co-operation.

But even here the two parties mentioned above develop two different lines of argument as to how such an elementary ontological and epistemological common ground can exist. The first line of argument – that of the *representation* party – is based on a certain form of *limited scepticism*. The debate about the validity of statements is reduced to comparing the various representations of the one (and only) external reality. Under these conditions, the chances of coming to an acceptable conclusion are considerable; one only has to continue prodding until the reality reveals itself, thus ending the argument. But a certain degree of scepticism is still needed at this point, as it is possible that this might not be the reality, but an intermediary revealing itself. In other words, the representation of a reality might actually be but a performance by an intermediary, which does not exist beyond the intermediary itself. (Think of various optical illusions that can be produced by optical instruments.) Despite this ever present sceptical caution, the representation party does not lose hope that eventually truth will prevail.

This line of argument rests on the conviction that statements are scientifically valid when they are absolutely free of all influence of the speaker and the context. In this sense, the modern scientific ideal is of an aperspectival objectivity that chronicles the naked truth from a "view from nowhere" (Nagel, 1986/1992). Robert Merton described in 1945 the social embeddedness of this conviction as resulting from the emerging type of society:

> With increasing social conflict, differences in the values, attitudes and modes of thought of groups develop to the point where the orientation which these groups previously had in common is overshadowed by incompatible differences. Not only do there develop distinct universes of discourse, but the existence of any one universe challenges the validity and legitimacy of the others. The co-existence of these conflicting perspectives and interpretations within the same society leads to an active and reciprocal *distrust* between groups. Within a context of distrust one no longer inquires into the content of beliefs and assertions to determine whether they are valid or not, one no longer confronts the assertions with relevant evidence, but introduces an entirely new question: how does it happen that these views are maintained? (1945/1968: 511).

Sociology of science is authorised to answer this question; it is exempt from the general distrust in that it claims aperspectival objectivity for itself. But sociologists of science can only maintain this authority for as long as they deny all other parties the capacity for such objectivity – otherwise one is back to the beginning.

The other line of argument – that of *performative production of realities* – is not satisfied with this limited form of scepticism and rejects the assumption of even a remote possibility of an aperspectival objectivity. It pleads instead for an *unlimited* scepticism. In the text cited below, Merton, standing somewhat in between these two parties, has provided a taste of what happens when various pretenders to "aperspectival objectivity" give up their more ambitious goals and switch to the performative idiom.

> What these schemes of analysis have in common is the practice of discounting the *face value* of statements, beliefs, and idea-systems by re-examining them within a new context which supplies the "real meaning". Statements ordinarily viewed in terms of their manifest content are debunked … by relating this content to the attributes of the speaker or of the society in which he lives. The professional iconoclast, the trained debunker, the ideological analyst and their respective systems of thought thrive in a society where large groups of people have already become alienated from common values; where separate universes of discourse are linked with reciprocal distrust (1945/1968: 512–13).

If the professional iconoclasts and debunkers – people like Merton – are drawn into the general feeling of distrust, and begin to doubt the claims of aperspectival objectivity themselves, that is, when the issue of objectivity is turned reflexively on itself, all safe foundations are lost. Answering the already difficult question of how to distinguish between good and less good descriptions of the world has become dramatically more demanding. In the section of this chapter entitled "The bazaar" I will try to show that while this question remains demanding on an epistemological level, there is a mundane practice that permits a convincing pragmatist solution.

Merton's prescription for avoiding the maelstrom of unlimited scepticism was to (sometimes ironically) clothe his own revelations in the rhetoric of aperspectival objectivity, while remaining well aware of its social provenience. More recent proponents of such generalised scepticism have turned more radical, and argue that if a discourse aspires to the label "scientific", it must not take for granted that which it desires to explain – be it God or reality. From the point of view of such agnostics, the "realists" among scientists are not really scientists because they, like religious believers, take for granted what they want to explain – and thus move in tautological circles (Bloor, 1976/1991).

These contrasting views (with Merton standing in-between) can be presented in another way. The first stance of limited scepticism drawing on aperspectival objectivity is a "science of error." It "enlightens" people by showing how differing worldviews are culturally shaped ("local") and therefore erroneous. The second stance, that of the agnostic's unlimited scepticism, is a "science of truth" insofar as it prefers to deal with knowledge that is considered valid – not only in popular understanding but also according to current scientific opinion.

Post-Mertonian social constructivism, for instance, assumes that objective knowledge about reality, understood as an interpretation and analysis of reality uninfluenced by the instruments of observation or analysis, is in principle impossible, and therefore not worth considering as an ideal. Consequently, the so-called "errors" are much less interesting study objects than what modern humanity touts as the "truths" based on science. Investigative attention is shifted from the usual suspects – the losers of modernity and the deviants – to the central institutions of modernity that determine its norms.

This shift is specified by the new sociology of knowledge's *principle of symmetry*. The principle of symmetry demands that truth and error, losers and winners, fictions and facts be treated equally. The shift consists in the contrast to the traditional sociology of knowledge where if one were to examine, for example, the argument that the world is flat, it would be unthinkable to even consider the possibility that the world may have been flat some time ago. And yet Earth has become a "blue planet" because that is what it looks like from the Moon (Sachs, 1994). The reason why this is so has been found to lie in the unique nature of the atmosphere. But the atmosphere is millions of years older than our present-day image of the blue planet. Thus the question arises of whether the Earth in the future might not take on completely different forms and characteristics that will make its current perception seem as naïve as the flat world arguments of the past.

The new social constructivism asks how it is possible that humanity can time and again agree on interpretations of reality as objective and true, despite the fact that history suggests that they will invariably change. One way of answering this question is excluded, though: namely that reality will reveal itself in its finally true shape. Truth is something that needs to be patiently fashioned and defended.

There is something else which becomes clear in the example of the blue planet, and it is this point I want to engage with in this chapter. Wolfgang Sachs traces down to minute detail that which he calls a socio-technical construction of the image, but he treats the history of the scientific and technical, military and political developments that has contributed to the existence of the contemporary image of the blue planet as an external reality – which he wants to describe truthfully and correctly.

It is at this point that the epistemological complications examined here enter the equation. For somebody interested more in the argument than the object of that argument, somebody interested in showing how an object is constructed, the characteristics of the product of that construction have to be bracketed. But the problem will re-emerge on another level. The process of construction, if it is to be described and analysed at all, can only be described as an element of an external reality. It is possible to say that one is interested in the process of the construction of a new car concept without being interested in the actual car thus produced, but this process will be described in a way analogous to the technical description of an assembly process (see e.g. Bragd, 2002). Social constructivist analysis cannot avoid legitimising itself by claiming an accurate description of an external reality, a description that can be verified by comparing it to reality, that is, the reality of the reality production. The problem remains, but it has been shifted. An important impulse for this shift can be found in anthropology, even if the credit for this impulse has long been relinquished to others.

The Anthropological Shifts

Due to its particular position, anthropology deals with this epistemological problem as if it were an empirical problem. Since the beginning of the 20th century, anthropology has faced the challenge of analysing and describing foreign cultures so as to shield them against the allegation of being irrational.[3]

---

[3] The question whether this challenge is rooted in colonial expansion interested in the construction of rational subjects, who were no longer to be exterminated but ruled and exploited, is irrelevant to the logic of the rehabilitation of supposedly irrational savages.

When anthropology set for itself the challenge to translate alien and apparently irrational reality models into its own language and thus explain them – i.e. to transform alienity into alterity – it set these reality models into the context of their cultural situation. A leading position in this translation project was taken by British social anthropology, drawing on the work of Emile Durkheim. Viewed in the context of their thus constructed socio-cultural situation, even the most baffling practices and perceptions seemed plausible and reasonable, in that they contributed to the maintenance of social order. The peoples in question, however, considered their convictions rational for wholly other reasons – namely, because they corresponded to the world as it is. They hence found themselves being no less the subject of denunciation than if they were directly accused of irrationality or superstition.

In anthropology, the epistemological justification paradox presented in the previous section becomes a translation paradox (Rottenburg, 2003). The Platonian cave metaphor has found, since Johann Gottfried Herder, a particular form there. Assuming (with Herder) that there can be such a thing as an objective description of a foreign culture, free of a culturally conditioned frame of reference, and also assuming (again with Herder) that cultures while being epistemologically different are all equally legitimate, one finds oneself in a quandary. Where does such a description come from, if it is free of cultural influence? From what position is it possible to judge whether cultures are equal or not? In which code is a judgment of such equality to be formulated? Four ways of answering these questions can be discerned within relativist anthropology.

Within the first position, known as *cultural relativism*, it seems reasonable to exclude the researchers from such relativism. Anthropologists move from one cultural cave to another and peer in. They observe the residents of the respective cave see their own shadows as realities independent of the observer. To describe these observations, the anthropologists use a metacode into which all the cultural codes or cave languages can be translated without deficit. In other words, anthropologists explain the worldviews and meaningful narratives of foreign cultures by demonstrating how these views and narratives relate to their respective economic, social and political context.

When anthropologists working within this paradigm stress in their prologues and epilogues that they describe foreign worldviews "from within", that they are interested in the rehabilitation of these foreign worldviews, warning bells should ring. Such attempts at rehabilitation lead unavoidably to the conclusion "Were I sitting in that cave, I too would consider my shadow an autonomous agent." The implication in this statement is thus that the speaker finds him/herself outside the cave and considers him/herself alone in that position. This form of rehabilitation is bought at the price of a radical denunciation: while the people living with the worldview and narratives are assumed to be unaware that they are captured in their own semantics and social structure, the lonely and marginal anthropologist knows that. Culture, from this point of view, proves to be a collective mistake made by others. A particularly adamant proponent of this position was Ernest Gellner (1992/1995).

To avoid this trap, a second, more radical version, an *epistemic relativism* is proposed. It assumes that anthropologists do not have a status of neutral observers and are not wizards of a metacode. Statements made outside the cultural frame of reference are thus avoided on principle. This means that the anthropological observers find themselves in the same epistemological situation as the residents of the cave, and have the same competencies to reflect on the illusionary nature of their worldviews. The resulting analyses and descriptions are not principally different; they are only less pretentious. Through external observation one does not see *more*; one merely sees something *different* from the people living "within" the studied semantic system. Clifford Geertz represents this approach, and he draws on the sociology of Max Weber and the hermeneutics of Hans-Georg Gadamer (Geertz, 1983/1993).

Ethnographies claiming this perspective are remarkable less for their explanations of "local" versions of the world in terms of "objective conditions" than for their desire to give a voice to these versions, which are heard outside the local context. A great deal of value is placed on conserving the heterogeneity and the polyphony of the foreign culture even at the expense of the consistency of its description. Nevertheless, in the end this approach leaves the initial question unanswered. If it were only an issue of providing the Other with an opportunity to represent themselves in their own voice, the question of one or many realities would not be a problem. Yet, it was exactly this that was impossible in the first place. This approach thus plays down the challenge of alienity in that it conceals the translation of alienity into alterity.

A third version attacks the denunciating effect of the cave metaphor more consistently. As in the second version, it is assumed that the cave dwellers and their anthropological observers inevitably find themselves in the same epistemological situation, and have the same competencies to reflect on the illusionary nature of their perception. But the third version goes further to include the observation that the cave dwellers are also in a position to gaze back into their observer's own cave.

The view into the cave of the Other is helpful mainly because it in turn gives access to the view of the Other onto the Self (called *le regard éloigné* by Lévi-Strauss, 1983/1993; see also Malinowski, 1937). The genuine goal of anthropological study becomes the examination of the Self through the Other. The validity of anthropological analysis in this third version is measured not in terms of agreement with a foreign reality but in terms of how well it manages to describe one's own model of reality and decentre it. In terms of Walter Benjamin's translation theory, this is an attempt at shifting and expanding one's own language through the language of the Other, instead of holding fast to its own coincidental historical position (Benjamin, 1977).

In the fourth version, scholars interested in studying the evolution of notions of reality are advised to replace the cave metaphor with that of the *bazaar* (Rorty, 1991).[4] The bazaar metaphor suggests a constant debate between various models of meaning and reality. Actors are no "cultural dupes"; they are competent enough to anticipate the expectations of others, to recognise these expected expectations as such, and to reflect on them. Most importantly, though, the actors are able to avoid negotiations over matters which would deviate from their purpose at hand. The observers cannot position themselves outside the bazaar and its negotiations; they are always, whether they like it or not, implicated in them. Their descriptions and analyses are never neutral or harmless; they invariably result in feedback and are themselves the result of power-laden bazaar negotiations.

Among the various bazaars, one can distinguish those that are comparatively homogenous or "cold". These are bazaars where most things occur with relatively little friction, where little needs to be negotiated, because the given rules and fundamental assumptions are rarely questioned. The cultural Other is usually not familiar with many of the implicit, unquestioned rules and fundamental assumptions, and her behaviour can easily become a breaching experiment (a process the ethnomethodologists also call "garfinkeling"). Professional Others can thus reveal the rules and the related tensions and debates concealed below the surface by the concerned actors who have an interest to ensure the undisturbed running of things. At the same time, the observers will become aware of their own fundamental assumptions, whose contingency they will now be able to recognise.

Even more revealing are heterogeneous or "hot" bazaars where different forms of knowledge or different principles, ensuing for instance out of a crisis, are openly debated, with the purpose of making collaboration possible. An agreement on exactly how to manage a crisis or to initiate eventual collaboration can only be reached when a common platform has been agreed upon. The negotiation of a common platform – i.e. shared procedures of evidence – assumes that at least a minimum of commonality already exists. In a bazaar that which is to be achieved needs always to be there in some rudimentary form if the negotiations are even to begin.

---

[4] Peter Galison operates within science studies with the same metaphorical shift under the name of "trading zone"; see Galison, 1997, esp. Chapter 9 "The trading zone: coordinating action and belief", pp. 781–844. Anselm Strauss' "arena" concept captures the same point (as in arenas of negotiation); for the most explicit formulation of this concept see Clarke, 1991.

This means that the translation paradox is not solved through bazaar negotiations, yet it is effectively avoided (or, in Luhmannian terminology, processed) by insinuating sufficient commonality. Anthropologists working within this framework as professional Others have a good chance to realize that their own translation paradox is not unique, but constitutes a daily routine of all bazaar actors, and they may now observe how others work to process it. The central interest of an investigation of this type is thus how procedures of evidence are agreed upon in heterogeneous bazaars.

The four anthropological models sketched here are in reality not this clearly separable. The differences are more a matter of different foci and priorities set by various authors, epochs and schools. It is also possible to describe the work of anthropology in other terms and bundle the approaches differently. The classification presented here intended merely to recapitulate the introductory dilemma in new terms: Is it possible and advisable to avoid the controversy of the one or of the many realities by investigating the shifts between metacode and cultural code or, between idiom of representation and idiom of performance?

At the Bazaar

In bazaar negotiations it must, firstly, be clear whether one starts with or without old debts and other obligations and what exactly is part of the deal. All those aspects of the exchange of goods and of the relations of the actors which may lead to undesired complications when articulated must be bracketed. Secondly, to have a bazaar transaction it is necessary to find a scale of comparison for those things that are to be exchanged. The communicative ideal of the bazaar is the minimization of factors and information to the absolutely necessary (or, formulated in other terms, the maximization of externalities to be kept out of the deal; Rottenburg et al., 2000). The extreme case of this minimization strategy is what is known in anthropology as silent trade. After one party deposits its goods (say, salt) at a known spot and withdraws, the second party approaches to deposit as much of its own goods (say, wheat) beside the original submission. The first party then returns to pick up the traded goods, assuming it is happy with the offer made; if not, they are left there indicating that the second party needs to add to its offer. If the trade is successful, it can be repeated in the future; if not, it can easily be discontinued.[5]

At a bazaar where the issue is not that of trading goods but of co-operation under heterogeneous conditions, the same basic mechanism is at work,

---

[5] Max Weber uses the silent exchange to make another point: it is strangers who exchange goods and thereby develop an interest to develop a sufficient level of trust, and hence the principle of honesty is the best policy (Weber, 1922/1972: 383).

in many complex variations. One prominent example is development co-operation. The negotiation technique "goal-oriented project planning" (gopp) has been developed for this field in an explicit recognition of the problem of heterogeneity. Two pictures will help to explain the logic of this concept. In the first, a group of administrators, engineers, managers and financial experts is "gopping" in a Tanzanian town in 1996, to define the presuppositions, goals and procedures for a development project. In the background a panel can be seen, on which inscribed pieces of paper have been pasted. The second picture shows two hydro engineers, a consultant and an anthropologist. A notebook computer is in the middle, with Microsoft Excel on the screen.

In such situations, all information that is not absolutely necessary and thus may cause interference is excluded so that a negotiation can take place. Those pieces of information that form the basis of the negotiations are presented in a *standardised* form, which has been agreed upon in advance. My claim here is that the so-called ultimate justifications for the truth of statements (*Letztbegründungen*), i.e. criteria for differentiating reality from fiction, have been replaced by *formalized procedures of evidence* (Porter, 1992; 1995; this point was already made by Heidegger 1938/2003: 84). In this way, pragmatic progress with respect to concrete co-operation is possible. *All* statements made in the course of the negotiations are recognised as relating to reality. This means that the claim that a statement is founded in reality can never be questioned on principle, without breaking the negotiations. Arguments about individual errors or deceptions can only be carried out on the basis of this provisional construction, justified only insofar as they might be seen as leading to an agreement about the intended co-operation.

A *metacode* is therefore required for this purpose, of a kind which claims to be removed from the particularist cultural codes, and to have a direct contact with outer reality. Like the trading language of the bazaar, the metacode must be able to communicate all necessary information, and exclude all unnecessary and potentially interfering knowledge.

The pragmatic and provisional agreement represented in the metacode thus shifts attention from the question of correspondence between individual statements to outer reality, to the question of correspondence of the statements to one another (*Anschlussfähigkeit*). The problem of *external reference* is pushed into the background in favour of the *coherence criterion* and hence the question of *transversal reference*.[6] In other words, the *procedure* receives priority over the *matter* being discussed. The actors need, at least for the duration of the negotiations, to avoid making the preference of the transversal reference over the external reference an issue. The negotiation proceeds under the assumption that the metacode is valid because it is anchored in an external reality, and therefore transcends all particular frames of reference. Such goal-oriented negotiations are possible at all only on the condition of the concealment of the actual dependency of the metacode on the bazaar as a frame of reference, and the procedural rules valid within that frame. Otherwise, the only possibility would be to conclude that the debated matters can be seen differently from each respective point of view and any decision can look arbitrary and therefore illegitimate.

Court procedures are a particularly obvious example of this process. One argues in court about the truth, but the rules by which it is argued are agreed upon before, to allow an ordered argument. This begins with the indictment: if it cannot be formulated in proper legal terms, the prosecution will draw

---

[6] On the coherence theory of truth see e.g. Davidson, 1986/1992.

attention away from the actual facts to other facts which can be translated into the legal procedure (an action which often goes against common sense). This process continues in the verification of the evidence; the immediate veracity of the evidence is not as important as the formal criteria of its validity as evidence.

My argument can be illustrated in a four-field scheme (adopted and reinterpreted from Mary Douglas and Aaron Wildavsky, 1982) showing the pragmatic iteration process that facilitates cooperation under conditions of heterogeneity.

		Knowledge	
		Certain	Uncertain
Consensus on Goals and Means	Complete	4 Problem: Technical Solution: Calculation	2 Problem: Information Solution: Research
	Contested	3 Problem: Disagreement Solution: Negotiation	1 Problem: Knowledge Solution: Move to Field 2

The first photo above shows a "gopp" discussion, which should be located in Douglas and Wildavsky's Field 3, where the knowledge about a given situation is certain but the goals and the means by which to achieve them are contested.

The table does not depict a necessary order of operations; it is an iteration process in which any field can be used as the starting point. As soon as a problem emerges, a search process is initiated, which can ideally be separated into four steps that are taken repeatedly. Negotiations in fact rarely begin in Field 1. Some negotiations might be drawn back into Field 1, though. Here it is uncertain what kind of situation one is in, what is its purpose, can it be achieved at all, who the affected parties are, who is legitimized to speak for them, how these affected parties see the situation, and what they want. It is even uncertain how to acquire the knowledge necessary for clarifying the situation. If the negotiations in Field 1 are to have any chance at all, the actors must move together into Field 2. In Douglas and Wildavsky's terms, this means that the actors need to improve and substantiate these elementary questions. In my terms, the consensus necessary for the move into Field 2 is achieved primarily by bracketing those dimensions that would challenge a common definition of what it is all about, i.e. by agreeing on a provisional definition of the common ground (a form of bluffing). This agreement is inspired more by the envisaged goal than by deep convictions about the "reality out there". Already here, in this provisional agreement, earlier power relations play a decisive role. Yet at the same time the imitation of seemingly successful models taking place here attributes power to these models that they did not have before.

In Field 2 a consensus must be reached on aperspectival, objective facts, which may lead to making the right decisions. This is facilitated by choosing procedures and instruments that carry the weight of being the best models available for the purpose at hand. These models and artifacts are utilized as boundary objects that are able to link heterogeneous fields because they are functional in several fields independently of the diverging basic assumptions in these fields (Star and Griesemer, 1989; Fujimura, 1992).

But the actors must move on to Field 3 if they intend to realize a concrete cooperation, because the verified scientific knowledge of Field 2 does not necessarily include evaluative and prescriptive information. As also Douglas and Wildavsky would agree, no definite formula for how to proceed emerges out of the objective description of a series of facts. It is at this point that my argument will differ from theirs, as I will explain later. In any case, in Field 3 the parties to the negotiation need to come to an agreement as to goals, and how these are best to be achieved based on acquired objective knowledge. The gopp discussants in the first photo are in the process of agreeing on how to best organize an urban water supply system.

Once a prescriptive agreement has been reached in Field 3 through consensus – in this case via a gopp procedure – the only remaining problem is to calculate the technical aspects of the intended cooperation. In the table this is signified by the move to Field 4. The planned cooperation is conducted and controlled on the basis of the agreed resolution. The activities represented in the second photo with the notebook in the middle can be located in Field 4. The figures in this scene know what they want, and are aware of their respective capabilities; they only need to calculate how they can best realize their goals.

The four-field scheme is built on two axes: differentiation of knowledge on the horizontal axis and consensus on the vertical one. This distinction corresponds to the difference between facts and values, or between what is true and what is good. In more abstract terms, the key difference here is between a *denotative language game* and an *evaluative* or a *prescriptive language game* (Lyotard, 1979/1986). In the course of this process of differentiation, the denotative language game comes to be understood as an event outside of society, which is only consensual (in Field 2) to the degree that it appears to be founded on the facts supposedly valid for all participants. From this perspective, i.e. the one taken by Douglas and Wildavsky, society, and with it the problem of coming to an agreement about goals and means, only becomes an issue in Field 3, at which time the application of neutral objective knowledge becomes value-laden.

This distinction is not convincing, though. Science, at least in unsettled, hot areas, historically does not seem to be converging on a single, increasingly valid version of reality. On the contrary, more conflicting versions of reality are constantly being produced. The growing numbers of answers being found do not seem to be reducing the numbers of questions being asked. There is no such thing as scientific expertise that could not be subject to a counterargument. The initial question is shifted from "how does one prove the objectivity of a statement?" to an unfathomable "how does one prove the proof?"

The work in Field 2 and the shift to Field 3 are, from this point of view, not activities taking place outside of society. They are activities that cannot draw on a neutral objectivity because they are interwoven, already in Field 2, with values and interpretations that depend on a chosen point of view. And the other way around, the problem of disagreements in terms of ideas about goals and means in Field 3 cannot be reduced to "evaluative" and "prescriptive" aspects. Every actor can draw, based on their ideas about goals and means, on other "denotative" statements from Field 2 to make their own ideas about these goals and means appear more realistic.

According to my thesis, the Douglas and Wildavsky table is nevertheless accurate, although in a sense other than that intended by the authors. The four-field scheme helps to see how and why the parties to a negotiation under conditions of heterogeneity need to pragmatically restrict themselves to a limited number of questions, to agree on a procedure, and to represent all that they do to achieve cooperation as founded in objective reality. They are aware that they are operating within an endless iteration process that they can bring to a stop only by avoiding fundamental questions relating to Fields 1 and 2 once they have moved back and forth several times. A persistent revisiting of Field 1 would result in an infinite loop in which the actors remain unable – at least for a time – to come to a denotative solution in Field 2, and an evaluative solution in Field 3. Without the determinations in Fields 2 and 3, arriving at Field 4 would never occur, and hence the intended cooperation would not materialize. Aside from the use of force, the only way to avoid an infinite loop is the staging of the selection of a chosen path as an event based on facts that are grounded in reality. It has been mentioned above that this selection is guided by the goal at hand, and that power and imitation play an important role here.

The assumption of a single reality with its metacode has a second, equally indispensable function, besides that of enabling cooperation under heterogeneous conditions. The participants in a bazaar negotiation are usually not acting in their own or only in their own name. They are representatives of collective actors to whom they are accountable, and in arguing their positions, they have to refer to generally agreed upon procedures. These procedures are again the result of similar negotiations.

From the perspective chosen here, the assumption of a single and attainable reality with its respective metacode is a political and juristic necessity.

A set of rules, the elementary principle of which is the key differentiation between denotative and evaluative language games, is necessary to remove from negotiation processes any sense of arbitrariness or ambiguity. But to ensure that this set of rules does not itself become a central instrument of hegemony, it is politically rational to keep these petitions to a single reality what they initially were – provisional agreements necessary within the limits of a particular framework, used to enable cooperation under conditions of heterogeneity. The uncertainty that results from such an assumption is insurmountable and simply has to be endured. The only consolation one can find is among epistemological and moral equals whom one meets in the evening, after leaving the bazaar, "in the club" (Rorty, 1991: 209). But the greatest comfort you get in the sort of club we are talking about here – the comfort that Rorty does not like to stress, although he is well aware of it (Rorty, 1991: 207) – is the particular kind of confirmation of one's superiority: a superiority that is not based in the belief of being in possession of ultimate truth but in the belief that one can self-reflectively relativize one's convictions after a bazaar experience.

Self-reflective questioning means nothing less than shifting back from the object of the negotiations to one's own frame of reference as an outside observer. The result is a constant switching back and forth between a meta-code with theoretical pretensions to correspondence with reality and a meta-code with theoretical pretensions to coherence with the cultural frame of the negotiations. Compared to aspirations of solving once and for all the justification paradox of objective statements through an absolute differentiation between reality and fiction, a code-switch seems a more reasonable alternative.

References

Aaker, David A. (1991) *Managing brand equity: Capitalizing on the value of a brand name*. New York: Free Press.

Aaker, David A. (1996) *Building strong brands*. New York: Free Press.

Abrahamson, Eric (1991) Managerial fads and fashions: The diffusion and rejection of innovations. *Academy of Management Review*, 16: 586–612.

Abrahamson, Eric (1996a) Technical and aesthetic fashion. In: Czarniawska, Barbara and Sevón, Guje (eds.) *Translating organization change*. Berlin: de Gruyter, 117–138.

Abrahamson, Eric (1996b) Management fashion. *Academy of Management Review*, 21: 254–285.

Abrahamson, Eric (1996c) Management fashion, academic fashion, and enduring truths – Response. *Academy of Management Review*, 21: 616–618.

Abrahamson, Eric, and Fairchild, Gregory (1999) Management fashion: Lifecycles, triggers and collective learning. *Administrative Science Quarterly*, December: 327–340.

Abramson, Alan J., Salamon, Lester, and Steuerle, C. Eugene (1999) The nonprofit sector and the federal budget: Recent history and future directions. In: Boris, Elizabeth T., Steuerle, C. Eugene (eds.) *Nonprofits and government: Collaboration and conflict*. Washington, DC: Urban Institute Press, 99–140.

Alchian, Armen (1950) Uncertainty, evolution, and economic theory. *Journal of Political Economy* 58: 211–221.

Alexander, Victoria D. (1996) Pictures at an exhibition: Conflicting pressures in museums and the display of art. *American Journal of Sociology*, 101: 797–839.

Appelbaum, Eileen, Bailey, Tom, Berg, Peter, and Kalleberg, Arne (Forthcoming) Organizations and the intersection of work and family: a comparative perspective. In: Thompson, Paul, Ackroyd, Stephan, Tolbert, Pam, and Batt, Rosemary (eds.) *The Oxford handbook on work and organization*. Oxford: Oxford University Press.

Arcangeli, Giuseppe and Zanellato, Gianluca (2002) Come riconoscere il vero "stoccafisso". *IL PESCE*, 2: 135–136.

Audit Commission (2001) *London Borough of Harrow – Refuse collection service. Best Value inspection*. London: Audit Commission.

Bagnasco, Arnaldo (1977) *Tre Italie: La problematica territoriale dello sviluppo italiano*. Bologna: Il Mulino.

Barnett, Michael N. and Finnemore, Martha (1999) The politics, power, and pathologies of international organizations. *International Organization*, 53(4): 699–733.

Barry, Andrew (2001) *Political machines. Governing a technological society*. London: Athlone Press.

Barthes, Roland (1967/1983) *The fashion system*. New York: Hill and Wang.

Benders, Jos, and van Veen, Kees (2001) What's in a fashion? Interpretative viability and management fashions. *Organization*, 8(1): 33–53.

Benjamin, Walter (1977) Die Aufgabe des Übersetzers. In: Benjamin, Walter, *Illuminationen*. Frankfurt am Main: Suhrkamp, 50–62.

Berg, Per-Olof (2003) Magic in action. Strategic management in a new economy. In: Czarniawska, Barbara, and Sevón, Guje (eds.) *The Northern Lights: Organization theory in Scandinavia*. Malmö: Liber, 291–315.

Bergevärn, Lars-Erik, and Olson, Olov (1987) *Kommunal redovisning då och nu. Längtan efter likformighet, rättvisa och affärsmässighet.* Lund: Doxa.

Berkovitch, Nitza (1999) *From motherhood to citizenship: Women's rights and international organizations.* Baltimore: Johns Hopkins University Press.

Bigg, Ada Heather (1893/1973) The evils of "fashion". In: Wills, Gordon and Midgley, David (eds.) *Fashion marketing.* London: Allen & Unwin, 35–46.

Bloor, David (1976/1991) *Knowledge and social imagery.* Chicago: University of Chicago Press.

Blumer, Herbert G. (1969/1973) Fashion: From class differentiation to collective selection. In: Wills, Gordon and Midgley, David (eds.) *Fashion Marketing.* London: Allen & Unwin, 327–340.

Borch, Odd Jarl, and Korneliussen, Tor (1995) *Norsk tørrfisknæring. Markedstilpasning og eksportorganisering.* Bodø: Nordlandsforskning, Report No. 2.

Borsuk, Richard. (1999) Chicago Business School picks Singapore – University to open permanent campus for Executive MBA students. *The Asian Wall Street Journal,* 25 January, p. 6.

Bourdieu, Pierre (1977/1980) The production of belief. Contribution to an economy of symbolic goods. *Media, Culture and Society,* 2: 261–293.

Bourdieu, Pierre (1984) *Homo academicus.* Paris: Èd. de Minuit.

Boyer, Robert, Charron, Elsie, Jürgens, Ulrich and Tolliday, Steven (1998) Between imitation and innovation. The transfer and hybridization of productive models in the international automobile industry. New York: Oxford University Press. Christensen, Tom and Laegreid, Per (2001) *New Public Management. The transformation of ideas and practice.* Aldershot: Ashgate.

Boyne, George A. (1999) Processes, performance and Best Value in local government. *Local Government Studies,* 2: 1–15.

Boyne, George A., Martin, Steve, and Walker, Richard (2001) *Explicit reforms, implicit theories and public service improvement: The case of Best Value.* Cardiff: Cardif University, Local & Regional Government Research Unit Discussion Paper No. 4.

Bragd, Annica (2002) *Knowing management – an ethnographic study of tinkering with a new car.* Gothenburg: BAS.

Braithwaite, John and Drahos, Peter (2000) *Global business regulation.* Cambridge, UK: Cambridge University Press.

Briers, Michael, and Chua, Wai Fong (2001) The role of actor-network and boundary objects in management accounting change: A field study of an implementation of activity-based costing. *Accounting, Organizations and Society,* 26: 237–269.

Brorström, Björn, and Siverbo, Sven (2001) *Institutioner och individer: om utveckling i framgångsrika kommuner.* Lund: Studentlitteratur.

Brorström, Björn, and Solli, Rolf (2000) Förändrad styrning och avsedda effekter – Om formella styrsystem i samklang med värdeförskjutningar. *Økonomistyring & Informatik.* 6: 457–475.

Brown, Steve (2002) Michel Serres: Science, translation and the logic of the parasite. *Theory, Culture & Society,* 19(3): 1–28.

Brunsson, Karin (1998) Non-learning organization. *Scandinavian Journal of Management,* 14(4): 421–432.

Brunsson, Nils (1989) *The organization of hypocrisy: Talk, decisions and actions in organizations.* Chichester: John Wiley & Sons.

Brunsson, Nils, and Olsen, Johan P. (1993) (eds.) *The reforming organization.* London: Routledge.

Brunsson, Nils, and Sahlin-Andersson, Kerstin (2000) Constructing organizations: The example of public sector reform. *Organization Studies*, 21(4): 721–746.

Brusco, Sebastino (1982) The Emilian model: Productive decentralization and social integration. *Cambridge Journal of Economics*, 6: 167–184.

Bryntse, Karin (2000) *Kontraktsstyrning i teori och praktik*. Lund: Lund Business Press.

Butler, David (2004) Memorandum. School of Hotel Administration, Cornell University, available at: http://web.cornell.edu/UniversityFaculty/FacSen/041013 SenateMtg/CAPP-SINGAPORE%20MEMO%2091704%201.htm, accessed 21 March 2005.

Callahan, Raymond (1962) *Education and the cult of efficiency*. Chicago: University of Chicago Press.

Callon, Michel (1980) Struggles to define what is problematic and what is not: The sociologic of translation. In: Knorr, Karin, Krohn, Roger G., and Whitley, Richard (eds.) *The social process of scientific investigation: Sociology of the sciences*. Dordrecht: D. Reidel, 197–219.

Callon, Michel (1986) Some elements of a sociology of translation: Domestication of the scallops and the fishermen of St Brieu's bay. In: Law, John (ed.) *Power, action and belief. A new sociology of knowledge?* London: Routledge & Kegan Paul, 196–229.

Callon, Michel (1991) Techno-economic networks and irreversibility. In: Law. John (ed.) *A sociology of monsters. Essays on power, technology and domination*. London: Routledge, 132–164.

Castells, Manuel (2001) *The internet galaxy. Reflections on the internet, business, and society*. Oxford: Oxford University Press.

Chang, Mariko Lin (2000) The evolution of sex segregation regimes. *American Journal of Sociology*, 105: 1658–1701.

Chapin, F. Stuart (1928) *Cultural change*. Dubuque, IO: Wm. C. Brown.

Christensen, Tom, and Lægreid Per (eds.) (2001) *New Public Management – The transformations of ideas and practice*. Aldershot: Ashgate.

Chua, Beng Huat (1997) *Political legitimacy and housing: Stakeholding in Singapore*. New York: Routledge.

Chui, Stephen, Ho, Kong Chong, and Lui, Tai-Lok (1997) *City-states in the global economy*. Boulder: Westview Press.

Clammer, John (2001) The dilemmas of the over-socialized intellectual: the universities and the political and institutional dynamics of knowledge in postcolonial Singapore. *Inter-Asia Cultural Studies*, 2(2): 199–220.

Clark, Terry N. (1969) Introduction. In: Clark, Terry N. (ed.), *Gabriel Tarde on communication and social influence*. Chicago: The University of Chicago Press, 1–69.

Clark, Timothy (2004) The fashion of management fashion: A surge too far? *Organization*, 11(2): 297–306.

Clarke, Adele E. (1991) Social worlds/arenas theory as organizational theory. In: Maines, David R. (ed.) *Social organization and social process. Essays in honor of Anselm Strauss*. New York: Aldine de Gruyter, 119–158.

Coe, Neil, and Kelly, Philip (2000) Distance and discourse in the local labour market: the case of Singapore. *Area*, 32(4): 413–422.

Coe, Neil, and Kelly, Philip (2002) Languages of labour: representational strategies in Singapore's labour control regime. *Political Geography*, 21: 341–371.

Cohen, Michael. D., March, James G., and Olsen, Johan P. (1972) A garbage can model of organizational choice. *Administrative Science Quarterly*, 17(1): 1–25.

Crainer, Stuart and Dearlove, Des (1999) *Gravy training: Inside the business of business schools*. San Francisco: Jossey-Bass.

Creed, William E.D., Scully, Maureen A., and Austin, J.R. (2002) Clothes make the person? The tailoring of legitimacy accounts and the social construction of identity. *Organization Science*, 13: 475–496.

Czarniawska, Barbara (1999) *Det var en gång en stad på vatten, Berättelser om organisering och organisering av berättelser i Stockholm*. Stockholm: SNS Förlag.

Czarniawska, Barbara (2001) Anthropology and organizational learning. In: Dierkes, Meinholf, Berthoin Antal, Ariane, Child, John and Nonaka, Ikuijro (eds.) *Handbook of organizational learning and knowledge*. Oxford: Oxford University Press, 118–136.

Czarniawska, Barbara (2002) *A tale of three cities, or the glocalization of city management*. Oxford: Oxford University Press.

Czarniawska, Barbara (2004a) Metaphors as enemies of organizing, or the advantages of a flat discourse. *International Journal of Sociological Linguistics*,166: 45–65.

Czarniawska, Barbara (2004b) On time, space and action nets. *Organization*, 11(6): 777–795.

Czarniawska, Barbara (2004c) Gabriel Tarde and city management. *Distinktion*, 9: 119–133.

Czarniawska, Barbara, and Hernes, Tor (2005) Constructing macro-actors according to ANT. In: Czarniawska, Barbara and Hernes, Tor (eds.) *Actor-network theory and organizing*. Malmö: Liber, 1–8.

Czarniawska, Barbara, and Joerges, Bernward (1995) Winds of organizational change: How to translate into objects and actions. In: Bacharach, Samuel, Gagliardi, Pasquale, and Mundell, Brian (eds.) *Research in the sociology of organizations*, vol. 13. Greenwich: JAI Press, 171–209.

Czarniawska, Barbara, and Joerges, Bernward (1996) Travels of ideas. In: Czarniawska, Barbara and Sevón, Guje (eds.) *Translating organizational change*. Berlin: de Gruyter, 13–48.

Czarniawska, Barbara, and Sevón, Guje (1996) Introduction. In: Czarniawska, Barbara and Sevón, Guje (eds.) *Translating organizational change*. Berlin: de Gruyter, 1–17.

Daniel, Carter (1998) *MBA: The first century*. London: Associated University Press.

Daston, Lorraine (2001) *Wunder, Beweise, Tatsachen. Zur Geschichte der Rationalität*. Frankfurt am Main: Fischer.

Davidson, Donald (1986/1992) A coherence theory of truth and knowledge. In: LePore, Ernest (ed.) *Interpretation and truth: Perspectives on the philosophy of Donald Davidson* Oxford: Blackwell.

Davis, Gerald F. (1991) Agents without principles? The spread of the poison pill through the intercorporate network. *Administrative Science Quarterly*, 36: 583–613.

Davis, Gerald F., Diekmann, Kristina A., and Tinsley, Catherine H. (1994) The decline and fall of the conglomerate firm in the 1980s. *American Sociological Review*, 59: 547–70.

Davis, Howard, Downe, James, and Martin, Steve (2001) *External inspection of local government – Driving improvement or drowning in detail?*. Layerthorpe: York Publishing Service Ltd.

Dees, Gregory, Emerson, Jed, and Economy, Peter (2001) *Enterprising nonprofits: A toolkit for social entrepreneurs.* New York: John Wiley.

Deibert, Ronald J. (2000) International plug 'n play? Citizen activism, the internet, and global public. *Policy International Studies Perspectives*, 1(3): 255–272.

del Río, A. Belén, Vázquez, Rodolfo, and Iglesias, Víctor (2001) The role of the brand name in obtaining differential advantages. *Journal of Product & Brand Management*, 10(7): 452–465.

den-Dulk, Laura (2001) Work-family arrangements in organisations: A cross-national study in the Netherlands, Italy, the United Kingdom, and Sweden. Amsterdam: Rozenberg.

Dicken, Peter (2003) *Global shift: Reshaping the global economic map in the 21st century.* (fourth edition) London: Sage.

Diedrich, Andreas (2004) *Engineering knowledge – How engineers and managers practice knowledge management.* Gothenburg: BAS.

DiMaggio, Paul J. (1983) State expansion in organizational fields. In: Hall, Richard H., and Quinn, Robert E. (eds.) *Organizational theory and public policy.* Beverley Hills, CA: Sage, 147–161.

DiMaggio, Paul, J. (1987) Classification in art. *American Sociological Review*, 52(4): 440–455.

DiMaggio, Paul J., and Powell, Walter W. (1983/1991) The iron cage revisited: Institutional isomorphism and collective rationality. *American Sociological Review* 48: 147–160. Reprinted in: Powell, Walter W., and DiMaggio, Paul J. (eds.) *The new institutionalism in organizational analysis.* Chicago: University of Chicago Press, 63–82.

DiMaggio, Paul J., and Powell, Walter W. (1991) Introduction. In: Powell, Walter W., and DiMaggio, Paul J. (eds.) *The new institutionalism in organizational analysis.* Chicago: University of Chicago Press, 1–38.

Djelic, Marie-Laure (1998) *Exporting the American model. The postwar transformation of European business.* New York: Oxford University Press.

Dobbin, Frank R. (1993) The social construction of the Great Depression: Industrial policy during the 1930s in the United States, Britain, and France. *Theory and Society*, 22: 1–56.

Dobbin, Frank, Sutton, John R., Meyer, John W., and Scott, W. Richard (1993) Equal opportunity law and the construction of internal labor markets. *American Journal of Sociology* 99(2): 396–427.

Dobers, Peter (2001) Netting the information infrasystem of Stockholm. An idea spreads throughout the world. In: Glimell, Hans and Juhlin, Oskar (eds.) *The social production of technology. On the everyday life with things.* Göteborg: BAS, 189–206.

Dobers, Peter (2002) Broadband – boom and bust in the New Economy. In: Holmberg, Ingalill, Salzer-Mörling, Miriam, and Strannegård, Lars (eds.) *Creating the future. An exploration of the "New Economy".* Stockholm: Bookhouse, 79–104.

Dobers, Peter (2003) Image of Stockholm as an IT City: Emerging urban entrepreneurship. In: Bjerke, Björn, Delmar, Frédéric, Hjorth, Daniel, and Steyaert, Chris (eds.): *New movements in entrepreneurship.* Aldershot: Edward Elgar, 200–217.

Douglas, Mary, and Wildavsky, Aaron (1982) *Risk and culture. An essay on the selection of technical and environmental dangers.* Berkeley, CA: University of California Press.

du Gay, Paul, and Pryke, Michael (2002) *Cultural economy. Cultural analysis and commercial life.* London: Sage.

Eco, Umberto (1989) *The open work*. Cambridge, MA: Harvard University Press.

Eco, Umberto (1990) *The limits of interpretation*. Bloomington, IN: Indiana University Press.

Edelman, Lauren (1990) Legal environments and organizational governance: The expansion of due process in the American workplace. *American Journal of Sociology*, 95: 1401–1440.

Efmd (1998) *Annual report*.

Elsbach, Kimberley D. (1994) Managing organizational legitimacy in the California cattle industry. *Administrative Science Quarterly* 39: 57–88.

Engwall, Lars (1992) *Mercury meets Minerva. Business studies and higher education, the Swedish case*. Oxford: Pergamon Press.

Engwall, Lars, and Pahlberg, Cecilia (2001) *The diffusion of European management ideas*. Uppsala: Uppsala University, Department of Business Studies, CEMP Report No. 17.

Engwall, Lars, and Zamagni, Vera (eds.) (1998) *Management education in historical perspective*. Manchester: Manchester University Press.

Enright, Dennis, Joseph (1969) *Memoirs of a mendicant professor*. London: Chatto and Windus.

ERC (2002a) *Report of the ERC Subcommittee on Services Industries: Part I*, Singapore: ERC, available at: http://www.erc.gov.sg/frm ERC ErcReports.htm (accessed 1 December 2003).

ERC (2002b) *Developing Singapore's Education Industry*, Singapore: ERC, available at: http://www.erc.gov.sg/frm ERC ErcReports.htm (accessed 21 March 2005).

Erlingsdóttir, Gudbjörg (1999) *Förförande idéer – kvalitetssäkring i hälso- och sjukvården*. Lund: KFS AB.

Erlingsdóttir, Gudbjörg, and Jonnergård, Karin (2006) *Att trolla med kvalitetssäkring – en jämförelse mellan hälso- och sjukvården och revisorbranschen*. Lund: Studentlitteratur.

Ernst, Berit, and Kieser, Alfred (2002) In search of explanations for the consulting explosion. In: Sahlin-Andersson, Kerstin, and Engwall, Lars (eds.) *The expansion of management knowledge*. Stanford, CA: Stanford University Press, 47–73.

Esping-Andersen, Gösta (1999) *Social foundations of postindustrial economies*. New York: Oxford University Press.

Financial Times, 25 January 1999. *Ranking Can Both Help and Rankle*.

Financial Times, 8 September 2000. *Consensus the Ideal*.

Finkelstein, Joanne (1989) *Dining out. A sociology of modern manners*. Cambridge, UK: Polity Press.

Finnemore, Martha (1996) *National interests in international society*. Ithaca, N.Y.: Cornell University Press.

Fish, Stanley (1989) *Doing what comes naturally: change, rhetoric, and the practice of theory in literary and legal studies*. Durham and London: Duke University Press.

Fiskerinæringens Felles Kompetansestyre (1990) *Stockfish, agreement on quality*. Tromsø: Fiskerinæringens Felles Kompetansestyre.

Fligstein, Neil (1985) The spread of the multidivisional form among large firms, 1919–1979. *American Sociological Review*, 50: 377–391.

Florida, Richard (2002) *The rise of the creative class. And how it's transforming work, leisure, community and everyday life*. New York: Basic Books.

Flügel, J. C. (1930/1973) The forces of fashion. In: Wills, Gordon and Midgley, David (eds.) *Fashion marketing*. London: Allen & Unwin, 229–239.

280

Flyvbjerg, Bent (2001) *Making social science matter. Why social inquiry fails and how it can succeed again.* Cambridge, UK: Cambridge University Press.

Fogiel-Bijawi, Sylvie (1997) Women in Israel: The politics of citizenship as a non-issue. *Israel Social Science Research*, 12:1–30.

Foley, Caroline A. (1893/1973) Consumer fashion. In: Wills, Gordon and Midgley, David (eds.) *Fashion marketing.* London: Allen & Unwin, 157–169.

Forty, Adrian (1986) *Objects of desire. Design and society 1750–1980.* London: Cameron.

Fountain, Jane E. (2001) *Building the virtual state: Information technology and institutional change.* Washington D.C.: Brookings Institute Press.

Freudenberger, Herman (1963/1973) Fashion, sumptuary laws and business. In: Wills, Gordon and Midgley, David (eds.) *Fashion marketing.* London: Allen & Unwin, 137–146.

Friedland, Roger, and Alford, Robert R. (1991) Bringing society back in: Symbols, practices, and institutional contradictions. In: Powell, Walter W., and DiMaggio, Paul J. (eds.) *The new institutionalism in organizational analysis.* Chicago: University of Chicago Press, 232–263.

Fujimura, Joan H. (1992) Crafting science: Standardized packages, boundary objects, and "translation". In: Pickering, Andrew (ed.) *Science as practice and culture.* Chicago: University of Chicago Press, 168–211.

Galinsky, Ellen (2001) Toward a new view of work and family life. In: Hertz, Rosanna (ed.) *Working families.* Berkley, CA: University of California Press, 168–186.

Galison, Peter (1997) *Image and logic: a material culture of microphysics.* Chicago: University of Chicago Press.

Geertz, Clifford (1983/1993) From the native's point of view: On the nature of anthropological understanding. In: Geertz, Clifford, *Local knowledge. Further essays in interpretive anthropology.* London: Fontana Press, 55–70.

Gellner, Ernest (1992/1995) *Descartes & Co. Von der Vernunft und ihren Feinden.* Frankfurt am Main: Junius. (English original, 1992: *Reason and culture: A sociological and philosophical study of the role of rationality and rationalism,* Oxford: Blackwell).

George, Cherian (2000) *Singapore: The air conditioned nation: Essays on the politics of comfort and control 1990–2000.* Singapore: Landmark Books.

Gibson, William (1993) Disneyland with the death penalty. *Wired*, September/October, available at http://www.wired.com/wired/archive/1.04/gibson.html, accessed 22 March 2005.

Gibson, William (1999) *All tomorrow's parties.* New York: Viking.

Gill, John, and Whittle, Sue (1993) Managing by panacea: Accounting for transience. *Journal of Management Studies*, 30(2): 281–295.

Girard, René (1977) *Violence and the sacred.* Baltimore, MD: John Hopkins University Press.

Glaser, Barney. G., and Strauss, Anselm L. (1967) *The discovery of grounded theory. Strategies for qualitative research.* Chicago: Aldine.

Glass, Jennifer (2000) Envisioning the integration of family and work: Toward a kinder, gentler workplace. *Contemporary Sociology*, 29: 129–143.

Glass, Jennifer (2004) Blessing of course: Work-family policies and mothers' wage growth over time. *Work and Occupations*, 31.

Goffman, Erving (1959) *The presentation of self in everyday life.* Garden City, NY: Doubleday.

Goffman, Erving (1967) *Interaction ritual: Essays on face-to-face behavior*. Garden City, NY: Anchor Books.

Gornick, Janet C., and Meyers, Marcia. (2003) *Families that work: Policies for reconciling parenthood and employment*. New York: Russell Sage Foundation.

Granovetter, Mark (1973) The strength of weak ties. *American Journal of Sociology*, 78: 1360–1380.

Greenwood, Royston, Suddaby, Roy, and Hinings, C. R. (2002) Theorizing change: The role of professional associations in the transformation of institutionalized fields. *Academy of Management Journal*, 45: 58–80.

Greimas, Algirdas Julien, and Courtés, Joseph (1982) *Semiotics and language. An analytical dictionary*. Bloomington, IN: Indiana University Press.

Haas, Peter M. (1992) Introduction: Epistemic communities and international policy coordination. Special issue of *International Organization*, 46 (1), *Knowledge, power and international policy coordination*: 1–35.

Hacking, Ian (1999) *The social construction of what?* Cambridge, MA: Harvard Univ: Press.

Hall, Peter Dobkin (1997) Business giving and social investment in the United States, 1970–1995. *New York Law School Review*, 41: 789–817.

Hall, Peter Dobkin (2006) A historical overview of philanthropy, voluntary associations, and nonprofit organizations in the United States, 1600–2000. In: Powell, Walter W., and Steinberg, R. (eds.) *The nonprofit sector: A research handbook*, 2nd ed. New Haven, CT: Yale University Press.

Hansen, Hans Krause (1998) Governmental mismanagement and symbolic violence. Discourses on corruption in the Yucatán of the 1990s. *Bulletin of Latin American Research*, 17 (3): 367–386.

Hansen, Hans Krause (2002) ¿Salidas de una mala administración? Racionalidad administrativa y prácticas de comunicación en el campo político: el caso de un municipio en el norte de México. *Gestión y Política Pública*, XI (1): 157–181.

Hansen, Hans Krause, and Salskov-Iversen, Dorte (2005) Remodelling the Transnational Political Realm: Partnerships, Benchmarking Schemes and the Digitalization of Governance. In: Alternatives, Volume 30, Number 2, 2005.

Hansen, Hans Krause, Langer, Roy, and Salskov-Iversen, Dorte (2001) Managing political communications. *Corporate Reputation Review*, 4(2): 167–184.

Hansen, Hans Krause, Salskov-Iversen, Dorte, and Bislev, Sven (2002) Discursive globalization: Transnational discourse communities and New Public Management. In: Ougaard, Morten and Higgot, Richard (eds.) *Towards a global polity*. London: Routledge.

Hansen, Katja Øder (2004) *"At gøre INDTRYK med det rigtige UDTRYCK" – en antropologisk undersøgelse af event markedsførg i en dansk kontekst*. Copenhagen: Copenhagen University, Department of Social Anthropology, Master Thesis 320.

Hansen, Lee (ed.) (1998) *Academic freedom on trial: 100 years of sifting and winnowing at the University of Wisconsin-Madison*, Madison: Office of University Publications.

Hark, Helmut (1997) *Jungianska grundbegrepp från A till Ö*. Stockholm: Natur och Kultur.

Hauan, Arnulf (2000) *Kunnskap-i-kontekst, Betydningen av kunnskap-i-kontekst for samhandling i økonomiske verdikjeder*. Bodø: Siviløkonomutdanningen i Bodø.

Hedmo, Tina (2004) *Rulemaking in the transnational space: The development of European accreditation of management education.* Unpublished doctoral thesis, No 109, Department of Business Studies, Uppsala University.

Hedmo, Tina, Sahlin-Andersson, Kerstin and Wedlin, Linda (2006) The emergence of a European regulatory field of management education. In: Djelic, Marie-Laure, and Sahlin-Andersson, Kerstin (eds.) *Transnational Governance: Institutional Dynamics of Regulation.* Cambridge: Cambridge University Press.

Heide, Jan B., and John, George (1988) The role of dependence balancing in safeguarding transaction-specific assets in conventional channels. *Journal of Marketing,* 52: 20–35.

Heidegger, Martin (1938/2003) Die Zeit des Weltbildes. In: Heidegger, Martin, *Holzwege.* Frankfurt am Main: Klostermann, 67–113.

Higgot, Richard A., Underhill, Geoffrey R.D., and Bieler, Andreas (eds.) (2000) *Non-state actors and authority in the global system.* London: Routledge.

Hirsch, Paul M., and Lounsbury, Michael (1997) Ending the family quarrel: towards a reconciliation of "old" and "new" institutionalism. *American Behavioral Scientist,* 40,4: 406–418.

Ho, Wah Kam, and Gopinathan, S. (1999) Recent developments in education in Singapore. *School Effectiveness and School Improvement,* 10(1): 99–117.

Hobsbawm, Eric, and Ranger, Terence (1993) *The invention of tradition.* Cambridge, UK: Cambridge University Press.

Hochschild, Arlie Russell (1997) *The time bind: when work becomes home and home becomes work.* New York: Metropolitan Books.

Hofstadter, Richard (1955) *Academic freedom in the age of the college.* New York: Columbia University Press.

Holm, Petter, and Nielsen, Kåre Nolde (2004) *The cyborg fish and the invisible hand: Making market models work in the fisheries.* Norwegian College of Fishery Science, University of Tromsø.

Hood, Christopher (1995) The "New Public Management" in the 1980s: Variations on a theme. *Accounting, Organizations and Society,* 20(2/3): 93–109.

Högdahl, Elisabeth (2003) *Göra gatan. Om gränser och kryphål på Möllevången och i Kapstaden.* (Doing the street. On borders and loopholes in Möllevången and Cape Town) Hedemora: Gidlunds förlag.

Islas, Ottavio, and Gutierrez, Fernando (2003) Los amigos de Microsoft. *Revista Mexicana de Comunicación,* 79 (January–February): 1–7.

Izraeli, Dafna N. (1993) Work/family conflict among women and men managers in dual-career couples in Israel. *Journal of Social Behavior and Personality,* 8: 371–388.

Izraeli, Dafna N. (1995) Gender and trade unions. *Industrial and Labor Relations Review* 49: 173–174.

Izraeli, Dafna N. (2003) Gender politics in Israel: The case of affirmative action for women directors. *Women's Studies International Forum* 26: 109–128.

Izraeli, Dafna N., and Tabory, Ephraim (1988) The political context of feminist attitudes in Israel. *Gender & Society,* 2: 463–481.

Jacobs, Jane (1961) *The death and life of the great American city.* New York: Random House.

Jacobsson, Bengt (1995) Le organizzazione come oggetto volontario di standardizzazione. *Rivista Trimestrale di Scienza dell'Amministrazione,* 3: 5–26.

Jaukkuri, Maaretta (1999) *Artscape Nordland.* Bodø: Nordland Fylkeskommune.

Jentoft, Svein and Kristoffersen, Trond (1989) Fishermen's co-management: The case of the Lofoten fishery. *Human Organization,* 48(4): 355–365.

Johannesen, Petter, and Magipinto, Massimo (1996) *Stoccafisso – il tesoro delle Lofoten*. Trento: Sirio Film.

Johnson, Richard (1986–7) What is cultural studies anyway? *Social Text*, 16: 38–80.

Jönsson, Sten (1995) *Goda utsikter*. Stockholm: Nerenius & Santérus.

Karsteinsen, Kari (2001) Flere kommuner halvert. *Nordlands Framtid:* January 19: 28.

Katz, Stanley N. (2004) *What does it mean to say that philanthropy is "effective"? The philanthropists' new clothes*. Paper delivered to American Philosophical Association annual meeting, Philadelphia, PA.

Kelly, Erin L. (2003) The strange history of employer-sponsored child care: Interested actors, uncertainty, and the transformation of law in organizational fields. *American Journal of Sociology*, 109: 606–649.

Kelly, Erin L. (1999) Theorizing corporate family policies: How advocates built "the business case" for "Family-Friendly" programs. *Research in the Sociology of Work*, 7: 169–202.

Kelly, Erin L., and Dobbin, Frank (1998) How affirmative action became diversity management – Employer response to antidiscrimination law, 1961 to 1996. *American Behavioral Scientist*, 41: 960–984.

Kelly, Erin L., and Dobbin, Frank (1999) Civil rights law at work: Sex discrimination and the rise of maternity leave policies. *American Journal of Sociology*, 105: 455–492.

Kieser, Alfred (2002) Managers as marionettes? Using fashion theories to explain the success of consultants. In: Kipping, Matthias, and Engwall, Lars (eds.) *Management consulting: Emergence and dynamics of a knowledge industry*. Oxford, UK: Oxford University Press, 167–183.

Klein, Naomi (2000) *No logo: No space, no choice, no jobs, taking aim at the brand bullies*. London: Flamingo.

Kong, Lily, and Yeoh, Brenda (2002) *The politics of landscape in Singapore: Constructions of "nation"*. Syracuse: Syracuse University Press.

Koolhaus, Rem, and Mau, Bruce (1995) *Small, medium, large, extra-Large*. Rotterdam: 010 Publishers.

Korneliussen, Tor (2000) Marketing relationships outside the marketing realm [CD-ROM]. In: Ford, David, Naude, Peter, Ritter, Thomas, Turnbull, Peter W., and Leek, S. (eds.): *Proceedings of the 16th Annual Industrial Marketing and Purchasing Conference*. Bath: University of Bath School of Management.

Korneliussen, Tor, and Pedersen, Pål A. (2001) Quality assessment in international industrial markets: The case of Norwegian stockfish [CD-ROM]. In: Håkansson, Håkan, Solberg, Carl Arthur, Huemer, Lars, and Steigum, Lillian (eds.): *Interactions, relationships and networks: Strategic dimensions. Proceedings of the 17th Annual Industrial Marketing and Purchasing Conference*. Oslo: The Norwegian School of Management BI.

Kossick, Robert M. Jr (2003) *Tramitament. Transforming the delivery of government services*. Mexico, D.F: Institute for Connectivity in the Americas, Centro de Investigación y Docencia Económicas (CIDE).

Kracauer, Siegfried (1930/1998) *The salaried masses. Duty and distraction in Weimar Germany*. London: Verso.

Kurlansky, Mark (1997) *Cod. A biography of the fish that changed the world*. New York: Vintage.

Latour, Bruno (1986) The powers of association. In: Law, John (ed.) *Power, action and belief*. London: Routledge and Kegan Paul, 261–277.

Latour, Bruno (1987) *Science in action: How to follow scientists and engineers through society*. Cambridge, MA: Harvard University Press.

Latour, Bruno (1990) Drawing things together. In: Lynch, Michael and Woolgar, Steve (eds.), *Representation in scientific practice*. Cambridge, Massachusetts: MIT Press, 19–68.

Latour, Bruno (1996a) *Aramis or the love of technology*. Cambridge, Massachusetts: Harvard University Press.

Latour, Bruno (1996b) *Petite réflexion sur le culte moderne des dieux faitiches*. Le Plessis-Robinson: Synthélabo.

Latour, Bruno (1998) *Artefaktens återkomst*. Stockholm: Nerenius & Santérus.

Latour, Bruno (1999) *Pandora's hope*. Cambridge, MA: Harvard University Press.

Latour, Bruno (2002) Gabriel Tarde and the end of the social. In: Joyce, Patrick (ed.) *The social in question*. London: Routledge, 117–132.

Law, John, and Hetherington, Keith (2000) Materialities, spatialities, globalitites. In: Bryson, John R., Daniels, Peter W., Henry, Nick, and Pollard, Jane (eds.) *Knowledge, space, economy*. London: Routledge.

Lawrence, Thomas B., Hardy, Cynthia, and Phillips, Nelson (2002) Institutional effects of interorganizational collaboration: The emergence of proto-institutions. *Academy of Management Journal,* 45(1): 281–291.

Leblebici, Huseyin, Salancik, Gerald R., Copay, Anne, and King, Tom (1991) Institutional change and the transformation of interorganizational fields: An organizational history of the U. S. radio broadcasting industry. *Administrative Science Quarterly,* 36 (September): 333–363.

Lee, Kuan Yew (1966) *Academic freedom and social responsibility*. Speech given at the Historical Society, University of Singapore, 24 November, available at: http://stars.nhb.gov.sg/public/index.html, accessed 20 March 2005.

Lee, Kuan Yew (2000) *From third world to first: The Singapore story, 1965–2000*. Singapore: Times Editions.

Lee, Michael, and Gopinathan, S. (2003) Reforming university education in Hong Kong and Singapore. *Higher Education Research & Development*, 22(2): 167–182.

Lehtovuori, Panu (2001) Public space as a resource for urban policy – Notes on 1990s Helsinki. In: Czarniawska, Barbara and Solli, Rolf (eds.) *Organizing metropolitan space and discourse*. Malmö: Liber, 67–89.

Leopold, Ellen (1992) The manufacture of the fashion system. In: Ash, Juliet, and Wilson, Elizabeth (eds.) *Chic thrills: A fashion reader*. Berkeley, CA: University of California Press, 101–118.

Letts, Christine, Ryan, W., and Grossman, A. (1997) Virtuous capital: What foundations can learn from venture capitalists. *Harvard Business Review,* Mar–Apr: 2–7.

Lévi-Strauss, Claude (1983/1993) *Der Blick aus der Ferne*. Frankfurt am Main: Fischer. (English version: *The view from afar*, Chicago: Chicago University Press, 1992).

Lewis, Jane (2001) The decline of the male breadwinner model: Implications for work and care. *Social Politics,* 8: 152–169.

Lewin, Kurt (1951) *Field theory in social science: Selected theoretical papers*. New York: Harper & Brothers.

Light, Paul (2004) *Sustaining nonprofit performance*. Washington, DC: The Brookings Institution.

Lindbeck, Assar, Molander, Per, Persson, Torsten, Petersson, Olof, and Swedenborg, Birgitta (2000) *Ekonomirådets rapport 2000: Politisk makt med oklart ansvar.* Stockholm: SNS.

Lindberg Kajsa (2002) *Kopplandets kraft. Omorganisering mellan organisationer.* Gothenburg: BAS.

Litvin, Deborah R. (2002) The business-case for diversity and the iron cage. In:Czarniawska, Barbara, and Höpfl, Heather (eds.) *Casting the other: the production and maintenance of inequalities in work organizations.* London: Routledge, 160–184.

Locke, Robert (1989) *Management and higher education since 1940. The influence of America and Japan on West Germany, Great Britain, and France.* Cambridge: Cambridge University Press.

Löfgren, Orvar (1999) *On holiday. A history of vacationing.* Berkeley: University of California Press.

Löfgren, Orvar (2003) The New Economy: A cultural history. *Global Networks. A Journal of Transnational Affairs*, 3: 239–254.

Löfgren, Orvar, and Willim, Robert (eds.) (2005) *Magic, culture and the New Economy.* Oxford: Berg.

Lubove, Roy (1965) *The professional altruist: The emergence of social work as a career 1880–1930.* Boston: Harvard University Press.

Luhmann, Niklas (1991) Sthenographie und Euryalistik. In: Gumbrecht, Hans Ulrich, and Pfeiffer, K. Ludwig (eds.) *Paradoxien, Dissonanzen, Zusammenbrüche. Situationen offener Epistemologien.* Frankfurt am Main: Suhrkamp, 58–82.

Lukes, Steven (ed.) (1986) *Power.* Oxford: Basil Blackwell.

Lyotard, Jean-Francois (1979/1986) *A postmodern condition: A report on knowledge.* Manchester: Manchester University Press.

MacIntyre, Alasdaire, C. (1981) *After virtue: A study in moral theory.* London: Duckworth.

Malinowski, Bronislaw (1937) Introduction. In: Lips, Julius E., *The savage hits back or the white man through native eyes.* New Haven: Yale University Press.

March, James G. (1999) A learning perspective on the network dynamics of institutional integration. In: Egeberg, M. and Laegreid, P. (eds.) *Organizing political institutions.* Oslo: Scandinavian University Press, 129–155.

March, James G., and Olsen, Johan P. (1998) The institutional dynamics of international political orders. *International Organization, 52,* 4: 943–969.

Martin, John Levi (2003) What is field theory? *American Journal of Sociology,* 109(1): 1–49.

Mathiesen Hjemdahl, Kirsti (2000) Oplevelsesindustri på Sörlandet. (www.kulturviter.no).

Mauser, Elizabeth (1998) The importance of organizational form: Parent perceptions versus reality in the day care industry. In: Powell, Walter W., and Clemens, Elisabeth (eds.) *Private action and the public good.* New Haven, CT: Yale University Press 114–123.

Mazza, Carmelo, and Alvarez, José-Luis (2000) Haute couture and prét-à-porter. The popular press and the diffusion of management practices. *Organization Studies,* 21(3): 567–588.

Mazza, Carmelo, Sahlin-Andersson, Kerstin, and Strandgaard, Jesper (1998) *MBA: European Constructions of an American Model.* SCORE Report 1998: 4.

McKenna, Christopher (2005) *The world's newest profession: Management consulting in the twentieth century.* Cambridge, UK: Cambridge University Press.

Mead, George H. (1934) *Mind, self and society: From the standpoint of social behaviorist.* Chicago: University of Chicago Press.

Melin, Frans (1999) *Varumärkesstrategi: om konsten att utveckla starka varumärken.* Malmö: Liber.

Menand, Louis (ed.) (1996) *The future of academic freedom.* Chicago: University of Chicago Press.

Merton, Robert K. (1945/1968) The sociology of knowledge. In: Merton, Robert K., *Social theory and social structure.* New York: The Free Press, 510–542.

Merton, Robert K. (1965/1985) *On the shoulders of giants: A Shandean postscript. An Italianate edition.* New York: Harcourt and Jovanovich.

Metiu, Anca (2002) *Escalation of disengagement across multiple boundaries.* Paper presented at EGOS, Barcelona July 1–3.

Metzger, Walter (1955) *Academic Freedom in the Age of the University.* New York: Columbia University Press.

Meyer, John W. (1994) Rationalized environments. In: Scott W. R. and Meyer, J. W. (eds.) *Institutional environments and organizations: Structural complexity and individualism.* Thousand Oaks, CA: Sage, 28–54.

Meyer, John W. (1996) Otherhood: The promulgation and transmission of ideas in the modern organizational environment. In: Czarniawska, Barbara and Sevón, Guje (eds.), *Translating Organizational Change.* Berlin: Walter de Gruyter, 241–272.

Meyer, John W. (2002) Globalization and the expansion and standardization of management. In: Sahlin-Andersson, K., and Engwall, L. (eds.) *The expansion of management knowledge: Carriers, flows, and sources.* Stanford, CA: Stanford University Press, 33–46.

Meyer, John W., Boli, John, and Thomas, George M. (1994) Ontology and rationalization in the western cultural account. In: Scott W,. Richard and Meyer, John W. (eds.) *Institutional environments and organizations: Structural complexity and individualism.* Thousand Oaks, CA: Sage, 9–27.

Meyer, John W., and Rowan, Brian (1977/1991) Institutionalized organizations – Formal structure as myth and ceremony. *American Journal of Sociology,* 83 (2): 340–363. Reprinted in: Powell, Walter W., and DiMaggio, Paul J. (eds.) *The new institutionalism in organizational analysis.* Chicago: University of Chicago Press, 41–62.

Miele, Mara, and Murdoch, Jonathan (2002) The practical aesthetic of traditional cuisines: Slow food in Tuscany. *Sociologia Ruralis,* 42(4): 312–328.

Mikunda, Christian (2002/2004) *Brand lands, hot spots & cool spaces. Welcome to the third place and the total marketing experience.* London: Kogan Page.

Miller, Peter, and Rose, Nikolas (1990) Governing economic life. *Economy and Society,* 19(1): 1–31.

Mintzberg, Henry (1979) *The structuring of organizations.* Englewood Cliffs, NJ: Prentice Hall.

Mintzberg, Henry (1994) *The rise and fall of strategic planning.* New York: Free Press.

Mizruchi, Mark S., and Fein, Lisa C. (1999) The social construction of organizational knowledge: A study of the uses of coercive, mimetic, and normative isomorphism. *Administrative Science Quarterly,* 44: 653–683.

Mohr, John W. (2005) Implicit terrains: Meaning, measurement, and spatial metaphors in organizational theory. In Ventresca, Marc, and Porac, Joseph (eds.) *Constructing industries and markets.* New York: Elsevier.

Mohr, John W., and Duquenne, Vincent (1997) The duality of culture and practice: Poverty relief in New York City, 1888–1917. *Theory and Society*, 26/2–3: 305–356.

Moon, Hyeyoung (2002) *The globalization of professional management education, 1881–2000: Its rise, expansion and implications*. Unpublished Doctoral Dissertation, Stanford University, Stanford, CA.

Morino Institute (2001) *Venture philanthropy: The changing landscape*.

Nagel, Thomas (1986/1992) *Der Blick von nirgendwo*. Frankfurt am Main: Suhrkamp. (English original: *The view from nowhere*, New York: Oxford University Press.)

Nalbandian, John (1991) *Professionalism in local government: transformations in the roles, responsibilities, and values of city managers*. San Francisco: Jossey-Bass Publishers.

Newell, Sue; Robertson, Maxine, and Swan, Jacky (2001) (eds.) *Management fads and fashions*. Special issue of *Organization*, 8(1).

Newton, Tim (1996) Agency and discourse: Recruiting consultants in a life insurance company. *Sociology*, 30(4): 717–739.

Nirmala, M. (2001) *"Campus courtships"*. Straits Times, 24 June, p. R1.

Norsk Bransjestandard for Fisk (1998) Sortering av tørrfisk. Bergen: Prosjekt bransjestandard for Fisk.

Nystrom, Paul (1928/1973) Character and direction of fashion movements. In: Wills, Gordon and Midgley, David (eds.) *Fashion Marketing*. London: Allen & Unwin, 193–205.

Oakes, L. S.; Townley, Barbara; and Cooper, David (1998) Business planning as pedagogy: Language and control in a changing institutional field. *Administrative Science Quarterly*, 43: 257–292.

O'Connor, Julia S.; Orloff, Ann Shola; and Shaver, Sheila. (1999) *States, markets, families: gender, liberalism, and social policy in Australia, Canada, Great Britain, and the United States*. New York: Cambridge University Press.

O'Dell, Thomas (ed.) (2005) *Experiencescapes: Tourism, culture and economy*. Copenhagen: Copenhagen Business School Press.

O'Keefe, Brendan (2004) Asian toast with Singapore fling. *The Australian*, 21 April, p. 23.

Olds, Kris, and Thrift, Nigel (2005a) Assembling the "global schoolhouse" in Pacific Asia. In: Daniels, Peter; Ho, Kong Chong; and Hutton,Thomas (eds.) *Service industries, cities and development trajectories in the Asia-Pacific*. London: Routledge.

Olds, Kris, and Thrift, Nigel (2005b) Cultures on the brink: reengineering the soul of capitalism – on a global scale. In: Ong, Aihwa; and Collier, Stephan (eds.) *Global assemblages: Technology, politics and ethics as anthropological problems*. Malden, MA: Blackwell, pp. 270–290.

Olds, Kris, and Yeung, Henry (2004) Pathways to global city formation: a view from the developmental city-state of Singapore. *Review of International Political Economy*, 11(3): 489–521.

Olsen, Johan P., and Peters, Guy B. (1996) Learning from experience? In: Olson, Johan P., and Peters, Guy B. (eds.) *Lessons from experience*. Oslo: Scandinavian University Press, 1–35.

Olson, Olov; Guthrie, James; and Humphrey, Christopher (eds.) (1998) *Global warning: Debating international developments in New Public Financial Management*. Cappelen. Oslo.

Ong, Aihwa (2005) Ecologies of expertise: technology and citizenship in Asian knowledge society. In: Ong, Aihwa; and Collier, Stephan (eds.) *Global assemblages: Technology, politics and ethics as anthropological problems*. Malden, MA: Blackwell, pp. 337–353.

Ong, Aihwa, and Collier, Stephan (eds.) (2005) *Global assemblages: Technology, politics and ethics as anthropological problems*. Malden, MA: Blackwell.

Panozzo, Fabrizio (2001) Den överbefolkade ledningen. In: Czarniawska, Barbara, and Solli, Rolf (eds.) *Modernisering av storstaden: Marknad och management i stora städer vid sekelskiftet*. Malmö: Liber, 74–83.

Partington, Angela (1992) Popular fashion and working-class affluence. In: Ash, Juliet, and Wilson, Elizabeth (eds.) *Chic thrills: A fashion reader*. Berkeley, CA: University of California Press, 145–161.

Pedersen, Kristian (2002) Räddas torsken så räddas yrkesfisket. *Göteborgs-Posten*, November 15: 4.

Pfau-Effinger, Birgit (2000) Conclusion: gender cultures, gender arrangements and social change in the European context. In: Duncan, Simon, and Pfau-Effinger, Birgit (eds.) *Gender, economy, and culture in the European Union*. London: Routledge xv, 288.

Pfau-Effinger, Birgit (2004) Socio-historical paths of the male breadwinner model – an explanation of cross-national differences. *British Journal of Sociology*, 55: 377–399.

Phillips, Nelson, and Hardy, Cynthia (1997) Managing multiple identities: Discourse, legitimacy, and resources in the U.K. refugee system. *Organization*, 4(2): 159–185.

Pine, B. Joseph II, and Gilmore, James H. (1999) *The experience economy. Work is theatre & every business is a stage*. Harvard, MA: Harvard Business School Press.

Porter, Michael E., and Kramer, Mark R. (1999) Philanthropy's new agenda: Creating value. *Harvard Business Review*, Nov–Dec: 121–130.

Porter, Theodore M. (1992) Objectivity as standardization: The rhetoric of impersonality in measurement, statistics, and cost-benefit analysis. *Annals of Scholarship*, 9 (1–2): 19–60.

Porter, Theodor M. (1995) *Trust in numbers. The pursuit of objectivity in science and public life*. Princeton: Princeton University Press.

Powell, Walter W. (1991) Expanding the scope of institutional analysis. In: Powell, Walter W., and DiMaggio, Paul J. (eds.) *The new institutionalism in organizational analysis*. Chicago: University of Chicago Press, 183–203.

Power, Michael (1997) *The audit society: Rituals of verification*. Oxford: Oxford University Press.

Puccetti, Roland (1972) Authoritarian government and academic subservience: The University of Singapore. *Minerva*, X(2), April: 223–241.

Pyhrr, Peter A. (1973) *Zero-base budgeting: a practical management tool for evaluating expenses*. New York: Wiley.

Rabinow, Paul (1997) Science as a practice. In: Downey, Garee Lee, and Dumit, Joseph (eds.) *Cyborgs & cytadels: Antropological interventions in emerging science and technologies*. Santa Fe, NM: School of American Research Press, 193–208.

Rabinow, Paul (2003) *Anthropos today: Reflections on modern equipment*. Princeton: Princeton University Press.

Rapoport, Rhona (2002) *Beyond work-family balance: Advancing gender equity and workplace performance*. San Francisco, CA: Jossey-Bass.

Rapoport, Rhona, Bailyn, Lotte, and Ford Foundation (1996) *Relinking life and work: toward a better future*. New York, NY: Ford Foundation.

Robertson, Roland (1992) *Globalization. Social theory and global culture*. London: Sage.

Rodan, Garry (1989) *The political economy of Singapore's industralization: National state and international capital*. London: Macmillan.

Rogers, Everett (1962/1983) *Diffusion of innovation*. New York: Free Press.

Rogers, Steve (2002) *Best Value under svenska förhållanden*. Presentation at KOM-MEK, Malmö, August 22.

Rorty, Richard (1991) On ethnocentrism: A reply to Clifford Geertz. In: Rorty, Richard, *Objectivity, relativism and truth: Philosophical papers I*, 203–210.

Rose, Niklas, and Miller, Peter (1992) Political power beyond the state: Problematics of government. *British Journal of Sociology*, Vol. 43 (2).

Roth, Wolff-Michael, and Bowen, G. Michael (1999) Digitizing lizards: The topology of "vision" in ecological fieldwork. *Social Studies of Science*, 29 (5): 719–764.

Rottenburg, Richard (1996) When organization travels: On intercultural translation. In: Czarniawska, B., and Sevón, G. (eds.) *Translating organizational change*. Berlin: Walter de Gruyter, 191–240.

Rottenburg, Richard (2002) *Weit hergeholte Fakten. Eine Parabel der Entwicklungshilfe*. Stuttgart: Lucius.

Rottenburg, Richard (2003) Crossing gaps of indeterminacy. Some theoretical remarks. In Maranhão, T., and Streck, B. (eds.). Translation and ethnography. The anthropological challenge of intercultural understanding. Tucson, AZ: University of Arizona Press.

Rottenburg, Richard, Kalthoff, Herbert, and Wagener, Hans-Jürgen (2000) Introduction. In search of a new bed: Economic representations and practices. In: Kalthoff, Herbert, Richard Rottenburg and Hans-Jürgen Wagener (eds.) *Facts and figures. Economic practices and representations*. Marburg: Metropolis, 9–34.

Røvik, Kjell Arne (1996) Deinstitutionalization and the logic of fashion. In: Czarniawska, Barbara and Sevón, Guje (eds.) *Translating organizational change*. Berlin: de Gruyter, 139–172.

Røvik, Kjell Arne (2000) *Moderna organisationer: trender inom organisationstänkandet vid millennieskiftet*. Malmö: Liber.

Rumbold, Judy (1992) An A–Z of sportswear. In: Ash, Juliet, and Wilson, Elizabeth (eds.) *Chic thrills: A fashion reader*. Berkeley, CA: University of California Press, 162–166.

Sabel, Charles (1989) Flexible specialization and the re-emergence of regional economies. In: Hirst, Paul Q. and Zeitlin, Jonathan (eds.) *Reversing industrial decline*. Oxford: Berg: 17–70.

Sachs, Wolfgang (1994) Satellitenblick. Die Ikone vom blauen Planeten und ihre Folge für die Wissenschaft. In: Braun, Ingo, and Joerges, Bernward (eds.). *Technik ohne Grenzen*. Frankfurt am Main: Suhrkamp, 305–346.

Sahlin-Andersson, Kerstin (1996) Imitating by editing success: The construction of organization field. In: Czarniawska, Barbara & Sevón, Guje (eds.) *Translating organizational change*. Berlin: de Gruyter, 69–92.

Sahlin-Andersson, Kerstin (2000) Arenas as standardizers. In: Brunsson, N., Jacobsson, B. and assoc. *A world of standards*. Oxford: Oxford University Press, 100–113.

Sahlin-Andersson, Kerstin (2001) National, international and transnational constructions of New Public Management. In: Christensen, Tom, and Lægreid, Per (eds.) *New Public Management: The transformation of ideas in practice.* Ashgate: Aldershot, 43–72.

Sahlin-Andersson, Kerstin and Engwall, Lars (eds.) (2002) *The expansion of management knowledge.* Stanford: Stanford University Press.

Sahlin-Andersson, Kerstin and Hedmo, Tina (2000) Från spridning till reglering: MBA-modellers Utbredning och Utveckling i Europa. *Nordiske Organisasjonsstudier,* 2(1): 8–31.

Sahlin-Andersson, Kerstin and Sevón, Guje (2003) Imitation and identification as performatives. In: Czarniawska, B. and Sevón, Guje (eds.) *The Northern lights: Organization theory in Scandinavia.* Malmö: Liber, 249–265.

Sainsbury, Diane (1994) *Gendering welfare states.* Thousand Oaks, CA: Sage.

Salamon, Lester M. (1987) Partners in public service. In: Powell, Walter W. (ed.) *The nonprofit sector: A research handbook.* New Haven, CT: Yale University Press, 99–117.

Salamon, Lester M. (ed.) (2002) *The resilient sector: The state of nonprofit America.* Washington, DC: Brookings.

Salskov-Iversen, Dorte (2005 forthcoming) *Global Interconnectedness: The Case of Danish Local Government in Network Society.* In: Hoff, Jens, and Hansen, Hans Krause: *Digital Governance://Networked Societies. Creating authority, community, and identity in a globalized world.* Copenhagen: Samfundslitteratur.

Sapir, Edward (1931) Fashion. *Encyclopedia of the Social Sciences.* New York: McMillan, 139–144.

Schatzki, Theodore, R. (2001) Introduction. Practice theory. In: Schatzki, Theodore R., Knorr Cetina, Karin, and von Savigny, Eike (eds.) *The practice turn in contemporary theory.* London: Routledge, 1–14.

Schatzman, Leonard, and Strauss, Anselm L. (1973) *Field research – Strategies for a natural sociology.* Englewood Cliffs, NJ: Prentice-Hall.

Schlesinger, Mark (1998) Mismeasuring the consequences of ownership. In: Powell, Walter W., and Clemens, Elisabeth (eds.) *Private action and the public good.* New Haven, CT: Yale University Press, 85–113.

Schneiberg, Marc, and Clemens, Elisabeth (2005) The typical tools for the job: Research strategies in institutional analysis. In: Powell, Walter W., and Jones, D.J. (eds.) *How institutions change.* Chicago: University of Chicago Press.

Schrecker, Elen (1988) *No ivory tower: McCarthyism and the universities.* Oxford: Oxford University Press.

Schulze, Gerhard (1995) *Die Erlebnisgesellschaft: Kultursoziologie der Gegenwart.* Frankfurt am Main: Campus.

Scott, W. Richard (1987) The adolescence of institutional theory. *Administrative Science Quarterly,* 32: 493–511.

Scott, W. Richard (2003) Institutional carriers: Reviewing modes of transporting ideas over time and space and considering their consequences. *Industrial and Corporate Change* 12(4): 879–894.

Scott, W. Richard, Reuf, Martin, Mendel, Peter J., and Caronna, Carol (2000) *Institutional change and health care organizations.* Chicago: University of Chicago Press.

SCT (Secretaría de Comunicación y Transportes) (2003) *Internal Document.* México, D.F: SCT.

Sellerberg, Ann-Mari (1994) *A blend of contradictions. Georg Simmel in theory and practice.* New Brunswick, NJ: Transaction.

Serres, Michel (1982) *Hermes: Literature, science, philosophy.* Baltimore, MD: John Hopkins University Press.

Sevón, Guje (1996) Organizational imitation in identity transformation. In: Czarniawska, Barbara and Sevón, Guje (eds.) *Translating organizational change*. Berlin: de Gruyter, 49–67.

SFS 1989: 164. *Lag om kontroll genom teknisk provning och om mätning*. Stockholm: Näringsdepartementet.

Shakespeare, William (1978) *The complete works of William Shakespeare*. London: Murrays Sales & Service Co.

Sievers, Bruce (2001) *If pigs had wings: The appeals and limits of venture philanthropy*. Address to the Waldemar A. Nielsen Issues in Philanthropy Seminar, Georgetown University, Nov. 16.

Simmel, Georg (1904/1971) Fashion. In: Levine, Donald N. (ed.) *Georg Simmel on individuality and social forms*. Chicago: University of Chicago Press, 294–323.

Simmel, Georg (1905/1997) The philosophy of fashion. In: Frisby, David, and Featherstone, Mike (eds.) *Simmel on culture*. London: Sage, 187–205.

Sims, Rob (2000) *Public sector financial management*. Paper presented at Public Sector Research Unit Continuous Learning Workshop, Melbourne, May 11.

Slaughter, Anne-Marie (2004) *A new world order*. Princeton: Princeton University Press.

Snow, David A., and Anderson, Leon (1987) Identity work among the homeless: The verbal construction and avowal of personal identities. *American Journal of Sociology*, 92: 1336–1371.

Solli, Rolf, and Czarniawska, Barbara (2001) Vad är på modet i storstaden? In: Solli, Rolf, and Czarniawska, Barbara (eds.) *Modernisering av storstaden: Marknad och management i stora städer vid sekelskiftet*. Malmö: Liber, 5–14.

Solli, Rolf, Sims, Rob, and Demediuk, Peter (2000) Chief Finance Officer in local government – Sweden vs Australia. Gothenburg: Förvaltningshögskolans rapporter, 24.

Sombart, Werner (1922/1967) *Luxury and capitalism*. Ann Arbor, MI: University of Michigan Press.

SOU (1993:16) *Nya villkor för ekonomi och politik: Ekonomikommissionens förslag: betänkande*. Ekonomikommissionen. Stockholm: Allmänna förlaget.

SOU (2001:75) *www.kommundatabas.NU!* Betänkande från Utredningen för en fortsatt utveckling av en kommunal databas. Stockholm: Finansdepartementet.

SOU (2001:76) *God ekonomisk hushållning i kommuner och landsting*. Betänkande från Ekonomiförvaltningsutredningen. Stockholm: Finansdepartementet.

SOU (2003:123) *Utvecklingskraft för hållbar välfärd*. Betänkande av den studiesociala utredningen. Stockholm: Finansdepartementet.

Spri (1990: 287) *Kvalitetssäkring i svensk sjukvård – förslag till nationell strategi*. Stockholm: Spri.

Ståhlberg, Krister (1999) Anpassningspolitiken i finländska och svenska kommuner under 90-talet – en jämförelse. *Kommunal ekonomi och politik*, 3 (1): 7–36.

Stanton, K. (1995) *Laboratory accreditation – Origins of a concept, http://www. nata.asn.au/*

Star, Susan Leigh, and Griesemer, James R. (1989) Institutional ecology, "translations" and boundary objects: Amateurs and professionals in Berkley's Museum of Vertebrate Zoology, 1907–39. *Social Studies of Science*, 19: 387–420.

Steele, Valerie (1992) Chanel in context. In: Ash, Juliet, and Wilson, Elizabeth (eds.) *Chic thrills: A fashion reader*. Berkeley, CA: University of California Press, 118–126.

Stinchcombe, Arthur (1965) Social structure and organizations. In: March, James G. (ed.) *Handbook of organizations*. New York: Mc-Graw-Hill, 142–160.

Stockholm Challenge (2002) Brochure, Stockholm City.

Stone, Diane (2003) The "Knowledge Bank" and the "Global Development Network". *Global Governance*, 9(1): 43–61.

Stone, Geoffrey (1995) Academic freedom and responsibility. The aims of education address. *The University of Chicago Record*, October 12.

Storr, Richard (1966) *Harper's University: The beginnings*. Chicago: University of Chicago Press.

Straits Times (Singapore) (2001) NUS academics free to express views to media. 12 April, p. 1.

Strang, David, and Macy, Michael (2001) In search of excellence: Fads, success stories, and adaptive emulation. *American Journal of Sociology*, 107: 147–182.

Strang, David, and Soule, Sarah A. (1998) Diffusion in organizations and social movements: From hybrid corn to poison pills. *Annual Review of Sociology*, 24: 265–290.

Sturdy, Andrew (2004) The adoption of management ideas and practices: Theoretical perspectives and possibilities. *Management Learning*, 35(2): 155–179.

Svendsen, Reinert (1916) *Historiske efterretninger om Værøy og Røst*. Kristiania: Aschehoug & Co.

Tan, Tony (2002) Speech by Dr Tony Tan Keng Yam, Deputy Prime Minister and Minister for Defence, at the Graduation Ceremony of the University of Chicago Graduate School of Business held on Saturday, 9 February 2002, at Raffles Hotel, Jubilee Hall, available at: http://www.sedb.com/edbcorp/sg/en_uk/index/in_the_news/2003/2002/speech_by_dr_tony.html, accessed 19 March 2005.

Tarde, Gabriel (1890/1962) *The laws of imitation*. New York: Henry Holt.

Tarde, Gabriel (1893/1999) *Monadologie et sociologie*. Paris: Institut Synthélabo.

Tarde, Gabriel (1902/1969) Invention. In: Clark, Terry N. (ed.), *Gabriel Tarde on communication and social influence*. Chicago: University of Chicago Press, 149–164.

Taussig, Michael (1993) *Mimesis and alterity. A particular history of the senses*. London: Routledge.

Teigland, Kristin R., and Mangseth, Lise (1998) *Analyse av det italienske tørrfiskmarkedet*. Tromsø: Eksportutvalget for fisk.

Teo, Chee Hean (2000) Speech by Teo Chee Hean, Minister for Education and Second Minister for Defence at the Alumni International Singapore (AIS) Lecture on 7 Jan 2000 at the NUSS Guild Hall, available at http://www.moe.gov.sg/speeches/2000/sp10012000.htm.

Thornton, Patricia H. (2004) *Markets from culture*. Stanford, CA: Stanford University Press.

Thrift Nigel (2005) Making sense: An afterword. In: Löfgren, Orvar, and Willim, Robert (eds.) *Magic, culture and the New Economy*. Oxford: Berg.

Tolbert, Pamela. S., and Zucker, Lynne G. (1983) Institutional sources of change in the formal structure of organizations: The diffusion of civil service reform, 1880–1935. *Administrative Science Quarterly*, 28: 22–39.

Tolbert, Pamela S., and Zucker, Lynne G. (1996) The institutionalization of institutional theory. In: Clegg, Stewart R., Hardy, Cynthia, and Nord, Walter R. (eds.) *Handbook of organizational studies*. London: SAGE, 175–190.

Tougaard, Ole (2002) EU-komissionen vill inte ha ett stopp. *Göteborgs-Posten*, November 15: 4.

Tremewan, Christopher (1994) *The political economy of social control in Singapore*. London: St. Martin's Press.

Tyack, David (1974) *The one best system.* Cambridge, MA: Harvard University Press.

Utley, Robert M. (1993) *The lance and the shield: The life and times of Sitting Bull.* New York: Ballantine Books.

Van der Lippe, Tanja, and Van Dijk, Liset (2002) Comparative research on women's employment. *Annual Review of Sociology,* 28: 221–241.

Van Doorne-Huiskes, Johanna, den Dulk, Laura, and Schippers, Johannes (1999) *Work-family arrangements in Europe.* Amsterdam: Thela Thesis.

Veblen, Thorsten (1899/1994) *The theory of the leisure class.* New York: Dover Publications.

Wade, Robert (1990) *Governing the market: Economic theory and the role of government in East Asian industrialization.* Princeton: Princeton University Press.

Warren, Roland L. (1967) The interorganizational field as a focus for investigation. *Administrative Science Quarterly,* 12: 396–419.

Warren, Roland L., Rose, Stephen M., and Bergunder, Ann F. (1974) *The structure of urban reform. Community Decision Organizations in stability and change.* Lexington, MA: Lexington Books.

Weber, Max. 1922/1972. *Wirtschaft und Gesellschaft.* Tübingen: Mohr. Abrahamson, Eric (1991) Managerial fads and fashions: The diffusion and rejection of innovations. *Academy of Management Review,* 16(3): 586–612.

Wedlin, Linda (2006) *Playing the ranking game: Field formation and boundary-work in European management education.* Cheltenham: Edward Elgar.

Weick, Karl E. (1979) *The social psychology of organizing.* Reading,MA: Addison-Wesley.

Weick, Karl E. (1995) *Sensemaking in organizations.* Thousand Oaks, CA: Sage.

Weisbrod, Burton (1988) *The nonprofit economy.* Cambridge, MA: Harvard University Press.

Weisbrod, Burton (ed.) (1998) *To profit or not: The commercial transformation of the nonprofit sector.* New York, NY: Cambridge University Press.

Weiss, Linda (1998) *The myth of the powerless state: Governing the economy in a global era.* Cambridge: Polity Press.

Westney, D. Eleanor (1987) *Imitation and innovation: The transfer of western organizational practices to Meiji Japan.* Cambridge, MA: Cambridge University Press.

Wikan, Unni (1992) Beyond the words: the power of resonance. *American Ethnologist* 19(3): 460–482.

Williams, Joan (2000) *Unbending gender: Why family and work conflict and what to do about it.* New York, NY: Oxford University Press.

Wilson, Elizabeth (1985) *Adorned in dreams. Fashion and modernity.* Berkeley, CA: University of California Press.

Wittel, Andreas (2001) Toward a network sociality. *Theory, Culture & Society,* 18(6): 51–76.

Wold, Helge A. (1986) Torsken-livsnerven i nord. *Ottar, populærvitenskapelig tidsskrift fra Tromsø Museum,* 164: 3–16.

Wold, Helge A. (1987) *Tørrfesk. Fra Lofotskrei til stoccafisso* (Video). Oslo: Statens filmsentral.

Wold, Helge A. (1991) *I paradisets første krets: Om drømmen om ære og rikdom, om et grusomt forlis, om et opphold på Røst i Lofoten 1432: italieneren Pietro Querinis egen beretning i ny oversettelse: med et tillegg om en reise til Røst i vår tid for å lete etter det tapte paradiset.* Oslo: Cappelen.

Wong, Ting-Hong (2005) Comparing state hegemonies: Chinese universities in post-war Singapore and Hong Kong. *British Journal of Sociology of Education*, 26(2): 199–218.

Woo-Cumings, Meridith (ed.) (1999) *The Developmental State*. Ithaca, NY: Cornell University Press.

Wood, Stephen J., de Menezes, Lilian M., and Lasaosa, Ana (2003) Family-friendly management in Great Britain: Testing various perspectives. *Industrial Relations*, 42: 221–250.

World Bank (1997) *The World Development Report*, World Bank: Washington D.C.

Young, Agnes Brook (1937/1973) Recurring cycles of fashion. In: Wills, Gordon and Midgley, David (eds.) *Fashion marketing*. London: Allen & Unwin, 107–124.

About the Authors

Petra Adolfsson is a researcher and lecturer at the School of Business, Economics and Law at Göteborg University, Sweden. Her research interests relate to organization studies and environmental issues. Her main publication is the thesis *Environment's many faces –Air and water quality monitoring and organizing in Stockholm* (in Swedish; BAS 2003).

Barbara Czarniawska holds a Science Research Council/Malmsten Foundation Chair in Management Studies at Gothenburg Research Institute, School of Business, Economics and Law, Göteborg University, Sweden. She is also a Titular Professor at the European Institute for Advanced Studies in Management, Brussels; Fellow at Center for Cultural Sociology, Yale University; and Visiting Professor at Management Centre, University of Leicester. Her research takes a constructionist perspective on organizing, most recently in the field of big city management and finance. She applies narratology to organization studies. Her recent books in English are *A Tale of Three Cities* (Oxford University Press, 2002), and *Narratives in Social Science Research* (Sage, 2004). She has recently edited *Northern Lights* (with Guje Sevón, 2003), *Narratives We Organize By* (with Pasquale Gagliardi, 2003), and *Actor-Network Theory and Organizing* (with Tor Hernes, 2005).

Peter Demediuk is Senior Lecturer in accounting and finance at Victoria University, Melbourne, Australia. He holds BCom (University of Melbourne, Australia), DipEd (State College of Victoria, Australia), and MEc (University of New England, Australia). He has experience in public sector resource and financial management as a practitioner, consultant, educator and researcher. He is an active member of the Public Sector Research Unit and the Value Reporting Research Group at Victoria University and member of several international organizations, such as, for example, the Asian Academy of Management and Western Decision Sciences Institute. He has been publishing articles about different aspect of accounting based on date from the public sector and the wine industry.

Gudbjörg Erlingsdóttir is an Assistant Professor at the Department of Business Administration, School of Economics at Lund University. She is working at present with two research projects: "Auditing – institutionalizing new forms of control in society" and "From professional autonomy to external standard setting – effects of changing institutions of control?" Both projects deal with the initiation, implementation and effects of quality assurances, and related control forms, in Swedish health care and Swedish auditing business. Her research mainly focuses on organizational change, new institutional theory, and travels of ideas, in the perspective of sociology of translation and theories of professions and control.

Michal Frenkel is an Assistant Professor of Sociology and Anthropology at the Hebrew University of Jerusalem. She studies the cross-cultural translation of managerial models and theories in Israel, emphasizing the contested aspect of translation and the various geopolitical, inter-societal and organizational tensions that affect this process. She is especially interested in how translated models influence the translating society by constructing and legitimizing alternative social hierarchies and transforming underlying assumptions that are usually taken for granted. Her work has been published in such journals as *Organization Studies, Organization,* and the *Scandinavian Journal of Management*.

Denise L. Gammal is managing director of the Stanford Project on Emerging Nonprofits, the major research initiative of the Center for Social Innovation at Stanford Graduate School of Business. She received her doctorate from Cambridge University (UK) in social and political sciences. Her research interests include public and social sector management, crisis communications, and media relations.

Hans Krause Hansen has a MA in Latin American Studies and Political Science (1991), and a Ph.D. from the University of Copenhagen (1997). He is working as Associate Professor at the Department of Intercultural Communication and Management, Copenhagen Business School. His major current research interests include the role of new media in organizational change from global and local perspectives. He is the author and co-author of a number of articles in books and international journals, such as *Bulletin of Latin American Research, Alternatives, Global Society, Corporate Reputation Review, Gestión y Pública* and *Critical Quarterly*.

Tina Hedmo is an Assistant Professor in the Department of Business Studies at Uppsala University. She received her PhD in 2004 on a thesis entitled *Rule-making in the transnational space. The development of European accreditation of management education*. Her main research interests are soft regulation, transnationalization and non-governmental organizations. She is presently studying the emergence of European regulation in the health care sector.

Hokyu Hwang is senior social science researcher for the Stanford Project on Emerging Nonprofits at Stanford Graduate School of Business. He received his doctorate in sociology from Stanford University. His research interests include comparative sociology, organizations, and institutional theory.

Tor Korneliussen is Associate Professor of Marketing at Bodø Graduate School of Business, Norway. His research focuses on internationalization, cross-national cooperation, and international distribution and export barriers. He is particularly interested in the complexities of issues related to catch, production and international trade in fishery products. Recently he has published in journals such as: *Supply Chain Management: An International Journal, Journal of Business Research, Tourism and Hospitality Research*, and the *Scandinavian Journal of Management*.

Kajsa Lindberg received her Ph.D. at School of Business, Economics and Law, Göteborg University and is now a researcher at Gothenburg Research Institute in the same School. Her research focuses on transformation of ideas into actions. Two studies are in progress: interorganizational change within the health care sector, and the impact of e-commerce on business organizing.

Orvar Löfgren is Professor of European Ethnology at the University of Lund, Sweden. His research interests concern identity politics, transnational processes and the relations between economy and culture. He is currently in charge of a multidisciplinary research project on the attempts to create a transnational region, linking Copenhagen and Southern Sweden. His latest books include *On holiday. A history of vacationing* (University of California Press, 2001) and *Magic, culture and the new economy* (coedited with Robert Willim, 2005.)

Kris Olds is Associate Professor of Geography, University of Wisconsin-Madison. His research interests include global economic networks, transnational communities, and services industries (esp., architecture, property development, and higher education). Recent publications include (as co-editor) *Globalisation and the Asia-Pacific: Contested Territories* (Routledge, 1999), *Globalisation of Chinese Business Firms*, (Macmillan, 2000), and (as author) *Globalization and Urban Change: Capital, Culture and Pacific Rim Mega-Projects* (Oxford University Press, 2001), as well as articles and book chapters on the relationship between immigration and foreign investment, global city formation processes in the Asia-Pacific, and the globalization of business education and research.

Fabrizio Panozzo is Associate Professor of Business Studies at the Ca' Foscari University of Venice and Associate Scholar at the European Institute for Advanced Studies in Management, Brussels. He likes to study calculative practices within organization. His most recent books are *Dalla produzione alla regolazione* (From production to regulation, Cedam, 2000) and *Pubblica amministrazione e la competitività territoriale* (Public administration and regional competitiveness, Einaudi, 2004). His articles have been published in *Accounting, Organizations and Society*, the *Scandinavian Journal of Management* and the *European Accounting Review*.

Walter W. Powell is Professor of Education and affiliated Professor of Organizational Behavior, Sociology, and Communication at Stanford University. He has worked in the areas of organization theory, economic sociology, and the sociology of science. For the last decade he has been engaged in research on the origins and development of the commercial field of the life sciences, including work on the evolving network structure of the biotechnology industry and mapping the university-industry interfaces.

Powell is also known for his contributions to institutional analysis, beginning with his article, with Paul DiMaggio, "The iron cage revisited: Institutional isomorphism and collective rationality in organizational fields" (*American Sociological Review*, 1983, the most cited paper in that journal's history) and their subsequent edited book, *The new institutionalism in organizational analysis* (University of Chicago Press, 1991). This line of work continues in a forthcoming edited book, *How institutions change*, and in his current research on the professionalization of management in the San Francisco Bay Area nonprofits community.

Richard Rottenburg holds a Chair of Social Anthropology at the Martin-Luther-Universität Wittenberg. He has written and edited books on the Sudan (*Ndemwareng. Wirtschaft Gesellschaft in den Morobergen*, München 1991), on organisations (edited together with von Oppen, *Organisationswandel in Afrika: Kollektive Praxis und kulturelle*, Berlin 1995), on economic anthropology (edited together with Herbert Kalthoff and Hans-Jürgen Wagener, *Facts and figures. Economic representations and practices*, Marburg 2001), and on the transcultural production of objectivity (*Weit hergeholte Fakten. Eine der Entwicklungshilfe*, Stuttgart 2002).

Kerstin Sahlin-Andersson is Professor of Management at Uppsala University. She has published books and articles on the global circulation of management models and standards, organizational changes in public sector, transnational regulations, and the organizing of large projects. She recently co-edited, with Lars Engwall, *The expansion of management knowledge: Carriers, flows and sources* (Stanford University Press, 2002). She is presently conducting research on emergent transnational regulations in the fields of higher education, corporate social responsibility and health care.

Dorte Salskov-Iversen has an MA in Modern Languages and Area Studies from Copenhagen Business School (CBS) in 1984, and a Ph.D in Industrial Relations & Cultural Studies, also from CBS, in 1992. She is Associate Professor at the Department of Intercultural Communication and

Management at CBS, and Vice Dean for Education at the Faculty of Economics and Business Administration. Her research is located at the interface between management & organizational change and international political economy, with (co-authored) publications in journals, e.g. *Discourse & Society*, *Alternatives*, *Corporate Reputation Review*, *Global Society*, *Critical Quarterly*, and in anthologies, e.g. Cary L. Cooper, Sue Cartwright and P. Christopher Earley's *The international handbook of organizational culture and climate*, (Wiley, 2001), and Morten Ougaard and Richard Higgott's *A global polity?* (Routledge, 2002).

Guje Sevón is Professor of Organization Psychology at Stockholm School of Economics. She has published books and articles in the research areas of management and organization. She has recently co-edited, with Barbara Czarniawska, *The Northern Lights – Organization Theory in Scandinavia* (Liber 2003) and, with Lennart Sjöberg, *Emotioner och värderingar i näringslivet* (Emotions and evaluations in business life) (EFI, Stockholm 2004). Her present research concerns translation of ideas with a specific interest in ideas about companies among different interest groups and partners of corporations.

Robert Sims is Senior Lecturer in Accounting and Finance at Victoria University, Melbourne, Australia and holds several academic degrees: MBus (Victoria University, Australia),BEc (Monash University, Australia), Dip Ed (Monash University, Australia), GradDip Comm Data Proc (Footscray Institute of Technology, Australia). He has been co-ordinating off-shore programmes in Singapore, Kuala Lumpur and China for the last four years and is now Associate Dean for International Relations at Victoria University. His publications deal with public administration and small businesses.

Caroline Simard is a research assistant for the Stanford Project on Emerging Nonprofits and a doctoral candidate in communications at Stanford University. Her dissertation focuses on knowledge networks in San Diego's wireless technology cluster. Her research interests include high-technology clusters, network analysis, the circulation and transfer of knowledge, as well as new media emergence, adoption, and use.

Rolf Solli is Professor of Management Studies at Gothenburg Research Institute (GRI), School of Economics and Commercial Law, Göteborg University, Sweden. His research focuses on accounting, management and leadership especially regarding public administration. He has published more than ten books, among which an edited volume *Organizing metropolitan space and discourse* (with Barbara Czarniawska, Liber, 2001), *Fictitious role models – reflections about movie heroes as leaders* (in Swedish, with

Björn Rombach, Studentlitteratur, 2002) and *Low-voiced control. Perspective on civil finance officers in local government* (SNS, 1999).

Professor Solli has been Head of various research and teaching departments for the last fifteen years and is now, besides doing his research, the Head of Gothenburg Research Institute (www.gri.gu.se).

David Suarez is a research assistant for the Stanford Project on Emerging Nonprofits and a doctoral candidate in education at Stanford University. His dissertation investigates the emergence and development of human rights education in Latin America. His research interests include comparative education, social movements, and organizational behavior.

Linda Wedlin is Assistant Professor at the Department of Business Studies at Uppsala University. She received her PhD in 2004 on a thesis entitled *Playing the ranking game. Field formation and boundary-work in European management education.* Her main research interests include the forming and expansion of rankings and classification activities, and other transnational regulatory systems, in higher education and in the business sector. Her present research concerns the forming of transnational monitoring systems within the EU.